PERSPECTIVE

THE
FINAL
TRANSITION

EDITED BY

RICHARD A. KALISH

ᏏᎧ Baywood Publishing Company, Inc.

Library of Congress Catalog Card Number: 85-21415

ISBN: 0-89503-043-8

Library of Congress Cataloging in Publication Data
Main entry under title:

The Final Transition

    (Perspectives on death and dying series; 5)
    Includes bibliographies.
    1. Death—Psychological aspects—Addresses, essays,
lectures. 2. Death—Social aspects—Addresses, essays,
lectures. 3. Bereavement—Addresses, essays, lectures.
4. Terminally ill—Counseling of—Addresses, essays,
lectures. 5. Death—Study and teaching—Addresses,
essays, lectures. I. Kalish, Richard A. II. Series.
HQ1073.F56   1985   304.6'4   85-21415
ISBN 0-89503-043-8

Editor's Preface

Another reader on death and grief? Well, yes and no. Aren't there already enough such readers? Well, yes and no. Is this one really needed? Does it really add something to what is already available? Well, yes and yes.

This volume is not just "another reader on death." Rather, it is a carefully-developed book, created specifically for those persons whose major interests are either death education, death counseling, or, of course, both. The audiences which this book addresses include (1) persons who have had either experience in death counseling or education or previous academic work; (2) those who are contemplating professional work in the field or who are already in the process of developing this area as one of their fields or competence; and (3) individuals who are already either counselors or educators or otherwise involved in the fields of mental health or education and who wish to learn more about the relationship of death and grief to their work. The book is not for beginners or for the casual reader, unless it is used to supplement a more basic reading, such as Kastenbaum's *Death, Society, and Human Experience, 2nd edition* (St. Louis: Mosby Publishing Company) or my own *Death, Grief, and Caring Relationships, 2nd edition* (Monterey, CA: Brooks/Cole Publishing Company).

In addition to the Preface, this volume consists of five major parts and an appendix that, itself, consists of several brief parts. Following an introductory section, which discusses the basic issues of death, dying, and grief, is a section on institutional care of the dying and a section on death and grief in a cross-cultural context. The final two sections cover counseling and psychotherapy and death education. An epilogue and an appendix, which details the kinds of classroom and non-classroom activities that would make a course or even an individual reading of the book more valuable, close the volume.

It is the two final sections and the appendix that we believe are unique among readers that deal with death and grief. The counseling and education sections total twelve chapters, almost half of the book, and the various chapters discuss relevant issues, offer applications, are concerned with evaluation and effectiveness, and provide programmatic ideas that can be modified for agencies and communities.

The appendix offers suggestions as to how the ideas discussed in the twenty-seven chapters can be tested in the world of practice and how people can expand their horizons and gain experience. The various sections of the appendix include volunteer opportunities, places to visit, ideas for developing further information, topics for discussion groups, and exercises that can be used in a classroom or in the community.

In addition to the contributions of numerous authors and to the practical suggestions in the Appendix, I have introduced each section, and each chapter within the sections, with my own comments. The nature and the length of these comments vary considerably, sometimes more focused on providing a transition between chapters and sometimes more concerned with expressing some of my own thoughts. I hope that they offer both integration and a sense of cohesion about the individual chapters, with the epilogue offering a final commentary.

This volume is certainly not to be viewed as a series of final answers. Instead, we hope that it will open up ideas for thought, provide a variety of kinds of understanding and knowledge, and encourage critical awareness. Some chapters were selected to provide breadth of knowledge and understanding of death, dying, and grief, or of counseling or education; others were included to offer depth of knowledge and understanding on a particular issue; and still others were provided to serve as the basis for future applications.

Both the editor and the publisher would like to thank all the authors who have provided materials for this book, as well as all the unnamed people who contributed to individual chapters or to the volume as a whole. Recent knowledge concerning death and grief comes from many sources, represents many disciplines, arises from many kinds of experience. *The Final Transition* is evidence of this.

Richard A. Kalish, Ph.D.
Santa Fe, New Mexico

Table of Contents

Introduction

Although the Twentieth Century is certainly an era of specialization, there is danger inherent in over-specialization. The boundaries of personal and vocational interests need to be broad enough to encompass related sources of information and understanding. Thus, those individuals who wish to become death educators need to know about educational processes; those individuals who wish to become death counselors need to know about counseling and psychotherapy. And both groups need to know about the meaning of death, the process of dying, and grief and bereavement.

There is also great advantage in viewing one's interests within appropriate contexts. And two kinds of context seem especially relevant: a cultural context and a historical context. The first section, limited to one chapter only, provides an initial basis for both cultural and historical understanding.

People who wish to work with the dying and the grieving, like most other practitioners, frequently want practical information. And they ask questions like "When I was working in the hospital, the wife of a dying man came up to me and asked . . . And I said . . . Did I say the right thing?" Or "The patient asked me whether he was going to die, and the doctor had told me the patient didn't know, and . . . What should I have said?" Or "When my mother said she wanted to be cremated, my brother became furious with her. I was there, but I didn't know what to say. Was there something I should have said and can I do anything about it now?"

Specific answers to such questions are often impossible without knowing a great deal about the particular situation and about the particular individuals involved. However, it is possible to gain a general background and understanding from experience, from reading, and from talking with others. This general background doesn't answer questions directly, but it can provide a framework and a knowledge-based philosophy on which some answers to the questions emerge.

Section I provides the basis for this background, with chapters that describe the process of dying, the meanings of death, and the impact of loss on the survivors.

PART 1
Death, Dying, and Grief:
The Basic Issues

Fifteen years ago, a chapter with this title would begin by lamenting the scarcity of written materials available, then would make reference to the taboo nature of the topic. Today, scarcity has given way to abundance, and death as taboo has been replaced by death as fad or fashion, although good practice still lags far behind acceptable rhetoric.

There are many ways of coping with death. The famous psychiatrist and author, Elisabeth Kübler-Ross, describes five: denial, anger, bargaining, depression, and acceptance. A later author (McCoy, 1974) adds defiance, fear, laughter, tears, and a search for meaning. We might also include regression, curiosity, search for spiritual well-being, hurrying the process, and panic. The list could continue on.

It appears logical that we cope with our own foreseeable death in much the same manner that we cope with other highly stressful situations, although each source of stress brings its own unique components to bear, and the prospect of death—whether imminent or eventual—certainly does the same. In fact, how far in the future we see as the timing of our own death may very well influence our forms of coping.

This chapter will focus on the meanings of one's own death as well as a discussion of significant tasks for people as they cope with their deaths. Also included will be implications for practitioners and for others who are brought into personal contact with individuals for whom death is a pressing concern.

Editor's Note: The introduction to this chapter is extracted from portions of the first three pages of Richard A. Kalish, Coping with Death, in *Living and Dying with Cancer*, Paul Ahmed (ed.), Elsevier, New York, pp. 223-239, 1981. An additional segment of pages 224-225 has been deleted. Reprinted with permission of the publisher.

CHAPTER
1

Coping with Death

Richard A. Kalish

Is there a "best" style of dying or a "best way" to cope with death? The initial response to this question must be another question: Best for whom? For health professionals? Health professionals, especially those providing direct and on-going care, seem to prefer people who cope with death quietly, cheerfully, and self-sufficiently. If the death occurs in a health facility, the health professionals may also prefer that the patient have a support system of family members and friends who attend in small numbers, speak quietly, and make minimal demands on the staff.

Best for society at large? The response might then be in terms of dying inexpensively, to reduce costs to taxpayers and strain on health facilities. And dying with minimal disruption of others, so that the general stress level of the community does not rise as a result of the death. If the ways in which the fatally ill person copes with death take too severe a toll on the family members, they may do less well on their jobs, in their child rearing, and with their relationships with others.

Best for family members? The patient's style of coping with death should, one hopes, not be guilt inducing nor too disruptive of other tasks that need to be done. Remaining contacts should be rich, full, and relaxed. And, if at all possible, financial costs should be covered by health insurance.

Of course the previous paragraphs are unnecessarily cynical, but the kernel of truth in each setting should be familiar. When we discuss the best way of coping with death, we are referring implicitly to best for the patient, but we can persuade ourselves easily that what is best for us, the family member, the close friend, the physician, nurse, social worker, or chaplain, is also best for the patient. We need to keep in mind that cancer patients are aware of the needs and wants of other important individuals, and many patients, made vulnerable through their illness, will seem to agree with the implicit or explicit message they are receiving as to how they should cope with death, rather than risk the premature loss or abandonment of such significant persons.

Even if we accept the definition of best as meaning best for the needs and wants of the patient, with relatively little regard for our own needs and wants, we are still confronted with a complex situation. Each dying person is unique, both in what is brought into the situation from the past and in the nature of the immediate life-threatening situation itself.

Thus, styles of coping with death are influenced by experiences, values, and expectations of the fatally ill person; by available relationships and resources outside of the health setting; by the tolerance for pain, discomfort, and uncertainty; by financial status and sense of previous accomplishments; by prior expectations for future life and accomplishments; by age and sex and ethnicity. In addition, coping styles are affected by what is being coped with: pain, loss of capacity, need for hospitalization, much reduced life expectancy, kinds of treatment recommended and undertaken.

Underlying all else is the personality of the patient. In using this term, I am including the fatally ill persons' needs and wants, their values and beliefs, their ways of interacting with others, their cognitive competence and cognitive styles, their methods of expressing themselves, and related characteristics.

Fortunately, as service providers and care takers, we do not need to know everything about a person to accomplish our own job. Since we cannot know everything and since we are not accomplished mind readers, it becomes necessary to do a lot of listening, to keep two-way communication free and open, to remain flexible in our own thinking as to appropriate procedures, to avoid viewing coping from a doctrinaire, ideologic point of view.

AGE AND STAGE AS FACTORS
IN COPING WITH DEATH

The age of the person confronting death is certainly one major factor in the response to death. Younger people often believe they have not been given their allocated time for living, and they feel angry and cheated; middle-aged persons have many responsibilities and are often immersed in plans and projects that will now remain unfinished. In fact, the evidence is fairly consistent that older people are less fearful of their own deaths than are either middle-aged or younger individuals, with the middle-aged probably being most anxious [1].

There are many reasons for this. The elderly have had more opportunity to learn to cope with their own deaths because they have been required to cope with the deaths of many other persons. Also, in many instances their futures hold less allure and excitement than the futures of younger people; they know that if *this* illness does not cause their death soon, *that* illness will cause it a little later. Further, they may already have suffered so many losses, often irreplaceable ones, that they do not see death as taking so much from them. And they are less likely to be involved in long-term plans and projects that require their active participation [2].

Stage refers to an entirely different matter: stages occur during the living—dying interval, i.e., that period beginning when the person becomes reasonably aware of a fatal prognosis and ending at death [3]. The best known stage approach, proposed by Kübler-Ross [4], describes five consecutive, somewhat overlapping, steps in the living—dying interval, from denial to acceptance. The stages can also be interpreted as five ways of coping with death, each way being appropriate to a particular duration of time, beginning with denial that occurs at the initation of the living—dying interval.

The validity of Kübler-Ross's stages has come under serious questioning [5, 6]. However, whether you accept these stages as gospel, use them as a framework, or reject them as misleading, the idea of stages in the process of coping with dying and death serves as a reminder that styles do not remain the same throughout the living-dying interval. The prior comments on age serve as a similar reminder that styles do not remain the same throughout the life span.

A fifty-year-old cancer patient may find ways to cope with her own death that are quite different than that same individual would have found useful, had the cancer occurred when she was twenty years younger or twenty years older. In the same way, methods of coping with death that develop immediately following awareness of being fatally ill may be highly effective at that time, but may be replaced by other coping procedures six months later that are equally effective for the changed nature of the situation.

To sum up, then, the styles of coping with death vary as a function of the individual's prior experiences, the nature of the life-threatening disease, the unique personality characteristics, age and other demographic factors, and the ways in which the dying person is experiencing the living—dying interval.

COPING

What Do We Cope With?

Coping with death is an on-going process that begins early in life, as soon as a child begins to conceptualize death, and continues throughout the life span. It is a movie, not a snapshot, although we frequently discuss it as though it were a number of disconnected frames. There is some controversy about how young children view death: how long it is seen as reversible, how responsible children feel when their parent dies. There is no longer any controversy regarding the idea that awareness of death as loss and departure begins very early in life and that a mature understanding of the meaning of death is completed by the age of nine years and perhaps earlier [7, 8].

When death becomes reasonably predictable in the foreseeable future or, even more to the issue, when death becomes imminent, the demands of coping with death become greater. Throughout life, coping with death involves accomplishing some significant tasks that become more salient and more stressful when death is close at hand. Some of these appear to be especially important.

- *First*, coping with death is coping with an unknown.
- *Second*, coping with death means coming to grips with the meaning of death and, therefore, with the meaning of what death destroys: life. It also

means dealing with what comes after death, whether this is self-aware existence, nonaware existence, or nonexistence; whether it involves the original body, a new and ideal body, or no body at all; whether the basis for the belief is a leap of faith or an attempt to apply the scientific method.

- *Third*, to cope with their own death, people must handle the pain arising from the losses that will occur at death, especially the losses involving social roles and personal relationships.
- *Fourth*, a dying person, both in the living–dying interval and in anticipation of death, usually wishes to make appropriate practical arrangements for the people, the groups, and often the ideologies and even the things left behind.
- *Fifth*, effective coping with death most frequently requires some form of communication with others in an open awareness context, i.e., a setting in which both dying people and those in their social milieu are knowledgeable about the prognosis and both know the other is knowledgeable.
- *Sixth*, as people die, they need to reconcile the conflicting pressures to let go of life and die and to hold on to life and retain every moment of existence possible.
- *Seventh*, as people face their own death, they need to find ways to continue to live in as pleasurable and satisfying a way as possible, pressing their demands of themselves and of others to, and perhaps beyond, their anticipated limitations.

With an Unknown

We can speculate about, make assumptions concerning, or have faith in our ideas regarding the nature of the event of death and the state of being dead. Sometimes faith is so strong that, for some, the unknown is really known. Nonetheless, for most, having to cope with death means that we have to cope with what is unknown and, presumably, unknowable during this life. Conversely, we can know a great deal about the dying process. We can observe people who are dying; we can talk to people who are dying and ask them about themselves; we can read what they have written or view them on film. Although systematic research is sparse, there are rich clinical and literary writings describing the dying process from medical, psychologic, and social points of view.

This means we can provide people who are dying with information that may help them cope more effectively with the dying process and with their fatal condition. They can gain a sense of what to anticipate, both in terms of the course of the disease and in terms of their possible feelings, attitudes, and behavior. They can do some planning for their own future, within whatever restrictions are required by their health, income, and other resources. This permits them to maintain at least some control over their own lives and, presumably, helps reduce some of their fears and anxieties.

We can also work out some implicit or even explicit contracts, i.e., under-standings, with people who are dying. We can assure them that we will control their pain or that we cannot control the pain as much as we would like; we can assure them that we will visit them, or that we will not visit them as much as we would like; we can assure them their insurance will cover financial costs of the illness, or that it will not cover as many of their costs as we would like.

We do not have comparable kinds of information about the realities of death. People have not written about what it is like to be dead; we cannot talk to a per-son who has experienced death; we cannot watch a person be dead; we cannot tell people what to anticipate when they are dead and help them do some plan-ning; we cannot offer them control over their existences after they are dead; we cannot work out any kind of contract about what we will do for them after they are dead (although we can work out contracts about funerals or survivors).

Some people, of course, have a religious faith strong enough to know what death means and what follows death. Others have such an intense belief in the permanent existence of the human soul and of individual consciousness that, without having any internalized theologic belief system, they have an abiding faith in their perpetual existence. The popularity of recent books on this topic is good evidence of this [9].

But for the most part we cannot help a person cope with death itself in the same way that we can help a person cope with the dying process or with the fatal health condition. There is no generally accepted series of empirical observa-tions about the nature of death nor do we have the kind of indirect evidence available that might be compared to the assumptions eventually verified in the development of atomic theory.

With the Death of Self

Cancer patients coping with death need to incorporate the awareness that their death is now fairly foreseeable and fairly predictable into the self. This does not require that they give up either hope or life. Too many cancer patients given a fatal diagnosis have toasted the memory of their departed medical diag-nosticians; others need not give up all hope, although the time will eventually arrive when the last flutter of hope is gone. And too many cancer patients have continued to be engaged thoroughly with their own activities and with the acti-vities of those around them to assume that the initial prognosis of fatal cancer need terminate meaningful life.

The death of the self has many possible meanings. It can be viewed as an ending, as a beginning, as a transition or rite of passage, or as all three. It can be viewed as a reward or as a punishment or as partaking of both. It can be perceived as a base from which a series of losses develop: loss of people, loss of experiencing, loss of control, loss of competence, loss of capacity to complete plans and projects, loss of body, loss of things [2]. And it can be perceived as a gain: gain of release from the stresses of this world, gain of abiding with God, gain of enriched consciousness or of absolution from consciousness in some form or state in a subsequent existence.

It is an unusual adult who has not spent at least a few moments, and frequently many hours, contemplating the meaning of personal death, why it occurs, what it is that occurs. This is part of coping with death. When death becomes imminent, as with a diagnosis of terminal cancer, what has existed at a theoretical or "some day" level becomes totally personal and meaningful.

One way of coping with death is to develop an acceptable belief in what comes after death. The more intrinsic this belief, the more likely it seems that death will lose its fear-arousing capability, assuming that the intrinsically maintained belief does not create the spector of a frightening death or hellish afterlife.

Many individuals derive both comfort and strength from a deeply held belief that some form of personal, self-aware existence will follow death. Others appear to find equivalent satisfaction from believing death leads to total extinction. And a few persons view the entire matter as either unknowable or irrelevant or both. Those who are most fearful of death appear to be those who are most uncertain as to what death brings and who care that they do not know.

Personal and self-aware existence is not the only type of immortality or continuity possible. Continuity of the self can occur through achievements, through residing in people's memories, through descendents, through being inscribed in the *Guiness Book of Records* or on a tombstone. These kinds of secular immortality, although lacking permanence, can still offer many individuals a sense of continued presence in the world.

A firm belief in what happens after death, whether it is something or nothing, eliminates some of the difficulties that make coping with death so difficult. For example, death no longer leads to an unknown: it leads to something that is known. Second, the meaning of one's own life does not cease with the end of life: it continues, either in sacred form or in secular form or both. Third, for those who espouse a self-aware after-life, death does not erase all possibility for experiencing or eliminate the uniqueness and beauty of the human soul or existence: it is a passage to another form of experiencing and existing.

With the Pain of Loss

Each of us performs many roles: spouse, co-worker, lover, car pooler, political party member, taxpayer, child, home owner, church member. Through each of these roles, we have many relationships, some obviously overlapping. And to an appreciable extent our personal identity emerges from these roles and relationships.

When we become aware we have also been thrust into the role *terminal cancer patient* and its related relationships, we do not suddenly cease being all other things to concentrate on the "dying role." Rather, as with any system, the components of the human system restructure to integrate the new component. We do not stop being spouse or car pooler, nor sever the relationship with our spouse or our carpool companions. However, our new identity as terminal cancer patient now influences our role and our relationships as spouse and as car pooler.

Dying people must cope emotionally with the losses to come with their impending death, with the loss of others and with the loss of themselves, as well as with the interpersonal relationships that will be on-going during the living–dying interval. They will no longer be mothers or fathers, lawyers, pianists, friends, or anything else. They will no longer have relationships with their children, fellow lawyers, concert-goers group, friends, or anyone else. They need to deal with this eventuality, now no longer posited as in an indefinite future, and they need to deal with both its emotional aspects and its practical demands.

The pressures to cope with the stresses of the living–dying interval add their weight. Perhaps dying patients will have to help others become able to help them; they may need to free others from their guilt in not giving sufficient attention; patients are likely to confront the possibility of being isolated by those who cannot handle their death or their dying process; since time is limited by coming death, decisions must be made about priorities in relationships with others. Thus, once again, the dying person simultaneously is coping with the losses to be brought about by death and those already brought about by dying and by fatal illness.

With Practical Arrangements

Making appropriate practical arrangements with and for others produces some similar difficulties. Arrangements must be made for what will occur as a result of death: funeral, burial, providing for family members, disposition of property, seeing that wills and trusts are taken care of. Other arrangements are required by the nature of the illness: cancelling out of the Saturday morning golf game; making decisions concerning giving up the apartment; seeing that the cat is cared for; getting the library books returned; making certain that someone else understands the notations in the checkbook and the record system for the income tax file. Then arrangements may need to be made for paying medical and hospital costs, for getting to and from medical offices, for seeing that any dependent children receive proper care.

Some of these tasks concerning roles and relationships would need to be performed if the health problem were mononucleosis or a broken leg; or, perhaps more salient, cancer from which recovery was extremely probable. Other concerns either occur because death is foreseeable or are altered in their effects for the same reason.

It is important that dying people cope reasonably well with emotional pain of anticipated losses and with the practical considerations. Then they will find it easier to devote time and energy to whatever life is left. Because, in the final analysis, people are living until they are dead and it is at least as important to use time wisely for personal satisfaction when it is in very short supply as it is when time seems almost endless.

OPENING COMMUNICATION

Until about a decade ago, the most familiar attitude about coping with death was that the patient would be best off not knowing the prognosis until as late in the course of the disease as possible. The assumption was that, in many instances, patients already knew or would learn on their own and had no need to discuss death, while in other instances, being confronted with the knowledge of having a fatal condition would be tantamount to a death sentence and would only serve to eliminate all hope and lead to depression.

In this fashion, the patient, physician, and family would establish either closed awareness or mutual pretense [10]. The former refers to a situation in which the dying person does not know the prognosis; the latter describes a setting in which both patient and others in the patient's milieu are aware that the condition is fatal, but each pretends with the other that improvement or cure is imminent. Both of these situations, especially closed awareness, are likely to change as the condition worsens.

Of course, in both situations, open communication is impossible, which means that the tasks involved in effective coping with death become much more difficult and sometimes impossible to carry out. Since according to the pretense, the person is not going to die, there is no basis for doing anything that would suggest death as a possibility.

For the past decade, academic, professional, and popular literature has been inundated with books and articles attacking the earlier position. Although the prior view is still maintained in many instances, a countervailing trend has developed: there are those who appear so eager for dying people to communicate about their dying and death that they focus people more on their death than on the functional life that they retain.

The issue for me, then, is to provide a mutual awareness context, in which both the fatally ill and those important to them are all aware that death is probable and are able to communicate this awareness to each other [10]. This does not *require* communication regarding death. It means that such communication can occur any time either party desires and that the desire is not inhibited by anxiety about whether the dying person is emotionally prepared for death.

Conversely, if the dying person actually never becomes aware that death is going to occur (and sometimes, as with a sudden coronary or an automobile accident or delayed visit to the physician, this becomes unavoidable), there is no opportunity to complete unfinished business, to attend to the practicalities of arrangements, or to develop some of the truly rich, albeit painful, emotional experiences that can take place when separation and loss are imminent.

Similarly, dying people who learn the condition is fatal, but too late to attend to whatever they might have wished to accomplish, are likely to feel deceived and cheated. A frequent outcome is considerable anger, since the message is only too clear: they were considered insufficiently competent to take care of their own stress and, as with children or confused people, needed someone to make decisions for them.

The mutual pretense context also calls for deceit, except that each party is attempting to deceive the other. Once again, patients are told they lack the competence to handle stress, but this time they say the same thing to others. That is, the implicit, unstated message is that "I don't trust you to be strong enough to handle my knowing that I'm dying; therefore, let us continue the game."

When there is no communication, people can only relate at shallow levels. Thus, the wife of a dying husband, given open awareness, can hold him and weep, and he will understand and try to hold her also. The experience is painful, but can be enriching. If the same couple is engrossed in mutual pretense, the wife dare not weep, for fear she would be communicating the very message she wishes to avoid giving, nor may her husband show any unexpected affection since that might give him away. The husband in this situation is going to have to cope with his own death alone, without the kind of loving support that his wife might otherwise offer. The wife may feel guilty about not being supportive of her husband when he most needed it.

ACCEPTANCE AND "LETTING GO"

The power and influence of Kübler-Ross's five stages have made it virtually axiomatic that the optimum way of coping with death is that of acceptance [4]. This can be seen as both appropriate and "natural;" that is, if people are given the proper medical and psychologic care, they will eventually come to accept their death. This means they will stop fighting death and hanging on to life, although it in no way implies that they will become eager to die or become weary of life. It does seem to suggest that they will disengage rather extensively from previous attachments, including people, while retaining only those relationships most important to them.

Enabling people to accept their own death has become an implicit goal of many, probably most, people who work with the dying. Frequently it is also an explicit goal. In fact, it often is assumed as the operational definition of "coping with death."

Similarly, people who work with the dying speak about enabling a dying person to "let go." People are frequently not ready to die because they have unfinished business, perhaps with other people or perhaps within themselves. This might reflect an intimate relationship that is still deeply involving, an incomplete project that has not lost its allure, or some other undone task. Sometimes it may be a special date, such as Christmas or a birthday, for which a person will hold on to life; there is statistical evidence that this indeed occurs [11].

In effect, then, people hang on to life because there is still something they need to do or to experience, and this need is sufficiently strong to enable them to stay alive. Obviously, hanging on is not an infinite possibility, but it can extend life for a period of time. Further, it will sometimes extend life when it would otherwise appear to be to dying persons' best interests to die. These people cannot accept death (enter the acceptance stage) until it is possible to let go of whatever is binding them to continued life. Therefore, their capacity to cope effectively with death cannot be made complete, since one or more unresolved issues requiring continued life keep getting in the way.

Counselors and others who work with the dying are likely to help clients deal with whatever is pressing them to hang on to life, so the issue can be resolved and the dying can then relax their hold on life and die. The reward for acceptance and letting go is optimum peace of mind, a quiet and peaceful death that is as comfortable as the health condition permits. Death is neither urgently sought nor fervently fought.

In a sense also, accepting death is a reflection of perceived reality. As energy ebbs, the dying person is capable of fewer interactions with fewer persons. After a lengthy period of not circulating in previous social circles and work settings, the individual is likely to find many earlier social relationships have become less frequent and less intense. Disengagement, which has been widely condemned when it occurs in healthy elderly people and also with institutionalized elderly people, is often approved when a dying person is involved [12]. Thus, the dying person retreats both physically and psychologically from the social environment, which simultaneously constricts its options for the dying person.

The individual can thus cope with death by reducing affective involvement in life and attachments to others, so that life shades into death by degrees instead of by quantum leaps. People who meditate long hours every day or who are frequent users of certain psychotropic drugs often report similar blurring of the line between life and death. In fact, most of us have known people who dealt with their entire lives by keeping their affective engagement so minimal that they were virtually beyond emotional pain, and similarly beyond joy.

Acceptance (or letting go) is certainly adaptive for many dying persons. It is even more adaptive for persons who are, either professionally or personally, involved with dying persons. It becomes all too simple for health and social service professionals to make the implicit assumption that the best possible method for coping with death requires entering the acceptance stage and being able to let go of attachments. Through books and articles and, more powerfully, through verbal, nonverbal, and indirect messages, these professionals effectively program dying persons to follow their dictates, while sanctimoniously proclaiming that they are winning victories for humanity.

I personally believe that accepting death is an excellent way of coping with death, and I hope that, when I reach that point in my life, I am able to accept my death. I am less certain that I want to disengage from most of my attachments, but I recognize that my health condition may require it of me. Nonetheless, in addressing those who care for dying cancer patients, I am pressing you to take a position that avoids prejudging how another person wishes to cope with death. There is a strong tendency to hold acceptance and letting go as ultimate goals, rather than as intermediate goals that frequently lead to the ultimate goal: that of enabling fatally ill patients to die in the style they desire, at least to the extent that this is possible.

MAKING THE BEST USE OF TIME

When death is imminent, people often reduce both their number of attachments and the intensity of these attachments to other individuals, to groups, and to whatever other involements they had had. To some extent this disengagement is caused by reduced energy; to some extent, it results from being pressed by limited time to develop priorities; to some extent, it arises from working through the pain of the coming losses, to the point where the loss has been accepted and the tie to the relationship has diminished.

It can be uniquely difficult to make good use of the time when there is little left, whether or not options are further limited by illness and by treatment regimens. Most people are so oriented to anticipating a future and planning their daily lives with this future in mind that refocusing their thinking to a very brief future becomes an extremely difficult task. Nonetheless, it does happen: people confronting their own death frequently do become capable of focusing on the present and living in that present, not by excluding awareness of the future nor by denial of coming death but by having found an acceptable style of coping with the death that permits significant attention to be given to what is available, rather than having all energy drained in attending to what will not be available.

People vary considerably in what they consider optimum use of time, and this is just as true for the dying as for others. When 434 residents of the greater Los Angeles area were asked how they would spend their remaining six months, if that was what their prognosis offered, the greatest number (26%) said they would make no major changes in their life patterns. More than 20 percent stated that they would spend time with people they loved or indicated some other involvement with others. Another 20 percent would focus on inner life, such as prayer or meditation; 17 percent believed they would undertake some activity that would provide a marked change in their lives, such as traveling or doing something they had always wanted to do but had never had the opportunity; slightly under 10 percent said that they would complete some project they were working on; and the rest gave responses that could not be categorized [1].

The research participants were not completely typical of Los Angeles: approximately 75 percent of them were black, Japanese American, or Mexican American; their income and educational levels were slightly below that of the general area, and older people were somewhat overrepresented. Nonetheless, even though the percentages for each response category would differ in other respondent groups, the results provide some clues as to how people not presently facing death believe they would best spend their time if they were facing death.

In the final analysis, no one can cope with someone else's death for that person. No matter how deeply involved we are, no matter how fervently we feel, no matter how intense our professional motivation, we can only hover around the person who is coping with death. We can sometimes make the task easier, more pleasant, less stressful, less frightening. We can sometimes make it richer, fuller, more meaningful. But we cannot do it for someone else.

What we must do is permit other people to face their own death. An appropriated death is seldom an appropriate death [13]. We can give the dying person what that person wishes and asks for, in the process of coping with death. And we have the option to let the dying person teach us what it is like to cope with death, so that when we must cope directly and existentially with our own death, we can build on the skills of a knowledgeable teacher.

REFERENCES

1. R. A. Kalish and D. Reynolds, *Death and Ethnicity: A Psychocultural Study*, University of Southern California Press, Los Angeles, 1976.
2. R. A. Kalish, *Death, Grief and Caring Relationships*, Brooks/Cole, Monterey, 1980.
3. E. M. Pattison, *The Experience of Dying*, Prentice-Hall, Englewood Cliffs, New Jersey, 1977.
4. E. Kübler-Ross, *On Death and Dying*, Macmillan, New York, 1969.
5. R. J. Kastenbaum, Is Death a Life Crisis? On the Confrontation with Death in Theory and Practice, in *Life-Span Developmental Psychology: Normative Life Crises*, N. Datan and L. H. Ginsberg (eds.), Academic Press, New York, 1975.
6. R. Schulz, *The Psychology of Death, Dying and Bereavement*, Addison-Wesley, Reading, Massachusetts, 1978.
7. M. Bluebond-Langer, Meanings of Death to Children, in *New Meanings of Death*, H. Feifel (ed.), McGraw-Hill, New York, 1976.
8. M. H. Nagy, The Child's Theories Concerning Death, *Journal of Genetic Psychology*, *73*, pp. 3-27, 1948.
9. R. A. Moody, Jr., *Life After Life*, Bantam Books, New York, 1976.

10. B. G. Glaser and A. L. Strauss, *Awareness of Dying*, Aldine, Chicago, 1965.
11. D. P. Phillips and K. A. Feldman, A Dip in Deaths Before Ceremonial Occasions: Some New Relationships Between Social Integration and Mortality, *American Sociological Review*, *38*, pp. 678-696, 1973.
12. R. A. Kalish, On Social Values and the Dying: A Defense of Disengagement, *Family Coordinator*, *21*, pp. 81-94, 1972.
13. A. D. Weisman, *On Dying and Denying*, Behavioral Publications, New York, 1972.

The title of Herman Feifel's book, the one that sparked so much interest in the issues of death and dying over a quarter century ago, was The Meaning of Death. It was not "the meaning of dying," although most of the increased attention in the area of death awareness has been to the concerns of the dying. This is understandable, since the plight of the vulnerable, suffering, dying person cries out for immediate attention. Nonetheless, although we are all, at various times in our lives, affected by concerns of the dying, we are all, at all times in our lives, affected by the meanings of death. And we should not permit the very legitimate demand to provide better care for dying persons to distract from the importance to all of us of gaining a better understanding of the meanings of death.

Each of us has our own view of the meanings of death. These views may be specific or general, sharply outlined or vague, closely tied to a known religious ideology or largely unrelated. And many of us are troubled by our view of death. When David Meagher and I asked some 150 Brooklyn College undergraduates why they registered for a credit course on death, around half of them indicated that coping with their own fears and concerns regarding death was their major reason.

Chapter Two describes the findings of a research study conducted in Los Angeles a number of years ago. Although the data are not new, there has not been a comprehensive, community study conducted since, and I believe that the statistics would be similar if the study were to be conducted today. Those who wish to look into the methodology more carefully can review the original book;[1] for present purposes it seems sufficient to state that the information was obtained by at-home interviews of 434 persons, conducted by professional interviewers. The study's participants were approximately equally divided among 1) four ethnic groups (Blacks, Japanese, Hispanics—designated as Mexican Americans—and Anglos), 2) three age groups (20-39, 40-59, and 60+), and 3) men and women. Reasonably good controls were used to avoid strong socioeconomic biases.

[1] Death and Ethnicity: A Psychocultural Study, by Richard A. Kalish and David K. Reynolds, published by Baywood Publishing Company, 120 Marine Street, Farmingdale, N.Y. 11735.

CHAPTER
2

An Overview of Death Attitudes and Expectations

Richard A. Kalish
and
David K. Reynolds

Two eternal truths about human beings are, first, that people differ from each other and, second, that people are similar to each other. Any attempt to communicate psychological insights must straddle these two truths, with a bow to one truth often incurring a buffet to the other. In this chapter, probably more than any other in this book, we defer to the latter. We will emphasize the overall data with only modest attention to the role of such groupings as sex, age, education, and religiousness, which are discussed in other chapters.

ENCOUNTERING THE DEATH OF OTHERS

Relatively few people have not had some encounter with the death or dying of other persons (see Table 1). Only 18 percent of the entire sample did not know anyone who had died in the two years prior to the interview, while almost that many knew personally at least eight persons who had died. Most of the deaths encountered were from natural causes, but nearly one-third of the respondents had known at least one accident victim during the previous two years, although only a handful knew people who had died from suicide or homicide.

Over one-third of the respondents had visited or talked with at least one dying person during the previous two years, and two-thirds had attended at least one funeral during the same time interval, while one person in twelve had gone to eight or more funerals. About 60 percent had been to a funeral during the previous year, compared to 55 percent of a primarily Anglo American sample over a decade ago [1], and only 22 percent of a large British sample covering adults of all regions and socio-economic classes [2]. Visiting the grave (other than during funeral services) was less common, over half not having made such a trip during the past two years (Table 1). A fifty-nine-year-old Anglo man expressed one extreme reaction: "Don't keep running there. There's nothing there. I guess it's okay on Decoration Day." A Japanese American woman

Table 1

	B (%)	J (%)	M (%)	A (%)
How many persons that you knew personally died in the past two years?				
None	10	17	19	26
8 or more	25	15	9	8
How many persons who were dying did you visit or talk with during the past two years?				
None	62	58	61	68
2 or more	16	17	15	18
How many funerals have you attended in the past two years?				
None	33	16	40	45
8 or more	9	17	2	4
How often have you visited someone's grave, other than during a burial service, during the past two years?				
None	71	36	56	59
4 or more	4	39	17	15

provided the counterpoint with an explosive "Twice a week! *Important* to visit the grave!"

Two points strike us as especially significant in this context. First, except for visits to the grave, the Anglos are obviously less in contact with the dying and with death than are the other ethnic groups. Second, and more meaningful, death and dying are very much a part of the experience of adults. Druing a two-year period, over two out of three adults have attended at least one funeral, and more than 25 percent have attended three or more; most adults have been friendly with at least two persons who died, and 25 percent have known five or more, and nearly 40 percent have visited or talked with at least one dying person. Perhaps—and only perhaps—we have denial mechanisms that exclude the affective impact of death and dying, but we most certainly do not escape continuing contact with this ultimate reality of life. Even the intimacy of touching the body at the funeral was considered acceptable by a majority of all groups except for the Japanese (B—51%, J—31%, M—76%, A—51%), and, although Blacks and Japanese would hold back, over half the Mexicans and one-third of the Anglos would be likely to kiss the dead person. One woman explained, "I don't know why—I just couldn't do it—touch the body." (Kiss the body?) "Oh, no." She paused a moment. "I don't even like to kiss him *now*."

In 1915, G. Stanley Hall could write, ". . . it appears that the first impression of death often comes from a sensation of coldness in touching the face or hands of the corpse of a relative, and the reaction is a nervous start at the contrast with the warmth which cuddling and hugging were wont to bring" [3, p. 551]. Hall's data had been gathered some two decades earlier. Although much reduced in frequency, such experiences are undoubtedly still not uncommon. These findings, and others to be discussed later, cause us to believe—with Donaldson [4]—that we have proclaimed this to be a death-denying society too often, and that the concept should either be effectively operationalized or else discarded.

The term *denial* is used both sociologically and psychodynamically, with relatively little overlap between the two usages. We will use the term in this chapter only when there is evidence that the individual is utilizing defense mechanisms to protect himself against awareness of death or something death-related. We will use the term *death-avoiding* to cover—we feel with more precision—such acts as not liking to go to funerals. Parsons and Lidz also question the common assumption that ours is a death-denying society, stating, "American society has institutionalized a broadly stable, though flexible and changing, orientation to death that is fundamentally not a 'denial' but a mode of acceptance appropriate to our primary cultural patterns of activism" [5, p. 134]. And Kastenbaum and Aisenberg ask why we so fear the fear of death [6].

In integrating these findings, we see that Anglos are likely to have the least contact with the dying and the dead, are probably more death-avoidant, although they do not admit to greater fear of death. Perhaps more salient, our data suggest that the avoidance of death is not a global concept, but must be restricted to more specific occurrences, i.e., what kind of avoidance behavior to what kinds of death for what reasons.

Attendance at funerals correlates significantly with having visited a dying person, and the correlation is substantial ($r = 0.41$), but neither of these variables correlates substantially with willingness to inform a person of his own death ($r = 0.17$ and 0.19 respectively). Both individual uniqueness and cultural roles contribute to the variance. Thus, although age, sex and ethnicity are predictive of reliable differences in how one responds to each of the numerous kinds of death-related encounters, considerable variability is evident even within these categories. In short, being Black, being old, and being female all help predict how an individual will respond to each of several kinds of death-encounters, while being an elderly Black woman will be even more predictive. However, considerable individual variation does exist among elderly Black women. Furthermore, knowing how a person will react to one kind of death setting (e.g., attending funerals) provides only limited predictive accuracy in determining how they will react to another setting (e.g., informing a dying person).

Before leaving this issue, we should point out that for *some* individuals, death-avoidance is sufficiently pervasive that they do exhibit avoidant behavior in a wide variety of situations. Even when their overt behavior does not appear consistent with such avoidance, they pay a penalty in anxiety or extensive use of defense mechanisms. Sometimes they display counter-phobic behavior through a virtually ritualistic attendance to planning their own funeral or establishing their own claim to immortality. Probing this issue would require depth interviews or similar methodologies.

Kastenbaum (personal communication) offers an alternative way of viewing these variables. Rather than utilizing only the concept of death-avoidance, he suggests applying the approach-avoidance mode of traditional psychology. Thus any given behavior could be viewed as the result of the interaction between the motivation to approach and the motivation to avoid. Not visiting graves could then be interpreted as having a low approach value rather than a high avoidance value. This strikes us as an important refinement and may help avoid some non-parsimonious assumptions about motivation when the root of the behavior (or lack of behavior) can be viewed as an absence of felt need.

COMMUNICATING WITH THE DYING

Ever since Glaser and Strauss published their monograph, *Awareness of Dying*, the issue of whether the patient should be made aware of his coming death has been discussed—sometimes heatedly—among physicians, nurses, clergymen, behavioral scientists, and others [7]. More than half our respondents felt that a dying person (described as approximately the same age and of the same sex as the interviewee) should be told that he is dying, but many more Anglo Americans favored this approach than members of other ethnic groups (B—60%, J—49%, M—37%, A—71%). One black American stated, "I think the person would want to know. Those things should not be kept a secret unless they are too old and can't stand the shock." An older Anglo man explained, "Yes, but in a roundabout way. No two people are alike, so you can't treat them all the same. I know one person who was told, but the doctor was too blunt and it about killed the whole family. He should have done it in a more roundabout way—gradually—work up to it." A woman presented the opposite position: "I wouldn't want to know. If she knows, she would worry."

The task of communicating was left primarily to the physician, with some member of the family listed as the second most appropriate choice. All ethnic groups responded in this fashion. For example, "The doctor, assuming the guy can take it. Also have to take into account how well the doctor knows the patient, how much confidence the patient has in the doctor, the ability of the doctor to relate to the patient, what the family members think. . . . Cannot say definitely any one person." Although survey data often do not reflect it, respondents constantly express the need to approach matters individually, to take individual differences into account.

Although over half the respondents felt that dying friends should be informed, three-fourths wish, themselves, to be informed. Only among Mexican Americans

does this drop to as low as 60 percent (B–71%, J–77%, M–60%, A–77%).
Each ethnic group has a higher proportion of persons wishing themselves to be
informed than feeling that others should be told. The two groups that are most
familistic, the Japanese Americans and the Mexican Americans, show the
greatest discrepancy between their own desire to know and willingness to let
others know, reflecting a strong desire to protect and a note of paternalism
perhaps.

Physicians are also much less likely to feel patients should be informed than
the patients are, while both physicians and laymen, according to several studies,
are more likely to want to be told themselves than to feel others should be
told [8, 9].

The results of other studies do not differ appreciably from ours. Hinton
reviews four studies in which patients and their relatives were asked whether a
cancer patient should be enabled to learn about his condition: the results were
overwhelmingly affirmative, ranging from 66 percent to 89 percent. Feifel and
Jones found 77 percent wished to be informed, drawing from both physical and
mentally ill and normals [10]; Vernon in a primarily youthful sample found a
71 percent favorable response [11].

Numerous authors make a very strong case for informing a terminally ill
person [12]. Koenig has gone so far as to tabulate the articles that provide the
pros and cons, and ends up with a distinct majority favoring some method of
permitting the dying to become aware of their impending death [13].

That the task of informing the dying is not an easy one is attested to by the
admission of the respondents that only a handful (between 4% and 7% of each
group) had ever told anyone he was dying and that fewer than half of the remainder felt capable of serving as informant in such a situation (B–51%, J–47%,
M–19%, A–52%). An elderly Black American woman answered, "I don't think
I could tell anyone. I'd just tell him when the Lord's ready, He will call him."
An ex-medical technician was forced by circumstances to answer a man who
"was literally almost cut in half . . . I told him that it didn't look too good but
that we were taking him to the hospital where he would get the best of care. He
never made it to the hospital." Of 295 Catholic and Unitarian women who were
asked whether they were afraid of encountering a dying friend, Chenard found
that equal thirds were "a great deal," "some," or "a little or not at all" afraid
[14]. There was no difference between the two religious groups.

GRIEF AND MOURNING

The loss of others through death is immensely painful. Such loss gives rise to
sadness and melancholy, anger, resentment, guilt, fear and anxiety, and
sometimes to a search for meaning, a turning toward or against God, the desire
to lay blame on someone or something, the attempt to find a reason for
the death.

The death of another disturbs us in several ways. First, it may remind us of our own finite nature, of the obvious but avoided truth that we too shall come to a termination of our existence on earth—which, for some, means termination of all existence. Second, the death of someone close removes something from our own lives—we no longer can relate to that individual, no longer receive his warmth, friendship, support, no longer depend upon him or gain pleasure from his depending upon us. This is object loss—it is also objective loss. Sometimes the loss removes from the family, the business, the institutions, the community, an important part of that structure. The tragedy of the loss is often related to how much dislocation and upset occur in the lives of the survivors.

Third, the intricate set of social obligations and interactions that death brings to a close are often not ready for total finality. The survivors may be angry at being deserted and attribute the death, in an unconscious and mystical fashion, to willfulness on the part of the deceased (this response may be intense following a suicide). They may feel overwhelming guilt in their real or fantasized role in his death, for their perceived failures in offering attention or concern or—in some instances—for their relief that the death has finally occurred. Things undone and unsaid can no longer be compensated for, although the funeral service may offer some opportunity for self-absolution. Expressions of guilt have come up spontaneously in all subgroups, i.e., ethnic, age, sex, education.

In describing the feelings of a wife subsequent to her husband's heart attack, Schoenberg and Stichman point out that the woman often berates herself for not having made certain that her husband had eaten more moderately, worked less intensely, exercised more, and worried less [15]. Or, in the case of the wife that had done these things, the self-condemnation would be for having nagged her husband unduly and thus raised the tension level of the home. The double bind is evident in many instances following loss.

Although the ability to express one's grief openly is frequently encouraged by professionals in the mental health field, our respondents displayed considerable reluctance to do so. Fewer then half would worry if they could not cry (except for Mexican Americans, 50 percent of whom responded in the affirmative). Three-fourths of the Blacks, Japanese, and Anglos would "try very hard to control the way (they) showed (their) emotions in public," although less than two-thirds of the Mexicans agreed to this. Nonetheless, a great majority of all groups and almost all of the Mexican Americans would "let (themselves) go and cry (them)selves out" in either private or public (B—64%, J—71%, M—88%, A—70%). Apparently emotional expression is appropriate, even encouraged, in private, but is expected to be constrained in public. One woman explained her feelings about the entire matter: "I would do whatever felt natural." Here, however, our observations indicate a real discrepancy between expressed norms and observed behavior in the Black American community. Perhaps attempts are made to control public expression of feeling, but they do not appear successful, since crying, moaning, wailing and fainting are commonly observed.

Two-thirds of the Black Americans and over 80 percent of the others would carry out their spouse's last wishes even if they were felt to be senseless and inconvenient. Such responses might arise from guilt, but we feel that the motivation is more from a sense of obligation, a recognition of the importance of the dead person and perhaps a kind of denial (we would not assume this to be emotionally unhealthy) that the relationship has been severed. Simmons describes how effectively final wishes can bind the survivors in some cultures [16].

A family member would usually be sought for comfort and support in time of bereavement, although clergymen were also cited with moderate frequency. Less often selected was a friend, and about 8 percent of the respondents said they would not turn to anyone for comfort. Support for the bereaved is not only emotional, however. The death of a spouse requires practical help, such as keeping the household going. Most people would seek this help from relatives (B—50%, J—74%, M—65%, A—45%), but friends, neighbors, and fellow church members were picked by nearly one-fourth (B—42%, J—9%, M—14%, A—45%). Previously we found the Anglos least likely to participate in rituals for the dead; now we find that they have fewer expectations of their family in times of crisis. It would appear that the mutual obligation structure is weakest in Anglo families in the Los Angeles area.

The extent to which a particular death is perceived as tragic seems to vary as a function of the age, the sex, and the kind of death involved (Table 2). And the different ethnic groups differ considerably in their evaluations. Particularly striking were the strong Anglo feelings about slow deaths and about the deaths of infants and children, and the relative unanimity about the meaning of the deaths of the elderly.

Death and loss are not only personal matters. They are also social. Society prescribes standards for grief and mourning, and each individual grieves not only from his personal sorrow, but in a style which is the product of early socialization and later social dictates. This is especially obvious in the length of time the mourner is expected to refrain from returning to usual behavior patterns. Although nearly one-fourth of the respondents felt that the widow(er) could appropriately remarry at any time after the death of his spouse, over half the Japanese Americans and Mexican Americans felt at least one year's wait was necessary, many feeling that two years or more would be preferable and some stating that remarriage was never appropriate. Since the question (and those following) was asked in terms of the age, sex, and ethnicity of the respondent, answers to this item were related to age, i.e., many of those who said remarriage was inappropriate were speaking of an older person remarrying (see Table 3).

Respondents were understandably more lenient in stipulating how long the bereaved should wear black. Over 40 percent of the Japanese Americans and over half of all other groups felt that black clothing was unimportant and need not be worn. In a major study of bereavement in England, Gorer interviewed over 350 men and women who had lost a close relative during the previous five

Table 2. Which Seems More Tragic?

	B (%)	J (%)	M (%)	A (%)
Sudden Death	39	43	41	20
Slow Death	58	50	50	68
Equally Tragic	3	7	9	12
(Don't Know)	(—)	(—)	(—)	(6)
Man's Death	10	34	9	16
Woman's Death	38	29	36	25
Equally Tragic	50	36	55	52
Other	2	2	0	7
(Don't Know)	(6)	(—)	(5)	(13)

	Most Tragic	Least Tragic	Most Tragic	Least Tragic	Most Tragic	Least Tragic	Most Tragic	Least Tragic
Infant's Death (0-1 year old)	14	24	8	18	13	25	17	14
Child's Death (around 7)	26	5	24	2	25	1	44	0
Youth's Death (around 25)	45	2	43	1	48	0	32	2
Middle-aged Person's Death (around 40)	8	2	22	2	6	5	5	1
Elderly Person's Death (around 75)	6	67	1	74	6	69	0	82
Other	1	1	3	3	3	1	1	1
(Don't Know)	(2)	(—)	(—)	(—)	(4)	(—)	(2)	(—)

years [2]. Of these, 37 percent wore no symbolic clothing or armband, and only 20 percent wore anything for longer than three months. Relatively few of our respondents felt that black should be worn beyond six months, but we have no data directly corresponding with those of Gorer. Similarly, a majority of all ethnicities felt that a week or less was ample time to remain away from work, roughly half of these indicating that the bereaved person should be able to return to work as soon as he wished.

Going out with others of the opposite sex was treated more conservatively, although a young Mexican American woman made the point that this would be all right "As soon as you felt no guilt about it." Less than one-fourth felt that waiting was unimportant, with the median response being between six months and a year. The Blacks and the Anglos were consistently more casual than the Mexicans and the Japanese, seeming to form a pattern in keeping with funeral attendance and other family interactions. About 30 percent of those who responded stated that they would begin to worry that mourning was extended too long if crying and grieving lasted as much as a couple of weeks; a slightly larger proportion would not be concerned for at least six months; while

Table 3. In General, After What Period of Time Would You Personally Consider it All Right for a (Person of Respondent's Age Group, Ethnic Group, Sex)

	B (%)	J (%)	M (%)	A (%)
To remarry?				
Unimportant to wait	34	14	22	26
1 week–6 months	15	3	1	23
1 year	25	30	38	34
2 years or more	11	26	20	11
Other/DK/Never	16	28	19	7
To stop wearing black?				
Unimportant to wait	62	42	52	53
1 week–1 month	24	26	11	31
6 months	6	7	7	5
1 year or more	5	14	28	1
Other/DK	4	11	3	11
To return to place of employment?				
Unimportant to wait	39	22	27	47
1 day–1 week	39	28	37	35
1 month or more	17	35	27	9
Other/DK	6	16	9	10
To start going out with other men/women?				
Unimportant to wait	30	17	17	25
1 week–1 month	14	8	4	9
6 months–1 year	24	22	22	29
2 years or more	11	34	40	21
Other/DK	21	19	18	17

the remainder opted for an intermediate period, usually between one and three months.

How do you know when grief is not normal? Around 30 percent did not know, but the remainder displayed considerable variability. Half the Blacks indicated that they would look for abnormal behavior, compared to 27–29 percent of the others; one-third of the Blacks and one-fourth of the Anglos (compared to 15–16% of the others) would look for withdrawal and extreme apathy. The Mexicans were alert to the bereaved under-reacting, i.e., not showing any overt signs of grief or, as one said, "When they can't cry" (34% compared to under 10% of the others). Two out of five Japanese gave answers that could not be coded in our available categories. The issue needs to be pursued, because it gives promise of major differences in expectations of the various ethnic groups.

ENCOUNTER WITH THE DEATH OF SELF

Do people fear death? We don't know. All we can say with certainty is that study after study has shown that people *say* they do not fear death. How valid are these comments? Again, we don't know. University students displayed the same reaction time lags to death words that they did to sex words, while their galvanic skin responses and reaction times to death words were significantly and substantially greater than to neutral words [17]. But does this suggest greater fear? It could imply excitement, fascination, or even response to the unexpected.

Most studies of fear of death have been conducted with specific age groups, especially with either university students or the elderly. These are discussed in the chapter on age, so that comparisons can be made with proper age groups. However, a few investigations have cut across age lines. Neither Scott [18] nor Hall [19] asked directly about fear of death in their questionnaires, although Hall did say twenty years later, "We long to be just as well, strong, happy, and vital as possible, and strive against everything that impedes this wish or will. . . . We love life supremely and cannot have too much of it . . . while we dread all that interferes with it" [19, p. 569]. Feifel and Jones combined the seriously ill, the chronically ill and disabled, the mentally ill, and normals into one sample, with roughly equal numbers in each category [10]. Of this conglomerate, 71 percent verbalized no fear of death.

In Hinton's observations of the terminally ill, he felt that "as many as two-thirds of those who died under fifty-years of age were clearly apprehensive, whereas less than a third of those over sixty years were as anxious" [8, p. 84]. Of Chenard's Catholic and Unitarian women, 11 percent were very much afraid, 21 percent were not at all afraid, and the rest were split between some fear and little fear [14].

In a recent national survey, conducted by the Harris Poll organization under the auspices of the National Council on the Aging, individuals in a large sample were asked to respond to the open-ended question: What are the worst things about being over sixty-five years of age? Fear of death was given as an answer by 9 percent of the total sample, but by only 6 percent of those fifty years of age and older. This compares with 62 percent of the sample who indicated that poor health was one of the worst things about being old and 33 percent who stipulated loneliness. Blacks mentioned fear of death only 2 percent of the time, compared to 10 percent for the non-Blacks (other ethnic groups were not represented in sufficient numbers for breakdowns) [20]. When the same respondents were asked to list what they considered to be very serious problems of old age, fear of death was not among the twelve most common concerns listed either by those between eighteen and sixty-four or by those sixty-five and over.

Riley (in Riley *et al.*, 1968) reports that only 4 percent of his national survey sample "gave evidence of fear or emotional anxiety in connection with death" [21, p. 332]. Other studies, although based upon samples limited by geography, age, or education, found comparable results ranging up to around 10 percent or so indicating fear of death. Our respondents were either more frightened of death—or more truthful in their responses. We asked, "Some people say they are afraid to die and others say they are not. How do you feel?" The interviewer coded the response in the categories *terrified/afraid, neither afraid nor unafraid*, or *unafraid/eager*. Only two people could be clearly categorized as *eager*, and about 2 percent gave responses classified by the interviewer as *terrified*. Because of these small numbers, we combined those categories with adjacent ones, as indicated just above.

Using this approach, over a quarter of all respondents were classed as afraid of dying (B—19%, J—31%, M—33%, A—22%), while just over half were unafraid (B—50%, J— 50%, M—54%, A—53%). About 2½ percent were uncodable, and the rest were classified as neither afraid nor unafraid. Why we received such a low proportion of persons claiming to be unafraid is difficult to say. Perhaps their having already participated in some thirty minutes of death-related discussion heightened their anxieties—or perhaps it enabled them to reply with greater honesty. To be consistent with our policy of assuming face validity of any statements, unless substantial evidence suggests otherwise, we propose that our data represent accurately the feelings of the respondents at the time the question was asked.

One respondent commented, "So many say they are ready (to die), but I don't feel near ready. Judging from the way I got frightened at the earthquake, I'm not near ready." A Mexican American man said, "I *say* I'm unafraid, but if I had time to think about it, and I knew I would die shortly, I don't know—I guess I would certainly be concerned." And an Anglo American man put his view succinctly: "You are *nuts* if you aren't afraid of death."

This leads to the question, how stable are attitudes toward death? Ivey and Bardwick have shown that death anxiety of women varies as a function of their menstrual cycle—as do other kinds of anxiety [22]. We know of no other evidence on this issue. However, we suggest no mystique for death attitudes— they undoubtedly vary as a function of situation, mood, experience, and shifting cultural milieu, just as all other attitudes vary.

Whatever a person's attitude might be regarding death, what has influenced these feelings? For this question we provided the respondent a card with ten alternatives, plus an eleventh, "OTHER (SPECIFY)." Over one-third of the respondents selected the statement, "The death of someone close," as having influenced them the most (B—26%, J—41%, M—39%, A—35%). "My father died when I was 5-and-a-half years old. I was very close to him, and when I heard of his death, I ran away from home and went into the woods. I was gone for 2-and-a-half days. I felt as if my whole world had collapsed, as if I had no one to turn to any longer. I was desperate. I cried a lot." Second most frequently selected was, "Your religious background" (B—40%, J—13%, M—21%, A—25%). Nearly 19 percent stated that having been close to their own death, or believing themselves to be, was their greatest influence. Reading, conversations, the death of an animal, mystical experiences, funerals or other rituals, the media, were all listed by only 5 percent or less of the sample.

Shneidman's survey, while not drawing from a comparable sample, obtained some parallel results. Of his respondents, 35 percent stated that introspection and meditation most influenced their attitudes toward death; we did not include that alternative, but we doubt whether many of our respondents would have selected it. Second and third most frequently mentioned by Shneidman's sample were the death of someone else and religious upbringing (19% and 15% respectively); these fit quite well with our data. Over one-third of Shneidman's group stated that existential philosophy influenced their present attitudes toward their own death more than such concerns as pollution, violence, television, war, poverty, and so forth. We believe that very few of our respondents would have selected that alternative.

Although 19 percent of the respondents felt that either actually being close to death or thinking they were close to death had the greatest impact upon their attitudes, over twice that many had—at least once—believed that they were close to dying (B—48%, J—31%, M—49%, A—37%). Of these, exactly half of the Blacks and Japanese asserted that the experience had affected their lives, slightly under half of the Mexicans and Anglos agreeing also. Unfortunately, responses to the question of how the experience affected them were so scattered, that the categories became too small for serious consideration. Here, too, the response to near death was highly individualistic, varying with circumstances, cultural background, and other experiences before and after the event.

Do people often think about their own death? Kennard informs us that the Hopi "man who thinks of the dead or of the future life instead of being concerned with worldly activities, is thereby bringing about his own death" [23, p. 492]. Simmons does not mention any other example of this, but a number of respondents in our study—proportionately more Black Americans than others—referred to being worried that talking about death would bring it about [16]. Scott's sample of 226 adults indicated that only 7 percent never "dwelt on death or suicide," while 60 percent responded in such fashion that they obviously gave at least some thought to the matter [18]. Vernon's student sample showed only 45 percent who said they thought only "rarely" or "very rarely" about their death [11].

Additional studies add numbers, but little insight. Feifel and Jones in their investigation of a primarily mentally or physically ill sample, found that 44 percent thought of death "rarely" and 42 percent occasionally [10]. Fulton, using a mail survey with a limited percent of response, also found that 40 percent rarely or never thought about death, while 12 percent dwelled on it frequently or all the time [1]. And in 1963, Riley's national sample splits into almost equal thirds, stipulating "often," "occasionally," and "hardly ever/never" [24]. Shneidman found 5 percent of his respondents thought of their death once a day, while 21 percent contemplated it no more than once a year [25]. In a study of persons forty-five years of age and older, drawn from Black, Mexican, and Anglo American samples also in Los Angeles, 33 percent stated they thought about their own death "not at all," 58 percent "occasionally," and 9 percent "frequently" [26]. Interviews in retirement communities found that fewer than 10 percent stated that they thought of death very frequently, while nearly 15 percent claimed not to think of their own death at all.

How do our respondents compare? Sadly, almost none of the studies produced directly comparable data. Nonetheless, there is reasonable consistency. Over one in six thinks daily about his death, while over one in four contemplates his termination at least once a week (B–34%, J–10%, M–37%, A–25%). On the other hand, 25 percent say they never think of their own death, and over twice that proportion claim that once a year is the most often that thoughts of personal death arise (i.e., combining "Never," "Hardly Ever," and "At Least Yearly") (B–41%, J–69%, M–38%, A–47%). One person makes the valuable point that, "One does think about death, but doesn't remember how often."

If conscious thoughts of one's own death are highly variable in terms of frequency, dreaming about one's own death is much less common, with less than 30 percent admitting that they ever have such dreams. Middleton's university students reported equivalent figures, only 37 percent indicating such dreams [27].

Another much-discussed aspect of the process of dying is that of the efficacy of the will-to-live or, conversely, the will-to-die. Weisman and Hackett discussed the post-operative deaths of six persons, all of whom anticipated their subsequent deaths and none of whom died from obvious medical causes [28]. The professional and popular literature is filled with other examples [29]. Except for the Mexican Americans, the overwhelming majority of each group agreed that "People can hasten or slow their own death through a will-to-live or a will-to-die" (B–88%, J–85%, M–62%, A–83%).

One Japanese American funeral director suggested a statistical study to verify his own observations that a highly disproportionate number of deaths occur within one month of the deceased person's birthday. Such research has, in a sense, been conducted. Phillips and Feldman found a significant reduction in deaths during the month prior to the birth month and a substantial increase in deaths during the month of birth and the month following; this was verified on several independent samples, apparently confirming the perceptions of the funeral director [30]. This information suggests that the dying person has some control over the actual time of his demise. A most graphic case described to the senior author was by a young woman studying for her doctorate whose mother was terminally ill. Although the older woman had been seriously ill for several months, she appeared in good spirits and alert until the day following her daughter's doctoral preliminary orals (the most demanding single day of her graduate program), when the mother died peacefully in her sleep. She had frequently expressed the double concern of wanting to know that her daughter had been successful (she was) and of not wanting to place the burden of a death on her during the immensely important event.

Many supernatural and mystical feelings surround death. Thus nearly half of all respondents were affirmative in answering, "Have you ever experienced or felt the presence of anyone after he had died?" (B—55%, J—29%, M—54%, A—38%), and one-fourth of these were manifested while awake and were perceived through the senses. This issue and the data are discussed at greater length elsewhere [31]. Pursuing feelings of mysticism surrounding death, over one-third of the Mexicans and between 12 percent and 15 percent of the other groups had experienced the "unexplainable feeling that (they) were about to die." We explicitly eliminated from our count instances in which these feelings occurred during dreams.

Even more persons had had such a feeling about someone else (B—37%, J—17%, M—38%, A—30%), and over 70 percent of these respondents stated that the presentiment was validated by actual death on at least one occasion. We feel strongly that these data have an important message to professionals who work with the dying and the bereaved: mystical feelings, "being in touch with his ether," "sensing the vibes," or actually having vivid and realistic contact with the dead, all these experiences are commonplace to large segments of the American public, and it is time they cease being approached as inevitably pathological.

In some settings, people routinely express their desire to die, e.g., at the Japanese American nursing home, nurses told us that nearly all the patients express such a wish at some time or other during their stay. Other than those suffering severe physical or emotional anguish, however, extremely few people wish to die, whether or not they state that they fear death. What is there about life that they cherish? Diggory and Rothman described seven values destroyed by death, and they obtained ratings of the importance of these values from over 500 respondents [32]. Shneidman administered the same questions in his *Psychology Today* study. (Shneidman also reports on the same items administered to 120 Harvard and Radcliff students.) Although the Diggory-Rothman sample was not limited to college students, about two-thirds were under twenty-five years old, two-thirds were unmarried, and one-fourth were Jewish. Diggory and Rothman also presented the values on a matched pair basis, the respondent being required to select the alternative felt to represent the greatest loss, while we had our respondents indicate whether they felt the value was "very important," "important," or "not important." Results are, thus, not directly comparable to our study (see Table 4).

Our respondents were most concerned by the possibility of causing grief to their friends and relatives (based upon combining "very important" and "important"). Diggory and Rothman also found this to be the most important, but it ranked fifth for Shneidman, perhaps due to the different family roles of his subjects. Over half the Blacks and 75 percent each of our other groups also listed not being able to care for dependents as "important" or "very important," but

Table 4. Here Are Some Reasons Why People Don't Want To Die.
Tell Me Whether They Are Very Important To You, Important To You,
Or Not Important To You. (*Don't Know* Responses About 3%).

	B (%)	J (%)	M (%)	A (%)
I am afraid of what might happen to my body after death.				
Very important	3	5	8	5
Important	6	11	9	11
Not important	91	84	83	84
I could no longer care for my dependents.				
Very important	26	42	47	44
Important	26	33	29	29
Not important	48	25	24	26
I am uncertain as to what might happen to me.				
Very important	9	14	11	9
Important	16	19	21	19
Not important	75	66	68	72
I could no longer have any experiences.				
Very important	3	11	7	6
Important	9	26	27	23
Not important	88	63	66	70
My death would cause grief to my relatives and friends.				
Very important	19	14	38	29
Important	55	48	40	50
Not important	26	38	23	21
All my plans and projects would come to an end.				
Very important	10	14	15	14
Important	24	43	34	22
Not important	66	44	51	64
The process of dying might be painful.				
Very important	13	18	30	18
Important	41	38	27	36
Not important	46	44	43	46

this concern was ranked much lower by the other studies, depending as they did upon respondents not so likely to have dependents. However, Shaffer's study of just over thirty individuals who were concerned with making out their wills had results in keeping with ours [33]. Hall expresses the feeling, "Often the last thought as the soul launches out to cross the bar is for others. There is often a tenacious clinging in thought of . . . a friend, and there is very rarely . . . any concern for the individual's future . . ." [3, p. 554].

Between one-fourth and one-third of each ethnic group felt that being uncertain as to what might happen to them was important or very important, ranking it fifth, while not being able to have any more experiences distressed well under one-third of our respondents to rank sixth. Shneidman's high-achievement sample placed it first by a wide margin, while Diggory and Rothman's intermediate group listed it fourth. And all studies agreed that what happened to the body after death was least important.

Clearly, concern over survivors ranks most highly as a reason for not wanting to die, while the fate of the physical body is obviously of minor importance. Fear of pain was also a major consideration. Somewhat unexpected in these results was the relatively low concern for the inability to continue with plans and projects or to have on-going experiences. If, as Kastenbaum and Aisenberg contend, cessation of experience is the one characteristic that differentiates death from other occurrences, these respondents certainly do not give the matter much status in their lives [6]. Had we requested that the seven issues be rank-ordered, rather than rated, we could understand better the relegation of loss of experience to such a low level. The question we have, then, is not why the other reasons for not wishing to die were rated so highly, but why these two were not rated equally high. Why do two-thirds of these respondents state that loss of ability to have experiences is not important to them? Why do well over half make the same claim about the end of plans and projects?

One obvious answer is that many respondents do not actually believe that their death will result in the end of self-aware existence. Those who believe in a traditional Christian or Buddhist concept of after-life may not feel they need be concerned about these losses. Another explanation is simply that people are not that enthralled with life. This suggests the possibility that the elderly, who have presumably become disengaged to some extent with life, would care less about these matters than younger persons. Examination of the data does show that to be the case, but it can only explain away a portion of those who respond in that fashion.

We would opt for a different kind of explanation. When people think of death, they tend to think in terms of the loss of others, of pain, of financial difficulties. They seldom think about ceasing to have experiences, which inevitably constitute life itself. When philosophers and others have stated that people cannot conceptualize their own deaths, they are often referring to cessation, including cessation of experience. To contemplate this is to contemplate nothingness, absence, void—the task is overwhelming. It is to conceive of that which has never—and can never be—experienced. Therefore, the notion is not dealt with and it is not conceptualized as an important reason for not wishing to die. Shneidman's respondents being younger, more introspective, and more intellectually sophisticated, may have given more thought to this issue.

In our writing this report, we sometimes find ourselves focusing on statistics and theory, rather than exposing ourselves to the personal and existential meaning of pain, of loss, and of death. In this regard, we want to quote from the report of one of our research assistants who effectively combined the research demands of our project with her own desire to offer personal service.

> Mr. Z. was a friendly, gentle, gregarious individual in his early thirties whose physical appearance reminded me a great deal of another patient who had just died of leukemia. In all the time Mr. Z. spoke with me, he never once mentioned his illness by name—it was as though he had been afraid to say the word. On my second visit, he talked a lot about God and made frequent references to passages in the Bible, he spoke about faith and how one has to think of God as being *un Dios Posesiro*. He even read me a passage from the New Testment. I commented that I had't seen anyone with such fervent faith in a long time, especially a young Mexican man. I then asked him if he was Protestant. "Yes, I'm a Seventh-Day Adventist."
>
> My third visit. Mr. Z. recognized me and said hello. He told me he wasn't feeling well and was in pain, because some liquid had been drawn from his liver. The whole process was extremely painful, and Mr. Z. was very uncomfortable. He looked at me and said, "I'd rather be . . ." and then he stopped, without completing the sentence. (Was he afraid that if he put the word *dead* at the end of his sentence, it might become a reality?)
>
> My fifth visit. Walking into Mr. Z.'s room I could see the anguish and pain he was going through. He restlessly changed from his back to his left side to his right side, all in vain. He was desperately fighting that pain. On top of his nightstand, beside his bed, I noticed a vase with red roses. Mr. Z. noticed me looking at his flowers: "My wife brought them to me yesterday and look at them—they're all . . . all . . . dead." He stared emptily, as if all hope for life were gone for himself as well as for his flowers.
>
> Never having seen anyone in such pain, I felt helpless and upset because I couldn't think of anything to do. I also looked at the roses in desperation. Then my eye caught sight of one rose that had been hidden. It was alive and in full bloom! "Look!! You were too quick to judge. One is still alive!!" Mr. Z. looked over and smiled.
>
> My sixth visit. Mr. Z. was in such pain that he could hardly bear it. His only consolation was the news that he did not have cancer, but had a rare blood disease. The nurse had told him that he couldn't have any more medication and that he needed to relax. Then she left. "Will you stay with me a while?" he asked. I nodded and he stared at me.
>
> "Try to lie back and relax." He tried, but he couldn't. He still kept fighting. In a final attempt, I told him, "Lie back and hold my hand. Every time the pain comes, squeeze my hand as hard as you can." He did. I sat with him for about thirty minutes before I felt the pressure on my hand slowly relax. He had fallen asleep."
>
> [From the notes of Patricia Osuna Salazar]

Predicting the Future

We asked our respondents to look into their future for a few moments. How do they predict they will die? and when? Almost all of those who responded (many did not respond: B–37%, J–9%, M–34%, A–21%) predicted a natural death for themselves (about 90%), and median age at death of seventy-five. (The 25%ile was 69 years of age, and the 75%ile was 82, with a range from 27 to over 100.) Over two-thirds of Shneidman's much younger group picked "an old age," but specific year of death was not provided. Significant differences (based on t-tests) were found between the Blacks and each other ethnic group, with the former expecting to live longer. (A more detailed anlaysis is presented in Reynolds and Kalish [34] and Bengtson, Cuellar, and Ragan [26], in their study of ethnicity and aging, also found that Blacks had longer subjective life expectancy than Mexican Americans or Anglos.

But how do they want to die? Relatively few have difficulty answering this one (under 7%), and all but a handful want to die a natural death. (We did find that 2% of the Blacks and 3% of the Anglos wanted to die by suicide, while about 25% of the Japanese and 7% of the Mexicans wanted to die in an accident.) And when? The median age was eighty, while the 25%ile at seventy (virtually the same as for the expectation of death) and the 75%ile at ninety. The range was from forty to well beyond 100 again. And 66 percent of Shneidman's respondents also opted for "old age."

Although it is well-known that most people now die in hospitals and convalescent centers, many more of our respondents would prefer dying at home. Among the Blacks, the ratio was 2:1, and among the Mexicans, a little lower. However the Japanese and Anglos both preferred dying at home by better than 4:1.

We also asked how the person would spend his last six months, assuming he learned that he was dying from a terminal illness. Answers were coded by the interviewers, and they ranged over a number of categories. About one-fourth would make no change in life style (B–31%, J–25%, M–12%, A–36%), and another one-fifth would focus attention on their inner life (e.g., contemplate, pray). However about one-sixth would undergo a marked change in life style, such as traveling, satisfying hedonistic demands, essentially trying to soak up as many experiences as possible (B–16%, J–24%, M–11%, A–17%). Nearly 40 percent of the Mexicans and about half that proportion of the others would devote their remaining time to those they love. The categories described above were preestablished, based upon our pilot testing. However, the question was open-ended, and examination of the specific answers given by interviewees shows great diversity. Thus, devoting time to loved ones might mean taking a trip with the wife, returning to live with parents, or baby-sitting with grandchildren. Each of our categories encompassed numerous specific kinds of behavior.

How would these people die? A little more than one-third would fight death, rather than accepting it, with virtually no differences by ethnicity. Explanations varied greatly. A Black high school graduate said, "I believe if you're a Christian, you wouldn't fight—just get yourself ready to go. Ask forgiveness for your sins and put yourself in the hands of the Lord." Another Black woman interpreted the question somewhat differently: "If by fight, you mean seeking any medical aid available or through positive thinking and not giving up, then I would fight." A Mexican American woman made the differentiation, "If I was in the hospital and feeling very sick, I would just accept death. But if I was out in the world, I would fight it by enjoying life as long as I possibly could." Well over half the Blacks and Japanese, but somewhat under half the Mexicans and Anglos, would tell someone of their pain rather than enduring it in silence. One made the point that, "If it was the doctor, I would tell him of my pain. I think maybe I would tell my husband, but not my son" (who was still a child). A college graduate from the Japanese American community was more fatalistic: "If it's going to hurt, it's going to hurt. The doctor knows I'm hurting already and if there was a way to prevent it, he would prevent it." An Anglo American man was more demanding: "I would ask the doctor to give me some codeine or some other pain killer." Very similar proportions would refrain from encouraging their families to be with them, if it were inconvenient. A young Japanese American woman said, "No, I wouldn't ask them, but I would feel better if they did." A Mexican American woman of about the same age explained, "I would want my husband and my child there only—not the rest of my family. Not my parents—they would probably cry and have a lot of sympathy for me, but my husband, he'd be strong." And nearly 90 percent of the Mexican Americans, and over half the others, would call for a clergyman. Something has happened to customary ethnic stereotypes in these figures. The stoical Japanese Americans and the emotive Mexican Americans appear to reverse expected roles in terms of expressing their feelings of pain; the aggressive, competitive Anglos were no more likely to fight death than the more accepting Mexicans or Japanese. The highly familistic Mexican Americans do encourage their families to be with them, but not the highly familistic Japanese Americans. Our point is certainly obvious: situational factors and competing demands often weigh more heavily than even well-established modal group characteristics.

Preparing for Death

In Riley's national survey, about 80 percent of the respondents had purchased life insurance, around one-third had made some funeral or cemetery arrangements, and about one-fourth had made out a will. Our percentages were similar, understandably, given the economic bias in our sample. Nearly 70 percent had some life insurance (B—84%, J—70%, M—52%, A—65%), and about one-fifth had wills (more Anglos and fewer Mexican Americans). Around one-fourth of the Blacks, Japanese, and Anglos (and half that many Mexicans) had a financial investment in a cemetery plot, while slightly more than half that proportion had made funeral arrangements. The overwhelming majority of Shneidman's respondents believed in having a will and making prior arrangements, but no data were provided as to whether they had actually done so.

Riley learned that about half his respondents had discussed "the uncertainty of life" with those closest to them. We avoided the euphemism, and received a lower affirmative response (B—27%, J—16%, M—33%, A—37%). Also about one-fourth of the entire sample (more Anglos and fewer Japanese) had arranged for someone to handle their affairs. Among the Japanese, such arrangements are handled automatically by persons filling roles designated by long custom. Nowadays the role expectations are less dependable, but the practical business of making individual arrangements has not yet caught up with the change.

Funerals

The polemics of those who favor or oppose today's funeral industry have been widely disseminated through books [35, 36] and articles [37, 38]. But what do people want for themselves? The modal cost for an adequate funeral, as stated in our study, was an even $1,000; this was the mode for each ethnicity as well as for the entire sample. However, the means for the ethnic groups varied considerably. The mean cost expected by the Blacks was $1,075, with 30 percent expecting to pay under $700; comparable figures for the Japanese were $1,948 and 9 percent. In between were the Mexicans ($1,209 and 29%) and Anglos ($1,179 and 31%). There were highly significant t-tests of differences between the Japanese and each other ethnic group. Shneidman's young, well-educated liberal respondents felt funerals should cost under $300 (62%). (Recall that these interviews were conducted in 1970.)

The Japanese can expect to pay the most for their funerals because more of them anticipate that friends and family will share in the expenses (B—27%, J—43%, M—30%, A—27%). On the other hand, 92 percent of the Japanese (compared to between 79% and 89% of the others) rejected a big elaborate funeral, and 81 percent (compared to between 58 percent and 63 percent) wanted a funeral with only relatives and friends rather than many friends and acquaintances in attendance. For example, a Japanese American explained hesitatingly, "No . . . it's too . . . it takes away . . . I don't like something that's gaudy." Our observations indicate that, in spite of these expressed desires, fairly elaborate funerals are common for all these groups. About one-third of all respondents expected that a large percentage of their life insurance should go toward paying funeral expenses with a higher figure among Mexican Americans and a lower one among Anglos.

Most people want the clergyman presiding at the funeral to be selected by their family after their death, and most prefer that he be of their ethnic group (except that over half the Blacks are indifferent as are large proportions of the other groups). Similar figures were found for the selection of a funeral director of the ethnic group of the respondent; a slight majority of Blacks and Anglos were indifferent, while two-thirds of the Japanese and half the Mexicans preferred ethnic solidarity.

The desire for a wake varies greatly among the ethnic groups, with percentages pro and con being B–25% vs 53%, J–41% vs. 46%, M–68% vs. 15%, A–22% vs. 72%. The preferred location for the wake is the funeral home, except for the Japanese Americans who wish to use the church, often a necessity for the large turnouts that attend their wakes. Somewhat under one-fourth (more Anglos and fewer Mexicans) want the wake in their own home.

On the other hand, two-thirds of the Blacks and three-fourths of the Japanese want the funeral in a church, while half the Mexican Americans and half the Anglos want the services in a funeral home (only 4% overall want to use their own home). One Mexican American explained she disliked funeral corteges that sped along the freeway and that she preferred using the cemetery chapel. And about half of each group feels that children under ten should be permitted to attend their funeral.

Customs and rituals that pertain to disposal of the body after the ceremony are also of major concern. One in four Anglos and Blacks and one in three Mexicans and Japanese would object to an autopsy, suggesting a substantial resistance still remaining to physical violation of the remains. Feifel and Jones show 27 percent objecting [10]. About 20 percent overall, fewer Black Americans and more Japanese Americans, object to embalming, perhaps related to the latter preference for cremation. Burial is preferred by nearly 20:1 over cremation for the Mexicans and Blacks, by about 3.5:1 among the Anglos. However, over half the Japanese prefer cremation, compared to one-third who desire burial. One-third of Shneidman's group wanted to be cremated and another third would request donation to medical school or science; only 22 percent desired burial.

Where the body/ashes are finally deposited is also important. Over half of each group selected Los Angeles, but the reasons for selection were more varied (17% preferred a location outside of Los Angeles, but within the United States; an additional 9% opted for another country). The reasons for the selected location also vary substantially as a result of ethnicity. Most frequently mentioned was that the community was where many family members lived (B–41%, J–27%, M–30%, A–10%), but the second most frequently-mentioned was that the respondent himself lived there now (between 19% and 24%). A birthplace was cited by about 15 percent (more Mexicans and Blacks, fewer Japanese and Anglos).

ANOTHER KIND OF ANALYSIS

Because our focus has been primarily upon differences among ethnic groups, we decided to investigate which variables showed no significant differences, either for the entire sample or between pairs of ethnicities. There were thirty-two items for which we found no significant differences (having eliminated items with very small Ns, those with continuous data, and second or later choices, a total of 19).

These items, we feel, represent the human condition, at least for persons residing in Los Angeles of low to moderate income and education. These are characteristics, feelings, beliefs, expectations, behavior, that people have regardless of social class.

The items on which our subcultures essentially agreed fall into several classes. The first class of responses deals with the familiarity of contact with death. The four groups were fairly similar in regard to knowing persons who had died from 1) accidents, 2) natural causes, 3) war-related incidents and 4) suicide. Neither was there a difference in the frequency of visiting a dying person, nor of having known someone who died under circumstances in which a decision was made to tell him or not.

A second category of response dealt with the acceptance of death. Around 60 percent of all respondents stated they would tend to accept their own death peacefully, and over three-fourths doubted that death would ever be eliminated. The resignation toward the ultimate (not the immediate!) inevitability of death is at least in part related to the belief that God has a hand in life and death. Around 60 percent of all respondents felt that accidental deaths showed God working among men. When they think of the elimination of human life from the earth, they tend to think in terms of nuclear-explosions or God's judgment. There is also consensus that the deaths of old people are less tragic than those of other ages.

But despite this contact with death and this recognition of it, there are ways in which impact of death is ignored or abridged by our respondents. Is this denial? or avoidance? practical-economic necessity? or transcendance? We cannot say. But fewer than 15 percent have made funeral arrangements, only some 25 percent are paying on a funeral plot, and upwards of 80 percent don't care particularly what happens to their body after they die. Revealingly, fewer than half could recall ever having dreamed about their own death or dying.

There seemed to be general agreement on some role behavior related to death. For example, physicians were handed the task of informing patients of a terminal condition by a majority of each ethnic group; family members were next most likely to be given this job. And these ideals corresponded closely to the reality of cases our respondents knew about. About 50 percent of the respondents in each group saw a relative as an appropriate person to turn to for comfort if a spouse died. And there were fairly uniform views toward people who threaten suicide. Roughly equal percentages in all groups felt such threateners want attention, are emotionally sick, need sympathy, and need professional help. There is consensus on the proper period of grieving for those in the role of the bereaved with approximately a third of each group choosing times within the "two weeks or less," "one to three months," and "six months or more" categories.

A few scattered items that showed no significant differences may be of interest. About 80 percent of all groups felt a person dying of cancer probably sensed it without being told. The groups were almost equally split as to whether or not the pain of dying is an unimportant factor (ca. 45%) in not wanting to die. Some 25–30 percent of each group would object to having an autopsy performed on their body.

To summarize, we found each of our groups to be well acquainted with death, in some ways accepting of it, but in other ways unable or unwilling to admit its impact or plan for its coming. They showed agreement on some role behaviors and role expectations. The overall impression is one of a practical and reasonable approach to the handling of death with perhaps a dash of avoidance when personal-emotional aspects are touched upon.

CONCLUDING REMARKS

There seems little doubt that ethnic background is an important factor in attitudes, feelings, beliefs, and expectations that people have regarding dying, death, and bereavement. The survey results show this very clearly. We would also assume that these differences are translated into differing behavior in hospitals, at home, in health and social service agencies, and in the community. Indeed, other information that will be discussed in subsequent chapters support the assumption.

At the same time that our data show substantial ethnic differences, we are also aware that individual differences within ethnic groups are at least as great as, and often much greater than, differences between ethnic groups. We will come back to this point later.

REFERENCES

1. R. Fulton, The Sacred and the Secular: Attitudes of the American Public toward Death, Funerals, and Funeral Directors, in *Death and Identity*, R. Fulton (ed.), Wiley, New York, pp. 89-105, 1965.
2. G. Gorer, *Death, Grief, and Mourning*, Doubleday, New York, 1965.
3. G. S. Hall, Thanatophobia and Immortality, *American Journal of Psychology*, 26, pp. 550-613, 1915.
4. P. J. Donaldson, Denying Death: A Note Regarding Some Ambiguities in the Current Discussion, *Omega*, 3, pp. 285-293, 1972.
5. T. Parsons and V. Lidz, Death in American Society, in *Essays in Self-Destruction*, E. S. Shneidman (ed.), Science House, New York, pp. 133-170, 1967.
6. R. Kastenbaum and R. B. Aisenberg, *The Psychology of Death*, Springer, New York, 1972.
7. B. G. Glaser and A. L. Strauss, *Awareness of Dying*, Aldine, Chicago, 1965.
8. J. M. Hinton, The Physical and Mental Distress of the Dying, *Quarterly Journal of Medicine*, 32, pp. 1-21, 1963.

9. H. Feifel, *et al.*, Physicians Consider Death, *Proceedings of the 75th Annual Convention of the American Psychological Association, 2,* pp. 201-202, 1967.
10. H. Feifel and R. Jones, Perception of Death as Related to Nearness to Death, *Proceedings of the 76th Annual Convention of the American Psychological Association, 3,* pp. 545-546, 1968.
11. G. M. Vernon, *Sociology of Death: An Analysis of Death-related Behavior,* Ronald Press, New York, 1970.
12. E. Kübler-Ross, *On Death and Dying,* Macmillan, New York, 1969.
13. R. Koenig, Anticipating Death from Cancer-Physician and Patient Attitudes, *Michigan Medicine, 68,* pp. 899-905, 1969.
14. M. Chenard, unpublished doctoral dissertation, 1972.
15. J. Schoenberg and J. Stichman, *How to Survive Your Husband's Heart Attack,* David McKay, New York, 1974.
16. L. W. Simmons, *The Role of the Aged in Primitive Society,* Yale University Press, New Haven, 1945.
17. I. E. Alexander, R. S. Colley, and A. M. Adlerstein, Is Death a Matter of Indifference?, *Journal of Psychology, 43,* pp. 277-283, 1957.
18. C. A. Scott, Old Age and Death, *American Journal of Psychology, 8,* pp. 54-122, 1896.
19. G. S. Hall, A Study of Fears, *American Journal of Psychology, 8,* pp. 147-149, 1897.
20. National Council on the Aging, *The Myth and Reality of Aging in America,* National Council on the Aging, Washington, D.C., 1975.
21. M. Riley and A. Foner, *Aging and Society,* Russel Sage, New York, 1968.
22. M. E. Ivey and J. M. Bardwick, Patterns of Affective Fluctuation in the Menstrual Cycle, *Psychosomatic Medicine, 30,* pp. 336-345, 1968.
23. E. A. Kennard, Hopi Reactions to Death, *American Anthropologist, 29,* pp. 491-494, 1937.
24. J. W. Riley, Jr., What People Think about Death, in *The Dying Patient,* O. G. Brim, Jr., H. E. Freeman, S. Levine, and N. A. Scotch (eds.), Russell Sage, New York, 1970.
25. E. S. Shneidman, You and Death, *Psychology Today, 5:*6, p. 43ff, 1971.
26. V. L. Bengtson, J. A. Cuellar, and P. K. Ragan, Group Contrasts in Attitudes toward Death: Variation by Race, Age, Occupational Status, and Sex, 1976.
27. W. C. Middleton, Some Reactions toward Death among College Students, *Journal of Abnormal and Social Psychology, 31,* pp. 165-173, 1936.
28. A. D. Weisman and T. P. Hackett, Predilection to Death: Death and Dying as a Psychiatric Problem, *Psychosomatic Medicine, 23,* pp. 232-256, 1961.
29. R. A. Kalish, The Aged and the Dying Process: The Inevitable Decisions, *Journal of Social Issues, 21,* pp. 87-96, 1965.
30. D. P. Phillips and K. A. Feldman, A Dip in Deaths before Ceremonial Occasions: Some New Relationships between Social Integration and Mortality, *American Sociological Review, 38,* pp. 678-696, 1973.
31. R. A. Kalish and D. K. Reynolds, Phenomenological Reality and Post-Death Contact, *Journal for the Scientific Study of Religion, 12,* pp. 209-221, 1973.

32. J. C. Diggory and D. Z. Rothman, Values Destroyed by Death, *Journal of Abnormal and Social Psychology*, *63*, pp. 205-210, 1961.
33. T. L. Shaffer, *Death, Property, and Lawyers: A Behavioral Approach*, Dunellen, New York, 1970.
34. D. K. Reynolds and R. A. Kalish, Anticipation of Futurity as a Function of Ethnicity and Age, *Journal of Gerontology*, *29*, pp. 224-231, 1974.
35. R. M. Harmer, *The High Cost of Dying*, Cromwell-Collier, New York, 1963.
36. J. Mitford, *The American Way of Death*, Simon and Schuster, New York, 1963.
37. R. M. Harmer, Funerals, Fantasy, and Flight, *Omega, 2,* pp. 127-135, 1971.
38. H. C. Raether, The Place of the Funeral: The Role of the Funeral Director in Contemporary America, *Omega*, *2*, pp. 150-153, 1971.

Death has many meanings, and it can certainly mean many things to each of us at any given time. Its meanings will also change over time and will undoubtedly change as the result of a serious encounter with death. An amazing number of people, even younger people, have had close calls with death, the result of automobile accidents (or near-accidents), of health problems (or the medications and surgery designed to alleviate these problems), of near-drowning, and so forth. A great deal can be learned about the dying process and the meanings of death by having such individuals describe their experiences and the outcomes of these experiences.

In the past decade, increasing attention has been given to the nature of what is usually called near-death experiences. These refer to a variety of occurrences in which people have either come very close to their own death or have been declared clinically dead but have subsequently been resuscitated. Whether such individuals have actually been granted a view of what it is like to be dead or whether they have experienced a vivid and compelling fantasy is a theological or philosophic question, and it needs to be answered by each person for himself or herself. However, the nature of these experiences and the later effects on feelings, values, and behavior are relevant to the behavioral and social sciences as well as to theology and philosophy, and it is with these issues that Chapter 3 has dealt. The author, Russell Noyes, Jr., is recognized as a true pioneer in using empirical procedures to study near-death experiences.

CHAPTER
3

The Human Experience
of Death or,
What Can We Learn
from
Near-Death Experiences?

Russell Noyes, Jr.

In a recent article I presented material on attitude changes following near-death
experiences and commented upon their importance for our understanding of the
human experience of death [1]. Here, I would like to speak further about what
I think we have, and may yet learn, from our study of near-death experiences.
I believe that these experiences have revealed to us a fundamental strategy for
coping with the threat of death. They have also shown us an experiental source
of our belief in long or unending life, and I believe, they have drawn our
attention to a powerful force for change if we can find the means to control it.

Our findings with respect to attitude and personality changes following
near-death experiences [1] come from the accounts of 215 persons who survived
life-threatening danger, 138 of whom commented upon the impact their
experience had upon their subsequent lives. Accounts were obtained through a
variety of informal contacts. A number of persons responded to advertisements,
others offered unsolicited reports, and still others responded to personal contacts.
A total of 76 persons were personally interviewed. The life-threatening
circumstances included fifty-eight falls, fifty-four drownings, fifty-three motor
vehicle accidents, twenty-four miscellaneous accidents, and twenty-six serious

illnesses. Accounts were obtained from 144 men and 71 women having a median age of twenty-three at the time of their experiences.

Each respondent was encouraged to provide a detailed account of his or her experience according to a set of printed instructions or a semi-structured interview. Although the circumstances of the accident or illness and the subjective response to it were emphasized, the subsequent impact of the experience was also explored. A total of 138 persons offered at least brief affirmative replies to the question, "Has your attitude toward life or death changed as a result of your experience?" The remainder reported no change in attitude or did not comment on any modification that might have taken place. Let us first examine the changes that occurred and then consider what they may mean.

DATA ON ATTITUDE CHANGE

A pattern of favorable attitude change resulting from near-death experiences was described that included the following: 1) a reduced fear of death, 2) a sense of relative invulnerability, 3) a feeling of special importance or destiny, 4) a belief in having received the special favor of God or fate, and 5) a strengthened belief in continued existence [1]. Of these interrelated elements the reduction in fear of death was the most often reported and the most emphasized. Of the 138 who commented, fifty-seven (41%) made specific mention of this. Some said they had lost their fear of the process of dying whenever that might occur. Others claimed that they were somehow no longer troubled by the temporary nature of their existence.

A smaller number claimed that their accident had resulted in a sense of invulnerability or calm in the face of uncertainty together with relative disregard for danger. They expressed the feeling that, having survived, they were somehow no longer subject to death. For thirty (21%) persons, this sense of invulnerability took on a larger meaning. They came to feel that they had survived because they were destined to do so. Consequently, they saw themselves as chosen to fulfill missions which gave a sense of uniqueness to their lives. Although most had not determined the specific nature of the mission to which they had been called they felt assured of continued life so long as it lay ahead.

In connection with the sense of destiny just described, twenty-four persons (17%) identified a responsible agent. Often this agent was God, an identification consistent with pre-existing religious beliefs. But this was not true in every instance. Those who felt God had rescued them believed they had been specially favored. Also meaningful for some was a strengthened belief in life beyond death. This belief was reported by fourteen (10%) and was in addition to the assurance of continued existence already described.

These findings are strikingly similar to those of others. Moody commented upon the effects of near-death experiences upon the lives of 150 persons he

interviewed [2]. Many of them reported that their lives were broadened and deep-
ened by their experiences. Life became more precious for some, and almost all lost
their fear of death. The reason for this, he said, was to be found in the removal
of doubts about survival. Survival of bodily death became "a fact of experience"
rather than an abstract possibility.

Ring reported similar effects among 102 persons who survived serious
accidents and illnesses [3]. His subjects described a heightened appreciation of
life and renewed sense of purpose in living. Some felt stronger and more
self-confident, while others reported that they became more religious and
developed greater conviction about life after death. Those who had what the
author termed a "core experience" reported that their fear of death was reduced
thereafter.

COPING WITH THE THREAT OF DEATH

Many respondents in our study claimed that they lost their fear of death as a
result of their accident or illness. For the observer who regards death as a distant
and impersonal event, such claims may seem puzzling. Is the fear of death so
widespread that experiences of this kind regularly reduce it, or have we not
completely understood what is meant by such a loss of fear? The question is
important because it pertains to the most fundamental change resulting from
near-death experiences.

In comments on their lessened fear, some respondents referred to the process
of dying, whenever that might occur. Others spoke of their impermanence in
this world or the next, and still others referred to the fear of death as they
experienced it in their daily lives. Of these three interrelated aspects, it is the
last one—what we shall call the fear of "deadness"—that is important for our
understanding. Deadness, and its opposite, "aliveness," are qualities of
existence quite apart from the biological state of the organism.[1] Because our
notions of life and death are so rooted in biological thinking, we tend to neglect
the psychological, social, and spiritual frames of reference. Consequently, the
terms "deadness" and "aliveness" may help us to think more clearly about these
aspects of our subject.

How, then, shall we define these opposing but interrelated qualities? The
participants in our investigation have done this for us [1]. As a result of their
near-death experiences, many reported greater aliveness. They described this in
terms of a feeling of invulnerability and of special importance or destiny. In
addition, some described having received the special favor of God or fate and a
strengthened belief in continued existence. In psychological terms, these changes
might be summarized as heightened sense of omnipotence, experienced
affectively as a feeling of invulnerability and cognitively as a belief in continued

[1] I am indebted to Mansell Pattison for the terms "aliveness" and "deadness."

existence, and as increased self-esteem, experienced cognitively as a belief in the special importance of one's life. Both—heightened omnipotence and self-esteem— were expressed in the religious dimension in terms of increased favor of an all- powerful being. By contrast, deadness may be defined as a sense of helplessness, low self-esteem, and meaninglessness that, in the religious dimension, may take the form of separation from an omnipotent being.

In aliveness, we see a basic human strategy for coping with the threat of death, one having its origin in the experience of birth. Just such an experience can be recognized in the pattern of responses reported in our study. In fact, many of our respondents, as well as those of Ring, described themselves as having experienced their own death and rebirth [3]. It was the aspect of being reborn that they emphasized in their comments on the subsequent impact of their accidents or illnesses. This renewal or rebirth seemed to directly affect the threat of death as they had experienced it. It appeared to replace this threat with a sense of permanence or continuing existence. This sense of permanence seemed to be independent of a person's intellectual belief or disbelief concerning life after death.

Studies of the fear of death have generally failed to take this existential dimension into account [4]. The fear of death, as with fear in general, is forward looking and relates to unpleasant future possibilities. One of these is an end to biological life, which presents a drastic, albeit unknown, change. Another is the process of dying with its attendant helplessness, suffering, and despair. But still another possibility is the threat of deadness. This, of the three, is the one most immediate and palpable. Deadness is a part of everyday experience as a person moves, in the course of events, first toward and then away from it. Unlike the other aspects, it is not dependent upon biological events. Indeed, in some circumstances, biological developments may spare a person from a death that might otherwise occur in the social, psychological, or religious spheres.

DIRECT EXPERIENCE OF SURVIVAL

Having freed ourselves from the reductionistic (biological) view of death, we have little difficulty in understanding that a person need not die in the physical sense to experience death or deadness. In fact, upon reflection we see that many times and in varying degrees each of us has experienced and re-experienced death. In the course of major life transitions such as adolescence, marriage, career change, and retirement or with the deaths or births of others, we again and again encounter death and rebirth. Freed of the biological absolute, we may look upon death or deadness as a relative matter.

Rarely will deadness be experienced in its self-obliterating completeness, although we observe this in the psychotic dissolution of acute schizophrenia and the hopeless despair of melancholia [5]. Likewise, the height of aliveness in its transcendent extreme will not commonly be experienced, although in peak and mystical experiences we catch a glimpse of this occurrence [5, 6]. Yet, in the course of separations and reunions, endings and beginnings, defeats and triumphs, illnesses and recoveries, we approach first one and then the other. In the ebb and flow of existence, there is constant movement between the poles of deadness and aliveness.

Grof and Halifax, in their fascinating book describing research on the administration of LSD to cancer patients, similarly call attention to the fact that rites of passage are associated with death-rebirth experiences [7]. They claim, with justification, that the effects of LSD are not unique but reflect a universal potential. These authors hypothesize that such experiences originate in the unconscious mind. According to their Jungian interpretation, LSD simply releases the symbolic death-rebirth content from the unconscious. How it came to reside there remains a mystery. Much simpler is the explanation offered here that, with LSD, a person experiences his own self-dissolution and reintegration, and that this psychological death and rebirth is reflected in the content of his altered state of consciousness. Such an explanation is consistent with the notion of deadness according to which death can be, and repeatedly is, experienced without involving biological cessation.

This brings us to an important observation about the near-death experiences we have been discussing. It is that the name assigned them may mislead us. Consistent with our notion of deadness, we should recognize these as "death-rebirth" experiences. In doing so we call attention to the fact of survival. We should not forget that those who report experiences to us have survived accidents or illnesses. In fact, we might refer to them as experiences of survival. It is precisely this aspect that persists in the form of attitude and personality changes. It is not too surprising, then, that the experiences we are discussing point toward some kind of survival of death. After all, persons who report them have survived! Being aware of this should make us cautious about our attempts to find evidence for life after death among these experiences.

We have evidence from our study that a sense of permanence or continuing life can be directly experienced, and that this emotional reaction may not be limited by prior beliefs about life beyond death [1]. Many respondents indicated that the more unique and valuable their lives seemed to become the more confident they grew of their continued existence to the point of feeling somehow indestructable. For some, this sense of assurance seemed to influence beliefs about life after death. If they experienced this assurance, their belief was strengthened. Thus, the experience of rebirth may bring with it an assurance of survival that is reflected in the content of the experience. Here we speak of psychological mechanism but not of any ultimate interpretation or truth about the matter.

A POWERFUL FORCE FOR CHANGE

Ultimately, we are interested in near-death experiences because of their power to change attitudes, personality, and beliefs. If we could learn their secrets, we could put a potent therapeutic force at our disposal. Their effects strike at the very core of existence and are produced in the briefest span of time. Indeed, the acuteness of their action suggests the use of words like conversion or transformation and prompts us to compare them with religious experiences of a similar kind [8, 9]. The changes themselves are variable both in intensity and duration. But, temporary or permanent, those that occur in some persons are impressive and bear continuing study.

To begin with, we wish to know whether there is one experience or many, and under what circumstances they occur. Our discussion would suggest that they are not limited to serious illnesses and accidents but may accompany major life crises and transitions. Certainly, the development and recovery from major psychiatric illnesses may be the stimulus for such experiences. In these instances, the content of the psychosis may contain death-rebirth symbolism [7, 10]. In many respects, religious conversions arising from existential crises resemble death-rebirth experiences [8, 9]. Also, as Grof and others have demonstrated, LSD and other consciousness-altering drugs are capable of producing them [7]. Profoundly altered states of consciousness, however they are produced, may prompt the kind of dynamic shifts within personality that we are considering [11].

Although the experiences we are discussing occur under a wide variety of circumstances, more than mere circumstances appear necessary for their development. A receptive attitude or giving-in to them may also be required. From our study of accident victims, we learned that persons involved in efforts to rescue themselves were more likely to experience anxiety and less likely to report reduced fear of death afterwards [1]. Similarly, for a mystical experience to occur under the influence of LSD, it may be necessary for the person to submit to the effects of the drug [12]. An attitude of surrender that accompanies religious conversions has been considered an essential ingredient by some observers [8, 9]. These observations from divergent sources seem to support the notion that a receptive attitude may be of importance.

Certainly, there can be little doubt but that personality and life circumstances have a bearing on the outcome of death-rebirth experiences. In our study, for example, a young woman reported that an existential crisis in her life had been resolved by her accident experience [1]. Of course, had there been no crisis none would have been resolved. Similarly, a number of specific fears and personality styles were changed only because they existed and were, therefore, subject to modification. From the descriptions we have of the pattern of change that may occur following a death-rebirth experience, we can catch a glimpse of the attitudes, personality traits, and beliefs that experiences of this kind are capable of modifying. For example, existential crises, life patterns designed to ward off the fear of death (deadness), and certain neurotic fears that have their origin in death anxiety appear likely candidates [13, 14].

We might carry our speculation to considerable lengths and generate a number of interesting, even testable, hypotheses. But, we would sooner or later come to the practical question of how death-rebirth experiences can be made available for therapeutic purposes. Do we have techniques for calling them forth, and if so, can we do so ethically? Of course, LSD and related drugs are capable of producing this experience and of causing profound changes in some persons [7]. Administration of these drugs to cancer patients has confirmed that death-rebirth experiences may have varied benefits. Still, LSD has fallen into disfavor and is presently not available even to most researchers.

However, death-rebirth experiences are probably operative in certain therapies that are presently being employed. We may observe their operation in the alcoholic who "hits bottom" prior to achieving sobriety in Alcoholics Anonymous [15]. Their influence may also be seen in certain marathon groups during which breakdown and restoration of personality contributes to the final result [16]. We may further our understanding of these and other therapeutic processes by recognizing the role of the death-rebirth experience in their inner workings. Perhaps if we can begin to understand how the experience brings about change we can find other ways of putting its healing potential to use. This is the critical challenge.

CONCLUSION

We have seen that near-death experiences may provide some persons with direct experiences of aliveness including assurances of continuing life. Can they also provide us with scientific evidence of life after death? The answer to this question would appear to hinge on whether appropriate methods are available [17]. Survival research has been the province of parapsychology and has been plagued by possible alternative explanations for findings since its inception a century ago [18]. New methods that satisfactorily respond to questions raised have not been forthcoming, although they may yet be developed.

As we have pointed out, persons are capable of experiencing a sense of permanence without undergoing biological death. Such experiential transcendence of the limits of time and space naturally influences personal beliefs. It also provides confirmation of shared beliefs about life after death and tells us something about the human experience of death and rebirth, although not necessarily about the reality of death. That remains an unknown. Still, we are on no firmer ground in interpreting the experience according to some psychological mechanism than we are in offering it as evidence for the reality of life after death. Students of the psychology of religion, including William James, have shown great caution in interpreting religious experiences on psychological grounds [8, 9]. We should follow their example with respect to death-rebirth experiences.

If we are to keep this area of research alive, we must avoid becoming overly committed to the survival question [19]. Because adequate methods do not appear to be available, we run the risk of making statements of belief that are without scientific foundation and, in the process, of drifting away from our data base. When this occurs, we tend to lose our legitimacy as scientific investigators. As I have attempted to point out, there are a number of other reasons for our interest in death-rebirth experiences and a number of testable hypotheses of great interest.

Ultimately, these experiences interest us because of their power to produce change. As natural occurrences we are interested in their potential for producing and modifying psychopathology. In connection with suicide attempts, for example, we are vitally concerned with their influence on pre-existing disorders and subsequent suicidal behavior [20]. Understanding of these experiences may teach us something, as well, about adaptation to cardiac arrests and other life-threatening circumstances that are survived with ever increasing frequency [1].

We are also interested in these experiences because they have much to teach us about the human experience of death. They can assist us to understand forms of psychopathology related to the ubiquitous but ill-defined fear of death and can help us to learn about how, as individuals, we cope with this threat from day to day and from one period of life to another. What we learn from extreme situations may provide a valuable perspective on more ordinary ones and get us to think along lines that we might not have otherwise. In addition, the concepts of deadness and aliveness may prove useful within the framework of personality functioning. The work of Maslow on the relationship of personality to peak experiences suggests this very thing [5].

Other reasons for interest include the mystical or religious nature of many of these experiences. That a dying person may have a religious experience as part of a final alteration in consciousness is a matter of keen interest to believers of many faiths. Experiences of this kind and reports of them will have their influence, supporting as they do certain spiritual realities. Certainly, the interpretation of these aspects should remain within the religious framework. We can note those factors and circumstances that contribute to them but should limit ourselves to that.

What can we learn from near-death experiences? As long as our objectives remain clearly before us, and we retain the objectivity essential to a scientific endeavor, we can learn a great deal. We should not simply resort to faith which, in our dealing with religious matters, is always a temptation.

REFERENCES

1. R. Noyes, Jr., Attitude Change Following Near-Death Experiences, *Psychiatry, 43,* pp. 234-242, 1980.
2. R. A. Moody, Jr., *Life After Life,* Mockingbird Books, Atlanta, 1975.

3. K. Ring, *Life at Death, A Scientific Investigation of the Near-Death Experience,* Cowan, McCann and Geoghegan, New York, 1980.
4. J. A. Durlak and R. A. Kass, Clarifying the Measurement of Death Attitudes: A Factor Analytic Evaluation of Fifteen Self-Report Death Scales, *Omega, 12*:2, pp. 129-143, 1981.
5. A. M. Maslow, *Religious, Values, and Peak-Experiences,* Viking Press, New York, 1964.
6. N. Stace, *Mysticism and Philosophy,* Lippincott, Philadelphia, 1960.
7. S. Grof and J. Halifax, *The Human Encounter with Death,* Dutton, New York, 1977.
8. W. H. Clark, *The Psychology of Religion,* Macmillan, New York, 1958.
9. W. James, *The Varieties of Religious Experience,* Longmans, London, 1929.
10. A. T. Boisen, *The Exploration of the Inner World,* Harper, New York, 1936.
11. C. T. Tart, *Altered States of Consciousness,* Wiley, New York, 1969.
12. J. N. Sherwood, M. J. Stolaroff, and W. W. Harman, The Psychedelic Experience—A New Concept in Psychotherapy, *J. Neuropsychiat., 4,* pp. 69-80, 1962.
13. J. E. Meyer, *Death and Neurosis,* M. Nunberg, (trans.), International University Press, New York, 1975.
14. I. D. Yalom, *Existential Psychotherapy,* Basic Books, New York, 1980.
15. J. Clancy, Motivation Conflicts of the Alcohol Addict, *Quart. J. of the Study of Alcohol, 25,* pp. 511-520, 1964.
16. I. D. Yalom, *The Theory and Practice of Group Psychotherapy,* Basic Books, New York, 1970.
17. I. Stevenson and B. Greyson, Near-Death Experiences: Relevance to the Question of Survival After Death, *J.A.M.A., 242,* pp. 265-267, 1979.
18. I. Stevenson, Research into the Evidence of Man's Survival After Death, *J. Nerv. Ment. Dis., 165,* pp. 152-170, 1977.
19. R. Noyes, Jr., Near-Death Experiences; Their Interpretation and Significance, R. Kastenbaum, (ed.), *Between Life and Death,* Springer, New York, pp. 73-88, 1979.
20. K. Ring, Do Suicide Survivors Report Near-Death Experiences?, *Omega, 12*:3, pp. 191-208, 1982.

Working with dying persons has been one major foci for death counselors; working with the survivors of death has been another. We all confront our own death, but the greatest emotional pain often comes when we confront the death of someone we love. Providing services for the survivors is much more than intervening at one point in time; rather, it requires on-going consideration, since the issues that affect the survivors prior to death are altered at the time of death and continue to change over time. This does not mean that every survivor of death requires an active intervention; far from it, since most people have adequate supports and use them effectively. However, people who are personally and professionally involved with grief need to pay particular attention to the grieving trajectory, which often begins days or even weeks or months before the death.

Almost every death in almost every culture is followed by some form of ceremony and ritual that provides for 1) the "soul" of the dead person to enter the next state of its existence, 2) the support and re-integration of the bereaved, and 3) the disposal of the body. Chapter 4 offers a description of what occurs in one region of the United States as the familiar ritual of the funeral takes place.

Is it possible to apply Rodabough's observations to other religious groups, such as Catholic or Jewish? Or to other regions of the country, such as the northwest or the New England states? It's difficult to know, but it seems very likely that many, perhaps most, of the "characters" described in Chapter 4 have their counterparts at funerals provided by other religions and in other parts of the country.

The funeral provides an opportunity for the expression of grief in a supportive setting. However, as Chapter 4 indicates, not everyone expresses this grief in the same fashion, nor with the same motives, and some may not even be expressing grief. At the very least, the expression of grief combines with the expression of other thoughts and feelings, and the outward manifestation are highly varied.

CHAPTER
4

Funeral Roles:
Ritualized Expectations

Tillman Rodabough

A funeral is defined here as the set of behaviors surrounding the disposal of a body from the time the participants enter the church until the cemetery observances are completed. A ritual is a set routine faithfully followed, often in an elaborate manner, in performing certain religious or solemn acts. This chapter does not propose to describe the procedures common to funerals while detailing such differences as those occurring between regions, denominations, ethnic groups, and social classes. Rather, certain differences between individuals occupying similar positions at different funerals are described, and a model is constructed of the process by which these differences become formalized into rituals with complementary expectations from those in other roles.

Rituals in funerals, as in other important social or religious events, serve as standardized ways of fulfilling certain social functions. Traditionally, the funeral has served many functions. Among these, it has functioned as a declaration of the deceased person's status in society, as a religious rite of passage, and as a means of disposing of the corpse. Sociologically, it functions to reaffirm the continued existence of the social system after the loss of one of its members [1]. The funeral also serves to compel survivors to acknowledge their loss; and, finally, it facilitates normal grief work [2].

Although a funeral literature exists, much of it focuses on the functions of the funeral as a ceremony or rite [3]; the funeral director [4]; the relationship between the minister and the funeral director [5]; the debate over how, when, where, and by whom the funeral should be conducted [6-8]; and what makes it Christian [9]. The duties of the minister, as well as some of his shortcomings, are set forth in some of this literature [10, 11]. For example, Hertz suggests that the function of the minister at the funeral service is [12, p. 121]:

> ... to bring a word of honest comfort and consolation to the family of the deceased and to his friends, to assure them that solace can come from God, and to offer a fervent and sincere prayer that the Almighty may strengthen their hearts and their courage for the difficult days ahead.

While ministers' performances are differentiated in dealing with the bereaved [11, 13], the roles at the funeral itself have received no comparable analysis. The bulk of the material concerning the minister has examined his ministry to the dying [14-16] or his ministry to the bereaved [8, 17, 18]. The purpose of the present research is to provide some insight into the reciprocal expectations of those participating in church funeral services. The particular function or functions emphasized in a specific funeral, or set of funerals—i.e., those conducted in a specific church—will determine to some degree which sets of complementary roles evolve.

METHODOLOGY

Although there are many strategies by which thanatological issues are researched [19], the data upon which this chapter is based were gathered through four years of participant observation of one hundred funerals in Mississippi among Southern Baptists—the predominant denomination there and the largest protestant denomination in the United States. Fifty of the funerals were conducted in churches whose average Sunday morning attendance was less than 150 persons. The other half of the sample consisted of observation of funerals occurring in churches where average attendance was more than 300 per Sunday. A total of ten churches, five churches in each size category, were used to gather the data. The number of funerals attended at each church varied according to their occurrence, so the churches are not uniformly represented. Funeral participants were unobtrusively questioned when necessary to clarify relationships between the deceased and the bereaved.

ROLES OF FUNERAL PARTICIPANTS

Depending upon their relationship to the deceased, there are three categories of participants in the funeral: the professionals, the family, and friends. The professionals consist of the funeral home personnel and the church staff. Because funerals conducted in funeral homes were excluded from the research sample, the responsibilities of the funeral home staff were limited to directing the body in and out of the church, displaying the flowers, and arranging the seating. Since observation of different styles of performance under these conditions was restricted, role variation of the funeral home staff is excluded from this study. Similarly, the other members of the church staff such as the organist, soloist, and music director are also excluded from analysis. Among professionals, this leaves the variation among roles enacted by the minister, whether pastor or invited guest minister, for examination.

Ministers

As with the description of the family roles and the friend roles, actual role performances are less exaggerated and more overlapping than presented here. Admittedly, some role descriptions approach the point of caricature, but one or more persons in the sample fit each description closely.

The Young Seminarian—The novice is easily recognizable not only by his age but also because he epitomizes the "social comparison" process [20]. He attempts to interpret, as surreptitiously as possible, the reactions of others to his performance. When he perceives reactions as negative, he quickly alters his behavior hoping for a more favorable response. This may well be a survival response since the churches in this particular denomination are relatively independent of hierarchical control and are responsible for employing their own ministers. Under these conditions, pleasing the congregation (of whom many of the other funeral participants are a part) is a primary concern. Frequently, the young seminarian shares the funeral responsibilities with some older minister known longer by the family and invited to participate in the funeral. Since the younger minister may never have attended any funeral, and since he may also be wary of the local congregation's reactions to the funeral services outlined in the Minister's Handbook, these older pastors serve as valuable role models. After further experience, the young seminarian moves by the process to be described later into one of the following roles or into some combination of them.

The Master Performer—This minister uses the whole funeral as his stage and manages to keep himself the center of everything. Even his eulogy tells more about himself than about the deceased. "When I was twenty-eight years old and had just completed my doctorate, I Met Mr. _____ at First Church of _____ where I had just become their youngest pastor." Frequently, the master performer is a visiting pastor who uses the eulogy or the sermon to inform the audience of his major accomplishments. The true master performer is so smooth that his self-centeredness may go undetected as such by most of the congregation. In fact, most of the other participants are likely to be as impressed by his revelations as he desires. Again, these "verbal vitae" may also be related to the denominational practice of allowing the churches to secure their own pastors.

The Political Gladhander—This minister makes the effort to greet all of the family and friends—even the distant ones. Although appropriately sorrowful, he easily breaks into a big, apparently genuine, smile which can give the person being greeted the impression that it is Monday noon at the Rotary Club. He may recall common acquaintances and be fairly adept at small talk during the less structured times before and after the funeral or during the ride to the cemetery. The other participants, particularly the more distant family members, are later likely to remember and appreciate his warm attention.

The Eternal Evangelist—Everyone is faced with the choice of where to spend his or her afterlife destiny, and this minister is concerned about that to the extent that everything else is overshadowed. The funeral is an object lesson; it is used to make the point that life ends and that the participants should be spiritually prepared for their own demise. Usually, if the minister believes that the deceased person was prepared, the point is heavily emphasized. The minister in this role set conducts the funerals as if it were the "invitation" time during the decision night concluding a revival meeting.

The Scripture Quoter— This style is epitomized by the minister who uses every scripture he can find dealing with death, resurrection, eternal life, judgment and trumpet calls. It almost seems that he is unable to speak to the issue of death personally or otherwise except from a secondhand perspective. Using scripture rather than eulogizing or philosophizing appears to help him avoid intimate contact with death. Occasionally, it is clear that this minister sees the use of scripture as more impactful for the other participants because it consists of God's Word rather than his own. The situation may elicit its use; it is most likely to occur if the deceased was unknown or had less than the best reputation.

The Harried Professional—This minister perceives his role as that of a professional, and he tries to accomplish his responsibilities in a cool, businesslike manner. However, because so many ministerial duties also entail interpersonal relations, he may find himself overwhelmed with the total set of responsibilities. He is very careful to let those with whom he interacts—here, the funeral audience —know how busy he is; his crisp personal style is designed to communicate success.

The Ebullient Eulogist—The rewards for this role are obvious—relatives appreciate hearing the deceased person praised. And to this minister, the person being memorialized at each funeral is, in turn, the most wonderful person who has ever lived. Although each eulogy is supposed to be just that—good words— this minister provides too much of a good thing. As one relative later remarked about the funeral for his aunt, "There wasn't anything remarkable about her. As a matter of fact, she was ornery, very negative, couldn't get along with anybody and couldn't care less. But you would never have guessed the preacher was talking about her. He praised her to the highest heaven and said all sorts of good things about her. Clearly, he didn't even know her!"

The Pessimistic Griever—The death, regardless of the way that it occurred or of how much "grief work" has already been accomplished, is regarded as a tragedy—as a time of intense suffering. "Nothing works out right in this life." This minister communicates to the family and friends the message that if they really cared about the deceased, their concern should be demonstrated through open grief. Also, the depth of their concern or love is measured by the intensity of their apparent grief; there is no room here for concealed grief. A funeral is not successful unless most of the friends and relatives are openly grieving at its conclusion. For example, one visiting minister was heard to remark to the pastor as they led the procession from the church to the cemetery, "Did you see that? I got a few tears!"

The Comforting Shepherd—This is the minister, who realizing the impact of loss with its accompanying grief upon those who are bereaved, attempts to provide support for them through his manner and words. He does not try to get them to cry, nor does he necessarily attempt to keep them from it. Their grief, no matter how expressed, is accepted and supported. Of the ministerial roles described here, this is one of those most likely to extend beyond the funeral ceremony. This is the basic pastoral role, e.g., the shepherd who takes care of his flock.

There are a number of other identifiable roles that the minister uses. Among them are: the *humorist* who provides nonoffensive entertainment with humorous anecdotes from the life of the deceased; the *poet* who describes the event and the underlying feelings in beautiful words and carefully constructed sentences; the *philosopher* whose reasoned presentation provides explanation of both the unique and the universal meanings surrounding the death experience; and the *manipulator* who maintains close control of the ritual and of the feelings expressed relative to it. However the manipulator defines the situation, he usually has sufficient skill to induce others to perform according to his expectations.

Family Members

Since neither the family nor the friends are as actively engaged in carrying out a ritual performance as is the minister, the varieties of expression available to them appear more limited. In any case, fewer roles were detected.

The Coping Griever—Most family members appear to fall into this category. The individual is still somewhat numb from the impact of the death. Full realization of the finality of the loss, although not completely comprehended, is beginning to occur. The funeral serves as a focal point of attention during this period. If this person has already grieved deeply alone and/or in the company of family and close friends, the funeral may function to elicit the personality resiliency necessary for emotional rebound. If the grief has not begun to occur, the funeral service may, by its function as a social marker of the passage, direct attention to the loss and elicit expressions of grief. Wherever this person is in the grief process, his or her major concern is with surviving the moment.

The Bewildered Novice—This person is usually one young enough to have experienced no previous deaths of close friends or family members.

Occasionally, an older person who has successfully avoided earlier funerals for various reasons may fit this role category. Lacking previous funeral experience and unsure of what to expect, this family member, to the extent that he or she is not numb with grief, behaves much as a tourist acts in a new country. Other funeral participants are closely observed as models of the appropriate behavior. The frequency with which the other family roles, discussed in this section, occur and are viewed positively (rewarded) by others will determine which role or combination of roles will be adopted by the newcomer.

The Hysterical Performer—To observe this person in action, one would think that he or she was the person closest to the deceased and, therefore, the most distraught. But follow-up questions about the relationship revealed that some individuals were very close, some were not, and several who had lived near the deceased had not bothered to visit during, what was in some cases, a lengthy terminal illness. Neither hypothesis that loss or guilt was the causal factor in the performance could be ruled out. However, there are two alternative hypotheses. The first is that this role is a style accepted through socialization combined with an exhibitionist personality. The second is suggested by Hammon's research [21] which found that the severe grief displayed by distant relatives upon closer examination was revealed to be older repressed grief triggered by the current occasion. The truth probably includes some combination of these explanations.

The Stoic Spartan—The eyes tell all. The body is held rigidly erect; facial muscles are immobilized. But the eyes bespeak intense suffering. In some instances this appears to be a performance because of the ease with which this eye communication is turned on and off. The person appears to be communicating, "I'll show you how much I'm suffering and also how I can take it in silence." In other cases, the individual appears to be a victim of the "stiff upper lip" cultural syndrome and is afraid that deep expression of grief are not socially acceptable. Afraid that any expression of grief may lead to emotions too intense to control, no expression is permitted.

The Party Queen—Although the word "Queen" is used, this person may be male or female. In the observations she was most frequently female. The funeral is used as a social gathering—that is, as a vehicle for presenting self to others. Dress, poise, and behavior are used to attract attention, and the funeral becomes a kind of "Easter parade." A combination of "clotheshorse" and fashion model, this person exudes "class". Two types of behavior were observed: on one hand, the person occupying this role was quiet, dignified, and noninterfering; and on the other, the behavior might be confused with that of a wedding director. This person felt responsible for insuring that every other person was in the appropriate place at the proper time.

The Cosmopolitan Protester—This person, usually in the young adult to middle age age range, has lived away from the family and the home church and has been exposed to alternative ideas—particularly as they pertain to funerals. He or she wants others to know that old traditions are not approved. The funeral is attended under protest, particularly if the suggested "improvements" are not utilized. The bored look affected at the funeral cannot be mistaken—the unwillingness to be fully involved in a disapproved funeral style.

Friends

Five major roles as enacted by friends or nonfamily funeral participants were detected in this study.

The Respect Payer—Out of obligation, social expectation, or respect for the deceased or the survivors, the respect payers attend the funeral to make their concern known. Funeral attendance is a quiet means of demonstrating support for the survivors and/or friendship with the deceased. For the friends of the deceased person, it is the final goodbye when memories of that person receive full and formal public attention for the last time. Society's continuation is affirmed as is also the previous societal importance of the deceased person. The bulk of the nonfamily funeral attenders appear to fit this category.

The Party Goer—Any social event is better than no social event, so this person has to make do with the funeral as a social event—particularly in the smaller communities. Although behavior is modified to be appropriate with the occasion, the interstitial areas in the funeral are occupied with the same "chitchat" that usually fills the time between Sunday school and church or the intermission time at the movies. For the party goers, the funeral provides a time to go out and be with other people.

The Status Accountant—This person has a pocket calculator instead of a brain. Everything is observed at the funeral in terms of cost. If the costs tally high, the status of the family is enhanced and vice versa. The status accountant is recognized by such remarks, particularly as they occur in series, as "The casket was one of the finest I've ever seen; must have been very expensive!" "Did you see the beautiful dress she was buried in and with all of her jewelry on?" "The church was filled with flowers, and some of those arrangements cost a mint." "I understand that they flew Brother _____ back from Texas to do the funeral!"

The Family Supporter—Concern with providing support for the family members during their time of loss and grief is the primary motivation of the family supporter. As opportunity presents itself during the funeral, those family members most in need are provided physical and emotional support. The concern of these close friends usually extends both directions in time from the actual funeral ceremony. That is, concern is expressed both preceding and following the funeral. Sometimes, months later, these friends are still providing the support needed by the survivors to work through the grief process.

The Professional Griever—This individual attends all, or most, funerals in the community and grieves for the deceased. Sometimes, open expressions of grief rivaling those of the immediate family occur. More frequently, the professional griever is identified by his or her continued presence at funerals without regard to personal closeness to the deceased or to the survivors. I asked about the relationship to the deceased of a woman who lifted her preschool age daughter to look into the casket as the body was being viewed after the funeral sermon. The reply was, "Oh, she didn't even know her (the deceased); she just comes to all the funerals!"

ROLE OVERLAP

Again, it must be emphasized that while the roles described here are the dominant performances of certain individuals, role enactments were rarely mutually exclusive. For example, among the ministers, it was not unusual to observe the "young seminarian" move into "scipture quoter" and, eventually, "comforting shepherd" role after backing off from the "humorist" role when no support was received. It was even more commonplace to observe the "master performer" move easily between the "political gladhander," "ebullient eulogist," and "harried professional" roles. The family member usually moved from the "bewildered novice" role into one of the other roles by his or her second or third funeral. And the "coping griever" would occasionally move into one of the other roles. Even the "cosmopolitan protester," when resettled in the community, moved into a less conflictive role. Among the nonfamily participants, the "party goer" and the "status accountant" were sometimes interchangeable roles, and the "respect payer" would move into one of the other styles periodically.

The situation, in many instances, appeared to determine which role would be enacted by an individual. Because several funerals were observed in each church, there was a large overlap in attendance from one funeral to the next. If a participant displayed dramatically different role performances at different funerals, situational differences were examined for possible explanations. And the situation was frequently found to be a causal factor. For example, ministers were observed to enact at different funerals the following dominant roles: "harried professional" when the week had been particularly full and hectic; "scripture quoter" when the funeral was for a woman killed in a car accident while drunk after barhopping all night; "ebullient eulogist" when a highly respected deacon died; "pessimistic griever" when an infant of a couple who had waited thirteen years before being able to give birth died an instant crib death; and "master performer" when invited to assist in a funeral at another church. Most pastors do not display a great variety of dominant roles but rather display a particular role consistently with only modest deviation. Similarly, the role enactments of family members and friends were usually consistent with some variation noted by situation. The "bewildered novice" and the "hysterical performer" roles were most likely to occur following a sudden and unexpected death. And death occurring in a family with an extended network of friends was more likely to bring in "family supporters" and "respect payers" than death occurring in a less gregarious family.

VARIATION IN ROLE ENACTMENT BY CHURCH SIZE

No church in the sample had an average Sunday morning worship attendance of less than 50 or more than 550. Therefore, the congregations were fairly well informed about the occurrence of deaths and were aware of the various related family needs. Differences between roles enactments in the churches with under 150 and those with over 300 average attendance were relatively few. Table 1 gives the distribution by church size category of both the total number of ministerial roles observed and the distribution when each minister is assigned only one dominant role. The figures in the dominant role assignment category

Table 1. Ministerial Role Enactments Observed by Church Size

Role Titles	Number of Total Roles Observed[a]		Number of Dominant Role Assignments[b]	
	Small Church[c]	Large Church[d]	Small Church	Large Church
Young Seminarian	14	4	12	1
Master Performer	4	8	2	6
Political Gladhander	9	11	3	6
Eternal Evangelist	12	7	10	3
Scripture Quoter	5	7	4	3
Harried Professional	5	12	3	10
Ebullient Eulogist	7	7	2	3
Pessimistic Griever	8	1	5	1
Comforting Shepherd	32	40	20	26
Humorist	3	2	0	0
Poet	0	2	0	1
Philosopher	2	4	1	1
Manipulator	3	3	1	1
Totals	104	108	63	62
Grand Totals		212		125

[a]Each minister may be observed in more than one role enactment.

[b]Each minister was assigned one role on the basis of the length and intensity of enactment.

[c]These churches had 150 members or less, although the average attendance was considerably less.

[d]These churches had 300 members or more.

total more than fifty funerals for each church size because more than one minister was involved in many of the funerals. Actually, more ministers were involved than the total number recorded, but the involvement of some was too brief to allow classification.

The "young seminarian" role rarely occurred in the larger churches, and the "harried professional," "political gladhander," and "master performer" were more likely to occur there. The "pessimistic griever" and "eternal evangelist" roles were more likely to be enacted in the smaller churches. The "scripture quoter," "ebullient eulogist," "comforting shepherd," and "manipulator" occurred approximately equal in both categories. The "humorist," "poet," and "philosopher" appeared too infrequently in the sample to allow enumeration. Of the family roles, the "hysterical performer" appeared most frequently in the smaller churches. The "cosmopolitan protester" seemed to appear more frequently in the smaller churches, but this may be an artifact of the ease of identification through observation of smaller funerals and in the questions asked afterwards. Likewise, among the roles of the nonfamily participants, the "professional griever" seemed to turn up only at the smaller churches—again, perhaps an artifact of the ease of identification where more people know each other.

ROLE RECIPROCITY

Role reciprocity means that within a certain set or network of roles each role meshes with the others in a supporting fashion. The roles described in this chapter were not observed in isolation but in conjunction with other roles. Most received support, but a few did not. Each unique combination of roles helps to shape the function filled by that particular funeral. There are several easy examples. When a "comforting shepherd" minister, "coping griever" family members, and "family supporter" nonfamily participants are linked in interaction, the funeral functions as a catharsis experience facilitating individual grief work. Link a "scripture quoter" with "stoic Spartans" and "respect payers," and the funeral functions as a rite of passage—quiet, contained, with little emotion. But if one or two "pessimistic grievers" are linked with "hysterical performers" and "professional grievers," the funeral becomes an emotional marker. In the one instance observed where this occurred, over an hour passed after the funeral oratory was completed before the participants quieted down and regained their emotional composure.

In some interactions networks or role sets, some roles may be interchanged and still serve the same function. For example, either the "harried professional," the "ebullient eulogist," the "master performer" or the "political gladhander" may interact with either the "party queen" or the "bewildered novice" and with either the "party goer" or the "status accountant" to fill the social cohesiveness need. Any combination of the roles listed in that example will serve the same function.

Certain combinations are nonreinforcing. The "master performer" and the "hysterical performer" compete for attention. However, if the "master performer" moves to the "pessimistic griever" role, the roles can mesh. The "young seminarian" and the "bewildered novice" fail to support each other, because there is no one to give direction to the event. When these types discover each other early enough in the process of preparing for the funeral, open communication and conscious decision-making can alleviate the problems. Almost anyone except, perhaps, the "poet" and "philosopher" has trouble with the "cosmopolitan protester". The problems are usually minimal because there are so few "cosmopolitan protesters". If there are enough to make a difference, the funeral is changed, thereby resolving some of the conflict.

When multiple ministers are involved in a funeral, the role enactments usually support each other. The "political gladhander" and the "ebullient eulogist" mesh well as do the "scripture quoter" and the "eternal evangelist". Occasionally, the roles conflict as happened when a "comforting shepherd" and a "pessimistic griever" approached the congregation with different intentions. The "pessimistic griever" swayed the audience; but at the next funeral, the "comforting shepherd" set the tone. The "pessimistic griever," a former pastor invited back, never returned to do another funeral at that church.

THE PROCESS OF ROLE DEVELOPMENT, STABILIZATION, AND CHANGE

Reciprocal expectations in an interpersonal reactions model format [22] constitute the process by which both pastoral and participant roles are formed. Each person in the interaction reacts to the expectations of the other as he or she perceives them—particularly as such behavior is rewarded by the other. Reward or reinforcement consists of whatever is valuable to the individual. For the minister, this ranges from approbation to keeping his job. For the family and friends, reward may consist of the feeling that the funeral was properly conducted, that the eulogy was fitting, that others care about the deceased person, that the minister performed well, and/or that one has received comfort in his or her grief. The power to enforce expectations varies across situations. The "young seminarian," relatively powerless, is likely to mold his role to match his perceived expectations of the congregation which controls his rewards. In contrast, the older "comforting shepherd" or "pessimistic griever" is more likely to be able to enforce his will upon the congregation and the other funeral participants. If the minister has been in the church or has been known by the congregation for a long period of time, he has usually accumulated credits which allow him some authority or freedom to choose his behavior [23]. He rewards those who support his role selection in much the same manner that he, himself, was rewarded for conforming to congregational expectations earlier in his career. This reciprocal response or cyclical reward system maintains the stability of traditional funeral roles. In many communities certain role configurations dominate over the years, while in others a different set of complementary roles are supported.

Such a stable system based upon mutual reinforcement may seem impervious to change. That change does occur and is stabilized in the form of ritualized interactions is obvious from observing the variation in funerals as one moves from one local church to another within the same conservative denomination in one of the most religiously traditional regions of the United States. Change occurs in several ways. Enough people of one role persuasion move into a church and gain enough power through continued attendance and assumed responsibility that they are able to socialize the next pastor, if not the present one, into the reciprocal role. A new church, or "mission," may be started which attracts people of a certain orientation, and a pastor is selected who shares that orientation. Attitudes toward role enactments at funerals usually fit consistently into broader perspectives on the role of the church in the community. Therefore, this broad orientation is what is looked for in a pastor—not funeral role enactments *per se*. On the other hand, the pastor may change the congregation to fit his expectations, particularly if he has the power or credits mentioned above.

Reciprocal role reinforcement does not operate in a closed system. The minister is subject to many external forces. His seminary training, the expectations of and models provided by older, highly respected ministers, the information received through the voluminous reading necessitated by his vocation, and the internalized expectations of previous congregations all exert influence affecting his selection of a role or a combination of roles to enact. Likewise, the other funeral participants have received input from a number of sources other than the performing minister(s). Affecting their role selection are performances by and expectations of previous pastors; exposure to funerals for family members in other churches, in other regions of the country, or in other denominations; expectations of other family members and friends; and mass media communications. However selected, once established, this new role set becomes fixed and functions by the same mutual rewards systems that supported the previous, traditional pattern.

CONCLUSION

Funerals can serve their many functions through a variety of role enactments by ministers, family members and nonfamily participants. The function receiving major emphasis elicits certain combinations of role interactions. Over time in a specific location among a given population, mutual expectations reciprocally reinforced become ritualized into a set routine. These ritualized expectations provide the stable support so valuable during a time of emotional upheaval. Role expectations vary across situations and actors. These expectations evolve over time into other sets of mutual expectations as functions and participating persons change. The funeral is as static or as dynamic as its participants desire.

REFERENCES

1. R. Fulton, The Sacred and the Secular, R. Fulton, (ed.), *Death and Identity,* Wiley, New York, pp. 89-105, 1965.
2. _____, Death and the Funeral in Contemporary Society, H. Wass, (ed.), *Dying: Facing the Facts,* McGraw-Hill, New York, pp. 236-255, 1979.
3. V. R. Pine, A. H. Kutscher, D. Peretz, R. C. Slater, R. De Bellis, R. J. Volk, and D. J. Cherico, (eds.), *Acute Grief and the Funeral,* Charles Thomas, Springfield, Ill., 1976.
4. V. R. Pine, Grief, Bereavement, and Mourning: The Realities of Loss, V. R. Pine, et al., (eds.), *Acute Grief and the Funeral,* Charles Thomas (ed.), Springfield, Ill., pp. 105-114, 1976.
5. R. Fulton, The Clergyman and the Funeral Director: A Study in Role Conflict, *Social Forces, 39,* pp. 317-323, 1961.
6. V. E. Huff and K. M. Dimick, Death Rites: An Alternative Approach, *Pastoral Psychology, 20,* pp. 35-38, 1969.
7. P. E. Irion, *The Funeral: Vestige or Value,* Abingdon, Nashville, 1966.
8. A. Kutscher and L. Kutscher, (eds.), *Religion and Bereavement,* Health Sciences, New York, 1972.
9. E. N. Jackson, *The Christian Funeral: Its Meaning, Its Purpose, and Its Modern Practice,* Channel Press, New York, 1966.
10. R. Flesch, The Clergy on the Firing Line, V. R. Pine, et al., (eds.), *Acute Grief and the Funeral,* Charles Thomas, Springfield, Ill., pp. 179-187, 1976.
11. R. B. Reeves, Jr., The Pastor's Problem With His Own Discomfort, V. R. Pine, et al., (eds.), *Acute Grief and the Funeral,* Charles Thomas, Springfield, Ill., pp. 188-190, 1976.
12. R. C. Hertz, What Comes After the Funeral, A. Kutscher and L. Kutscher, (eds.), *Religion and Bereavement,* Health Sciences, New York, pp. 121-122, 1972.
13. M. K. Bowers, E. N. Jackson, J. Knight and L. LeShan, *Counseling the Dying,* Thomas Nelson and Sons, New York, 1964.
14. T. Fuller and A. Reed, More Alive than I, *Pastoral Psychology, 23,* pp. 33-40, 1972.
15. J. Wood, The Structure of Concern: The Ministry in Death-Related Situations, L. H. Lofland, (ed.), *Toward a Sociology of Death and Dying,* Sage Publications, Beverly Hills, 1976.
16. R. Kastenbaum and R. Aisenberg, *The Psychology of Death,* Springer, New York, 1976.
17. T. F. Garrity and J. Wyss, Death, Funeral and Bereavement Practices in Appalachian and Non-Appalachian Kentucky, *Omega, 7,* pp. 209-228, 1976.
18. P. E. Irion, *The Funeral and the Mourners,* Abingdon, New York, 1957.
19. T. Rodabough, How We Know About Death: Research Strategies, *Death Education, 4,* pp. 315-336, 1981.
20. L. Festinger, A Theory of Social Comparison Processes, *Human Relations, 7,* pp. 117-140, 1954.
21. G. C. Hammon, Dealing with Grief, A. Kutscher and L. Kutscher, (eds.), *Religion and Bereavement,* Health Sciences, New York, pp. 119-120, 1972.
22. T. Rodabough, Alternatives to the Stages Model of the Dying Process, *Death Education, 4,* pp. 1-19, 1980.
23. E. P. Hollander, Conformity, Status and Idiosyncrasy Credit, *Psychological Review, 65,* pp. 117-127, 1958.

The funeral is probably the most important death-related ritual for most deaths that occur in this country, although some individuals probably find other ceremonies (e.g., the wake or sitting shiva) as equally or more significant. But the funeral is only one brief event in the lengthy process known as mourning.

We all find ourselves, either as professionals or as concerned human beings, involved with the grieving process of others and of ourselves. While we wish to limit the pain and disruption of this process, we also need to avoid any act that would rob the loss of its meaning. In fact, the only way to keep the death from hurting is to keep the dead person from having been important to us. So we need to mourn and suffer our grief when we are bereaved, but we can also attend to the grieving process so that it occurs in a supportive environment and so that the grieving persons are not disabled by their grief.

There is often confusion as to the meanings of the terms grief, bereavement, and mourning, although they can justifiably be used interchangeably under some circumstances. Grief refers to the feelings that are experienced in response to a significant loss; bereavement describes the social status of a person who has suffered such a loss; and mourning is the behavior that is exhibited. Thus, it is possible for a bereaved person to display mourning behavior without actually feeling grief, or for a bereaved person to feel grief without exhibiting the behavior expected of a mourner.

It is unusual for an individual to reach his or her middle years without having been bereaved by the death of at least one close family member, and many persons experience the death of a parent, brother or sister, or other very close person at much younger ages. Grief, then, is very much a part of the human condition.

Chapter 5 provides an overview of the meaning of grief and bereavement to those persons who have experienced a serious loss through death.

Editor's Note: R. Kalish, Death and Survivorship: The Final Transition, *ANNALS, AAPSS, 464*, November 1982, pp. 163–173. Reprinted by permission of Sage Publications, Inc.

CHAPTER
5

Death and Survivorship:
The Final Transition

Richard A. Kalish

Relatively little has taken place during the past quarter century to alter the perspective insights of Marion Langer in *Learning to Live as a Widow*.

You had no training, no preparation to help you handle this crisis [of widowhood] in your life. You did not know what you could reasonably expect of yourself and other people [1].

The transition from wife to widow, from husband to widower, is still as distressing as ever, and it still leaves the survivor just as lonely, confused, uncertain, depressed, and financially vulnerable as ever. This is not to say that the status quo has prevailed in the availability of services and in the general professional awareness:

- widow-to-widow support groups have been established all over the country;
- a useful, albeit modest, flow of research and writing has provided insight to service-providers and to widows themselves;
- the fact that more women are familiar with work and careers has undoubtedly served to reduce a little of the stress of the transition;
- crisis intervention centers provide significant services.

Each of these is helpful, facilitative of better physical, mental, emotional, social, and spiritual well-being, but all taken together, they still do not invalidate Ms. Langer's point.

WITH TIME ON THE ABSCISSA

Time is a factor in the transition from the role of spouse to that of survivor in at least three ways. The first is the way in which the death occurs in time: the extent to which it is sudden, expected, and timely. Second, as the death approaches, then occurs, and finally recedes in time, the feelings of grief, the status of the bereaved, and the rituals of mourning all change. And third, the way in which transition to widow(er)hood occurs differs as a function of the age and of the stage in life of the individual experiencing the transition.

Sudden, Expected, and Timely

People die suddenly and they die slowly and in all stages in between; their deaths can be expected, unexpected, and all stages in between; they can have timely deaths, untimely deaths, and all stages in between. And each of these continua will affect the kind of transition experienced by the survivor.

In thinking of sudden versus slow deaths, the assumption is frequently made that the slow death is necessarily a painful death, while the sudden death is not painful. This is often, but not always, a valid assumption. If the sudden death is instantaneous, such as a gunshot or sudden coronary causing either immediate death or a comatose state until death, then there is no pain; if the slow death is from cancer in a particularly painful site, then there is intense pain.

Sudden death, especially when it is also unexpected, leaves the survivors unprepared and often precludes the dying person's making appropriate arrangements for survivors. Victims of sudden, unexpected death have no time to get their financial affairs in order, no opportunity to explain to their spouses how the household works or where important documents are, and no chance to make arrangements to see family members or to offer or receive absolution for long-past deeds that have produced family schisms. In short, I view sudden deaths as being the cruelest for the survivors. One study of eighty widows has shown that sudden death does, in fact, lead to stronger grief reactions than death following a more prolonged illness; in this instance, sudden death was defined as occurring fewer than five days from the onset of symptoms [2].

Although sudden deaths are frequently also unexpected deaths, and although unexpected deaths by definition cannot be prolonged, sudden and unexpected are not by any means synonymous. A man has a coronary at age forty-eight and recovers; in his fifties he has several strokes that slightly incapacitate him; at sixty he has a massive coronary and dies. A middle-aged woman, depressed makes a serious suicide attempt that is thwarted; six months later she succeeds in committing suicide. Both of these deaths are sudden; neither can be considered unexpected. The spouse of a man with a life-threatening coronary problem or of a woman who is depressed and potentially suicidal lives in a very different family system than someone living with a spouse with terminal cancer or multiple sclerosis.

Deaths are often seen as untimely when they occur either too soon or too late in terms of a person's career, family relationships, fame and prestige, and so forth. The death of someone with significant responsibilities for work or family or someone whose creativity is still developing is often viewed as untimely; conversely, we may think that an elderly person has lived too long when he or she lives to see the deaths of children and grandchildren, or the disintegration of values held dear, or the deterioration of a business or farm that had been part of his or her life. Both kinds of death are out of sync. In the former, the spouse undoubtedly suffers a great deal; in the latter, the surviving spouse is likely to welcome the death.

Grief is Not Static

The grieving process is far from static. A spouse legally and statistically becomes a widow(er) in a moment, but the same person may begin the psychological role of widow early in the marriage or even before being married, through fantasizing the meaning and feelings associated with that role. This rehearsal for widow(er)hood is reported more frequently by women than by men [3]. Grieving, in a more familiar fashion, often begins with anticipatory grief, when the spouse who will survive learns that the husband/wife is now going to die in a foreseeable and moderately predictable future.

When does grieving end? Certainly not a week later, by which time the survivors are expected to return to work, school, housekeeping, and similar roles. The variability in duration is immense: a year or, more probably, two years will be needed to recuperate from the grief, and some people never fully cease grieving. Although the trend is for feelings of grief to become less intense and for episodes to become less frequent over time, this is not a simple linear trend; a recent report showed that some widows have a second depressive reaction some years after the death, and that this is often more intense than their depression at the time of death [4].

Grieving, it must be emphasized, is not a point but a process, one that changes constantly and, to a modest extent, predictably over a period of time. Various attempts to delineate stages of grief have been made, one of which proposed four stages: numbness, pining, depression, and recovery [5]. These stages are not to be seen as rigid, irreversible, or universal, but they do describe modal behavior that can be viewed across time.

Mourning behavior, the rituals associated with the state of bereavement and the feelings of grief, is more readily given boundaries. In a Los Angeles study roughly one-third of the respondents stated that the bereaved person should feel free to remarry within six months of the death, could return to work within one week of the death, and could start going out with other men/women within a month after the death [6].

Grieving as a Function of Age and Stage

Time is also on the abscissa when we consider the transitions caused by the death of one's spouse, as these transitions are affected by the age of the survivor and the stage of life of that survivor. Although the use of a life-span perspective to view human behavior is gaining acceptance in the behavioral and social sciences, it is still more widely ignored than integrated into research and writing in these fields. The application of life-span perspectives to policy and programs is even more tenuous.

It is immediately obvious that the transitions encountered by the twenty-five-year-old widower differ in a variety of ways from those met by the forty-five-year-old widower, the sixty-five-year-old widower, and the eighty-five-year-old widower. Recent research [7, 8] on adult developmental stages suggests that men at different ages are also at different stages in the ways they see themselves, their work and career, and their families. The death of a spouse would enter dynamically into the equation along with these other factors to produce a very different kind of transition to widow(er)hood as the result of age and related stage.

Not only will this transition differ because of the psychological factors just outlined, but it will also differ because of the sociological factors. The younger man is just beginning a career; the middle-aged man may well have children in both high school and college; the elderly man is likely to have some chronic health condition for which his wife provided ministering.

Adult development research findings on women are just beginning to filter in, but there is no doubt that the age and stage of women will also influence the meaning of their transition. A forty-year-old widow may be earning considerably less and have less earning potential than her forty-year-old male equivalent, so she faces a different financial stress than does the widower. Similarly, a fifty-year-old widow may have finished her formal education only a decade or so before and may have had only a handful of years climbing the career ladder, while a man of the same age has probably been pursuing his career for twenty-five years or more. Thus both age and stage will influence the meaning of the transition to widowhood.

THE GRIEVING PROCESS

Grieving, as I have emphasized, is a dynamic process and not a static occurrence. Having said that, I want to discuss a variety of concerns that develop immediately following the death—and frequently preceding it—and that continue, although often with diminishing intensity and frequency, for an extended period of time. These are physical and health changes, psychological and emotional distress, social and relational concerns, and practical issues.

Physical and Health Changes

In his now-classic article on grief, Erich Lindemann described numerous physical changes that occur in the very early stages of grief: somatic distress occurring in waves of twenty minutes or more, tightness in the throat, choking and shortness of breath, need to sigh, empty feeling in the abdomen, lack of muscular power [9]. Other symptoms have also been observed, including lack of physical strength, loss of appetite, reduced sexual drive, and restless and aimless hyperactivity [5, pp. 34, 50].

Immediately after the death some people feel the pangs of grief just described, while others experience a numbness that appears to be comparable to a state of shock, leaving the widow(er) without the anticipated feelings of or physical responses to grief. This stage will pass, normally within a few days [5, p. 39].

Several studies have shown that health problems accompany grief. In one study eighty widows ranging in age from very young to age seventy-five were interviewed between six and nine months after the death of their spouses. The physical symptoms that were most frequently mentioned were sleeping problems (71%); restlessness (68%); fatigue (61%); loss of appetite (61%); and drug usage (48%). For the first three symptoms listed, 29 percent or more indicated that their symptoms were severe or occurred often; for the latter two, 14 percent described the symptom as severe or frequent [2, pp. 218-225].

Two other investigations offer further confirmation. The recently bereaved were found to suffer from such symptoms as headache, dizziness, muscular ache, menstrual irregularity, loss of appetite, sleeplessness, fainting spells, skin rashes, indigestion and vomiting, chest pains, and heart palpitations. In fact, it appears that as many as 40 percent of widows consulted a physician within eight weeks following their bereavement [10, 11].

The evidence points to a definite increase in both illness and death rates of widows and widowers within the six months following their bereavement [12]. We cannot be certain, however, how much of this increase arises from the changes in health practices during the period before the death, since those caring for dying spouses often neglect their own health; how much is due to the stress that accompanies the death and related losses; and how much is a function of the new and often unanticipated stresses that face recent widow(er)s as they attempt to adapt to their new roles and circumstances.

Psychological and Emotional Distress

The health problems just discussed are undoubtedly also indications of emotional distress. Sleeplessness, for example, or loss of appetite can be caused directly by physical illness or indirectly by the reactions of the body to stress and distress. Psychological and emotional responses to grief are not limited to those with identifiable somatic correlates. Lindemann listed "an intense subjective distress described as tension or mental pain" [9, p. 141] among the symptoms he observed.

In a Minnesota study of 434 widows and widowers, substantial percentages indicated confusion about the future (30%), depression and unhappiness most of the time (20%), a lack of feeling that life was worthwhile (18%), and difficulty in concentration (11%). At the same time, many respondents also described changes in a positive direction. Since the death, they had become more appreciative of others (41%), more sensitive to the feelings of others (35%), and warmer toward others (27%) [13]. It appears that although widows and widowers feel severe loss and distress, they also view their losses as having led to personal growth, particularly in terms of relationships with others.

Social and Relational Concerns

It is not surprising to learn that loneliness is the most significant problem experienced by recent widow(er)s [2, p. 324; 14]. Even loneliness, however, is not always a totally negative experience. Many widows and widowers come to appreciate the new autonomy that comes from not having anyone at home who requires care. There seems nothing inconsistent in grieving deeply for the deceased spouse and simultaneously welcoming opportunities to explore new roles and relationships and reduced responsibilities. This would be especially true for persons whose spouse required a great deal of care and attention over a lengthy period of terminal illness.

The widow(er) is still obviously in need of ongoing social relationships to provide nurturance, to satisfy intimacy needs, and to offer companionship and stimulation. These can be satisfied through friends, relatives, work associates, organizational involvement, service-providers, and—at a somewhat different level—God, pets, self, fantasies, and the deceased spouse [15].

Friends and relatives would normally present the most available pool for establishing or maintaining relationships, but interactions with these people often undergo a noticeable change. Friendships have likely been established on a couple-to-couple basis, and most widow(er)s and divorced people are familiar with the difficulty in continuing these relationships as a threesome. It may be true that "old friends are the best friends," but widow(er)hood often requires the development of new friendships. Previous friendships established on a one-to-one basis are probably more likely to continue.

Relationships with relatives—children, brothers and sisters, parents, and perhaps cousins—are likely to continue and even to grow stronger. In-laws provide another source of relationships, but many of these people are doing their own grieving and may not have the ability to be supportive at this point. Also, once the surviving spouse begins to move into a new life, perhaps seeking new relationships that will replace the lost relationship, in-laws can feel threatened and displaced [15, p. 6].

Work associates and people met through social, political, recreational, or religious organizations may offer social relationships. Relationships established in these ways may compensate to some extent for the loss, but they seldom provide the needed kinds of nurturance and intimacy. Service-providers supply limited forms of relationship, but while appreciated, they cannot take over the role of family member or friend. Interestingly enough, and in spite of their bad press, funeral directors often receive warm commendations for their important support, exceeding those for physicians, nurses, chaplains, social workers, clergy, and neighbors [15, p. 8, 14, p. 172].

The ongoing relationship with the deceased spouse deserves special mention. The presence of the dead person is felt on numerous occasions. Rather than being viewed as pathological, this experience needs to be understood as normative, since it occurs with great frequency [10, Chap. 8; 5, p. 57ff]. In some instances the surviving spouse reports an awareness of the presence of the dead person in such terms as "I felt he was close to me, and it was like I heard his voice although I didn't," or "I was dozing off to sleep and I felt her next to me."

On less frequent occasions the occurrence is that of actually seeing, hearing, smelling, or being touched by the dead person. The experience is almost always a positive one. Although research evidence is lacking, it seems likely that these encounters offer support and solace to the widow(er) and may be facilitative of a normal response to bereavement.

The feeling of presence is not the only way that widows and widowers maintain the dead spouse in their lives. Over one-third of a large sample of such persons agreed that "everything around me seems to remind me of [the deceased]" [13, p. 16]. Another familiar kind of statement is "I still find myself waiting for his key in the lock at 5:30 each afternoon," or "I sometimes set two places at the table without thinking anything of it."

The sexual relationships of widow(er)s have received very little attention. It is as though the death eliminates all sexual needs, which initially seems to be the case for some widows who described a period of early avoidance of sex and of disgust with men, followed by a period of acute sexual needs and fantasies [4, p. 98]. Widows often receive sexual advances from men who take it upon themselves to satisfy what they see as the obvious sexual needs of the poor, deprived widow. It is not unusual for the man who makes such an advance to be a close friend of the husband or the husband of a close friend of the recent widow. Sometimes companionship, love, and comfort accompany the proposition; often is a blatant proposal for direct, immediate, and presumably rapid sex.

Although once again the literature is devoid of research, it is highly likely that extremely few of these early sexual overtures are accepted by recent widows—whether the situation for widowers is comparable is more problematic. Nonetheless, widows, like divorced women, are often seen by the still-married women as threats to their marriage. The assumption seems to be made, often implicitly and perhaps unconsciously, that a formerly married woman, especially one whose sexual needs have presumably been satisfied until recently, will entice husbands into affairs. This dynamic undoubtedly adds to the tendency of couples to withdraw friendship from the recently widowed.

The Practical Issues

Recent widows and widowers face innumerable practical problems, created or exacerbated by the death. If the dead person had contributed a large share to the family income, financial problems will loom large, with insurance often being insufficient to compensate for the loss or compensating only for a limited period of time. If the dead person had been primarily a housekeeper, rather than direcly producing income, the survivor must either take over those chores or pay someone to do them. In the event that small children remain in the home, the surviving spouse virtually always must work outside the home, and care for the children becomes a major logistical and financial problem.

Household chores are also a practical issue. Whether the household tasks had been divided along traditional sex-role lines or more egalitarian bases, the loss of a spouse diminishes the tasks to be done by very little and leaves the performance of the tasks to one person. Children, of course, may be helpful in taking up the slack if they are old enough and still living at home, but if they are not old enough to help—or if the widow(er) does not know how to incorporate them into performing household tasks—they merely add to the practical difficulties, even though they may offer emotional support and companionship.

Schools, churches, and other public and private organizations still work on the assumption that adults come in pairs and that children have two functional parents. Although this is slowly changing and although many churches have developed groups for single persons, usually emphasizing the divorced, activities are often planned with little regard for single parents or single persons. Making matters worse for widows, the fear of criminal victimization will often keep single women home, especially at night, further restricting their involvement in activities. This seems to be particularly true for older people.

Other practical issues also emerge, as time, money, energy, and patience are found to be in short supply, with one person now having to accomplish most of what two people had been accomplishing. Some examples include getting ready for holidays (also depressing for many widow(er)s, especially Christmas and birthdays); arranging for home/car/appliance servicing (telephone intallers and plumbers continue to assume that someone in the household is going to be home anyway, and that it does not matter if the appointment is early, late, or postponed for the day); finding care in case of illness or disability; finding companionship for a movie, concert, or Sunday stroll; moving the household to a new home and neighborhood.

FACTORS INFLUENCING THE TRANSITION

Factors influencing the stressful nature of the transition to widowhood are obviously numerous, including the ego strength of the survivor, the nature of the previous relationship, the availability of support from others, the perception of the effectiveness of the health professionals and health facilities, and the secondary losses that accrue as a result of the death, such as loss of income, change in parenting requirements, anticipated loneliness, and consideration of relocating.

The nature of the illness itself and of the death trajectory is also a factor, although not widely discussed in the literature. One available study compared widows whose husbands died from cancer with those whose husbands died from cardiovascular problems. Compared to the latter, those women who were widowed through a cancer death 1) perceived the illness as more stressful, 2) felt their role was more passive and that they were forced to watch suffering, 3) experienced more anxiety and saw their own role as wives as less essential, 4) were more angry with the health-care system and ruminated more about health care, and 5) had more nightmares about the final illness [16].

Predicting Later Adjustment

Most of those who write about the concerns of the dying and the bereaved have speculated that the ability to maintain an open communication system concerning the terminal prognosis would make the dying process easier. Recently a study of widows of cancer patients found that this shared communication did make it easier to cope with the subsequent grief [16, p. 5]. This result fits with the finding, discussed earlier, that the grief from sudden death was more intense than the grief following a more prolonged death [2, pp. 314-315]: when the death occurs suddenly, there is much less opportunity—and sometimes no opportunity at all—to talk together and to share feelings and concerns.

In one well-known study, sixty-eight young widow(er)s were interviewed shortly after the bereavement and then again a year later. Those who were adjusting least well had experienced a short terminal illness and had had no opportunity to talk and share feelings and fears with the dead spouse, again confirming the findings mentioned previously. They were also the people who, in the initial interview, were most likely to 1) indicate high anxiety, 2) express a strong yearning for the deceased, 3) feel no one cared about them, 4) welcome their own death, and 5) describe themselves as feeling empty [17]. All these expressions could be readily translated as indicating not only considerable fear and anxiety, and perhaps a reduced capacity to cope with the demands of the world, but also a high level of depression.

Differences between Widows and Widowers

Are widowers better off or less well-off than widows? The answer is partly a function of how one reads the research and observational findings and how one decides what makes someone better off than someone else. Thus a British study showed that widows are more likely to be living with relatives, usually their children (46% versus 29%), while widowers are more likely to live alone (65% versus 49%) [18]. Is the widow better cared for? Is the widower more autonomous and better off financially? Answers may be in the eye of the beholder.

Findings from several comprehensive studies of elderly widows and widowers are relevant here. In two studies widowers were found to be more likely to participate in social organizations, to reach out more to friends, and to be less likely to say they were lonely [14, p. 169; 19]. Conversely, in another study, widows were found with great consistency to have greater resources and less overall need than widowers, with the latter experiencing lower morale, greater loneliness and dissatisfaction with life, less adequate diet, and more negative attitudes toward community services [20]. Clearly we need to be cautious before coming to conclusions when the research findings are still so inconclusive.

A study of somewhat younger persons (median age of 57), concluded that widowers were better adjusted than widows, and the author speculated that this was because of 1) the loss of identity that the wife suffered, because her identity was more involved in her husband's than vice versa; 2) the greater difficulty widows have in remarrying; and 3) the greater stress generated by the practical problems of making decisions, handling money, and so forth [14, p. 167].

Experience and logic suggest numerous differences between widows and widowers. Compared with widows, widowers will

- be older and, therefore, less healthy;
- be less numerous and, therefore, have more difficulty in finding older men with whom to establish friendships, but will find it easier to remarry or to develop relationships with women;
- have more money;
- be less capable of accomplishing the traditional female tasks of house-keeping and child care, but more capable of accomplishing the traditional male tasks of earning money and home maintenance. It seems possible that fewer of these advantages will accrue to the widower in old age, since the occupational role has normally ceased anyway;
- have developed fewer social and verbal skills and be less willing to reach out for help;
- be more likely to drive and to be willing to be out after dark; they are also more likely to be willing to go places alone;
- have had more experience in making financial and related decisions.

There are undoubtedly other differentiating characteristics that might be hypothesized, but two conclusions seem apparent from these assumptions. First, the determination as to whether widows or widowers do better after bereavement depends on which variables one examines; and second, other factors, such as age, social class, and income, interact with gender in determining the relative problems of coping with the death of a spouse.

CONCLUDING REMARKS

This article has not attempted to prove anything or to make a specific point. Its purpose has been to examine the effects of the transition from wife to widow, from husband to widower, and to describe some of the processes and events that accompany this transition. Certainly there is always the temptation, during the summing up, to call for more research. The call is just as valid for this topic as for most others, although it is important to recognize that the research cited here is only a sample selected from a much larger body of work now available.

Perhaps the issue is not so much more research as research that recognizes differences in age, sex, education, ethnicity, income, and health. Certainly a life-span perspective seems essential. And if the criteria of physical, mental, emotional, social, and spiritual well-being are applied to topics to determine their worthiness for conducting research and for creative, constructive thought and writing, the topic of widow(er)hood will be a popular one for at least the remainder of this decade.

REFERENCES

1. M. Langer, *Learning to Live as a Widow*, Gilbert, New York, p. 12, 1967.
2. J. F. Ball, Widow's Grief: The Impact of Age and Mode of Death, *Omega*, *74*, pp. 314-315, 1976-77.
3. R. A. Kalish, Sex and Marital Role Differences in Anticipation of Age-producted Dependency, *Journal of Genetic Psychology, 119*, pp. 53-62, January 1971.
4. C. J. Barrett and K. M. Schneweis, An Empirical Search for Stages of Widowhood, *Omega, 11*:2, p. 98, 1980-81.
5. C. M. Parkes, *Bereavement: Studies of Grief in Adult Life*, International Universities Press, New York, p. 7, 1972.
6. R. A. Kalish and D. K. Reynolds, *Death and Ethnicity: A Psychocultural Study*, University of Southern California Press, Los Angeles, 1976; reprinted New York: Baywood, 1981, pp. 212-213.
7. D. J. Levinson, *The Seasons of a Man's Life*, Knopf, New York, 1978.
8. G. E. Vaillant, *Adaptation to Life*, Little, Brown, Boston, 1977.
9. E. Lindemann, Symptomatology and Management of Acute Grief, *American Journal of Psychiatry, 101*, pp. 141-142, Sept. 1944.
10. I. O. Glick, R. S. Weiss, and C. M. Parkes, *The First Year of Bereavement*, John Wiley, New York, Chap. 4, 1974.
11. D. Maddison and A. Viola, The Health of Widows in the Year Following Bereavement, *Journal of Psychosomatic Research, 12*, p. 297, Dec. 1968.
12. K. F. Rowland, Environmental Events Predicting Death for the Elderly, *Psychological Bulletin, 84*:2, pp. 349-372, Nov. 1972.
13. G. Owen, R. Fulton, and E. Markusen, Death at a Distance: A Study of Family Survivors, paper presented to the Midwest Sociological Society, Omaha, NE, April 14, 1978, pp. 16-18.
14. R. G. Carey, Weathering Widowhood: Problems and Adjustment of the Widowed During the First Year, *Omega, 10*:2, p. 169, 1979-80.
15. C. J. Barrett, Intimacy in Widowhood, mimeograph, circa 1978, pp. 3-13.
16. M. L. S. Vachon, K. Freedman, and S. I. J. Freeman, Cancer and Bereavement, paper presented at the Symposium on Coping with Cancer, Toronto, pp. 7-8, April 24-26, 1977.
17. C. M. Parkes, Determinants of Outcome Following Bereavement, *Omega*, *6*:4, pp. 303-323, 1975.
18. A. Cartwright, L. Hockey and J. L. Anderson, *Life Before Death*, Routledge and Kegan Paul, London, p. 203, 1973.
19. R. C. Atchley, Dimensions of Widowhood in Later Life, *The Gerontologist*, *15*:2, p. 177, April 1975.
20. C. J. Barrett, Sex Differences in the Experience of Widowhood, paper presented to the American Psychological Association, p. 6, September 1, 1978.

There was a time when most people assumed that children never thought about sex, in fact that they were totally unconcerned with sex. We no longer make that assumption, but we continue to assume that children are unaware of any serious meaning of death and that the best way to help them cope with death is to try to limit their awareness as much as possible. As with sex, hiding death from children does not work and often becomes counterproductive. Although children do not develop a mature understanding of death until fourth or fifth grade, they have their own views of what death and dying mean, and they most certainly grieve those who have died. Their grief may represent a response to the grieving they experience going on around them or to their awareness that an important person has been removed from their lives (whether they perceive this as being permanent or not is a function of how mature their conceptualizations are). More specifically, this chapter describes the phenomenon of the anniversary reaction and how children respond to the anniversaries of death. Essentially, it discusses many aspects of the ways in which children grieve.

CHAPTER
6

Children's Anniversary Reactions to the Death of a Family Member

Sandra Sutherland Fox

Professional mental health literature is replete with theoretical formulations and clinical descriptions of the impact of parent or sibling death on children and the occurrence of anniversary-related adult emotional and physical disorders. These reports of causal connections between childhood bereavement and adult anniversary pathology mandate the careful exploration of *children's* anniversary reactions to the death of a family member. If childhood responses to bereavement become *pathological* in adulthood, it is essential that we study those early anniversaries and develop strategies for prevention. We must understand when, why, and for what children anniversaries become problematic.

The Family Support Center of Judge Baker Guidance Center in Boston, Massachusetts, has conducted an exploratory study of children's anniversary reactions to the death of a family member. This study had two broad goals:

1. to identify and understand symptomatic behavior that may occur as a part of a child's anniversary reaction to the death of a family member; and
2. to differentiate children's normal and predictable anniversary responses from pathological reactions.

Five specific hypotheses were proposed:

1. There is a predictable anniversary response in children to a family member's death that can be identified by expected emotional, physical, and/or behavioral patterns around a specific time period.

2. The selection of the anniversary time will vary according to times of special significance for each child. Children will have the clearest anniversary reactions at times when the dead family member's image is quite strong such as birthdays, holidays, and family celebrations.

3. The pattern of behaviors during an anniversary reaction will differ depending on the developmental stage of the child at the time of the death of the family member.

4. Normal and pathological anniversary reactions in children can be identified by different patterns of behavior.

5. Specific external variables will influence the child's anniversary reaction. These factors will include, among others:
   a. the nature of the death (sudden or anticipated);
   b. the location of the death (home, hospital, etc.);
   c. the child's information about the death (what he or she observed or was told);
   d. the child's involvement in the funeral and/or other services;
   e. the religious or cultural orientation of the family;
   f. the parent's/caregiver's pattern of grieving;
   g. the child's changed role in the family structure; and
   h. the availability of a support system to the family at times of crisis.

For this study, anniversary reactions are defined as *psychological, physical, and/or behavioral responses occurring at a time of special significance related to the death of a family member.* "Family members" are defined by each family and generally include the nuclear and extended family and partners of adults in the family.

LITERATURE REVIEW

One dimension of this study has been an extensive literature review addressing the following areas:

1. Children's anniversary reactions to the death of a family member
2. Anniversary reactions in adults
3. The development of the child's concept of death
4. The development of the child's concept of time
5. Children's mourning (with relevance to anniversary reactions)

Only three papers have been identified that make reference to *children's anniversary reactions to the death of a family member.* Dopson reports on a fifteen-year-old girl with chronic lymphedema of the hand [1]. The onset of symptoms was triggered by the first anniversary of her grandmother's death. In a paper discussing children's disturbed reactions to the death of a family member, Cain, Fast, and Erickson state, "The children were often convinced not only that they, too, would die, but that they would die... at precisely the same age... as the dead sibling." [2, p. 747] Cain and Cain writing about children who are used by parents to "replace" a dead sibling, write, "Two [replacement] children who were approaching the age at which their sibling died solemnly announced that they did not want to have any more birthdays." [3, p. 450] They were convinced they would die at the same age as their sibling.

The richest, though most perplexing, literature discusses *adult anniversary reactions.* Many anniversary reactions in adults appear as *physiological* problems. A particularly striking example is a woman who developed incapacitating headaches on the forty-second anniversary of her brother's murder by a bullet in the head [4]. Other presentations include ulcerative colitis [5-8], rheumatoid arthritis [9], dermatologic conditions [10], migraine headaches [11, 4], severe cardiac problems [12, 13], conversion reaction back pain [4], cancer [14], and glaucoma and other opthalmic conditions [15-18].

The relationship between anniversaries of parent or sibling death and adult psychiatric symptoms is reported in a number of retrospective studies [19-21]. Hilgard and her colleagues suggest causal relationships between psychiatric hospitalization and the adult's reaching the age at which his or her parent died, or the adult's child reaching the age the patient had been when his own parent died [22]. Depression, suicide, and psychosis are noteworthy presentations of anniversary reactions to parent or sibling death in childhood [23, 24].

Most discussion of adult anniversary reactions is found in clinical reports [25-33]. The earliest describes Freud's awareness of the anniversary nature of recurrent memories in the case of Elizabeth von R. He writes, ". . . This lady celebrated annual festivals of remembrance at the point of her various catastrophies, and on these occasions her vivid visual reproduction and expressions of feeling kept to the date precisely." [28, p. 163] Engel [4] describes his self-analysis of anniversary reactions over the ten years following the unexpected death of his forty-nine-year-old identical twin brother and as he lived through his fifty-eighth year and approached the age of his father at the time of *his* sudden death [34].

Formulations about the dynamics of adult anniversary reactions propose they are evidence of incomplete mourning and generally suggest they are pathological. For example, in his classic papers on anniversary reactions Pollock writes, "[An anniversary reaction is] the reaction to a temporal trigger that permits the emergence of repressed conflict, which may or may not have defensive qualities that can be manifested in symptoms." [35, p. 348] He believes the anniversary reaction is "a manifestation of a previous traumatic fixation." [35, p. 363] In a later paper he states, "Anniversary reactions derive from pathological or uncompleted mourning. With the resolution of intrapsychic conflicts through analysis, these symptoms disappear leaving only a memory as a memorial." [36, p.123] Others describe anniversary reactions as examples of pathological mourning [37], a response to "unresolved feelings related to a traumatic episode of the past" [38, p. 749], "an attempt to relive or reexperience the traumatic event again in a repetitious way, in anticipation of being able to master the trauma which was not mastered previously" [39, p. 210], and as a striking clinical manifestation of repetition compulsion [4]. Ferenczi, in his 1919 paper on Sunday Neuroses says, "We know . . . since Freud established it psychoanalytically, that psycho-neurotics—so many of whom . . . suffer from repressed memories—cheerfully celebrate the anniversary or the time of year of certain experiences significant to them by an exacerbation of their symptoms." [40, p. 174] Those who wish to be involved in theoretical discussion of anniversary reactions are advised to investigate such concepts as identification; repetition compulsion; traumatic neurosis; psychic injury; cumulative, retrospective, and anterospective trauma; conditioned reflexes; and the unconscious sense of time [41].

Literature on *the child's developing understanding of the concept of death* is extensive. The classic works by Nagy [42] and Anthony [43, 44] are confirmed in more recent studies that detail the development of both cognitive and affective understanding of death [45, 46]. It is not until about age nine that most children see death as final and as something that will someday happen to them.

There is limited discussion in the literature of *children's development of the concept of time*, though the notion of time is a critical component in understanding children's anniversary reactions. Piaget's 1946 experiments on various cognitive-developmental problems include an exploration of the growth of temporal perspective in children [47]. A child of three years has memories from as much as a year earlier. By age five the child is capable of simple estimates of duration, and by age seven or eight learns to measure time [48]. Basic time concepts are usually in place by late childhood to early adolescence [45].

The concept of time is important because of the *variety of temporal markers* associated with adult anniversary reactions [49-51]. As Pollack writes, "For the vulnerable individual a specific time of day, a specific day of the week, a specific season of the year, or a specific holiday can serve as a trigger or activator for the appearance of a symptom related to anniversary reactions." [36, p. 123]

The final area of the literature review explores *children's mourning*. Numerous analytically oriented case studies discuss the reactions of specific children to bereavement [52-58]. Most report on young children. None comment on the children's responses to significant dates or times that might represent anniversaries. Most end before the first calendar anniversary of the family member's death.

The age at which children are capable of mourning is relevent to the current study of children's anniversary reactions. Mourning is defined as "the mental work following the loss of a love object through death." [52, p. 34] In order to mourn, a child requires:

1. Sufficiently stable and differentiated self and object representations in the inner world so that the integrity of the self representation can withstand the threat implicit in the death of someone else;
2. Sufficient ego mastery over the id so that the concept of death can be relatively more integrated within the ego's expanding pool of knowledge rather than utilized for the arousal of instinctual derivatives;
3. The ability to distinguish animate from inanimate and thus have a concept of the living as opposed to the nonliving;
4. Some ability to understand time in terms of the past, present, and future; and
5. Sufficient secondary-process causal thinking to understand that since something is dead, it can no longer do certain things [59, p. 325].

While Kliman [60] and Furman [61] believe young children *do* mourn when active clinical efforts are made to facilitate that process, Wolfenstein [62] and most other psychoanalytically oriented writers take the position "that children, in comparison to adults, do not pass through mourning when the latter is defined, following Freud, as including the gradual and painful emotional detachment from the inner representation of the person who has died." [63, p. 714] They believe the ego functions necessary for mourning are not firmly established before adolescence.

The literature review raises several important questions for this study of children's anniversary reactions to the death of a family member:

1. *Can children have anniversary reactions to the death of a family member?* What developmental level of the capacity to mourn must a child have achieved to make anniversary reactions theoretically possible?
2. *What theoretical formulations explain children's anniversary reactions to the death of a family member?* Such a formulation must consider current ideas about object relations, concept development in children, and anniversary reactions in adults.
3. *Are all anniversary reactions to death signs of incomplete mourning or pathological ego adaptation?* Is there a place for anniversary reactions in the theoretical framework of predictable responses to crisis? Can they, for at least some people, represent efforts at healthy integration of loss?

THE EXPLORATORY STUDY

This study explores children's anniversary reactions—psychological, physical, and/or behavioral responses occurring at a time of special significance related to the death of a family member. The Family Support Center, a preventive mental health program, provides counseling to children and families coping with diagnosis of a life-threatening illness or situation; sudden death caused by accident, illness, murder, or suicide; anticipated death resulting from illness or aging; and jailing of a family member.

The Sample

Twenty-one families who have been seen at the Family Support Center because of the death of a family member have been invited to participate in the study. Five families declined, four agreed but then did not keep their initial or rescheduled appointments, and one family felt their reactions were clouded by the death of another family member during the week of the first anniversary of the original family member death. Eleven families (52%) agreed to participate. Eighteen children and twelve parents/guardians have been interviewed. Each child has passed the first anniversary of the death; four who first came to the center more than a year after the death, were interviewed soon after the second or third anniversary. These eighteen children ranged in age from four to seventeen years and included seven boys and eleven girls. Family members who died included parents, siblings, grandparents, and partners of parents. Causes of death included accidents, illnesses, and suicide. All eleven families had funeral services, nine with open caskets.

Methodology

Each family invited to participate in this study received a letter describing the research. About a week later a member of the research team called. If the family members were willing to participate, a home or office appointment was arranged, informed consent was discussed, and copies of the Informed Consent Form were mailed so the family could review them before the day of the interview.

On the interview day the children and adults met briefly with the interviewer to raise any questions and to review and sign the consent forms. The children's interviews were usually completed first; an interview with the parent(s)/guardian(s) followed. Each interview required about thirty minutes. The children were then invited to draw a picture of their family before or after the family member's death or to draw something they thought about during the interview.

A number of families who met the study's criteria were not contacted. Several families still involved with the center were excluded at the request of their therapists who felt participation in the research might interfere with ongoing clinical work. Others were not contacted for a variety of other reasons.

THE FINDINGS

Several questions were designed to identify experiences that were meaningful for the child at the actual time of the family member's death. The children were asked what special things they went to or participated in when the family member died, what they remember about that participation, and what else they remember that happened around the time of the family member's death.

Fourteen of the eighteen children went to the funeral, and most also participated in the wake and/or burial. Of the four children who did not go, three were told they were too young. One of these children (age 5) commented, "There was a funeral, but I didn't go. I'm too little. I sleeped in his bed. I wanted to. It felt good. Maybe I'll be next to him. He was looking down at me." Several children remembered special roles in the wake, funeral, and burial. One child (age 6) remembered she felt like pushing her divorced father's body out of the casket.

Eleven of the eighteen children remembered other things that happened around the time of the family member's death. They cited a friend's birthday, weather phenomena, holidays, and sports seasons.

A second group of questions aimed more directly at temporal and experiential markers and about anniversary reactions. The children were asked the date the family member died, what helps them remember when the family member died, and what special things their family has done to remember that person. They also identified the point during the past year when they missed the family member *most* and described any special things they did at that time. Finally, they described *other* times during the year when they found themselves missing the deceased relative.

Six children (33%), ranging in age from eight to eighteen, knew the month, day, and year of the death. Four children (22%), aged five to ten, were unable to say when the death occurred. Others gave dates one or two days before or after the death, gave an incorrect year or none at all, or indicated the time of death in relation to their own age or to the day of the week.

The children described several things that help them remember when the family member died including the weather, what they were doing, the month and the date. When asked what their family has done to remember the deceased relative, they note anniversary masses, taking flowers to the grave, telling a family member she looks just like the person who died, and visiting the cemetery.

The children identified a variety of points at which they *most* missed the dead family member during the previous year: times when they needed the relative's help or friendship, on holidays—especially Thanksgiving, Chrismas, and Easter; on the dead person's birthday; on the day of the week when the relative died; and for several children, every day. The *other* times during the year when they have found themselves remembering the dead family member include when they are doing things they used to do with the relative, birthdays, holidays, when they see a dead sibling's friends, and when they go to bed.

EXAMPLES

The responses of three children in the study illustrate the richness and diversity of their feelings and their memories.

Tanya was thirteen-years-old when her father died of a drug and alcohol overdose, apparently suicide. Prior to his death on a Monday, he had been at the family home on Saturday for Tanya's sister's birthday party and had spent the night. This raised the hopes of the girls for a reconciliation between their parents, who had divorced four years earlier. Several weeks following his death, the father's girlfriend's pregnancy with his child was confirmed. Tanya has established a relationship with her new "sister" and the baby's mother. Tanya was referred to the Family Support Center three weeks after her father's death following several emergency room visits for hyperventilation, muscle spasms, and a seizure-like presentation, apparently related to the death. She continues in treatment.

When asked what special things she participated in at the time of her father's death, Tanya replied: "It was awful. At the wake my cousins kept playing with my father's body in ways I didn't like. I had an argument with them. I closed the casket. That ended it for a while. His girlfriend [not really his girlfriend] fainted."

When asked what else she remembers that happened about that time, she replied: "The day before [my father] died he stayed over at our house. That was special because he was living with another lady. He and Mom are divorced. It meant that they might get back together."

Tanya knew the correct month, day, and year of her father's death. When asked what helps her to remember, she said: "How can I forget it? That's a day I'll never forget. Like your first birthday party or first graduation. You never forget." When the interviewer commented that it was about a year since her father died, Tanya said it had been a year, two months, and a week. She was asked what special things the family has done to remember him. She described ringing ears and a "funny feeling" in her stomach that were "premonitions." She continued: "When I heard the date I remembered. It didn't seem like a whole year. To this day my father still doesn't have a headstone. I'll save money to get him one. The only thing you see is a pile of dirt."

During the past year Tanya missed her father *most* at Easter. "He always came to take us somewhere. He always sees how nice we look. And on Christmas. At Christmas we went to my [maternal] grandmother's house. That's the first time I saw my baby sister. I feel so sorry for her. She'll never know my father. That's why I'm sticking around her." When Tanya was asked about *other* times during the year when she remembered her father, she replied: "Lots. I thought about him every day. But the thing that got me coming here [to the Family Support Center] was like seizures. The doctor said I should see somebody (my therapist)." Tanya connects her "seizures" with times when she thinks about her father.

When Tanya was asked to draw her family before or after her father's death, she drew a series of five identical heads with the largest, her father's, on the left and the smallest, her youngest sibling's, on the right. She said she couldn't make her father look right and added "his Afro wasn't this big either." She labeled each family member and at the bottom of the picture wrote,"We were an all together family!"

Emily was seven years old when her infant half-brother died of cardiac arrest secondary to fetal alcohol syndrome. With the exception of a twenty-four-hour period at home several weeks earlier, the baby's entire life had been spent in a pediatric intensive care unit. Emily and her mother visited frequently. The baby's father had been jailed on criminal charges prior to the birth. Her mother was referred to the Family Support Center by the hospital social worker three months after the baby's death. Her continued depression and its impact on Emily were ongoing concerns, as was her difficulty terminating with the hospital staff.

Emily went to her baby brother's funeral "up by my aunt's house." She and her mother were the second ones there. She remembers the baby was "frozen" because "when we kissed him he was cold." When asked what else she remembered about that time, she said: "My friends came to my house because they liked my brother a lot. They were going to pray for him."

Although Emily's brother had died sixteen months ealier, she stated he died "last week." It is of interest that her mother gave the month of the baby's birth when asked the date of his death. Emily could identify no special things her family has done to remember the baby. During the past year Emily recalled missing her brother most "when I'm dreaming. I dreamed I was standing there looking at him. Then I opened the box and saw him and he was floating up in the air like angels." Emily also finds herself thinking about her brother when she is getting ready to go to bed. She adds, "Once in a while I think about God."

Emily drew two pictures with a black crayon to try to illustrate her dream of standing and looking at her dead baby brother, opening the box, and seeing him "floating up in the air like angels." She printed "My drim is this" at the top of both pictures. First she drew a large rectangle with a small stick figure standing at the bottom of the box. She then turned the paper over and drew an outline of an angel.

Gretchen was a young adolescent when her ten-year-old sister, Kia, died. Kia was slightly retarded and had a seizure disorder. Kia's school was cancelled because of bad weather, and since she was not dressed, she stayed home while her mother drove Gretchen, who had overslept, to school. When the mother returned home, Kia was in the bathtub, apparently dead. Although it is assumed she had a seizure and drowned, the autopsy revealed no water in her lungs so the family still is not certain about the cause of death. Six months after the death the mother called the Family Support Center because of her concern about how she and Gretchen were handling the death.

Gretchen attended Kia's funeral, which she found "boring." She added, "Kia would have fallen asleep!" The burial was close to the family home. Gretchen commented that the bus she takes to school goes right through the cemetery, but she is usually talking and doesn't "think about it." When asked what else she remembers that happened about that time, Gretchen said: "I was late for school that day. I just slept late. I didn't want to get up. Mom had to drive me to school and Kia drowned while we were gone."

Gretchen remembered the exact date of Kia's death. Kia's bed and other belongings, which are still in the bedroom they shared, help Gretchen remember. She volunteered that it doesn't bother her that Kia's things are still there. When asked what her family has done to remember Kia, Gretchen reports they go to the cemetery. Also her great aunt frequently dresses up one of Kia's dolls and fixes the doll's hair. Her mother added that they are getting a grey marble marker for the grave, which they had hoped to have for Kia's birthday but will instead have by Memorial Day. Gretchen's mother had wanted a pink headstone, but Gretchen objected, saying, "pink wouldn't go with the green dress Kia was buried in." They also put a memorial notice in the newspaper on the anniversary date. Gretchen said there was no special time when she missed Kia most during the past year and no other times when she found herself remembering her.

Gretchen had appeared very poised, mature, and self-contained during the interview. When invited to draw a picture, she put her head on her arm on the table and kept it there the entire time she drew her family. She began at the right side of the page moving to the left, and drew her dead sister "who loved the color green and was buried in a green dress, " her mother who "should have on all white clothes because she's a nurse, but the white won't show up," herself (no comments), and "Mikey-Mikey," a brown teddy bear with a circle around him. She told me Mikey-Mikey was buried with Kia. Gretchen said she 'gouged out" Mikey-Mikey's eyes several years ago after Kia gouged the eyes out of Gretchen's identical teddy bear, which, she noted, she still has.

DISCUSSION

This exploratory study and the associated literature review have generated rich clinical data and highlighted theoretical complexities about children's anniversary reactions to the death of a family member. The broad parameters of the sample, especially with regard to the age of the children and the particular family member who died, and its small size make it difficult to draw conclusions at this time. However, some impressions do emerge:

1. These children *do* describe psychological, physical, and/or behavioral responses occurring at times of special significance related to the death of the family member—that is, anniversary reactions.

2. The children's anniversary times are varied. Temporal and experiential markers of the times of special significance include birthdays, holidays, weather phenomena, and meaningful activities shared with the family member shortly before his or her death.
3. Only one-third of the children in the study knew the exact month, day, and year when the family member died. The remaining responses were incomplete or inaccurate. In two of the eleven familes the parent(s) could not give the correct date of death. It appears calendar dates are less significant than temporal or experiential markers for children's anniversary phenomena.
4. During the past year the children missed the dead family member *most of all* on holidays (especially Christmas), when they were doing special things they would have done with the dead person, at times when that person would have guided or protected them, and on the dead person's birthday.
   Identification of *other times* during the year when they remembered the family member was similar. Only one child mentioned the actual calendar anniversary in response to these questions.
5. Children's anniversary reactions seem to involve remembering rather than reliving (which seems to be more characteristic of the adult anniversary reactions described in the literature.)

THE FUTURE

This study describes anniversary reactions to the death of a family member in a broad but small sample. We hope to begin longitudinal studies of these children to follow their development into adulthood and monitor their anniversary reactions. It is hoped that this will increase our understanding of when and how apparently benign remembering becomes pathological reliving.

We will study in greater detail the particular variables we believe may significantly influence anniversary reactions—the nature and location of the death, the child's information about the death and involvement in the funeral and/or other services, the religious orientation of the family, the pattern of grieving in the family, the child's changed role in the family structure, and the family's support system.

We must also understand any relationship between children's anniversary reactions and the exacerbation of emotional disorders. In the only controlled study of bereaved children located in the literature, Rutter [64] reports over twice as many children attending a psychiatric clinic had lost a parent by death as would be expected from comparable death rates in the general population. Black [65] notes that 14 percent of the children at a child guidance clinic she studied had been bereaved of a close relative in the recent past. The human and economic importance of prevention requires that we be aggressive in our efforts to understand the possible correlations between children's bereavement, anniversary reactions, and mental health problems.

ACKNOWLEDGMENT

The assistance of Donna Plotkin, MSW and Sandra Payne, MSW in assembling a portion of the data and developing this study is gratefully acknowledged.

REFERENCES

1. C. Dopson, Unresolved Grief Presenting as Chronic Lymphedema of the Hand, *American Journal of Psychiatry,* pp. 1333-1334, 1979.
2. A.C. Cain, I. Fast, and M.E. Erickson. Children's Disturbed Reactions to the Death of a Sibling, *American Journal of Orthopsychiatry,* pp. 741-752, 1964.
3. A.C. Cain and B.S. Cain, On Replacing a Child, *Journal of the American Academy of Child Psychiatry, 3,* pp. 443-456, 1964.
4. J. O. Cavenar, J. L. Nash, and A. A. Maltbie, Anniversary Reactions Presenting as Physical Complaints, *Journal of Clinical Psychiatry, 39,* pp. 369-371, 374, 1978.
5. B. Bressler, Ulcerative Colitis as an Anniversary Syndrome, *The Psychoanalytic Review, 43,* pp. 381-387, 1965.
6. G. Engel, Studies of Ulcerative Colitis, *American Journal of Medicine, 19,* pp. 231-256, 1955.
7. I. Mintz, The Anniversary Reaction: A Response to the Unconscious Sense of Time, *Journal of the American Psychoanalytic Association, 19,* pp. 720-735, 1971.
8. P.E. Sifneos, *Ascent from Chaos: A Psychosomatic Case Study,* Harvard University Press, Cambridge, Massachusetts, 1964.
9. A. D. Ludwig, Rheumatoid Arthritis, in *Recent Developments in Psychosomatic Medicine,* E. D. Wittkower and R. A. Cleghorn, (eds.), J. B. Lippincott Co., Philadephia, 1954.
10. I. Macalpine, Psychosomatic Symptom Formation, *The Lancet,* p. 278, 1952.
11. M. Griffin, Some Psychiatric Aspects of Migraine, *Proceedings of Staff Meetings of Mayo Clinic, 28,* pp. 694-697, 1953.
12. J.O. Cavenar and J.G. Spaulding, Anniversary Reactions in Medical Practice, *Southern Medical Journal* (in press).
13. E. Weiss, B. Dlin, H. R. Rollin, et. al., Emotional Factors in Coronary Occlusion, *Archives of Internal Medicine,* XCIV, pp. 628-641, 1957.
14. W. S. Inman, Emotion, Cancer and Time: Coincidence or Determinism, *British Journal of Medical Psychology, 40,* pp. 225-231, 1967.
15. H.K. Fischer, B.M.Dlin, W.L. Winters, et al., Emotional Factors in Coronary Occlusion - II. Time Patterns and Factors Related to Onset, *Psychosomatics, 5,* pp. 380-391, 1964.

16. W.S. Inman, Emotion and Acute Glaucoma, *Lancet,* December 7, 1929.
17. W.S. Inman, Opthalmic Adventure: A Story of Frustration and Organic Disease, *British Journal of Medical Psychology, 35,* pp. 299-309, 1962.
18. W.S. Inman, Emotional Factors in Diseases of the Cornea, *British Journal of Medical Psychology, 38,* pp. 277-287, 1965.
19. J. R. Hilgard, Anniversary Reactions in Parents Precipitated by Children, *Psychiatry, 16,* pp. 73-80, 1953.
20. J. R. Hilgard, M. F. Newman, and F. Fisk, Strength of Adult Ego Functioning Following Childhood Bereavement, *American Journal of Orthopsychiatry, 30,* pp. 788-798, 1960.
21. D. Black, The Bereaved Child, *Journal of Child Psychology and Psychiatry and Allied Disciplines, 19,* pp. 287-292, 1978.
22. J. R. Hilgard and M. F. Newman, Anniversaries in Mental Illness, *Psychiatry, 22,* pp. 113-120, 1959.
23. J. R. Hilgard, Depressive and Psychotic States in Anniversaries of Sibling Death in Childhood, *International Psychiatry Clinics, 6,* pp. 197-211, 1969.
24. J. O. Cavenar, J. L. Nash, and A. A. Maltbie, Anniversary Reactions Masquerading as Manic-Depressive Illness, *American Journal of Psychiatry,* (in press).
25. M. Stein, Premonition as a Defense, *Psychoanalytic Quarterly, 22,* pp. 69-74, 1953.
26. C. Scott, A. Psychoanalytic Concept of the Origin of Depression, *British Medical Journal, 1,* pp. 538-540, 1948.
27. G. Zilboorg, Considerations on Suicide with Particular Reference to the Young, *American Journal of Orthopsychiatry, 7,* pp. 15-31, 1937.
28. S. Freud, Studies on Hysteria, *Standard Edition 2,* Hogarth Press, London, 1955.
29. P. Greenacre, The Family Romance of the Artist, *Psychoanalytic Study of the Child, 13,* International Universities Press, 1958.
30. P. Greenacre, The Relation of the Imposter to the Artist, *Psychoanalytic Study of the Child, 13,* International Universities Press, 1958.
31. R. B. Cornfield, J. S. Rosenthal, and N. Straker, Anniversary Reaction: Unusual Anniversaries in Medical Practice, *New York State Journal of Medicine, 79,* pp. 1597-1599, 1979.
32. J. O. Cavenar, A. A. Maltbie, and J. L. Sullivan, Aftermath of an Abortion: Anniversary Depression and Abdominal Pain, *Bulletin of the Menninger Clinic, 42,* pp. 433-438, 1978.
33. S. Axelrod, O. L. Schnipper, and J. H. Rau, Hospitalized Children of Holocaust Survivors, *Continuing Medical Education: Syllabus and Proceedings in Summary Form,* American Psychiatric Assocation, Washington, D. C., 1978.
34. G. Engel, The Death of a Twin: Mourning and Anniversary Reactions: Fragments of 10 Years of Self-Analysis, *International Journal of Psychoanalysis, 56,* pp. 23-40, 1975.
35. G. H. Pollock, Anniversary Reactions, Trauma and Mourning, *Psychoanalytic Quarterly, 39,* pp. 347-71, 1970.
36. G. H. Pollock, Temporal Anniversary Manifestations: Hour, Day, Holiday, *Psychoanalytic Quarterly, 40,* pp. 123-131, 1971.

37. G. Krupp and C. Landau, Variants of Pathological Bereavement, *Archives of the Foundation of Thanatology, 7,* p. 48. 1978.
38. B. M. Dlin and H. K. Fischer, The Anniversary Reaction: A Meeting of Freud and Pavlov, *Psychosomatics, 20,* pp. 749-755, 1979.
39. J.O. Cavenar, J.G. Spaulding, and E.B. Hammett, Anniversary Reactions, *Psychosomatics, 17,* p. 210, 1977.
40. S. Ferenczi, Sunday Neuroses, 1919, in *Further Contributions to the Theory and Technique of Psychoanalysis,* E. Jones, (ed.), Hogarth Press, London, 1950.
41. L.D. Siggins, Mourning: A Critical Survey of the Literature, *International Journal of Psychoanalysis,* XLVII, pp. 14-25, 1966.
42. M.I. Nagy, The Child's Theory Concerning Death, *Journal of Genetic Psychology, 73,* pp. 3-26, 1948.
43. S. Anthony, *The Child's Discovery of Death,* Kegan Paul, London, 1940.
44. S. Anthony, *The Discovery of Death in Childhood and After,* Penguin, London, 1973.
45. R. Lonetto, *Children's Conceptions of Death,* Springer Publishing Company, New York, 1980.
46. F. Ferguson, Children's Cognitive Discovery of Death, *Journal of the Association for the Care of Children in Hospitals, 7,* pp. 8-14, 1978.
47. J. Piaget, *Le Development de la Notion de Temps Chez L'Infant,* Presses Universitie de France, Paris, 1946.
48. P. Friasse, *The Psychology of Time,* Eyre & Spottiswodde, London, 1964.
49. F. Cohn, Time and the Ego, *Psychoanalytic Quarterly, 26,* pp. 168-169, 1957.
50. L. Szekely, Anniversaries, Unfinished Mourning, Time and the Invention of the Calendar: A Psychoanalytic "Apercu", *Scandanavian Psychoanalytic Review, 1,* pp. 115-146, 1978.
51. W. Stekel, Time and Its Relationship to the Neurotic, *American Journal of Urology, 14,* p. 437, 1912.
52. E. Furman, *A Child's Parent Dies: Studies in Childhood Bereavement,* Yale University Press, New Haven, 1974.
53. M.J. Barnes, Reactions to the Death of a Mother, *Psychoanalytic Study of the Child, 19,* International Universities Press, New York, 1964.
54. R.A. Furman, Death of a Six-Year-Old's Mother During His Analysis, *Psychoanalytic Study of the Child, 19,* International Universities Press, 1964.
55. Y. Gauthier, The Mourning Reaction of a 10½ Year Old Boy, *Psychoanalytic Study of the Child, 20,* International Universities Press, 1965.
56. A.S. Kliman, Eighteen Untreated Orphans, in *Psychological Emergencies of Childhood,* G. Kliman (ed.), Grune & Stratton, New York, 1968.
57. T. Lopez and G.W. Kliman, Memory, Reconstruction, and Mourning in the Analysis of a 4-Year-Old Child: Maternal Bereavement in the Second Year of Life, *Psychoanalytic Study of the Child, 34,* International Universities Press, New York, 1979.
58. B. Rosenblatt, A Young Boy's Reaction to the Death of His Sister, *Journal of the American Academy of Child Psychiatry, 8,* pp. 320-335, 1969.

59. R.A. Furman, Death and the Young Child: Some Preliminary Considerations, *Psychoanalytic Study of the Child, 19,* International Universities Press, New York, 1964.
60. G. Kliman, Facilitation of Mourning During Childhood, Presented at the Annual Meeting of the American Orthopsychiatric Association, New York, April, 1969.
61. R.A. Furman, A Child's Capacity for Mourning, in *The Child in His Family: The Impact of Disease and Death,* E.J. Anthony and C. Koupernik, (eds.), John Wiley & Sons, New York, 1973.
62. M. Wolfenstein, How Is Mourning Possible?, *Psychoanalytic Study of the Child, 21,* International Universities Press, New York, 1966.
63. J.B.M. Miller, Children's Reactions to the Death of a Parent: A Review of the Psychoanalytic Literature, *Journal of the American Psychoanalytic Association, 19,* pp. 697-719, 1971.
64. M. Rutter, *Children of Sick Parents,* Oxford University Press, Oxford, 1966.
65. D. Black. What Happens to Bereaved Children?, *Therapeutic Education, 2,* p. 15-20, 1974.

At what age is death most tragic? On this issue, the research is clear: the death of a child or young adult is fairly consistently seen as more tragic than the death of a middle-aged adult whose death, in turn, is seen as more tragic than that of an elderly person. The same question is not asked regarding the survivor, that is, at what age is surviving the death of a loved one the most tragic. Perhaps the question is not asked because the relationship of the dead person to the survivor is so important that the question loses its meaning. In our society, the deaths that probably carry the greatest significance are the parent (for a child not yet adult), the child (for a parent of any age), and the spouse.

Therefore, when we think of bereaved adults, we usually think of widows and widowers or, less frequently, of parents who have experienced the death of a child. Somehow the death of the elderly parent of a middle-aged child seldom comes to mind, even though this is the death experienced most often by young and middle-aged adults. The death of an elderly parent certainly lacks the impact that we associate with the death of a spouse or a child or the death of a young parent: the elderly are expected to die and the adult child is often assumed to be minimally affected. Perhaps because of these very assumptions, the death of an elderly parent may have ramifications for the well-being of the adult child that are frequently ignored by both friends and mental-health professionals. Chapter 7 brings some of these important issues to light.

CHAPTER
7

The Impact of Parental Death on Middle Aged Children*

Miriam S. Moss
and
Sidney Z. Moss

Separations and losses are crucial events over the life cycle and are the focus of much psychosocial literature on individuals and families. One loss that many persons in their mid-years experience is the death of a parent. This chapter explores the impact of that loss on adult children in their thirties and forties. It suggests a number of generic themes that may occur.

A search of the literature examining the impact of the loss of a parent reveals that with rare exceptions the focus is on parental loss by the young child, either as initially experienced [1, 2] or as a root of adult psychopathology or suicide [3, 4]. Only a handful of authors have explored the nonpathological impact of parental death in mid-life [5-8]. Why have we failed to examine the one type of death that outnumbers them all: the death of an older person and its impact on the surviving child? What is it about this modal type of death that appears to be so anathema?

Perhaps some of the explanation for ignoring the impact of the loss of a parent comes in our relative disregard of life tasks specific to middle age—a time when a large number of parental deaths occur. Parental loss may seem to pale

*An earlier version of this chapter was presented at the 38th Annual Meeting of American Association of Marriage and Family Therapy, Toronto, November 8, 1980.

in importance against the need to work out marital relationships, career goals, parent-adolescent conflicts and reassessment of the self. Further, traditional formulations in psychology have emphasized the individual at the expense of relationships. Only relatively recently—particularly with the increased emphasis on object relations and family therapy—has the meaning of relationships begun to be a primary focus in psychology.

In our culture parental death for an adult child is seen as relatively unimportant in comparison with death of younger persons [9]. Even cross cultural studies of death and dying pay scant attention to the adult child's loss of parent. Findings suggest that an adult losing a parent does not exhibit intense grief and aggression, and rarely necessitates the formal treatment which is normally given to persons in deep mourning [10]. On the other hand, the loss of parents may be so painful that we as researchers and clinicians flee from it to protect ourselves, to escape facing our unresolved guilts and frustrations. The child in each of us may feel abandoned in losing a parent, and we shy away from the topic.

From another perspective, the loss of a parent is quite positive: a relief from the real or potential burdens of caretaking, a welcome severing of destructive family ties, an opportunity to grow unhampered by parental expectations, and a realization of the all too small reward of an inheritance. Yet our cultural proscriptions inhibit open expression of these feelings. Finally, it may be that a personal response to the death of a parent follows no general patterns and is totally idiosyncratic and reflective of the unique relationship of the child and parent over the previous decades, combined with the current life situation of the child, and a wide range of special characteristics which defy generalization.

The older person is sometimes viewed as having outlived the parental role, as being in a "post parental" stage [11, 12]. Concurrently, the middle-aged adult may no longer be seen to need a parent. Does this suggest that the role relationship is severed? While we know something about frequency of interaction and extent of mutual assistance [13], few have examined the *quality* of the relationship between adult children and their parents [14, 15]. If parenting primarily connotes basic nurturance and meeting daily survival needs, then most middle aged persons neither need nor want parenting; however, if parenting is conceptualized differently as suggested above, there persists a viable and significant bond between adult children and their parents.

THE "ADULT CHILD"

The concept of the "adult child" is enigmatic. What does it mean to be a child and an adult simultaneously? Child brings to mind dependency, immaturity, and youth; adult connotes independence, maturity, and age. The dialectic of the adult child concept is appealing. The man or woman who has achieved mastery over life's tasks does not slough off the tie with a parent. The child in each of us persists throughout the years in which we have a parent (and some would suggest beyond). It is generally not a crippling link to the past, but a part of the human condition in which the past and present are melded. None of us is pure child or pure adult. A dialectic of contradictions allows for the interplay of the past and the present, the attachments and separations, the child and the adult [16]. This theme of a dialectic will recur throughout our discussion.

The next section of this paper examines the child-parent relationship, primarily from the vantage of the adult child. Factors that tend to weaken and to maintain the tie are examined. The assumption is that the bond is a dynamic bio-social one which persists throughout life.

Quality of the Adult Child-Parent Relationship

This paper focuses on normal, middle-aged children, generally married with children of their own. Their parents are generally in the "young old" category, live active independent lives, and are not subject to major impairments or incapacity. Thus, this section deals with the quality of relationship between basically independent adults and children, not with issues of long term primary care of the impaired elderly. For these adult children, their parent tie is the longest of life's relationships—the prototype of attachment. For three or four decades the image of the parent has been internalized. The infinite number of transactions throughout life—from infancy on—indelibly imprint the images of each on the other. Shared memories, rituals, and the emotional life in the family weave the past into the present. Unfortunately, there is little research that focuses on this area, and the ideas presented here are exploratory. First we examine factors that strengthen the tie.

The genetic tie underlies the parent-child bond. The link of flesh and blood is underscored in middle age when a look in the mirror most easily brings to mind a resemblance to the parent. A core of bio-socially based care eliciting behavior [17] is a vital aspect of the parent-child attachment. Each finds a need for and is satisfied in the bond. Each identifies with a pervasive sense of family that further cements the parent-child tie. A sense of family solidarity strengthens the bond. Values and beliefs are quite often congruent between generations [18], and this tends to provide continuity. Who else in the lives of adult children has offered the possibility of unconditional love? The marital bond, though more intense for most adults, has proved in recent decades to be quite fragile. It is not unusual for recently divorced persons to exhibit strong ties with their parents and to seek and receive considerable parental support—emotional, instrumental, and financial. Few would suggest that the severance of parental bonds has or will approach the soaring divorce rate.

We know little of the qualitative aspects of the tie, yet they play a crucial role in maintaining the relationship. Affection, caring and warm companionship persist in some situations. Yet, we do not know how pervasive these feelings are. The parent continues to be a model for the child and a parent's coping with transitions (child leaving home, retirement, diminished physical strength) provides continuing anticipatory socialization. More thought should be given to the dynamics of reciprocal socialization where each provides a model and a source of influence for the other [18].

The expectations of the partners in the relationship are significant to the bond—each trying to do the right thing for each other. Repeatedly we hear of older parents seeking to maintain independence from their children, with the pervasive fear of being a burden. On the other hand, the adult children, responding to internal as well as social pressures, seek to fufilll filial obligations in spite of conflicting responsibilities. Ideally this allows for progression toward filial maturity [19] when the child can be dependable in assuming some responsibilities for the parent, and the parent has the capacity to be appropriately dependent [20].

Central to the parent-child bond is trustworthiness built out of parental accountability and filial loyalty [21]. There is a deep sense of mutual committment and responsibility. Most adult children keep in touch with their parents, many live nearby and maintain persistent threads of mutual assistance. The way in which the bonds of duty are meshed with genuine caring in the relationship is yet to be ascertained. No matter how dependent the parent becomes on the child, however, there is no role reversal. In only the most superficial way can one equate an older person's inability to take care of some routine task (previously handled unassisted and with little thought) with the incapacity of a young child. Whereas the child is learning to become independent, the older person is losing some autonomy and dreads the inability to regain it.

In spite of the persistence of the bond with the parents, there is a range of factors that tend to weaken the attachment. The parent-child tie is permeated with conflicting elements and the overall quality is a synthesis of contradictions. The separation and individuation process of a child is a recurrent theme intensified in adolescence. There is a stigma for a young adult who is "too" tied to the parent and living at home. Thus by middle age, normal developmental processes have tended to weaken the bond. Old conflicts indigenous to the relationship may persist with issues of control and blaming often recurring. New conflicts are then superimposed upon the old, where the adult child must balance personal needs and those of the family of procreation as well as the responsibilities to another set of parents—the in-laws.

There is some indication that the parents view their adult children as more important in their lives than the children see them [22]. Each may be involved with the other, but most do not live in the same household, and although "intimacy at a distance" may well occur, the fact that the adult child lives with and responds to demands of a spouse and children may place the older parent on the periphery of the demands of everyday living.

There are real pulls that tend to separate parents from children. Parents have lives and interests of their own—they have friends and pleasures that are largely independent of their adult children. They may often be quite pleased that they can assume some distance from the middle-aged generation—struggling as it does to keep marriages together, to meet spiraling costs for expanding needs, to respond to women's issues and adolescent rebellion as well as strong themes of self-fulfillment. One of the major factors that serves to create stress in the adult child-parent relationship is the lack of clarity in the role expectations of each *vis a vis* the other. This is an anomic situation with guidelines generally missing to prescribe and proscribe patterns of interaction. Though the basic tie persists, the details of how it is to be acted out are vague, and each family may feel it must forge its own pattern.

Since the state now provides some basic care (e.g., social security and medicare) the child is released from some responsibility. Hess and Waring [14] suggest that the parental bond may be seen as primarily a voluntary one and that the model which most closely approximates it is that of friendship and homophily, stressing mutuality of respect, interests, and affect. Does this adequately explain findings that most of the care for older people is supplied by the family, not the formal service delivery network or friends [23]? We suggest crucial elements such as biosocial family underpinnings, life long patterns of interaction, and deep family loyalties should not be relegated to secondary status. Further, it is not clear whether increasing responsibility taken by the public sector tends to weaken the family tie (diluting the child's responsibility) or strengthen it (by reducing the fear of economic burden and supporting an affective base of the relationship) [13]. As the parent ages, the child is increasingly aware of small, often incremental deficits in the ability of the parent to equal or exceed past performance. These signs of decline are painful to the child who may wish to forestall the aging of parents in order to hold on to his or her own youth.

Another major factor in weakening the bond is anticipatory orphanhood, which flows throughout the child's life. From earliest childhood, there is the fear that the loved parent will leave or die. Weisman suggests that anticipatory grief begins as soon "as love is implanted." [24, p. 15] Thus, living and loss are intimately intertwined. When a child becomes aware of death of others there is a natural tendency to imagine the death of a parent. How often does a young child say "Mommy, when you die" or "Daddy if you die." The fear of orphanhood comes early. Parents live now, but parents will die. Each of us comes to anticipate the death of parents, yet this death has a place in "some legendary time." [25]

As children become middle-aged, they experience the death of parents of their peers. Each such loss has an impact and is a socialization to the death of their own parent. They learn that parents do not have to be very old or to be sick for a long period of time to die. They are braced for death if it should occur. The adult child recurrently considers and rehearses the potential death of a parent. There is less taboo in anticipating one's parent's death than the death of a spouse or a child. The cognitive and affective process of anticipatory orphanhood may occur over decades, thus preparing the adult child for the fact of parental death.

There is an interplay between the factors that serve to strengthen the child-parent bond and those that tend to loosen it. The elasticity of the bond enables it to transcend a life time. Troll says of child-parent relationships: "They seem to override geographic and socioeconomic mobility as well as developmental changes in a way no other relationships seem to do." [26, p. 84]

LIMITATIONS OF THIS DISCUSSION

Before discussing some generic aspects of the impact of the death of a parent on an adult child, we must stress that there are a number of factors in the situation that this paper does not consider, and each may be very important. These include the following:

- whether the death is of the first parent or the second parent;
- the quality and circumstances of the relationship over the life cycle;
- the degree, intensity and quality of the interacton between parent and child toward the end of the parent's life;
- the circumstances and timing of the last illness and death of the parent;
- social supports and the life situation of the surviving child;
- objective factors such as the gender of the parent and of the child, whether or not they lived in the same household, and the financial resources of each;
- the cultural, ethnic and religious characteristics of the family;
- the broader family and intergenerational implications of the loss; and finally
- the personality of the parent and the child.

IMPACT OF THE LOSS:
SEVERING AND MAINTAINING THE BOND

The last formal task of an adult child toward his or her parent is to cope with the death of the parent. The shock at the death generally initiates a brief period of numbing and denial, often followed by some degree of protest. Few young-old parents are seen by their children as having lived long enough; even fewer are felt to die in the right way and at the right time. Yet, the loss is no surprise.

The years of anticipatory orphanhood and anticipatory grief have laid a foundation for acceptance. This may decrease the ambiguity of what death means and increase the resources available to the child in coping with the loss. Yet even a profound sense of preparedness may not be equal to the reality of death.

Though the loss may be deeply felt by the child, society does not accept or support profound or extended mourning in this situation. This may leave the adult child in the position of outwardly denying the impact of the loss, while inwardly he or she may be grieving. The bond has been severed, and as part of the grief for a parent there may be an attempt to recapture the essence of the relationship, to dwell on past events and feelings in a life review. The parent who died is recalled in part as the parent of early childhood. Recollections are tinged with grief over unfulfilled wishes and entitlements. While mourning the loss of parents, one also mourns the loss of the family of origin in which they played a central part. The child in us receives the ultimate blow, our parent is dead, and only the image remains.

To the extent that feelings of anticipatory orphanhood had begun prior to the parent's death, there may have been an opportunity to work out some of the life review directly with the parents. But how many adult children can handle this—with the potential threats to self and the imagined threats to parents and to the relationship? Whatever the unfinished business with the parents, after their death the issue is unusually poignant because it cannot be worked out directly. Ambivalence persists and with it the gnawing questions of earlier childhood: Did they really understand me and love me for myself? Did they love a sibling more? What were the secrets I was never privy to?

Feelings of guilt and blame may also arise. There is usually no strong guilt in being a survivor, since it is right for a child to outlive a parent. As deBeauvoir writes, it is a guilt of "carelessness, omission, and abstention," one of "a thousand piercing regrets." [25, p. 108] Blame recurs for a life time when love was not always received in right measure or under the right conditions. Superimposed upon this may be an opportunity for the child to step back and with empathy see the relationship from the parent's perspective and allow for forgiveness instead of blame.

After the death most children continue much the same as they did when the parent was alive, keeping some values and attitudes of their parents and rejecting others. If continuity of life style is evidence of mastery of transition, then most people handle death of a parent quite well. There is, however, a spectrum of reactions ranging from the need to exorcize the ghost of the parent to identifying so strongly with the legacy of the parent that the child strives to complete the parent's tasks in lieu of his own goals. This may include taking on responsibility for another family member, carrying on a family business, or taking over as head of the clan.

Some have written of the "former" parent [27, 28] suggesting that after a parent's death the bond is gone. This paper argues that the tie persists, not only on an unconscious level, but viably in the here and now. This was strikingly demonstrated when Troll asked adults in their sixties and seventies to describe a man and a woman. The modal response for each was a parent [12]. Parents continue to be significant people after their death. Professionals working with very old people often hear emotion-laden references to parents who died three or four decades ago. In the symbolic remnants of the tie are images of parental supports, protection, or challenge, no matter how constricting or enabling they may have been in the past. The tie is not severed, and the image or presence of the parent continues both in the habitual patterns of daily life which previously involved the parent as well as in subsequent life transitions. Thus, a basic contradiction inherent in the loss is that of separateness and connectedness. The parent has died, the interaction has ceased, and yet the bond continues.

IMPACT OF THE LOSS: FINITUDE AND PERSONAL GROWTH

The second perspective from which we view the impact of the loss of a parent focuses on the surviving child as he or she faces both finitude and the challenge of personal growth. The death of a parent is a signal that life is transient and that one's personal time is not forever. It brings the child face to face with death. Note the following strikingly parallel accounts of a mother's death:

> . . . the hour in which I lost my immortality. . . in which I tried on my shroud for the first time. . . came to me when my mother died. I accepted death for both of us [29, p. 114].
> The only comfort I have. . . is that it will happen to me too. Otherwise it would be too unfair. Yes, we [sisters] were taking part in the dress rehearsal for our own burial [25, p. 115]

The loss of a parent represents the removal of a buffer against death. As long as the parent was alive the child could feel protected, since the parent by the rational order of things was expected to die first. Without this buffer, there is a strong reminder that the child is now the older generation and cannot easily deny his or her own mortality. A major task of mid-life is to cope with finitude, which is the acceptance of the fact that there is more time behind one than ahead and that death is coming closer. Kastenbaum suggests the possibility of defining the onset of middle age as the time when finitude is accepted [6]. Jacques has written sensitively of the pathology of persons who have been unable to meet this crisis [30].

Not only does the loss of a parent force the child to face death, but also to confront its polar opposite: life and personal growth. Successful coping with a parent's death involves neither reifying the past nor leaving it behind but assimilating it as one's psychological inheritance. The positive aspects of the parental tie can be owned and can enable the child in turn to be a better parent and family member to those remaining in his or her life. A conflict-ridden relationship can be terminated and release the child's energy for use in more satisfying directions. Burdensome injunctions of the parent may be challenged and placed in realistic perspective, thus freeing the person to generate a new core of expectations.

Death of parents may usher in a sense of needing to reorganize the self as a way to deal with the profound impact of the loss. What is desired is a feeling of autonomy that flows from a deep sense of one's identity. This can come out of the willingness to face life as it is or was, not as one would have liked or wanted it to be. This tough-mindedness seems essential particularly when evaluating one's relationship with parents. Personal growth does not demand a rejection of parental legacies but rather a selective integration of them into one's own value system [31].

As the bond is loosened, the child can reevaluate the dynamics of the tie and its personal meaning and come to a better understanding of who he was and who he is in the process of becoming. This calls for a shift in identity, in finding one's true roots, and in being less an extension of parents. Some may find the strength to discover and modify the legacies of their parents and value their own difference and creativity. Thus, loss of a parent may potentially free the person to trust more in the self and to risk new behaviors [32].

The need for attachment is strong. After the parent dies the child may look for other parental figures, not only as a substitute or a replacement, but as a way of retaining a hold on the intergenerational tie and as a surrogate buffer against death. Middle age may well be a time of cathectic flexibility. Reaching out for new relationships does not mean disloyalty to the parent. What we are suggesting, then, is that by the loss of parents, the life force of the child who faces his own death can potentially be synthesized into a stronger sense of identity, a renewed commitment to love and to relate to others, and a deeper cognitive grasp of the world.

In summary, this paper has examined the impact of the loss of a parent on a middle-aged child. A life long process of anticipatory orphanhood has been suggested as preparing for, and possibly reducing, the impact of the death. Reaction to the loss involves two dialectic themes which need to be dealt with by the surviving child: first, the breaking and the persistence of the bond, and second, the finitude and personal growth. It is hoped that the ideas presented can be an impetus to further exploration of parental loss in adulthood.

REFERENCES

1. J. Bowlby, *Attachment and Loss*, Volume 3, Basic Books, New York, 1980.
2. E. Furman, *A Child's Parent Dies*, Yale University Press, New Haven, 1974.

3. J. Birtchnell, Depression in Relation to Early and Recent Parent Death, *British Journal of Psychiatry, 116*, pp. 299-306, 1970.
4. J. Bunch, The Influence of Parental Death Anniversaries upon Suicide Dates, *British Journal of Psychiatry, 118*, pp. 621-626, 1971.
5. H. Anderson, The Death of a Parent: Its Impact on Middle-Aged Sons and Daughters, *Pastoral Psychology, 28*, pp. 151-167, 1980.
6. R. Kastenbaum, Death and Development Through the Life Span, in *New Meanings of Death*, H. Feifel (ed.), McGraw Hill, New York, 1977.
7. D. P. Malinak, M. F. Hoyt, and V. Patterson, Adult's Reactions to the Death of a Parent: A Preliminary Study, *American Journal of Psychiatry, 136*, pp. 1152-1156, 1979.
8. M. Schlentz, A Study of Grief: The Affect of Death of Parents on Middle Aged Adults, *Archives of the Foundation of Thanatology, 7*, p. 157, 1978.
9. C. M. Sanders, A Comparison of Adult Bereavement in the Death of a Spouse, Child and Parent, *Omega, 10*, pp. 303-322, 1979-80.
10. P. C. Rosenblatt, R. P. Walsh and D. A. Jackson, *Grief and Mourning in Cross Cultural Perspective*, HRAF Press, New Haven, 1976.
11. R. S. Cavan, *The American Family*, Thomas Y. Crowell, New York, 1963.
12. L. Troll, S. J. Miller, and R. C. Atchley, *Families in Later Life*, Wadsworth, Belmont, California, 1979.
13. M. Sussman, The Family Life of Old People, in *Handbook of Aging and the Social Sciences*, R. Binstock and E. Shanas (eds.), Van Nostrand Reinhold, New York, 1976.
14. B. B. Hess and J. M. Waring, Parent and Child in Later Life: Rethinking the Relationship, in *Child Influences on Marital and Family Interaction*, R. M. Lerner and G. B. Spanier (eds.), Academic Press, New York, 1978.
15. J. A. Peterson, The Relationship of Middle-Aged Children and Their Parents, in *Aging Parents*, P. K. Ragan (ed.), University of South California Press, Los Angeles, 1979.
16. K. Riegel, Dialectic Operations, *Human Development, 16*, pp. 346-370, 1973.
17. S. Henderson, Care-Eliciting Behavior in Man, *Journal of Nervous and Mental Disease, 159*, pp. 172-181, 1974.
18. V. L. Bengston and L. Troll, Youth and Their Parents: Feedback and Intergenerational Influence in Socialization, in *Child Influences on Marital and Family Interaction: A Life Span Perspective*, R. Lerner and G. B. Spanier (eds.), Academic Press, New York, 1978.
19. M. Blenkner, Social Work and Family Relationships in Later Life with Some Thoughts on Filial Maturity, in *Social Structure and the Family: Generational Relations*, E. Shanas and G. Streib (eds.), Prentice-Hall, Englewood Cliffs, New Jersey, 1965.
20. E. Brody, Aging Parents and Aging Children, in *Aging Parents*, P. K. Ragan (ed.), University of Southern California Press, Los Angeles, 1979.
21. I. Boszormenyi-Nagy and B. Krasner, Trust-Based Therapy: A Contextual Approach, *American Journal of Psychiatry, 137*, pp. 767-775, 1980.
22. S. Weishaus, Aging is a Family Affair, in *Aging Parents*, P. K. Ragan (ed.), University of Southern California, Press, Los Angeles, 1979.

23. U. S. Comptroller General, *Well Being of Older People in Cleveland, Ohio,*
    U. S. General Accounting Office, Washington, D.C., 1977.
24. A. D. Weisman, Is Mourning Necessary?, in *Anticipatory Grief,* B.
    Schoenberg (ed.), Columbia University Press, New York, 1974.
25. S. de Beauvoir, *A Very Easy Death,* Warner, New York, 1973.
26. L. E. Troll, Intergenerational Relations in Later Life: A Family System
    Approach, in *Transitions of Aging,* N. Datan and N. Lohmann (eds.),
    Academic Press, New York, 1980.
27. M. Taggart, Salvete et valete: On Saying Goodbye to a Deceased Former
    Parent, *Journal of Marital and Family Therapy, 6,* pp. 117-120, 1980.
28. D. S. Williamson, New Life at the Graveyard: A Method of Therapy for
    Individuation from a Dead Former Parent, *Journal of Marriage and Family
    Counseling, 4,* pp. 93-101, 1978.
29. B. Hecht, *A Child of the Century,* Simon and Schuster, New York, 1954.
30. E. Jacques, Death and the Mid-Life Crisis, *International Journal of
    Psychoanalysis, 46,* pp. 502-514, 1965.
31. D. J. Levinson, *The Season of a Man's Life,* Alfred Knopf, New York,
    1978.
32. L. Pincus, *Death in the Family,* Pantheon, New York, 1974.

Chapter 7 describes the impact of death fairly shortly after the death occurs. Chapter 8 discusses the impact of death a full year after the event itself. Also, in the previous chapters, the ideas are abstracted and generalized, based largely on the observations and experiences of the authors; Chapter 8 presents ideas that are both very personal and immediate and are based on the carefully-conducted research efforts of the author. These two approaches to knowledge and understanding serve to supplement each other.

Chapter 8 begins with a brief quiz that you can take if you wish. Keep in mind that the answers are based on Dr. Carey's own research and might differ from the results of other studies or the experiences of other practitioners. However, even though research findings vary somewhat from study to study, the results presented here are fairly typical of those reported in similar investigations.

Eventually people recover from their most intense feelings of grief, although the greiving process may take much longer than anticipated and although surges of grief often return years, even decades, later. In our culture, the emphasis is on experiencing the grief and, after a period of time, perhaps a year or perhaps two years, to return to a full, rich life. This does not mean that the mourners are supposed to forget their past relationship, but that they need to go on to new relationships. That is, life must go on. This view is not held in all societies. For example, there are communities in the world in which a widow is expected to spend the rest of her life mourning for her deceased husband. Therefore, as we encourage widows to adjust to their new circumstances and to regain the previous fullness of their lives, we need to remain aware that this definition of optimum adjustment is not universal.

CHAPTER
8

Weathering Widowhood: Problems and Adjustment of the Widowed during the First Year

Raymond G. Carey

Do you feel you know the problems of the widowed and what helps them through bereavement? Try the following quiz and compare your answers with those obtained from a recent study of 119 widowed persons interviewed after thirteen to sixteen months of bereavement [1].

1. Widows are: a. better adjusted than widowers; b. more poorly adjusted than widowers; c. about equally adjusted compared to widowers.
2. Forewarning about the death of a spouse will be an asset for adjustment during breavement: a. for both men and women; b. for women only; c. for men only.
3. Age is related to adjustment so that: a. younger widowed persons are better adjusted than older persons; b. older widowed persons are better adjusted than younger persons; c. there is no difference between age groups.
4. Level of income is a prime factor in adjustment: a. for widowers only; b. for widows only; c. for both widows and widowers; d. for neither.
5. The best adjustment after one year is experienced by widowed persons: a. who live with independent children; b. who live with dependent children; c. who live alone.
6. After family members, widowed persons obtained the most help from: a. physicians; b. nurses; c. neighbors; d. clergy; e. funeral directors.

Answers: 1. (b) 2. (b) 3. (b) 4. (d) 5. (c) 6. (e)

THE PRESENT STUDY

The purpose of this study was:

1. to develop a simple self-report measure of adjustment-depression;
2. to identify factors relating to adjustment so as to assist physicians, local clergy, and other helping agents predict which spouses would have the greatest difficulty during bereavement;

3. to identify problems of widowed persons;
4. to identify which people within and without the hospital helped widowed persons most and how they helped; and
5. to resolve some of the apparent contradictions in the previous research.

Every widow and widower seventy years of age and younger whose spouses died at an acute general hospital between January 1, 1974, and November 1, 1974, were considered possible respondents ($n = 161$). Those over seventy years of age were excluded so that the effects of advanced age would not be confused with the effects of bereavement. Every widow and widower seventy years of age and younger whose spouse was pronounced dead on arrival (DOA) at the hospital from April 1, 1974, to November 1, 1974, was also included in the study ($n = 60$), because one of the main items under investigation was the effect of forewarning and anticipatory grief.

Of the 221 possible respondents, 119 (54%) accepted the invitation to participate in the study, thirty-eight (17%) refused to participate, and sixty-four (29%) were not able to be reached. Of those who could be reached, 76 percent of widows and 75 percent of widowers accepted the invitation to be interviewed. Respondents were from twenty-eight to seventy years of age, with a median age of fifty-seven for both widows and widowers. None of the widows had remarried, although 20 percent of widowers had remarried. All respondents were white.

The widowed people were interviewed in their homes from thirteen to sixteen months after the death of their husband or wife.

A shortened version of the questionnaire was also given to 100 married people approached randomly in and around the hospital, the same area from which the widowed respondents came. Only those married people who appeared to be over forty years of age were invited to respond so that they would be of approximately the same age as the widowed. Of these, eighty-six responded. The age range for the widowed was twenty-eight to seventy as compared to thirty-six to seventy-seven for the married. The median age was fifty-seven for widowed and fifty-six for married. The married sample was 50 percent male, as compared to 34 percent male for the widowed sample. Of the married persons, 20 percent had college degrees, as compared to 13 percent of the widowed.

Results

Adjustment scale — An eight item self-report measure of adjustment-depression was developed that clearly differentiated widowed persons from married persons and widowed persons among themselves. This measure, called the Adjustment Scale, is a quantitative measure which can locate a person on a continuum between adjustment and depression. The Adjustment Scale correlated highly with the Bornstein-Clayton measure of depression [2], but is simple to administer and we feel provides a more exact measure of the level of adjustment.

As expected, married persons were significantly better adjusted than widowed persons as measured by the Adjustment Scale. This was true of both men and women. Only 3.5 percent of married persons were in the depressed category as compared to 25 percent of the widowed, and 82.5 percent of the married persons were in the well-adjusted category as compared to 50 percent of the widowed.

Factors in adjustment — The clearest, and perhaps the most important finding in the study was that widowers were significantly better adjusted than widows. This difference held up even when respondents were broken down by level of income, the amount of forewarning, level of education, and age.

The relatively better adjustment of widowers as compared to widows may be related to several factors. First, women are encouraged to build their identities around their husbands, as symbolized by taking the husband's name at the time of marriage. When a woman's husband dies, her life style is radically changed. This may be less true in the future because women today are more career oriented than in past years. Second, statistics show that women tend to live longer than men and men usually marry women who are younger than themselves. It is, therefore, easier for a man to remarry. Finally, the volunteered comments of respondents suggest that the difficulty widows experienced in making decisions and in handling financial matters alone, their concern about personal safety, and worry about dependent children outweigh the difficulty widowers experienced in maintaining their homes and handling the physical and emotional needs of children alone.

The second key factor in adjustment was the amount of forewarning about the death of a spouse. Widows who had forewarning about the approaching death of their husbands had a significantly higher level of adjustment than the widowed who had no forewarning. The critical amount of time was a minimum of two weeks; there was little difference between groups with longer periods of forewarning. Forewarning, however, was not a significant factor for widowers.

The reasons why forewarning was only a factor in the adjustment of women are not clear. The fact that 20 percent of widowers in this study had remarried as compared to none of the widows invites further study. Perhaps women do not work through their grief as quickly as men. Therefore, the opportunity for anticipatory grief would be more beneficial for women. Perhaps it is more important emotionally for women than for men to talk through their anxieties and grief. Widows more than widowers commented on the helpfulness of having their children, neighbors, or clergy act as sounding boards. Women may also have deeper emotional attachments toward their husbands than men do toward their wives. Another possibility is that men have somewhat more opportunity to remarry.

Age was a significant factor in adjustment. The widowed over the median age of fifty-seven were better adjusted than the widowed under the age of fifty-seven. The age factor, however, was more important for widows. Age may be positively related to adjustment because younger widowed persons are more inclined to feel cheated because their spouses had abbreviated life spans.

Widowed persons with college degrees were significantly better adjusted than those with a high school education or less. Education was a stronger factor in the adjustment of widows than of widowers. Education provides a person with more interests, more opportunities for meaningful employment, and more financial security. These advantages explain the positive relationship between education and adjustment and would be particularly important for women who were not working at the time their husbands died or who still had dependent children to support.

Widowed persons who received more than $10,000 annually from all sources were better adjusted than those who received less than $10,000. However, because 85 percent of men had an annual income over $10,000 and 83 percent of women had an annual income under $10,000, the effect of income largely reflected the influence of the sex variable on adjustment.

Widowed persons who lived alone were better adjusted than widowed persons with dependent children, and they in turn were better adjusted than those who lived with independent children. It is not clear from this study whether living with adult children beyond the first year of bereavement has a negative influence on adjustment, or whether living with adult children is a sign that the person has not yet made a good adjustment.

There was a curvilinear relationship between happiness in marriage and adjustment to bereavement. Those who reported that their whole marriage had been very happy were better adjusted than those who said that there had been some period of unhappiness in their marriage. However, those who had prolonged and serious problems (e.g., two women and one man who were married to alcoholic spouses and three widowers whose wives had committed suicide) appeared to be well adjusted. Apparently, where there had been a very severe problem, there was a great feeling of relief when it was ended. But, in general, married persons who are capable of working out a happy marriage are also those most capable of handling the period of bereavement.

Main problems of widowed persons – In response to the open-ended question: "What were the main problems you faced before your spouse's death (when anticipated)?" two problems were prominent. The first was the respondent's own difficulty in accepting the reality of the situation, that is, the slow deterioration and approaching death. The second problem was fear of what life would be like after the patient died, that is, how they would care for themselves and their children and what their goals in life would be.

Avoiding the subject of death also resulted in problems for many. Some women had no knowledge of the financial condition of their families because death was not discussed. One man said it was difficult to "fake for my wife that I had faith in a miracle when I knew there wouldn't be one." Another expressed his anguish about "keeping the knowledge that I knew she would die from my wife and also from the children."

With respect to the care of terminal patients, a few respondents said that medication for pain should be given to terminal patients as they want it, and that a spouse should be free to dismiss a physician's responsibilities regarding an overdose of drugs. Other respondents were opposed to continued testing on patients who were clearly dying. They felt such testing was not only futile, but caused unnecessary pain and discomfort.

When asked to name the main problems faced after the death of their spouses, loneliness was named by 27 percent of widowers and 54 percent of widows as being a great problem. Loneliness was particularly difficult at certain times of the day, for example, at the time of the evening meal and later in the evening. The widowed also feel lonely doing things by themselves, for example, going to the theater and shopping. Indecision about the future and a lack of personal goals were also problems for many. There is a need to be needed by someone. The widowed, especially those without children, found it difficult to find someone with whom to share their feelings and the burden of their grief.

For widowers, learning how to run their houses without their wives and handling the emotional and physical needs of their children were frequent problems. Getting younger children off to school and helping them with their homework were difficult for widowers whose wives had taken care of these needs.

For widows, making decisions alone without their husbands was often a source of anxiety because they repeatedly questioned whether they had made the right decision (e.g., to move, to sell their house, to go to work). Some women were fearful regarding personal safety and security and had nightmares about people breaking into their homes. For women who were not accustomed to handling financial matters, the ordinary routine of paying bills and making purchases presented difficulties.

Who Helped Out?

Respondents were asked which people within and outside the hospital gave them help (little? some? great?). If the widowed responded "great help," they were asked their reasons. Respondents who said they were disappointed in some person or group were also asked their reasons.

Physicians – Physicians were rated as offering great help by 47 percent of the widowers and 40 percent of the widows. They were considered of great help when they were honest, compassionate, available, not hurried, and comforting to the family. Some sample quotations from those who praised physicians were: ". . . he gave us all the information we wanted in language we could understand." ". . . he was honest, yet encouraging." ". . . he answered our questions kindly, with compassion." ". . . he called me to discuss taking my husband off the respirator. We made the decision together; the full responsibility was not mine." ". . . he took time with us; we didn't have to chase him."

On the other hand, 27 percent of widowers and 33 percent of widows expressed disappointment in their physicians. Most expressions of disappointment centered around allegations of failure to be honest with the patient and/or family, avoiding the family, lacking gentleness, having a "poor bedside manner," being cold, impersonal, unconcerned, and misdiagnosing patients.

Nurses — Nurses were rated as offering great help by 56 percent of widowers and 55 percent of widows. Usually they were praised for being solicitous and showing concern for the patient and/or relatives. People were also grateful for information regarding tests and equipment when this was not given by the physician.

Some quotations from those who were pleased with nurses were: ". . . they extended visiting hours." ". . . she put her arms around me." ". . . they gave me confidence that I could care for my husband when I took him home."

Only 12 percent of widowers and 15 percent of widows complained about nurses. It seemed that when relatives were not satisfied with overall hospital care, they vented all their feelings onto nurses. The major complaint was an attitude of coldness and unconcern.

Chaplains — Chaplains were rated as offering great help by 44 percent of widowers and 71 percent of widows. They were considered of great help when they consoled the widowed, helped patients talk about their approaching death, were available and attentive to patients and relatives. Only 5 percent of widowers and 7 percent of widows expressed disappointment in the chaplains.

Social workers — The majority of people had no contact with social workers. Some did not know they were in the hospital. This may explain why only 10 percent of the widowed said they received great help from social workers. Some said they wished they had met a social worker because they would have appreciated having a non-religious counselor with whom to talk.

A number of different services were mentioned by those who found the social workers of great help. The widowed appreciated help in making accommodations for patients sent home. For example, social workers contacted the Cancer Society to get hospital equipment at home. They also helped with financial advice, for example, getting state aid to pay a hospital bill. Social workers arranged for transportation for patients who had to return for outpatient treatments and also found people to stay with patients at home during the day.

Only 4 percent of the widowed said they were disappointed in social workers.

For example, some social workers allegedly failed to familiarize themselves with the case histories of patients (e.g., "I had to tell her over and over that my wife was terminal.").

Family — Of all non-hospital personnel, the family was rated as the most helpful group to the bereaved. The family was rated as a great help by over 80 percent of both widows and widowers. Family members were praised for offering emotional support and understanding.

Before the death of the spouse, family members helped most by taking care of the patients when they were at home and visiting them in the hospital while their spouses were at work. The family members that helped most with these needs were both teenage and adult children. The siblings of both the husband and wife helped most in those families where there were no children.

After the death of the spouse, the family helped widowed persons realize that they were not alone, for example, by making them feel loved and cared for through phone calls and visits, by keeping them busy, or taking them to dinner. A frequent note was that the family helped by "just being there." Invitations to dinner were appreciated most of all because many people find it difficult to eat alone. For example, one man said that he cooked his dinner at home and then threw it out and went to a restaurant to eat so that he would not have to eat by himself. Finally, the widowed praised family members who came in from out-of-town or at some personal inconvenience to visit the patient, to attend the funeral, or to visit them during bereavement.

Funeral directors — Funeral directors were said to be of great help by 76 percent of both widows and widowers. Funeral directors were second only to family members in receiving praise from the widowed. They helped to obtain social security benefits and insurance payments. They were praised for not pressuring people into expensive funerals and for not sending their bills immediately. They were frequently praised for being "courteous," "honest," and "professional." Only one respondent expressed disappointment in a funeral director.

Local clergy — The local clergy were rated as a great help by 56 percent of widowers and 62 percent of widows, while only 5 percent of widowers and 15 percent of widows expressed disappointment in the clergy.

The clergy helped in a number of ways. First, visits to patients both in the hospital and at home before the time of death were greatly appreciated by their spouses. Second, counseling the widowed both before and after the death of their spouses was also frequently mentioned with gratitude. Third, many widowed commented on the conduct of the funeral. The family appreciated the local clergy allowing them or their friends to take part in the funeral service and for giving permission to clergymen from their old neighborhood to say a funeral mass or conduct the services in their new church. One woman was grateful when her parish priest conducted the funeral service for her non-Catholic husband. On the other hand, one Jewish woman wrote a eulogy for her husband and was irritated when her rabbi refused to read it at the funeral because it was his policy not to read anything that he did not write. A minister was criticized for revealing confidential aspects of the husband-wife relationship that were complimentary, but private. Finally, visits by clergymen to the widowed following the deaths of their spouses were rare, but greatly appreciated.

Neighbors — Neighbors were rated as a great help by 56 percent of widowers and 68 percent of widows. Before the death of the patient, neighbors helped by checking on the sick at home while spouses were at work, by driving children to school, and by bringing in meals. After the death of the patient, neighbors were praised for attending the funeral, for sending cards and flowers, and for bringing food to the home after the funeral. Widowers frequently had food brought in for themselves and their children during the prolonged illness of their wives and also for weeks after the deaths of their wives. Widows were grateful for neighbors who provided a sounding board for them and who kept them busy, for example, by taking them shopping, to dinner, or to places of entertainment.

Only about 2 percent of the respondents expressed disappointment in the behavior of neighbors. However, a number of widowed people left old social groups and joined new ones to avoid accusations of being a "romantic threat" to other husbands and wives. Even a young widow in a wheelchair was subject to this accusation. An older widow was accused by her neighbor of flirting with her eighty-year-old husband. Another widow allegedly was propositioned by her neighbor (her husband's best friend) only five weeks after her husband's death.

Finally, while many neighbors would say, "Call me anytime," their availability usually only lasted a few weeks. Unless there is a visible need, neighbors stop offering help after a few months. For example, a young widow confined to a wheelchair continued to get a great deal of help from her neighbors.

Implications — Several major themes emerge from the findings of this study. First, physicians and counselors are well-adivsed to give special attention to the importance of anticipatory grief in women. This study suggests that a physician may assist adjustment in bereavement by clearly, gently, and tactfully informing a wife of the seriousness of her husband's condition as soon as this is evident. About 20 percent of widows of hospitalized patients were upset because they allegedly were not so informed, although few widowers complained they were not informed. A physician might also promote contact with nurses, chaplains, social workers, and other counselors who can assist a wife to deal with her emotions while her husband is still alive.

Second, it is apparently not standard procedure for clergy to make follow-up visits to the bereaved after a spouse's death. Many widowed who are church-goers expected such a visit, were grateful when they received it, and were dis-appointed when they did not. Third, the non-technical, humanistic aspects of health care delivery are seen as having great value by the families of patients who are seriously ill. Both physicians and nurses are esteemed as much for their honesty, gentleness, availability, and unhurried concern as they are for their technical competence. The importance of humanistic concern to patients is underscored by the large percentage of the widowed, especially widows, who found the chaplains of great help.

REFERENCES

1. R. G. Carey, The Widowed: A Year Later, *Journal of Counseling Psychology*, *24*, pp. 125-131, 1977.
2. P. E. Bornstein, P. J. Clayton, J. E. Halikas, W. L. Maurice, and E. Robins, The Depression of Widowhood After Thirteen Months, *The British Journal of Psychiatry*, *122*, pp. 561-566, 1973.

Health professionals in our society are beginning to encourage dying patients to remain in their homes as long as possible, even to the time of death. In this setting, they can receive care from family members and be surrounded by familiar objects; equally important, they remain more autonomous and can schedule their time more according to their own dictates rather than those of an institution. Nonetheless, most deaths occur in institutions, with over half of the deaths in the United States and Canada taking place in hospitals; others occur in long-term care facilities, such as nursing homes and the domiciliaries of the Veterans Administration. And, very recently, a new form of institution—the hospice—has been developed for the sole purpose of caring for dying persons.

An institution can be defined as a particular program in a particular building, so when we think of health-care institutions we usually think in terms of "a hospital" or "a nursing home." However, the term is also defined more broadly, in social terms, so that we talk about "the social institution of health care." Therefore, death counselors and death educators need to comprehend the ways in which these institutions—both defined as individual units and as social concepts—function, to understand what the dying and grieving persons experience and to improve their own capacities to work effectively within institutional boundaries.

A great deal of time and energy has been expended over the years in condemning the practices and bureaucracies of institutions. In some instances, the institution and its staff have been viewed virtually as villains. All this misses the point: the issue is to improve the well-being of the dying and the grieving. And this can best be accomplished by functioning within institutional settings while—for those who wish—simultaneously attempting to change institutional policies and practices. A better approach is probably to look on directors and staff members of institutions as individuals who are doing as well as they can, given the confines of the systems that seem to develop in all organizations. This is not to contend that the situation at institutions cannot be improved; rather, the point is that verbal attacks on these institutions are more likely to increase tensions than to improve care.

PART 2
Institutional Care

It has often been said that we must each die our own death and do so alone. That is, no one can die my death for me—I must do it myself. And in that way, the dying person is alone. Nonetheless, the dying process is a social process, involving people, laws, institutions, customs, rituals, and so forth. A number of years ago, Robert Kastenbaum wrote about "the death system," referring to the entire constellation of people, things, events, and ideas that surround the dying process, the meaning of death, and grief and bereavement. As each element of this system changes, each other element is affected. Thus, as the dying person comes closer to death, changes can be observed in the behavior of the health professionals and family members, in the uses of medication and other regimens, in the dying person's thoughts about wills and insurance, and so forth.

The authors of this chapter describe the final stages of dying for one person, and they show that the dying process of a given individual occurs within a social system. They do not suggest that we, as readers, try to generalize from their experience, but that we attempt to understand each individual dying process as they have attempted to understand the dying process that they encountered.

CHAPTER
9

A Group Awaiting Death:
The Social System's Perspective
on a Naturally Occurring
Group Situation

Steven Starker
and
Joan E. Starker

This study was undertaken in tragic circumstances. A critically ill relative lay in
the intensive care unit of a major New York City hospital after suffering a severe
heart attack. There followed a period of great stress for family and friends as
crises came and went, hope rose and ebbed. Life was sustained for twenty-one
days by medical chemistry and technology until mounting complications led to
coma and finally to death.

    The situation as described is hardly novel; we all endure and shall again suffer
experience with illness and death. If there is anything new or different in this
situation, it is the addition of a new technology which prolongs both the living
and the dying, and the location of this technology in the intensive care units of
modern hospitals. There have always been instances of both gradual and rapid
decline in health leading to death. A third category has been added—those who
probably would have died immediately but are kept alive by artificial means
until recovery or death. Such was the case described here.

In the twenty-one day period of artificially sustained life, a transient but powerful group formed, composed of family members and friends of the patient. We did not initially think of it as a "group," or, indeed, apply any professional perspective to this intensely personal situation. As the duration and level of stress increased, however, phenomena occurred that were difficult for us to accept or understand until we fell back upon our professional experience with groups. We had been thrust involuntarily into a naturally occurring group situation as participant-observers. We have used the construction of this report as one way of sorting out and attempting to comprehend a most overwhelming personal experience and because such groups are all too common and inevitable, we shall attempt to share our efforts in a form which might be of use to others both as mental health professionals and as potential participants.

The concepts provided by social systems theory seemed particularly helpful in the analysis, with its emphasis on the rational "work" of the group, primary and secondary "tasks," and the inevitable irrational side of group life which can impede or replace the work entirely [1-4]. This framework is more commonly and readily applied to classroom self-study groups [5-9], Tavistock workshops [10, 11], or complex organizations [4, 12, 13], and may seem alien to such an intensely personal, emotional and real-life experience as took place in the intensive care waiting room. The "work" or "tasks," for example, are not easily defined. Nonetheless, we shall proceed along these lines and attempt to demonstrate via this perspective some of the structural and dynamic aspects of this most unfortunate group situation.

Before proceeding, we must acknowledge some of the constraints upon this project. We shall be examining in detail only a single group experience rather than a representative sample of such groups. The single case study approach with individuals or groups is particularly useful for generating research hypotheses but not at all useful for proving them, therefore our goals and conclusions must be appropriately modest. Another difficulty is that both authors were personally and emotionally involved in the subject matter of the investigation and therefore vulnerable to all manner of bias and error. This problem is certainly shared by clinicians describing their own treatment cases and, to some extent, by anyone doing fieldwork in the participant-observer mode. We shall not even attempt to prove independence from such problems but instead leave it to other, more objective minds to determine the extent to which our formulations prove useful.

THE TASK STRUCTURE

It is difficult to identify a concrete primary task for this group as compared to work groups in organizational settings or even to psychotherapy groups. Group formation begins as friends and relatives receive word of the illness and a portion of these feel that they should "be there." For some, this is as far as the thinking goes, particularly where the response is experienced more as obligatory than voluntary. In general, however, the participants seemed to share and be bound together by three tasks:

1. comforting the patient, whom we shall call "Mr. A."
2. supporting and comforting the patient's spouse and, in lesser degree, the patient's two grown children.
3. insuring that "everything possible is being done" medically.

In this instance, the first task played a limited role in the overall group structure because of the restrictive visiting rules of the intensive care unit (ICU). Only immediate family members were allowed to visit the patient, two at a time, and for only ten minutes out of each hour. Hence the majority of group members never got to see the patient at all and were minimally involved in the performance of this task. The subgroup of immediate family, particularly spouse and children, did have this task in mind but found little they could actually do in this regard. They were, of course, partially incapacitated by their own anxiety and despair regarding the prognosis. After the first few days, the primary physician was consistently clear regarding the gravity of the situation and had left little grounds for hope. Hence, family members would spend their visitation time literally speechless, fearing they might say the wrong thing or even break down in tears if they attempted to speak. The patient, in turn, was cautioned by the medical staff not to attempt speech and was usually unable to speak because of medical apparatus. Mere physical presence and the holding of hands were the only ways in which the family could attempt to comfort the patient. In practice then, the task of comforting the patient fell largely to the very capable nursing staff. This serves to illustrate two points:

1. the degree and quality of stress on the family.
2. the presence of a latent task which was literally impossible to carry out because of the structure of the ICU and the application of considerable medical hardware. In simpler times, with the dying patient cared for at home, this task must have had far greater reality for such groups and engendered less feeling of helplessness and frustration.

The task upon which the group could more easily agree and act upon had to do with comforting the patient's spouse. When speaking of the importance of "being there," participants usually made reference to the need for emotional support for the patient's wife. Associated with this general task were many concrete jobs such as bringing her to and from the hospital, keeping her company at home, bringing food and beverage to her in the waiting room or else seeing to it that she went to the cafeteria; handling phone calls, offering minor tranquilizers, etc. Because it was shared by so many members and it defined so much of the rational activity, this seems to be the best candidate for "primary task." However, we must note some inherent difficulties with such a task. While it is true that many of the concrete jobs could be delegated and carried out as group "work," it is also true that limited comfort could be given in a situation which seemed so very grave medically. Knowing the seriousness of the situation, Mrs. A could accept but little in the way of encouragement or hope and remained understandably upset. Hence the work of the group, in a broad sense, could certainly not be accomplished in any satisfactory way. The emotional support of Mrs. A's children never really became a group focus, and they tended to be seen primarily in terms of their contributions to the support of Mrs. A.

The setting for this group experience was a modern, sophisticated, well-equipped ICU in a respected teaching hospital. The cardiac team and the internist had all been highly recommended. Nevertheless, it did not take long for doubts and suspicions to arise about the quality of the medical care. Before the patient was to expire, several more specialists would be either called in, consulted, or considered by the group members. Another task had emerged, that of monitoring the medical care to be certain that everything possible was being done. This task overlapped with the second task in that it was crucial to convince Mrs. A in this regard, but there was additionally an autonomous concern with amassing sufficient medical expertise to save the patient. We must note, however, that none of the most active members in this regard, was a physician or nurse. They weren't really in a position to judge either the primary clinicians or the various consultants or to know whether every avenue of possibility was being explored. Once again a potential "work" area for the group was frought with ambiguity and frustration.

The three potentially rational tasks for the group: comforting the patient, comforting the spouse and insuring quality care had built-in structural limitations and consequent frustrations. One might at this point begin to wonder whether our theoretical preoccupation with tasks is even applicable here. It is just this perspective, however, of a transient task group under enormous emotional pressure but with little hope of accomplishing much rational work that enables us to comprehend subsequent developments.

MEMBERSHIP STRUCTURE

The waiting room of the ICU was the physical location of much group activity although processes begun there frequently were continued in other settings, e.g. Mrs. A's home, telephone calls between various participants. Membership in the group required that the individual "be there," that is, be physically present in the waiting area at least part of the time and be available for telephone contacts when not present. Many members formed strong convictions about who "should be there" and how often and who was failing to fulfill obligations. We shall return to this aspect later.

The group consisted of the patient's wife, son and daughter, son-in-law, daughter-in-law, siblings and their spouses, long-time friends, neighbors and business associates. They were all notified by telephone immediately or shortly after Mr. A entered the hospital. The group may in some respects be said to have continued through the patient's death, burial and beyond, into the immediate mourning period but we will focus here on the twenty-one day period of its existence prior to Mr. A's death. Members could not, of course, know for what length of time their participation would be necessary; most had families, jobs, and other responsibilities to which they must return. This lack of definite time boundaries created an additional source of stress for the membership.

Leadership, which many investigators feel is the crucial element in group behavior, was ill defined. The designated authority, the physician in charge of the patient, was rarely seen or spoken with and hence not sufficiently "in" the group to provide leadership despite his powerful influence. Instead, leadership was passed around according to various criteria; those who had spoken last with the doctor; those who were closest to the patient; those who spent the most time at the hospital; those who felt they should be in charge by virtue of their position in the family; those who were aggressive enough to push for leadership given the power vacuum. Mrs. A was too upset to provide leadership but did provide direction from time to time by voicing dissatisfaction with some of the members' behavior and by defining her needs more clearly to the others. The absence of any clear leadership structure is another important variable in understanding subsequent group developments.

THE PROCESS UNFOLDS

The initial period following group formation may be characterized as a "utopian" phase. Family and friends drew together rapidly in response to the crisis; old family feuds and other family dynamics suddenly receded into the background and considerable effort was spent in supporting the patient and his wife. At this point, despite having suffered a "major heart attack," Mr. A was alert, responsive and able to converse with family visitors. The mood was one of initial shock followed by cautious optimism and concern.

It was at this time that the newly-formed task structure seemed most workable. That is, Mr. A could accept some comforting (task 1); Mrs. A could accept support and comfort because she was still hopeful of a positive outcome (task 2); the well-staffed and highly instrumented modern ICU provided material with which to assure one and all that "everything possible is being done" (task 3).

Membership was not a significant problem because everyone who was notified would drop their other commitments and respond to the crisis. Leadership requirements were minimal in an atmosphere of support, concern, and general agreement on the nature of the work (tasks) to be accomplished. To this point the stress and anxiety generated by severe and potentially fatal illness was handled in the group by a combination of clear task-orientation (work) and utopian fantasy. The latter might be expressed as follows: "if we all stick together and love one another, everything will turn out all right." This fantasy could not sustain the group for very long.

Gibbard and Hartman have explored the significance of utopian fantasies in "self-analytic" classroom groups [5]. They describe these fantasies as based on the assumption that intrapsychic and interpersonal conflict can be eliminated and replaced by unconditional love, nurturance and security. The emergence of the utopian fantasy is thought to be based on the individual's use of "splitting" such that a perfectly "good group" is created and the possibility of intense hostility, oedipal wishes, competitions, etc. is denied.

Gibbard and Hartman question the extent to which utopian fantasies are observable in other group situations [5]. They speculate that there are moments in the early life of many groups when "the relative absence of individuation and differentiation evokes fantasies of fusion with the group" which may be perceived as a good maternal entity. Our observation of the early phase of this naturally occurring group tends to support their speculation.

The mid-phase process began only a few days after group formation and continued until Mr. A's death. It was characterized by increasing stress, mounting frustration with the group's inability to do its "work," progressive loss of the task orientation and increase in the irrational side of group life (Bion's "basic assumption" activity), and the appearance of splitting as the major mode of dealing with the group's anxiety and frustration.

The passage of time brought increasing stress to each of the group members individually and to the group as a whole. Several individuals had attempted to resume their normal activities and to remain only peripherally involved once Mr. A's condition was "stabilized" and things seemed under control. This stability then yielded to several crises involving drops in blood pressure, cardiac arrhythmia, and various medical complications. On each of these occasions, many group members would hurry back to the intensive care waiting room with the awareness that Mr. A might be gone even before they arrived. The situation continued for nearly three weeks and resulted in enormous strain for all concerned. Although perfectly willing to drop their usual activities in the face of a crisis, an ongoing continuing crisis situation was enormously disruptive to member's other responsibilities. Only a few individuals who were retired, had grown children or a minimum of outside involvements escaped some of these problems.

As a group, the membership was losing its utopian defense. Clearly things were not going well and all the support and encouragement they provided was no longer enough to ward off approaching disaster. Mr. A was seen only by the immediate family and their reports were not encouraging. He was now looking really ill and was not communicative because of medical apparatus. Their distraught reactions to this scene and their agitation and depression about the poor prognosis would not be assuaged even by the most supportive comments and actions. Hence the first two tasks were becoming impossible. Moreover, the medical situation was getting more and more complex. If "everything possible" was being done, why was the downward trend continuing? Even when the medical staff attempted to explain the problems, few group members could appreciate the nature of the problem or even understand the medical terms involved. How then could the third task be accomplished? All of this frustration of the group's work generated mounting feelings of anxiety, helplessness and rage in the members and dissolved any vestiges of utopianism.

The mid-phase process is a study in dissension and splitting. Having lost the more benign utopian defense and much of the task structure, the group was now required to deal with some increasingly powerful feelings in another way. Gibbard notes that "The most common response of a group faced with frustration, ambivalence, or internal conflict is splitting and compartmentalization." [4]. In retrospect, looking at the kinds of heated disagreements which arose, we feel that these are well characterized as constituting another "splitting" defense. As Gibbard indicates, the price of such activity is some distortion and simplification of emotional life in the group. There were three major sources of dissension.

Good vs. Bad Prognosis

One subgroup became more and more convinced that the end was near for Mr. A. His condition was not improving and was not even remaining very stable. Moreover, his physician was quite consistent in indicating that the prognosis was poor given the seriousness of the coronary, the age of the patient, and the complications of emphysema and diabetes. This subgroup was, to some degree, entering an anticipatory mourning process in which the loss was already experienced. Not all group members felt that this was appropriate, however, and some felt strongly that "giving up hope" was premature and perhaps an abandonment of Mr. A. Moreover, these other group members struggled against acceptance of the medical prognosis and would sometimes "hear" the medical opinion differently or else devalue if it were too clearly negative. They would instead seize upon the notion that every day survived tended to improve the overall progress.

Good vs. Bad Doctor

Although the ICU at this particular hospital and its cardiac team had been highly recommended by several sources, the mid-phase process saw a gradual division among group members regarding its adequacy. This division was largely overlapping with the previous one in that the "good prognosis" subgroup tended to respond to pessimistic medical input by devaluing its source. These subgroups were not identical, however, as some of the "poor prognosis" members could obviously be persuaded to doubt the adequacy of a system that did not seem to be curing its patient.

It was the "bad doctor" subgroup that took the lead in contacting specialists to visit Mr. A and to contribute their opinions. The intensive care unit cardiac team had its own specialists, of course, but these were deemed inadequate. Some of the outside physicians indicated that their participation would not be necessary as Mr. A was already in extremely competent hands; a few agreed to visit but found little to contribute to the overall picture or treatment plan. The "bad doctor" subgroup never tired of its efforts to find the "good doctor" although he always seemed just out of reach; they never ceased considering more specialists until Mr. A finally passed away.

The "good doctor" subgroup found some measure of comfort in the notion that "everything possible is being done."

Good vs. Bad Members

Perhaps the most emotion-laden issue of all was the matter of which group members were "fulfilling their responsibilities" and which were not. The overt content involved the amount of time spent physically present in the intensive care unit waiting room or at home with Mrs. A. There were many reasons why various members could not remain physically present all or more of the three week period, e.g., job commitments, having to care for young children, personal illness, etc. These reasons, however valid, were frequently not accepted by those considering themselves "good members." Presumably, this had much to do with the need to maintain a large enough group to share and diffuse the stress. In fact, it may have been another important way of channeling some of the anxiety, helplessness and impotent rage inherent in this situation. It was an implicit confirmation of one's own contributions, a denial of the rather helpless, taskless situation which had developed. Inevitably, certain of the "bad" members were made special targets or scapegoats.

As time passed, anxieties and frustations mounted until the mid-process dissension and splitting grew to dominate the proceedings, overwhelming even the last vestiges of task orientation. Mrs. A, for example, repeatedly was invited to join one or another subgroup and to participate in the attacks on "bad" members, doctors, or thoughts. Her own mounting distress over such unproductive activity was largely ignored and she was left feeling that all concerned were being grossly insensitive to her plight. In some respects, of course, her own condemnations of some members as being particularly insensitive can be viewed as part of the proceedings, a division into good (sensitive) and bad (insensitive) members. However, Mrs. A also has the greatest investment in the rational work of this particular group and her contributions reflect as well an attempt to steer members back to a task orientation.

The end-phase process, occurring with the death of Mr. A, predictably involved a collapse of the subgroup structure and a return to a task-oriented work group. The long ordeal had ended, the helplessness and rage were suddenly replaced by loss and the redefinition of the task structure. That is, the death of

Mr. A meant that a variety of things needed to be done relating to the funeral arrangements and the estate. These concrete tasks provided new focus and simultaneously a channel by which members could attempt to maintain a sense of effectiveness and competence in an otherwise overwhelming human situation. With a task structure provided and the intense frustrations of the waiting period ended, the splits were no longer useful or necessary and therefore rapidly disappeared. This in no way implies the absence of new splits in the subsequent mourning group but this takes us beyond the scope of the present study.

CONCLUSION

The "primary task" of society, as conceived by Ernest Becker, is to convince its members that they have some primary value, some specialness, and above all a meaningful existence [15]. "Society everywhere is a living myth of the significance of human life." This is deemed necessary because to see the world as it really is would be "devastating and terrifying."

The group described herein is one in which denial of the human condition is severely challenged. Rage and terror are glimpsed from time to time as task-structures fail and members are confronted with their own helplessness in the face of the terrible, impersonal, biological imperative that is death. If only someone could be held responsible—the incompetent medical staff, the irresponsible relatives, anyone—then perhaps the illusion of human power and control could be maintained. The initial task-structure and utopian fantasy provided a first-line defense against perception of the existential dilemma; their failure prompted secondary, less satisfactory forms of defense. Only the emergence of a new task structure upon Mr. A's death permitted a "sealing over" process to occur as members picked up new and more manageable social roles.

Table 1. Sequence of Medical Events and Group Phases

Medical Events	Group Phases
1. Heart attack	1. No group
2. Hospitalization	2. Group formation
3. First four days (alert, responsive)	3. Utopian phase (supportive, cooperative, optimistic)
4. Days 4-20 (complications, deterioration)	4. Mid-phase (frustration, dissention, multiple splits)
5. Death	5. Restructuring (cooperation, task orientation)

Erickson, examining the psychosocial needs of hospitalized dying patients and their families, notes that an interdisciplinary team could be most useful in providing a powerful support system to help "clarify, understand and integrate the complexities of the entire situation." [16] He also notes that medical personnel, like the family members discussed here, frequently are faced with an impossible task. By virtue of their training and mission, they are expected to "cure" the dying patient. Hence they too are vulnerable to intense feelings of frustration, anger, helplessness and guilt. Undoubtedly this was one reason for the inability of the primary physician in this case to be of greater help to the family.

What is suggested by this application of a social systems perspective is that some specially trained staff member (nurse, social worker, psychologist) might assume leadership of the group created by the "death-watch" situation and attempt to provide it with sufficient task structure to minimize splitting, scapegoating, and other unhelpful behaviors. The notion of providing friends and family with a task-structure may not seem terribly empathic or humanistic. Nevertheless, our observations and deliberations suggest that this may be a most helpful and supportive type of intervention. Religion provides us with a set of customs and rituals regarding the funeral and mourning situations which define relatively explicit tasks and roles but it provides far less guidance as regards the anticipation of death. This may be an area in which mental health practitioners can make a significant contribution. Exactly what sort of tasks and roles would be most helpful is a difficult question which we will not attempt to tackle at this point.

We began with the question of whether the social systems perspective would be helpful in understanding this naturally occurring group situation. The phenomena we have observed and described (utopian fantasy, subgrouping, splitting defenses) seem quite compatible with the theory-based expectation of groups which lack sufficient internal differentiation as to tasks and roles to maintain a work-orientation under stress.

REFERENCES

1. W. R. Bion, *Experiences in Groups,* Tavistock Publications, London, 1961.
2. A. K. Rice, *The Enterprise and Its Environment,* Tavistock Publications, London, 1963.
3. _____ , *Learning for Leadership,* Tavistock Publications, London, 1965.
4. E. J. Miller and A. K. Rice, *Systems of Organization,* Tavistock Publications, London, 1967.
5. G. S. Gibbard and J. J. Hartman, The Significance of Utopian Fantasies in Small Groups, *International Journal of Group Psychotherapy, 23,* pp. 125-147, 1973.
6. _____ , The Oedipal Paradigm in Group Development: A Clincal and Empirical Study, *Small Group Behavior, 4,* pp. 305-353, 1973.

7. R. D. Mann, The Development of the Member-Trainer Relationship in Self-Analytic Groups, *Human Relations, 19,* pp. 85-115, 1966.
8. _____ , *Interpersonal Styles and Group Development,* John Wiley and Sons, New York, 1967.
9. _____ , *The College Classroom: Conflict, Change and Learning,* John Wiley and Sons, New York, 1970.
10. F. C. Redlich and B. M. Astrachan, Group Dynamics Training, *American Journal of Psychiatry, 125,* pp. 1501-1507, 1969.
11. M. Rioch, All We Like Sheep: Followers and Leaders, *Psychiatry, 34,* pp. 258-273, 1971.
12. I. Menzies, A Case Study in the Functioning of Social Systems as a Defense Against Anxiety, *Human Relations, 13,* pp. 95-121, 1960.
13. S. Starker, Case Conference and Tribal Ritual: Some Cognitive, Social and Anthropologic Aspects of the Interdisciplinary Case Conference, *Journal of Personality and Social Systems, 1,* pp. 3-14, 1978.
14. G. S. Gibbard, Individuation, Fusion and Role Specialization, in G. S. Gibbard, J. J. Hartman and R. D. Mann (eds.), *Analysis of Groups,* Jossey-Bass, Inc., San Francisco, 1974.
15. E. Becker, *The Denial of Death,* The Free Press, New York, 1973.
16. R. C. Erickson and B. J. Hyerstay, The Dying Patient and the Double-Bind Hypothesis, *Omega, 5,* pp. 287-298, 1974.

In the introduction to the previous chapter, we alluded to the usefulness of the systems approach in understanding what occurs when dying or grieving takes place. At this point, it seems appropriate to elaborate on the meaning of the systems approach. Thus, we can view the dying process as occurring as part of many systems. There is, for example, the physiological or biochemical system, that is, what goes on within the dying person's body; and there is the intrapsychic system, or the thoughts, feelings, expectations, and so forth of the dying person; third, there is the interpersonal system, his or her interactions with other people; then there is the organizational system, how the dying person interacts with the (perhaps) hospital, the staff, the record-keeping office, the x-ray machines, the billing procedures; and finally, there is the community system, which expands outwards from the hospital to the neighborhood, the Bureau of Vital Statistics, the work setting that the dying person has left (or, perhaps, the Senior Center), the offices of the insurance company where his/her records are being processed, and so forth. And not only does every element within each of these systems interact with every other element, but each system interacts with each other system. To understand fully the totality of what is going on, each of these systems must be understood in totality. Obviously, that is impossible, but it does suggest the immensity of even approximating a full picture.

Like Chapter 9, this chapter uses a qualitative research procedure, known as grounded theory, to investigate and describe what happens in an institution when an individual is dying. However, there are significant differences between Chapter 9 and Chapter 10. The author of the latter has abstracted from his observations of eleven different persons, children in this instance, while the authors of the former described one person in great detail. Also, the latter author was looking for principles and trends, while the former were looking for understanding the dynamics of one person's dying context. And the latter also framed hypotheses, while the former restricted themselves to description. Nonetheless, each offers a good example of a research process that differs considerably from the more familiar quantitative research studies.

CHAPTER
10

The Social Organization of Terminal Care in Two Pediatric Hospitals*

Kenneth J. Doka

In recent years, there has been a considerable amount of research done in the organization of behavior in hospital systems around death and dying most notably Sudnow [1], and Glaser and Strauss [2-4]. However, in this research, the particular problems of organizing behavior around the dying child has been neglected. These studies, particularly Glaser and Strauss [2], comment briefly that the death of the child, because of his high social value and the incongruity of his death, creates organizational strains upon the hospital system. However, the death of the child was tengential to the focus of the studies and seemingly an unusual occurrence in the hospitals studied. Other students such as Easson [5], Rothenberg [6], Binger *et al*. [7], Wiener [8] who have had the child as the central focus, have commented upon the strategies of avoidance and isolation that seem to insulate the staff from the child. Unfortunately, these studies are often based on case anecdotes rather than systematic empirical investigation.

THE HYPOTHESIS

It is expected that hospital staffs will develop broad strategies (that are observable) for the organization of behavior around young dying patients in order to minimize the impact of these deaths upon staff. It is also expected that these strategies will be most apparent and most useful in those cases in which a death is defined by the staff to be certain. Thus, if a death occurs in a patient whose prognosis is considered to be uncertain, the result should be more organizational strain than in the occurrence of a death which may be prepared for. Hence, one may hypothesize that staff efforts to adjust will be greater when

* This chapter is an abridgement of a master's thesis on file at St. Louis University. Basically, the findings are presented with few deletions and limited summarizations. Other sections dealing with the review of the literature, the research design, and the theoretical implications of this report for sociological consideration, are heavily abbreviated. This was done to avoid burdening the reader with concerns peripheral to major interests.

deaths which are not defined to be certain occur than they will when deaths which are defined to be certain occur.

For this study a death will be considered certain when staff define a patient, in verbal reports or written notations as having a disease that is fatal, even though a definite prediction of time may not be able to be stated. In some cases, this information is conveyed by the diagnosis. In other cases, the definition of "terminal" is only slowly accepted by staff when a patient fails to respond to treatment. A death will be considered uncertain when these conditions are not met. Staff effort to adjust will be operationalized in terms of the amount of communication passed between staff members involved and the duration of such communication. Those deaths which involve more members and more communication about the child and the conditions of his death will be characterized as involving greater efforts to adjust. This is based on an assumption that anything that is important or problematic to an organization will become apparent in information exchanges within that organization.

THE RESEARCH DESIGN

Research for this study was carried out in a midwestern city's two pediatric hospitals. The sample for this study consisted of all those patients, in both hospitals, who died within the course of this study (26 days). This consisted of eleven cases. In addition, four other cases in which the child was defined as in critical condition or suffering from a terminal disease, but who did not die during the course of the study, were also observed.

The basic source of data for this study was observations within the field supplemented by interviews with staff and review of staff notes. Aside from observations in the field, the other major source of data was the medical records of the patients. The method of analysis was one of case comparisons. A more concise discussion of the methodology employed, and the problems inherent in it, may be found in the original thesis.

THE FINDINGS

The Negotiation of Terminal Care

Strauss, Schatzmann, *et al.*, in a study of a mental hospital, characterized the hospital as "negotiated order," or a place in a constant process of negotiation, in which numerous agreements were forgotten while others were established or revised [9]. This model also fits the organization of terminal care in the two pediatric hospitals studied. For while broad patterns of care, which will be subsequently discussed, were discernible, it is more accurate to see these not as preconceived plans of action that are uniformly applied to each case, but rather as strategies that emerge as a result of various negotiations. Hence, it is necessary to describe briefly the context of these negotiations before turning to the patterns of care that emerge from them.

The two hospitals were very dynamic places. Patients were constantly being admitted and discharged. The census rose and fell. At times, auxiliary personnel, such as volunteers or nursing students, were available and helped to relieve the pressure of certain demands upon the nursing staff. Not only the number of patients on a floor at a given time varied, but also their ages and diagnoses. Naturally, younger or sicker patients placed greater demands on the time of the nursing staff than those who were older or who were ambulatory or in for minor illness or injury. Thus, nursing and other staff constantly had to make "priority decisions," i.e., what needed most to be done at a particular time. Thus, patients whose immediate needs were perceived as less pressing by staff had lesser claims on their time. As one nurse put it: "Care really depends on how many people we have on each shift."

An illustration of this is found in the neonatal unit at one hospital. This particular unit, a specialized intensive care unit for newborns, had ten beds. As each new patient was admitted, a decision had to be made on which child was to be moved to another floor in order to make room for the new one. The patient who "least" needed this type of care had to be defined by staff. This decision was made by the ranking doctor at that time, often in consultation with the head nurse, and based on information provided by the nursing and medical staff. Naturally, the definition of "least" varied with the diagnosis and needs of other patients on the unit at that time. A patient who is defined as "least in need of care" at one time may not be so defined at another time with another group of patients.

Thus, staff was constantly defining patients on the basis of staff definition of patient's claims on their time and organizing their behavior around their definitions of that patient's state and his needs. These definitions were not stable, but changed with changes in the patient's state and with new information about that patient. For example, one child who was initially defined as having respiratory distress of unknown cause was later diagnosed as having cystic fibrosis, a disease that is generally terminal. This new information led to changes in the way the staff defined the patient and organized their behavior around him.

The major goal of the two hospitals to which all staff subscribed was to return the patient, healthy, to the outside. Staff took great pride in recounting incidents in which they succeeded. One nurse stated: "We had a case a while ago in which a child came to the hospital with a real bad heart problem. He was real bad—his lips were blue and his fingers were swollen. After surgery, he was pink and really looked great—just beautiful. It's cases like that which are really exciting to work on. They really make work worthwhile." Another doctor stated: "I like pediatrics because I like to see things grow. There's nothing more fulfilling than looking at this (a bulletin board of pictures of former patients) and remembering their condition when they came." In terminal cases, this goal is not possible, hence, the goal rather becomes to maintain life for a period of time or to make death as painless and unstressful as possible. Thus, once a child is defined by the staff to be terminal, that is, that death is seen to be certain, he has a lower claim on staff time than a patient who is not viewed by staff in such a manner. The implications of this for care will be discussed in greater depth later in this paper.

Not only the negotiation of time, but also the negotiation of information was an important element in terminal care. Much of the staff communication during reports was to assess the state of information that various terminal patients had concerning their condition. Staff then attempted to match their behavior to the patient's state of information. However, this was often difficult because of organizational constraints. In one hospital, the standard policy was that children were not to be told their prognosis. In the other, there was no standard policy and the decision as to whether the child was to be told or not was left to the parents. Most of the children were not told and thus staff members were constrained not to tell the child anything, even in response to direct questions.

The result of this was that interaction with terminal patients became difficult, particularly to nurses. On one hand, there was always the problem that the child would say or ask something that would place them in a difficult position. For instance, in one case, an eleven year old boy with leukemia grabbed hold of a student nurse as she was taking his blood pressure and asked her: "I'm not going to be able to play again, am I? I'm going to die." The nurses were of the general opinion that most children, particularly in the later stages, were well aware of what was occurring. One nurse, for example, told of a six year old leukemia victim. The child had a number of toy horses that she guarded jealously. At the end of her last hospitalization, the child, although no one discussed her condition with her, began to give these horses to her favorite nurses. They interpreted this as a sure sign that the child knew that she was going to die. In another case, a nurse was watching television with a child who had leukemia but supposedly didn't know her diagnosis. An anti-leukemia commercial came on and the girl began to ask a number of questions about the disease. While the child did not connect herself with the disease, the nurse interpreted this as a sign that the child did know her diagnosis and wished to talk about it.

The nurses, then, were placed in a position, by the organization's constraints, of behaving in a manner inappropriate to the cues they received from the child, so that their interaction was thus disjointed. For example, in one case reported by one social worker, a patient announced to a student: "I'm going to die." The student responded: "You've got such a lovely view from here." As one nurse put it: "It puts us into an impossible box. We have to play it by ear and we can only play it so far. If we play it any farther we get called on the carpet."

The negotiation of information with critical cases (i.e., where death was uncertain) was not seen by staff to be an issue. Whenever a child asked if he was going to die, the nurse would respond with a comment like, "Not if we can help it," or "No, you're pretty sick but we'll be able to pull you through."

They seemed to believe that this type of response was not inappropriate or untruthful.

Patterns of Care

Two major patterns of care emerged from these negotiations. The first pattern may be described as the terminal pattern. This refers to those cases in which death was considered to be certain, albeit a time of death might not have been able to be estimated. Patients in this category had chronic and fatal diseases, such as leukemia or other forms of cancer.

As stated earlier, such patients had generally lesser claim on demands on staff time. In most cases, aside from routine tasks such as checking vital signs and administering medication, there was little staff did. While they might have offered a supportive role (i.e., attempting to offer some sort of emotional support and comfort), this task required time demands which often could not be worked in in terms of the other demands on staff time. And, as discussed previously, it was often made difficult because of the organizational rule against discussing the child's condition or prognosis with him. Interactive behavior in such a case became highly disjointed and awkward.

In addition, in the two hospitals, there was some confusion on just what staff was responsible for this task. Even in cases in which care needs of the terminal child were more immediate, such as those cases when the child took a sudden turn for the worse, his demands on staff time had to be worked in and negotiated against the demands placed by those whom the staff deemed a better risk.

The results of these negotiations was that staff had a tendency to interact less with terminal cases. This was particularly true in the latter stages of disease when the treatment of patient shifted from some treatment to merely palliative care. Generally, at this time family began to gather, and staff felt that any disruption, even for routine matters such as a bath, would be a resented intrusion. (In one particular case, two members of the staff had an argument over the propriety of just such a task at that time.)

The other pattern of care may be called the critical one, in which the death of a particular patient is defined by staff to be possible, but not inevitable. Examples of these are serious accidents or acute diseases. Such cases received high staff priority and interaction around these patients tended to be intense. Most of these patients were "specialed." Specialing meant that a child was assigned a nurse who took care of him as her sole or prime case. Naturally, this too had to be worked out against other demands on the time of staff. At some time, such as during the night shift, there may have been only one nurse on duty. Thus, this nurse would spend a majority of time with this particular patient, spreading the rest of her time among others. At other times, staff were borrowed from other floors, these "floaters" either specialed the child themselves, or freed the regular floor staff to do such intensive care. Because of the varying demands upon staff

Table 1. Interaction of Staff Around Terminal vs. Critical Patients

Cases	Staff Definition of the Inevitability of Death	Notations	Noters
1	uncertain	55	8
2	uncertain	56	9
3	certain	24	7
4	certain	27	6
5	certain	15	6

time, varying shifts, as well as days off of particular staff, these intenseive efforts were generally spread among a number of staff. Thus staff definition of a death as possible but uncertain led to increased effort and involvement of more of the staff until either the patient was defined as recovering or until new information led to a new definition of death as certain.

One way this was seen was that staff spent more time communicating among themselves as to what should be done next in regard to these patients and in arranging work schedules so as to assure constant coverage. An illustration of this is found in "reports," in which a disproportionate amount of information exchanged in a report involved such patients. For example, in four reports in which such communication was timed, an average of four minutes was spent discussing critical patients, while other patients averaged 1.3 minutes.

It is important to note that these definitions were subject to change. Not only the information conveyed in diagnosis, but other cues given by the patients served to either confirm or to suggest alterations of staff definitions.

To sum up so far, the staff organized their behavior around patients on the basis of various negotiations, the most important of which is the negotiation of time demands. The result of this is that the child who was defined to be terminal interacted with less than the child who was defined to be critical. An index of this can be constructed from medical records, in which each nurse would vote her visits. If the notations on the charts of patients were compared for the two days prior to death, one found that staff interaction around critical patients was over double that of terminal patients. See Table 1.

While this information was only available at one hospital, a comparison of interactions around patients during selected time periods at the other produced similar results. In the eleven cases compared, there did not seem to be any differences in the number of staff who interacted with each patient. Thus, the critical cases involved the investment of time by many, while in the terminal cases, a lesser amount of involvement was shared by approximately the same number of staff.

The evaluation of a patient, then, in regard to staff definition of life chance is the basis of the way staff organizes their behavior around that patient. Staff members have to work out various demands on their time. In general hospitals, evaluations of the patient seem to be based on a variety of factors, such as race, socio-economic class, or age, and these factors seem to validate or invalidate, or to rank patients' claim to care [1, 2, 10]. However, because of the high social value assigned to the child [1, 2], these types of variables do not seem to visibly affect care. The definition of staff in regard to the certainty or uncertainty of death does however serve as a basis for organizing demands on time.

Staff Efforts to Adjust Following the Deaths of Patients

One would expect that if staff interacted less with terminal patients, investing less time with them, staff efforts to adjust following their death would be less than in those cases in which staff involvement was greater. In the six cases characterized by staff as terminal, efforts to adjust following the death of the patient were classified as little or none. In all of these cases, news of the death was not deemed to convey much information value. For example, in these cases the news was not even volunteered to the next shift. At some time during report, the information was either remarked in passing or requested. Usually, the information was received with only a passing comment ("That's too bad.") or a request for brief additional information, such as family reaction. In these cases, communication did not exceed more than two exchanges of question and response. And, communication did not extend beyond this initial exchange. Even in one case in which a fourteen year old girl who had bone cancer took a quick turn for the worse and died earlier than staff believed she would, staff communications following her death were brief. The typical reaction was one of "It's better it happened this way than for her to linger."

Staff reactions to the deaths of critical patients varied from moderate to great. A moderate reaction was observed in two cases. In one of these cases, staff reaction was limited to two or three members of the staff who attempted to reconstruct events and, in general, discussed the child throughout the day. In the other, the patient had bronchitis and pneumonia and, even though the child began to decline two days prior to death, staff had hope that with time he could be pulled through. Before his death, the child was transferred to ICU. At his death, staff reaction may have been characterized as disappointed but not surprised. Nonetheless, communication about the child after his death continued throughout the day.

One case caused great efforts to adjust. In this case, the child was admitted to the hospital because of seizures. When the child began to react to medications, staff involvement was intensified and specialing techniques were instituted. The child was thought to have stabilized. However, she died on night shift. Information about the child's death was the first news exchanged that morning: in fact, it replaced any greeting. Through that day and the next few days, communication between the staff about the child and the events leading to her death was continuous. For instance, when a nurse came on the floor the first thing she would be likely to hear would be: "Did you hear about A__." The entire story would then be reconstructed. At the coffee shop when a nurse met a colleague from another floor she began her conversation with the comment: "We had a real rough one yesterday. A__ died last night. . ." An attempt was made to reconstruct events to see if any cues were misperceived or that if anything else could have been done. Attempts were also made to reassure staff, such as the night nurse, that all that could have been done to save the child was done.

In addition, the death of a child necessitates various tasks. The family has to be notified that death is imminent. Requests for autopsies have to be made and thus the doctor who has taken care of the case should be forewarned so that he will be available. When a death is certain, staff can organize around these events with some degree of surety. When a death is not certain these types of tasks cannot be so prepared. Thus, when a death that is uncertain occurs, the floor is disrupted as certain staff have to make time for other events such as notifying family. In the previously discussed case, the child's death totally surprised the staff and efforts had to be executed to call parents and doctor. As it took over three hours to contact parents, the work order of the staff was highly disrupted and thus this too added to staff efforts to adjust.

In summation, then, the death of a child who staff defined to be terminal did not require much effort to adjust on the part of the staff. This seemed to be due to two reasons. First, because of the fact that the child had a lesser claim on demands on time of the staff, and because interaction with the child was difficult because of organizational constraints on that interaction, the child was interacted with less than patients who were defined to be in danger of death but not terminal. Secondly, when a death was defined to be certain, staff could organize around the various tasks that needed to be done prior to the time of death. When a death was seen as uncertain, no such preparations could be made and demands on staff were intensified and the work order disrupted.

Thus, deaths that were uncertain involved greater efforts to adjust both in terms of their increased involvement with these patients and in requiring renegotiations in regard to work. Broad patterns of care were discernible, but these patterns were not preconceived plans of action that were applied in order to lessen the effect of deaths upon staff. Rather, they were strategies that emerged in the situation due to various types of negotiations which then had the effect of lessening staff efforts to adjust to deaths that could be anticipated.

Conclusions and Implications

This study suggests that the evaluation of the child in terms of "life chance" has effects on the way staff organize care around the patient and the way they adjust to his death. These evaluations arise in a process of interaction and guide such interaction. These effects do not seem to be the result of standardized strategies but rather emerge from negotiations that are guided by evaluations of the child. This is consistent with the work of others in the field of medical sociology such as Glaser and Strauss [2], Sudnow [1], and Roth [10]. This study adds a dimension in that it discusses a basic variable, certainty of death, that seems to be important in staff negotiations of demands upon time in the two children's hospitals studied.

In conclusion, three limitations of this study ought to be noted. First, the sample was limited to children who had died, or who were in risk of dying, during the course of the study. Systematic observation and comparison with other types of patients is lacking. Secondly, the study was limited in choice of setting. In both hospitals, staff was more likely to be exposed to specialized personnel and to various educational programs than might be found on pediatric units in other types of hospital settings. Finally, it is somewhat limited in methodology. Observational techniques are a good way to begin to get at the study of social process in an alien and under-researched setting. However, they can only be a beginning. Further research, with more stringent controls, is clearly necessary.

REFERENCES

1. D. Sudnow, *Passing On: The Social Organization of Death and Dying*, Prentice Hall, Englewood Cliffs, New Jersey, 1967.
2. B. Glaser and A. Strauss, The Social Loss of Dying Patients, *American Journal of Nursing, 64*, pp. 119-121, June, 1964.
3. _____, *Awareness of Dying*, Aldine, Chicago, 1965.
4. _____, *Time for Dying*, Aldine, Chicago, 1968.
5. W. Easson, *The Dying Child*, C. C. Thomas (ed.), Springfield, Illinois, 1970.
6. M. Rothenberg, Reactions of Those Who Treat Children With Cancer, *Pediatrics, 40*, pp. 507-512, 1967.
7. C. Binger, *et al.*, Childhood Leukemia: Emotional Impact on Patient and Family, *New England Journal of Medicine, 280*, pp. 414-418, 1969.
8. J. Wiener, Responses of Medical Personnel to the Fatal Illness of a Child, B. Shoenberg *et al.* (eds.), *Loss and Grief*, Columbia University Press, New York, pp. 102-115, 1970.
9. A. Strauss, *et al.*, The Hospital and Its Negotiated Order, E. Friedson (ed.), *The Hospital in Modern Society*, Free Press, Glencoe, Illinois, pp. 147-169, 1963.
10. J. Roth, Some Contingencies of the Moral Evaluation and Control of Clientele: The Case of the Hospital Emergency Service, *American Journal of Sociology, 177*, pp. 839-856, March 1972.

In the United States, Canada, Great Britain, and most European countries, more deaths occur in hospitals than at home or in other kinds of institutions. However, hospital care tends to be geared to health conditions that can be treated and reversed, with some likelihood of success, not to those conditions that will inevitably lead to death. About twenty-five years ago, some health and mental-health professionals began to believe that another kind of program was needed, one that would attempt to improve the well-being of individuals whose physicians viewed as having conditions that were no longer reversible or effectively treatable, and whose deaths were foreseeable. The first of these institutions was developed in England by Dr. Cicely Saunders, who applied the term hospice *to the care program. The past decade has seen a rapid spread of the hospice movement throughout the United States and Canada as well as western Europe.*

CHAPTER 11

Hospice Care
in the
United States:
The Process Begins

Robert W. Buckingham

Since the turn of the century, enormous changes have taken place within American society in our attitudes toward death and dying and the role death plays in our lives. Both the age at which a person is expected to die and the place where death typically occurs have changed radically. People die at home, on the street, and at their place of employment, but the greatest number of deaths take place in public institutions. Many elderly people die in extended care facilities and convalescent homes. Even in this case, when the aged who have been taken care of in a long-term institution begin to fail, they are frequently transported to an acute care hospital to die.

Recently, however, there appears to be a springback of public opinion with a return to the feeling that some of the problems with the care of the dying could be solved if the patient could die at home surrounded by his or her family. This feeling may be part of the "back to nature" culture which seeks to reintegrate each human being with the life cycle. This change in attitude is also influenced by the growing realization by young and middle-aged people that we are turning into a top-heavy society. The policy makers of our society are beginning to realize that when they are old they will be part of a population of aged for whom society, as it is presently structured, has no effective place. Indeed, the hospice movement can be seen as a springboard from which society is re-examining its attitudes toward bodily deterioration, death, and decay, which in turn will affect our attitudes toward all unproductive members of our society: mentally and physically handicapped, the weak, and the elderly. Hospice is a symbol of the revolt against excessive specialization. It represents a return to humanistic medicine, to care within the patient's community, to family-centered care and the view of the patient as a person.

Today, more than three-quarters of the terminally ill are consigned to institutions which are unprepared to deal with their final needs. The real terror of institutionalized dying is not death but the mechanical maintenance without medical purpose and the ultimate indignity of having one's final days controlled by strangers. Death is often perceived by those attending the patient, not as a perfectly natural event, but as a technological failure to use the machines at their disposal.

The hospice concept arrived in America with the incorporation of Hospice, Connecticut in 1971 and the rendering of service to patients and families in 1974. In the intervening years the concept has grown rapidly throughout the nation. Medical, governmental, and educational institutions have recognized the profound urgency for the advocacy of the hospice concept. Because 80 per cent of the health care dollar is spent in the last year of life, the National Cancer Institute has investigated this new method of providing improved, more appropriate care at less cost. Their findings resulted in the allocation of health care money. The National Cancer Institute recognized that the answer to at least a portion of the cancer problem lies in the provision of patient-family services rather than basic science research. This realization resulted in a considerable change in policy and attitude.

To enhance further discussion of this new attitude, it is necessary to define hospice. The definition cited by the National Hospice Organization is stated as follows:

> Hospice is a medically directed multidisciplinary program providing skilled care of an appropriate nature for terminally ill patients and their families to live as fully as possible until the time of death helps relieve symptoms during the distress (physically, psychological, spirtual, social, economic) that may occur during the course of the disease, dying and bereavement [1, p. 1902].

Although hospice exists as a *concept of care,* it is apparent that a distinction must be made between a hospice home care program and a hospice inpatient facility. For those patients that are alone, who do not have a family member or anyone else to act as a primary care person, and for those patients who need more medical care than that which can be offered at home, inpatient care is appropriate. The work of Henry J. Wald, *A Hospice for Terminally Ill Patients,* speaks to the issue of environment and the dying person: "The quality of the dying process is affected to a large extent by the physical surrounding in which the process occurs. The surrounding itself acts not only as a catalyst to initiate the most effective treatment for the patient as an individual but also can assist in managing the complex psychosocial interrelationship inextricably entwined with the patient's medical treatment." [2, pp. 12-13] It should be further stated that whatever environment aids in the fullfillment of the patient and family's needs (provided it can be arranged), that is the environment in which the patient should go through the dying process.

Basic methodologies must be established to accomodate the patient with adequate care. Hospice work begins with the question, "What does this person need?" [3, p. 216] Probably, the answer to this initial question will be either home care or inpatient care; both have their advantages and disadvantages. It is the needs of the patient and family that must be considered. Sandol Stoddard states the following on behalf of inpatient care:

> Inpatient care for hospice patients, when and if it becomes necessary, may have some subtle advantages over the best of the care that can be provided in patients' home. Families visiting there come into contact with others who are experiencing similiar emotions, and help to support one another during the process of loss and bereavement. Many take pleasure in offering small comforts and companionship to dying members of one another's families. Patients themselves, brought together at this time are often able to experience the sort of friendship which is unmasked and thus, however brief, very real and satisfying, "Time" as Cicely Saunders once remarked, "is not a question of length, it's a question of depth, isn't it?" Witnessing the peaceful sort of death that is made possible by good hospice care, patients and families alike can come to the realization that dying itself is not a horror, and is nothing to be feared, however grievous it may be in terms of parting and to the bereaved, of loss [3, p. 170].

Hospice home care programs have the same concepts and principles as inpatient facilities. The distinction lies in the involvement of the family in the actual care of the patient. If a patient remains at home, a member of the family is trained as a "primary care person" in nursing methods. "Such training allows someone in the family to participate actively in the care of the patient." [4, p. 5] There is a lot to be said for involving the family in the care of the dying patient; so many times families express the feelings of helplessness when a loved one is dying. In an earlier study, I found that both patient and family groups, when compared to a non-hospice group, were more independent. Feelings of personal inadequacy and inferiority accompanied by negative expectancies concerning interpersonal contacts with others were much more characteristic of non-hospice than of hospice primary care persons. Being able to take care of, provide assistance for, and give comfort to the dying patient relinquished some of the guilt and helplessness felt by the family. At the same time, when caring for a dying patient at home, there are adjustments that have to be made in the functioning of the family. Sylvia Lack and myself, in *The First American Hospice*, give the foundation for the "one unit of care" concept as follows:

> Because of the disruption of family life style caused by many changes that occur during the course of terminal illness, Hospice personnel recognize the importance of sustaining continuity of care. Terminal illness shatters the equilibrium of the family group; therefore it is the patient and the family who are designated as the unit of care. Medical care and supportive counseling involve both the patient and family by day in their homes. The team is also on call for emergencies at night and weekends [4, p. 4].

As stated earlier, treating the patient and family as one unit of care is effective hospice care. Problems of the patient and family are inevitably intertwined. It is virtually impossible for the family to provide care to a dying patient and camouflage their feelings; at the same time the dying patient will (and should) display his/her feelings openly. For this to remain a productive interchange, hospice staff is necessary for support.

> Patient's behavioral patterns often undergo a marked change, and overlapping defenses of denial and symptoms of depression dominate their relationships with others. At this time the medical personnel, and more especially the families, desperately need to understand that the patient's changed behavior is not a result of something they may or may not have done but a predictable response to a very difficult situation. Only when feelings of anger, guilt, and loneliness experienced by the family members are vented and dissipated can the unspoken sense of alienation in the dying patient be alleviated. Family problems are often too closely related to interaction with the terminally ill cancer patient to go unheeded [4, p. 5].

The point is made continually in the literature that the patient and family should not be separated. The patient needs to be listened to, cared for, and supported. The same applies to the family, with an added emphasis on education. The better informed family members are, the less anxiety that exists. An important task of hospice workers is to find out what the family's lifestyle was like before terminal illness; this necessary piece of information adds to more effective care of the patient-family unit. Wald discusses the New Haven Hospice and quotes from the Yale Planning Group's Philosophy:

> It is important to discover the patient's and family's life style so that we can adapt to them and help them include this experience of dying and bereavement in their life, in their own way. The patient and his family, therefore assume active roles in the decision making process. They also

become teachers for other patients and families and for staff members seeking to be more understanding and helpful during this moment of crisis in life experience. Thus, the work of hospice is shared among patients, families and staff, all cooperating in the caring task [2, p. 29].

Robert Kastenbaum, author of *Death, Society and Human Experience,* reiterates the focus of hospice: "Emphasis is upon the total well being of the terminally ill person—and the family—wherever they happen to be." [5, p. 226]

Hospice is significantly broadening the scope of reimbursed "skilled nursing services." Lack of recognition of the need of the dying for skilled nursing causes many patients to be consigned to custodial levels of care. As custodial care is not reimbursable in the home setting, dying patients must be sent to a nursing home. Nursing homes whose programs are ideally suited for care of the long-term geriatric patient are not usually able to cope with the multitude of rapidly changing problems presented by the dying patient; nor are they willing to deal with the acute crisis of the death itself. Many nursing homes return the patient to the hospital, which results in an unnecessary, expensive journey and high cost hospital care for the last day or two of life.

As the hospice movement grows, it does more than alter our treatment of the dying. Hospices and home care are de-escalating the soaring costs of illness by reducing the individual and collective burdens borne by all health insurance policy holders. Because hospices and home care use no sophisticated, diagnostic treatment, their overhead is basically for personal care and medication. The cost of a hospice stay is projected to be less than the hospital stay. At present, health insurance programs are not geared to cope with hospice techniques and will not reimburse their services. Ironically, getting a patient out of bed and out of his home usually disrupts his coverage. Hospice, Inc., has made formal recommendations that Medicare be extended to cover anyone of any age with a limited life prognosis.

Having discussed the hospice concept of care in general and the importance of caring for the patient and family as one unit, focus turns now to the needs of the dying patient and then to the needs of the family of the dying patient.

John Hinton, author of *Dying,* states that "the emphasis must always lie upon tending the person, not battling with his disease, treating the one who feels symptoms, not just treating the symptoms." [6, p. 111] This point is further expanded in *The Hospice Movement,* where Stoddard speaks of hospice as a "caring community," and within that community is a body coexisting with a belief that the patient is something more than his body [13, p. 166]. The dying patient needs not to be abandoned nor isolated from his usual sources of spiritual and emotional support. He needs to know that he matters as a *human being* to those around him at this time [3, p. 129]. Hinton and Stoddard are not the only ones who emphasize the holistic approach of caring for the dying—it is a concept that pervades the literature.

The primary message that must be conveyed to the dying patient is that he/ she is unique, and that his/her needs are special and will be met in an individual way. Although standard reactions may take place, we who care for the dying must not lose sight of the meaning these feelings hold for the individual. Even if a person does experience and express some feelings common with other dying people, he/she does so within the unique pattern of a life that no other person has lived and within a particular environment while suffering from a particular disease syndrome. What is distinctive about this person's life may be more significant as a particular moment than the universal situation he/she has in common with many others [5, p. 216]. Cicely Saunders says so well what should be said to all dying patients; "You matter because you are you. You matter to the last moment of your life, and we will do all we can not only to help you die peacefully, but also to live until you die." [3, p. 91]

Saunders' method of helping patients live until they die is accomplished through effective pain and symptom control. The first step in alleviating uncomfortable symptoms and easing the pain is listening to the patient, for he/she alone can best describe the suffering. Once the symptoms and nature of the pain have been identified, appropriate measures can be taken to alleviate them [7, p. 1817]. "Pain control it turns out is not so much a matter of what it is in the medicine, as it is of how and when it is administered." [3, p. 48]

So much of chronic pain in cancer patients is perpetuated by the letters "p.r.n."—meaning "whenever necessary." This expression dictates that the patient be given medication at the onset of pain. This is precisely where the problem lies. Medication must be given prior to the onset of pain. "The fear of pain increases pain itself by geometric proportions. When severe pain is experienced and is expected to continue indefinitely or even to get worse, the patient enters a world of horror and hopelessness that for many treated by conventional methods ends only with death. This is not necessary and with hospice care it simply does not happen. Knowing that it does not happen is, in itself, part of the comfort offered to hospice patients and families." [3, p. 48] The administration of medication whenever necessary fosters dependency on medication. Dying patients feel enough loss without having to sacrifice more of their independence [7, p. 1818].

It is for these very reasons that the alleviation of symptoms and the control of pain is of primary importance in terminal care. Kastenbaum states, "The hospice staff has made itself expert in the management of chronic pain. Relief from seemingly endless and meaningless suffering makes it possible for many terminally ill people to call upon their own personal resources to adapt to their situation and to be more responsive to others. When the high priority given to pain management is successful it makes a dramatic difference in the patient's sense of well being and obviously, a difference to family and staff as well." [5, p. 227]

Hospice has also affected government policies in the area of drug control. Judith Quattelbaum, horrified by Stuart Alsop's description of a terminal cancer patient in pain and inspired by the news of effective pain control with heroin in British hospices, formed the Committee for Change on Intractable Pain. Although British studies have shown that morphine is an effective oral analgesic for the vast majority of terminal cancer patients, there remains a small group of patients who need injectible narcotics and for whom the greater solubility of heroin proves of great benefit. At the urging of Miss Quattelbaum's committee and leaders of hospice in Britain and America, the President's Committee, headed by Dr. Peter Bourne, was formed to examine the use of restricted drugs for the terminally ill. The government feels strongly that the search into the possible therapeutic benefits should not be restricted by a drug's bad reputation. The government has now instructed the Department of Health and Welfare to change its policies in this area, stating that fear of addiction and uninformed biases against selected potent narcotics should not be allowed to interfere with the humane treatment of the terminally ill. If the administration of any drug could help alleviate pain or anxiety, it should be available to the medical profession.

Once the dying patient is treated as a unique individual whose suffering is at its absolute minimum, other needs may be met. Reference is made throughout the literature to the isolation and loneliness that the dying person experiences. It has been said that the fear of abandonment is the most critical and crucial fear that one feels when dying. One way of diminishing that fear is through availability—by being there when needed—even if it means just sitting in silence, holding the patient's hand. Sometimes "a gentle massage, a soft pillow placed just so, a subtle change in diet, a tempting drink, or time taken simply to be present, quietly caring and listening, recognizing the person as a unique and valued individual—these things can truly heal the dying, even when the cure has become impossible." [3, p. 49]

Throughout the discussion of the needs of the dying patient, it appears that the patient is doing all the receiving (i.e., he/she is treated as a unique individual, symptoms are alleviated, pain is controlled, people are accessible to the patient). Yet, it is of vital importance to realize that the dying are just as involved in giving as in receiving. We who care for the dying must be aware of this; we must allow this process to occur. "With the spread of the hospice concept in our culture, many of us may discover that we are learning from the sick how to be well again and from the dying how to live." [3, p. 36]

Through the use of metaphor, Martin Shepard, author of *Someone You Love is Dying,* describes the relationship between two people, one of which is dying. "You are to an extent like dancing partners, exerting subtle influences upon each other, guilding at times and following the lead on other occasions. The dying one and you can exchange real feelings, play act, support, encourage, or burden each other, depending upon your individual needs, temperaments and awareness. Coping with your emotions is intimately related to coping with the other person's, for like mirrors, we tend to reflect each other." [8, p. 213] Although the description may appear a bit romanticized, the message conveyed is that a special interdependence exists between caregivers and patients. Each possesses something that the other needs. The dying patient needs comfort and support from others, while at the same time, they have so much to teach others about the nature of relationships and the meaning of life. They have dropped their masks and ceased to worry about the inconsequentials of life [3, p. 75]. In the words of Elisabeth Kubler-Ross, we must remember to always regard them as persons who are going through a natural, rather than unnatural process [9, p. 64].

While caring for the dying patient, it is important not to ignore the needs of the family, for it is believed that the role they play and their reactions contribute a lot to the patient's response to his/her illness [10, p. 157]. Whether the dying patient is cared for at an in-patient facility or at home, hospice staff must remember that the family is just as much "patients" as the patients themselves. As hospice workers need replenishment, so do family members. This is, perhaps, one of the primary goals of attempting to meet the needs of the family. The hospice concept of care dictates that "the family is both an agency and a recipient of care." [5, p. 276] We must help family members to do one of the most difficult tasks—to go on living while their loved one is dying. This is the point at which guilt becomes the most intense emotion.

Kubler-Ross addresses this issue when she says, "I think it is more meaningful for the patient and his family to see that the illness does not totally disrupt a household or completely deprive all members of any pleasurable activities; rather, the illness may allow for a gradual adjustment and change toward the kind of home it is going to be when the patient is no longer around. Just as the terminally ill patient cannot face death all the time, the family member cannot and should not exclude all other interactions for the sake of being with the patient exclusively. He, too (the family member), has a need to deny or avoid the sad realities at times in order to face them better when his presence is really needed." [10, p. 159] It is for this reason (i.e., to place a limit on family involvement), "the hospice has established a weekly "family's day off." This allows a useful "vacation" without any sense of guilt attached." [5, p. 226] By encouraging the family to continue their lives with gaiety, when possible, the dying are not made to feel a burden; by lessening the dying patient's feelings of guilt, they are better able "to live until they die."

Another aspect of caring for the family of the dying is the degree to which they become involved in the care of the patient. As indicated earlier, participating in the care of the dying patient can significantly reduce common feelings of guilt and helplessness. "A family's active participation in care is also part of the separation process itself, which includes giving and receiving, coming together and letting go." [7, p. 1820] This "separation process" as Craven and Wald refer to it, is a crucial task that must be resolved if the family is to go on living after the patient dies. More commonly called "anticipatory grief" or "preparatory grief," it is a stage, much like the stage of the dying experience, where family members act as though their loved one has already died. This

process of "grieving begins before death occurs and continues after death."
[7, p. 1821] To further discuss anticipatory grief, a broad definition is given
below:

> Anticipatory grief work is the grief work we do as we try to prepare
> ourselves ahead of time for the loss. It is putting our house in order. It is
> setting the stage for a moving and perhaps difficult event. It is a
> forewarning of a condition which will demand energy and effort. It is
> working through the impact of an event ahead of time [11, p. 347].

The ideal would be for the patient and all those who care for the patient to go
through the process together. "All involved must let the life go. When everyone
does so simultaneously, it is easier, but this does not always happen. Hospice
staff members must be ready to provide the needed support before, during and
after the patient's death." [7, p. 1822]

Although the anticipatory grief period is a hard time for all involved because
the process of letting go has begun, perhaps the most difficult time for the
family is when the patient is very close to death and has begun the process of
detachment from the family. "It is at this time, 'Kubler-Ross asserts,' we can be
of greatest service to them if we help them understand that only patients who
have worked through their dying are able to detach themselves slowly and
peacefully in this manner. It should be a source of solace and comfort to them
and not one of grief and resentment. It is during this time that the family needs
the most support, the patient perhaps the least. I do not mean to imply by this
that the patient should be left alone. We should always be available, but a
patient who has reached this stage of acceptance and decathexis usually requires
little in terms of interpersonal relationship." [10, p. 170]

What about the dying patient who has not worked through his/her own death;
who is having a difficult time coping; who turns to his/her family for support?
Lack and Buckingham address this issue:

> Just as the patient must undergo a process of realization and adjustment
> before coming to terms with approaching death, the family will experience
> transitions in learning to adapt and reconcile themselves to such profound
> loss. Because family members are frequently given more information about
> the patient's condition during the earlier stages of the malignancy, they tend
> to accomodate to the difficult emotional demands of the situation earlier
> and are therefore ready to support the patient through the successive trials
> and disappointments of progressive deterioration. By virtue of their ability
> to postpone grief, close family members are also enabled to support the
> patient through increasingly difficult times. [4, p. 197-198].

This is not to say that the family does not experience anticipatory grief. Rather,
it is sometimes necessary, when caring for the dying, to put one's feelings away
until a later time and be there for the patient. "Grief over the anticipated loss of
a loved one," state Lack and Buckingham, "may begin as soon as the diagnosis is

confirmed and prognosis revealed. It has been postulated, although not confirmed empirically, that the individual awaiting bereavement undergoes stages similar to those which the dying person moves through before acceptance of his fate." [4, p. 201]

Perhaps what we can stress most when attending to the needs of the family is the importance of being real—of expressing feelings. We must encourage family members to share with each other and to share with the dying person while he/she is still alive. This may appear to be a frightening task but leaving things unsaid, finding out it is too late to convey a thought, is far more devasting.

According to the results of my study, both hospice patients and primary care persons reported greater satisfaction in their relationships with relatives, family, spouse, and children than did the non-hospice group. The study revealed that the hospice patients and care persons experienced less friction with family, friends, and social contacts.

Reports of debilitating attachment to family, submission, dependence, and anxious rumination were significantly fewer among the hospice group. Hospice primary care persons also felt significantly less inhibited in their communication with others than did non-hospice primary care persons.

As a result of involvement and communication with the patient, the family should experience greater ease saying "goodbye," to a loved one than the family that has distanced themselves. As Martin Shephard puts it, "Helping someone you love to the exit door—instead of leaving that job to others—can be one of the richest personal experiences in both your life and the life that is ending." [8, p. 154]

Keeping in mind that the hospice concept of care designates the patient and family as one unit, it follows that care would not end at the death of the patient but continue throughout bereavement. The hospice community embraces patient, family, and close friends, not only during the final days and weeks of the patient's life but long after death, offering consolation and support during the time of bereavement. It cannot be emphasized enough the necessity for the hospice staff to maintain contact with the family after death has occurred. Although the concern here is primarily the family, hospice workers who have been involved in the care of the patient feel a certain amount of loss also. Therefore, some degree of interdependence may exist. "Dying patients do not live in a vacuum," states Wald, "the suffering of the family begins—but it extends after the death." He continues, "Grieving is a process which again will vary, but includes relief, frozen isolation, open grief, anger and resolution. Those who have worked side by side with the patient and family are potentially in an excellent position to help in the resolution of grief because they have shared it and felt it in part." [3, p. 168] We must remember that there is nothing one can do to replace the void that one experiences having lost a loved one, but knowing that others share the loss, that others do care, that someone will be there to listen can offer more comfort and solace than ever imagined.

Many reasons can be attributed to the fact that the loss of a loved one is one of the most traumatic events in one's life. Throughout this paper, the interdependence of people has been referred to continually. Interdependence implies a relationship, and relationships foster physical, intellectual, and emotional involvement. Of these, experiencing emotional attachment is the force that gravitates human beings toward each other. It has been said that "the intensity of the sense of loss is largely a function of the intensity of the emotional attachments that have been built up over the years." [12, p. 217] It stands to reason that the closer one feels to someone who is dying, the deeper sense of loss one feels. Those people that find coping with loss so difficult that they prohibit themselves from becoming involved with people at an emotional level are truly depriving themselves of one of life's most enriching experiences. As a bereaved fiance once said after the death of her loved one, "The experience of knowing and loving him, is well worth all the hurt and pain I am experiencing now. If I had to do it over, knowing what I know today, I wouldn't have it any other way."

Having acknowledged the importance of involvement with people, dealing with the loss of these people is necessary. It should be remembered that feelings, reaction, and coping mechanisms vary from individual to individual. Therefore, common occurences cited in the literature will be stated. "The dying process of family members produces an immense range of emotional reactions, from guilt and anger to money worries to fear and anxiety. Also, the death of someone close to us is a reminder of our own vulnerability, which is fear-evoking itself." [12, p. 218] Of these feelings, anger and guilt frequently occur when losing a loved one from terminal illness. Richard Kalish explains the cycle containing anger and guilt: family members feel anger toward the dying person for abandoning them, for draining their emotional resources, for taking up their time and energy. Often this anger is repressed because rationally, the family knows that their loved one did not want to die, could not exercise control over his/her death, and the realization occurs that losing their life is a far greater loss than what they are experiencing. Therefore, they feel guilty for their own anger which serves to intensify their guilt, and in this way, the cycle perpetuates itself [12, p. 229-230]. Essential to resolving these feelings is the ventilation of them to another person, preferably a hospice worker skilled in the art of bereavement care. It is possible that family members will displace their anger towards the dead loved one onto the person offering comfort and support. It is important to recognize this for what it is.

Another reason that one may feel guilt is if a family member does not feel as sad and devastated as he/she feels he/she should. Western culture dictates what is appropriate and what is not appropriate. Therefore, reacting the way one really feels may not be in accordance with what is expected. "Letting go is usually preconceived as very painful for everyone involved," state Craven and Wald, "but it is important to recognize this is not always so, since interpersonal relationships include burdens and problems in addition to assets and love. If the perception of helpers is colored by romantic sentimentality, those survivors who feel a sense of relief in separation may feel inappropriately guilty because they don't weep and feel relieved, not grief stricken." [7, p. 1822]

Lily Pincus, author of *Death and the Family*, sums up the discussion of guilt by saying, "Ambivalence is inseparable from guilt, and there is always guilt at the death of an important person—guilt about what has been said or not said, done or not done, justified guilt and guilt which has no rational justification. Perhaps the most painful and confusing guilt is about the moments—however fleeting—of triumph that the other one is dead, and I am alive! Yet, just as with mixed feelings, guilt can also be based on realistic regrets about insufficient care and concern for the dead. Often it is a mixture of justified and unjustified feelings, and it is this mixture which makes it so difficult to live with guilt." [13, pp. 118-119]

Realizing the damaging effects unresolved guilt can have, one aim of bereavement care should be the alleviation or, at least, ventilation of these feelings. Assuming that the dying person was cared for by hospice, and the family was involved in that care, regrets about insufficient care would appear to be practically non-existent, therefore, reducing the fostering of guilt feelings.

Another aim of bereavement care is helping the family to renew contacts that may have been neglected while caring for the dying. It is important that the living go on living. Sometimes, it may be necessary to do intervention work with those people to whom the survivors are looking to for support. Sometimes out of ignorance of how to act or what to say, people ignore the bereaved, thus alienating them at a time when isolation can be quite damaging. According to Geoffrey Gorer, and reiterated by Lack and Buckingham, our society attempts to further cripple the bereaved by stigmatizing them. "In our death-denying society, the suffering of the bereaved is often exacerbated by the reactions of others to his or her plight. Loneliness due to loss of the loved one is intensified by the failure of others to support the survivor during the different period of transition and social adjustment. People become uncomfortable and embarassed in the presence of the bereaved. As if tainted by recent experience with death, the bereaved person is unwelcome socially." [4, p. 202]

It is to this issue that we must address ourselves. The people in our society need to be reeducated; more violence is done to people out of ignorance than can well be imagined. We need to know that dying is as much a part of living as being born. It is a natural part of the life process. We need to know that ending relationships is as important as beginning them; only through connecting with others do we complete ourselves. The hurt, anger, despair, loneliness, sadness, emptiness that one feels when someone close dies makes one wonder if it is all worth it. People often express a desire to withdraw from life; the bereaved may feel that they will never get over the loss, that a part of them has gone with the deceased.

The words of Elisabeth Kubler-Ross are appropriate at this point: "Learning to reinvest yourself in living when you have lost someone you love is very difficult, but only through doing so can you give some meaning to that person's death." [14, p. 74] This is the message that must be conveyed to the bereaved. Much as hospice operates on the belief that the quality of human life should be preserved at all costs, that the dying should live until they die, the same pertain to the bereaved: they, too, must live until they die.

REFERENCES

1. R. F. Rizzo, Hospice: Comprehensive Terminal Care, *New York State Journal of Medicine,* October, 1978.
2. H. J. Wald, A Hospice for Terminally Ill Patients, unpublished masters thesis, Columbia University, School of Architecture, May 21, 1971.
3. S. Stoddard, *The Hospice Movement,* Stein and Day Publishers, New York, 1978.
4. S. A. Lack and R. W. Buckingham, III, *First American Hospice: Three Years of Home Care,* Hospice, Inc., U.S.A., 1978.
5. R. J. Kastenbaum, *Death, Society and Human Experience,* The C. V. Mosby Co., Saint Louis, MO., 1977.
6. J. Hinton, *Dying,* Hunt Barnard Printing, Ltd., Great Britain, 1972.
7. J. Craven and F. S. Wald, Hospice Care for Dying Patients, *American Journal of Nursing,* October, 1975.
8. M. Shepard, *Someone You Love is Dying,* Crown Publishers, Inc., New York, 1975.
9. D. R. Longo and K. Sarr, Hospital Care for the Terminally Ill: A Model Program, *Hospital Progress, 59,* January-June, 1978.
10. E. Kubler-Ross, *On Death and Dying,* Macmillan Publishing Co., Inc., New York, 1969.
11. A. W. Reed, Anticipatory Grief Work, B. Schoenberg, et al., (eds.), *Anticipatory Grief,* Columbia University Press, New York, 1974.
12. R. A. Kalish, Dying and Preparing for Death: A View of Families, H. Feifel, (ed.), *New Meanings of Death,* McGraw-Hill Book Co., New York, 1977.
13. L. Pincus, *Death and the Family,* Random House, Inc., New York, 1974.
14. E. Kubler-Ross, *Death: The Final Stage of Growth,* Prentice-Hall, Inc., 1975.

In spite of their best intentions, people who work with the dying and the grieving often forget that there are vast differences among cultural groups in terms of relevant attitudes, values, expectations, roles, rituals, ceremonies, and so forth. This is especially true when we view the value systems of communities that are far distant from our own and at a different point in their economic development, but it is also true of communities within the United States.

There is a tendency to look at cultural and subcultural differences without seeing them in context. Thus, on one occasion many years ago, when I was in Nepal, I saw a body being cremated on a small structure right next to a river bank. People were walking past the burning body without apparent concern. Since I am not familiar with the ceremonies of the Nepalese nor of the values that underlie their ceremonies, the public nature of the cremation struck me as very strange. Later I came to understand the context in which it occurred.

The chapters in this section reflect the approaches of groups both within the United States and outside this country. In the former instance, I have selected ethnic communities that are not familiar to most readers, but we have previously (Chapter Two) provided an overview of attitudes and values of Black, Hispanic, and Japanese Americans. There are, of course, groups within groups within groups, and there are individual differences within all groups, but we can at least make a start here. In the latter instance, I have included one chapter that deals with an issue across societies and another that deals with one society across several issues.

PART 3
Death and Grief in a
Cross-Cultural Context

The myths and legends of the origins of life are familiar: God created Adam and then created Eve from Adam's rib; in the ocean was an immense egg, which eventually reached the shore and was hatched and from it came the human race.

The myths and legends of the origins of death are much less familiar, and we often forget that Adam and Eve were not only the first to have life but—except for Abel—the first to experience death. It would appear, from the chapter that follows, that each culture describes a period of time when there was life without death, since each myth—like the myth of the Garden of Eden—proposes that people already existed before death was brought to them. And while the people of the Judaic-Christian world are cursed with death because of their own misdeeds or sins that were under their control, the myths of other cultures describe death as much more benign and, in some instances, as arising from circumstances over which the people of these cultures had no control.

It might be worth pondering, however, whether the myth a given culture has of the origin of death establishes a tone that continues to influence that culture's view of death. "The wages of sin is death." There seems little doubt that in our cultural system, death is viewed as resulting from the misdeeds of a woman who sinned against God's commandment. Although the more recent Christian view of life after death proposes both union with God and personal reunion, we are still left with the Old Testament's admonitions. Thus death is presented as both punishment and reward in our theological history, leading to a dichotomy that is still very much present in our thought and feeling processes. "The good die young" and "God took him/her young because He wanted him/her near" are familiar comments. "He/She must have been loved by God to have lived to such a ripe old age" is also familiar.

CHAPTER
12

How Death
Came to Mankind:
Myths and Legends

Alain Corcos
and
Lawrence Krupka

The mythology of people who have lived or are still living in less complex societies suggests that death was, or still is, an accidental event; and that if it had not been for this accident humans would be immortal. These myths and legends indicate that death originated as a mistake, a misdeed, greed, or perhaps a joke on someone's part, and that we would all live happily forever if it had not been for such an unfortunate blunder. The reasons why death came to humankind vary from society to society, but major themes are evident, and often these themes are intermixed in the same tale. In this chapter, we shall examine these major themes.

THE FORBIDDEN FRUIT THEME

Disobedience to divine commandments results in the death of the offenders and their descendants. This is the theme of the forbidden fruit, which is common in both Africa and the South Sea Islands. The theme explains the origin of death, and not the origin of sin as in the Book of Genesis. The Wachagga, who live in the Kilimanjaro region, believe that death occurs from eating a certain tree's

165

fruit that their supreme god had forbidden [1]. A Hawaiian legend relates how Kumuhomua, the first man, lived with his wife, Lalohomua, in the land of Kane, until she met the Great Seabird. She was induced to eat the sacred apples of Kane, after which she and her husband were carried away by the Great Seabird into the jungle. There they were lost, and death became the penalty for both Kumuhomua and his wife for not obeying God's command [2]. The same idea is found among the pygmies. Death came to early people in the form of a cataclysm that obliterated the ancestral paradise at the source of the Nile. The following is one of the many versions [3]. God, who made the first man and woman, allowed them to live forever as long as they would not pick the fruit of the tahu tree. When the woman became big with child, she decided that she must eat that fruit and no other. Her husband warned her that God has forbidden them to eat the fruit, but the woman argued, cried, and screamed. In desperation, in order to quiet his wife, the husband picked the fruit, and they ate it together and hid its peel under leaves. God sent a wind to blow the leaves away and saw the peel. He became angry and punished both by condemning them to hard work, illness, and ultimate death. He punished the woman even more for initiating the problem and gave her the pain of childbirth. In Australia, some tribes have a slight variation on the forbidden fruit theme. Death is blamed on women who have gone to a forbidden hollow tree containing a bee's nest, searching for honey. A huge bat, the spirit of death, was released from the tree, and the bat roamed the world, providing death to all it could touch with its wings [4].

THE DELAYED OR GARBLED MESSAGE THEME

This theme centers upon the decision about whether God would allow his creation, humankind, to have immortality or death. Having made a decision, God sent a messenger to humankind. Unfortunately, while enroute, something happened to the messenger, and a second messenger had to be sent. The messages, however, were not the same, were misunderstood, or were changed by malice. The message that prevailed was that people must eventually die. A great number of variations of the myth exist. Animals are the usual messengers and include the lizard, chameleon, salamander, millipede, hare, or some kind of bird [5].

The legends of the Akamba of East Africa illustrate the messenger theme [6]. God had intended to endow his creation, humankind, with immortality, and chose the chameleon, slow but reliable, to convey this important message. The chameleon set off, but took the matter lightly, stopping now and then to catch flies. He finally arrived and began to give the message. In the meantime God had changed his mind and had sent a swift flying weaver bird with a new message. As the chameleon stood stammering, the bird quickly conveyed the new message, and humankind became mortal.

In another version, from the Amazalu of South Africa, the weaver bird is replaced by the Big Lizard [7]. In this tale, the first human beings emerged from the Marsh of Reeds and God sent a chameleon to them with the message that "Man will die, but he will rise again." The chameleon loitered on the way, eating fruit. Impatient, God sent the Big Lizard with a new message, "Man will die and rot." The Big Lizard with its swift gait soon overpassed the chameleon and delivered the death message. The chameleon finally arrived, but it was too late. Humankind had already accepted the message of the Big Lizard and death had become part of life.

In the two myths just described, the chameleon was chosen by God as the messenger of immortality. In the following legend from the Ba Wenda of Northern Transvaal [8], the chameleon has become the messenger of death.

> The Creator sent a millipede to go quickly to tell the people of the world that they would never die. On the way to deliver its message the millipede saw a tutulwa tree and feeling hungry, it wasted time eating the fruit. Meanwhile the chameleon was sent to tell the people that he was the messenger of death. He arrived first and delivered the bad news. When the millipede arrived, he was too late.

Today, in many parts of Africa, chameleons are always killed, as they are believed to be the instrument which caused death and so much sorrow in the world [9].

In the following story from Southern Nigeria the messengers are the dog and the sheep [10]. The legend relates how the Creator of men, women, and animals felt sorry whenever anyone died. Therefore he sent his head messenger, a dog, to tell all the people that whenever one died, the body was to be left on the ground, and covered with wood ashes, and after twenty-four hours it would regain life. Unfortunately, the dog went to sleep after a meal and forgot the Creator's message. When the dog did not return the Creator sent a sheep. The sheep, however, garbled the message and told the people to bury their dead. In the meantime, the dog remembered his mission, ran into town and gave the people the correct message. The people would not believe him since they had already heard the Creator's word from the sheep. For this reason, dogs are disliked and all dead bodies are buried. A similar story is told among the Ashanti of West Africa, but the dog as a messenger has been replaced by a goat [11].

Another messenger theme involving the moon as a deity is popular among the Hottentots and Bushmen [9]. Here we find the moon sending a hare to the people with a message indicating that humans will come back to life after death, in the same manner as the cyclic phases of the moon. Here again the hare distorts the message. When the hare came back, the moon found that the message given by the hare to the people was wrong. The moon struck the hare on the mouth, giving it a harelip. The hare has been running ever since. In defending itself, the hare scratched the moon, giving it its familiar spots.

In a variation of the above myth from the Dagomba of Toyoland [12], mankind's message to God is misinterpreted. The myth states that in olden times people did not die but passed their entire lives as slaves. They became weary of eternal bondage and sent a dog to God begging him to end their servitude. The dog stopped on the way and the message was carried on to God by a goat, who transformed it. The new message stated that people were tired of being slaves and now wanted to die. God agreed, and refused to change his mind, in spite of the dog's plea that this was not the people's wish.

THE MOLTING ANIMAL THEME

The origin of death in some societies is attributed to animals, in particular the lizard. Why is this so? Myths relate how the lizard and the snake cast off their skins periodically and are thought to renew youth, whereas people cannot and thus grow old and die.

The tales explain how jealousy arose between humans and those animals able to shed their skins. According to the folklore of the Guiana Indians [13], people also once had the power to undergo ecdysis for eternity, but had lost this power when God had observed them behaving badly. God took away their everlasting life and bestowed it upon those animals that we know as having the ability to molt. The Samoans tell the story of how this power was given to crustaceans [14]. The gods held a council to decide the fate of humans. One of the gods said,

> Bring men and let them cast their skin, and when they die, let them be turned into shellfish or to a coconut leaf torch which when shaken in the wind blazes on again.

However, another god, called Pasy, rose up and said,

> Bring men and let them be like the candle nut torch which once out cannot be blown up again. Let the shellfish change their skin, but let men die.

While the gods debated, a heavy rain came. As the gods ran for shelter they cried out, "Let it be according to the council of Pasy." Since that day people have died, but the shellfish casts off its skin.

The Amman of Indochina have the following myth concerning the origin of death [15]:

> God loved mankind but hated snakes and wished to kill them. So he sent a messenger from heaven to earth with the message that when men reached old age, they should change their skins and live forever, but when

the snakes grow old, they must die. The messenger delivered the right message, but unfortunately for man there happened to be a brood of snakes within hearing, and when they heard the doom pronounced on their kind they fell into a fury and said to the messenger to repeat the message but say exactly the contrary or they would bite him. That frightened the messenger who did what the snakes told him to say. That is why all the creatures are now subject to death except the snake, who when old, casts its skin and lives forever.

A legend similar to the above is known by the Melanesians [16], with one difference. In this case the messenger, either through blunder or malice, reversed the message. People had to die and the snakes lived forever.

According to the Mbang of the Cameroon [17], all animals met in council. The lizard suggested that once people died they should never rise from the dead again. The other animals agreed. Death came to humankind, and humans hate lizards to this day.

The toad is blamed for bringing death to humans in a Bantu legend [18]. In this tale, in the beginning death did not exist. Humankind slowly aged and was rejuvenated by God at a particular time. One day an old woman died and God ordered the toad to carry the woman's body away from the village. A toad nearby requested the job. The toad placed the corpse on his shoulders and attempted to cross a ditch, but the grass was wet and the toad slipped. God became very angry and wanted to kill the toad, but the toad hid in the mud. The woman's body slipped into the bottom of the water, and ever since every human being has had to fall in the ditch. Death had come to the world. The Nandi of East Africa believe death came to humankind because of the evil of a dog that was not treated properly [19]. The Wa-Sanniah, also of East Africa believe it came because of the evil powers of a lizard for no reason at all [20], and the Fijans believe it came because of the evil of a rat [21]. The Fijan myth is as follows:

> Once upon a time the moon contended that man should be like her. As she grows old, disappears, and comes in sight again, so men should grow old, vanish for a while, and then return to life. But the rat who was a Fijan god would not hear of it and today humans die like rats.

THE MOON THEME

Many death myths, like the Fijan tale, use the moon as an image of death and resurrection. As the moon wanes and waxes, perhaps people could also be immortal, dying only to rise again. Although the moon is a better image of death and resurrection than the skin-shedding reptiles who are also known occasionally to die at human hands, the moon is less commonly found in myths than are reptiles. The Votjobaluk of South Eastern Australia believe that at one time all animals were once men and women [22]. When one would die, the moon would say, "Get up, you" and the person would come to life again. One day, an old man said, "Let them remain dead." Since then nobody has ever come back to life except for the moon, which still continues to do so. A Kulin myth from Victoria states that moon wished to give old people water so that they would return to life after dying, but the "bronze-winged" pigeon would not agree [22]. The Dalabon at the other end of the continent relate a similar myth.

> The wallaby was married to the black-nosed python and the moon to the red-bellied water snake. The two men disputed as to whose urine their wives should drink. The wallaby wanted them to drink his, but the moon insisted that his be drunk instead. Eventually the women chose the wallaby's and that is why death is final. Had the moon's urine been chosen, people would have grown old and died, but like the moon would have returned.

The Rembarranga, neighbors of the Dalabon, have a similar myth in which a native cat is substituted for the wallaby as the moon's opponent [23].

THE BANANA AS THE IMAGE OF MORTALITY

If the waxing and waning of the new moon and the skin-shedding of snakes, lizards, and shellfish are emblems of immortality, the banana, which dies once it has produced fruit, is a symbol of mortality, and is commonly found in the folklores of the Pacific. The natives of Mias, an island off the coast of Sumatra [23], say that when the earth was created a certain being was sent by God from heaven to put the final touches to the work of creation. During this work the messenger was to fast for a month. However, after great hunger he ate some bananas. The choice of food was unfortunate, for if he had only eaten river crabs instead, people would be able to cast off their skins as crabs do and would live forever.

Another myth focusing on the banana is known by the natives of Poso of Central Celebes [23]. In the beginning, when the sky was very near the earth, the creator would lower his gifts to humans at the end of a rope. One day he lowered a stone, but the first father and mother refused to accept it and asked for something else. The creator complied and lowered a banana instead, which the first parent accepted. Then God spoke, "Because you have chosen the banana, your life shall be like its life. When the banana tree has offspring, the parent stem dies. So you shall die, and your children shall step in your place. Had you chosen the stone, your life would have been like the life of the stone, changeless and immortal." The first parents mourned over their fatal choice but it was too late.

THE OVERPOPULATION THEME

The idea that death was necessary to prevent there being too many people on earth is prevalent in American Indian folklore. The Cherokee believe that the creators had intended for people to live forever [24]. One of their gods, the sun, after passing over all the people, told the people on the earth that there wasn't enough room for everyone and that they had better die! The sun's daughter, who was on earth, was bitten by a snake and died. The sun changed his mind and said that man might live forever. He bad the people to fetch his daughter's spirit and place it in a box, and not to open the box until they arrived at the spot where his daughter had died. The people, moved by curiosity, opened the box too soon, and the spirit of death flew away. Since than all people have died. The story is similar among the Lipan Apache indians [25], but the sun is replaced by the Raven. Similar tales can be found for the Shalisman tribes [26], the Picarella Apaches [27], and the Mandan Sioux [28]. In the latter case the raven is replaced by a frog. For the Modocs of North America death came to humans also because of overpopulation [29]. In this tale, the daughter of the Indians' hero, Kumokums, died because he had decided that people should leave the earth forever after they die. Kumokums traveled to the Land of the Dead and asked its chief to give him back his daughter. He was told that he could bring his daughter back home as long as he never looked back. Kumokums disobeyed and his daughter, who was following, was turned into a pile of bones which eventually disappeared. Thus, death remained on earth.

The overpopulation theme for the origin of death also exists in Asia. The Bahmars of Vietnam have a myth which relates how in the beginning all people, when they died, would be buried at the foot of the Long Blo tree [30]. After a while they would rise from the dead as full grown men and women. The earth became very overpopulated. It became so crowded that a certain lizard could not take his walks without somebody stepping on his tail. This annoyed the lizard so that he suggested to the gravediggers that they ought to bury the dead at the foot of the Long Knung trees. The hint was taken, and from that day the dead have not come back to life again. The Long Blo tree was the tree of life, while the Long Knung tree was the tree of death.

According to the Melanesians of the Banks Islands [31], death came to earth in order to facilitate a more equitable distribution of property. Death used to live underground in a place called Panoi. People on earth changed their skins like snakes and had eternal youth. A practical inconvenience of immortality was that property never changed hands even though the population grew. The old monopolized everything. To remedy this problem, death was induced to emerge from the lower world.

The Mentras in the jungles of the Malay Peninsula explained the origins of death using a combination of the themes already presented [32, 33]. In this myth, individuals never died, but simply grew thin at the waning of the moon and then grew fat again as the moon became full. Population grew to an alarming extent. A son brought this to the attention of his father and asked what should be done. He replied that it would be best to leave things as they were. The man's second son responded that he would rather die like a banana, leaving offspring behind. The question was finally submitted to the Lord of the Underworld, who decided in favor of death. Today men cease to renew their youth like the moon, dying instead like the banana.

MISCELLANEOUS MYTHS

Many of the aforementioned myths blame the coming of death on the disobedience of divine commandments. Other myths relate the etiology of death to a specific ancestor who has misbehaved. For example, the Tiwi blame the loss of eternal life on the unfaithfulness of a woman [34]. Purukupali, a legendary hero, had a wife named Bima and an infant son. One day she was seduced by Tjapara, who persuaded her to leave her child in the shade of a tree while she slipped away with him. Bima returned late one day from her lover to find that her son had died from exposure to the sun, the shade having shifted in her absence. When Purukupali learned of this he drove Bima away and declared henceforth death would come to all in the world. Tjapara promised to restore the child to life in three days if he could have the body, but Purukupali ignored his pleas. Both men fought and hurt each other. Purukupali walked backwards into the sea with his child's body, and Tjapara rose in the sky and became the moon.

In the following myth, attributed to the Ba Ila, the onset of death is blamed on human's selfishness [35]. In the beginning, man descended from above accompanied by his mother, wife, mother-in-law, cattle, goats, and dog. Sometime later the man's mother-in-law died, and the wife said to her husband, "Let us go and bring back my mother. She must not be allowed to leave us like this." The husband responded, "Oh, it is alright. She will turn up on her own accord." After a while the man's dog died and he said to his wife, "Let us go and bring back my dog," but the woman refused saying, "You wish to go fetch your dog, but my mother went away and has not returned and you would not go fetch her." Then the man's mother died. Again the same story was repeated as with the dog. And that is why when people die they do not come back.

The Gouro of the Ivory Coast explain that death came to humans because of greed [36]. At one time people lived forever. An old man named Tara had ten goats, ten wives, and ten children, and was therefore very rich, but he was not charitable and never gave anything to anyone in the village. One day Tara became annoyed from the noise of his goats, wives, and children, and took his favorite wife and went into the bush and built a hut. Ga, a mythical being who lived in the bush, discovered the hut and killed both Tara and his wife. One of Tara's sons looked for his father and discovered the corpse. He returned home, but Ga had seen him, and followed him back to the village and began to kill people. That is why men and women now die.

The Balolo of the Upper Congo have another myth explaining the origin of death by stressing greed [37]. One day while man was working in the forest, a little man with two bundles, one large and one small, approached and asked him which bundle he would have. The large one contained knives, mirrors, cloth, etc., and the small one contained immortal life. The man said that he could not choose by himself and went to town to seek help in making the decision. While he was gone, some women arrived, and the choice was left to them. They tried the knives, wrapped themselves in cloth, and admired themselves in the mirrors, and then chose the big bundle. The little man picked up the small bundle and vanished. Today the people often say, "If those women had only chosen the small bundle, we would not be dying." A similar story exists among the Wemba of Northern Rhodesia [38].

The origin of death has also been attributed to a practical joke in the legend held by the Chingpaws of Upper Burma [39]. Apparently an old man pretended to be dead in the ancient days when nobody really died. However, the sun, who had the threads of human lives in his hand, detected the fraud, and in anger cut short the threads of life of the practical joker. Since then everyone else has died.

The Polynesians [40] and the Maoris [7] have an unusual explanation for the origin of death. Tane, the child of Father Sky, left the earth for a while. In his absence two of his nephews came down from the heavens. Their visit brought disastrous results to humanity. Tane's wife, the first woman, was curious to know where she had come from. Tane, who had created her, had always skillfully evaded her questions. She asked the two nephews, who told her that she was in reality a daughter of Tane. The first woman was filled with horror to find that her father was also her husband, and so she fled with her daughters. Tane returned to find his wife gone. By sniffing the wind he knew the direction his wife was going, and by hurrying he caught up with her. They argued, but he could not convince her to return. She told him, "You go back and rear our children and I will proceed and drag them down to me." Thus humankind has been brought to the abode of the Goddess of Death ever since, in spite of the efforts of Maui (the devine hero) who tried to conquer death.

The inhabitants of southeastern Madagascar blame the origin of death on God's jealousy of his own daughter [41]. The myth is as follows. In the beginning, God had created all things except man. He had a daughter, Vava, the earth, who enjoyed making little men out of clay. There were a lot of them since Vava enjoyed making them. One day, God visited his daughter and became interested in her toys. He blew life into them. They multiplied and became numerous, since death did not exist. They worked very hard, and Vava became very rich. God saw how rich Vava was and asked her to give him half the people. She refused and God became angry. He took away the breath of life that he had given to mankind. Vava became sad, and from that day death has come to people and earth still retains the bodies of her clay dolls.

For the Konos of the African region of Nzerekore death originated because of the wrath of a father [42]. A long time ago lived an old man called Sa, who had a wife and daughter. One day, a young man named Atlantaqua came to visit them, but criticized Sa for having built a house without vegetation or light. He offered to make their home more hospitable. Soon, he fell in love with Sa's daughter. Sa rejected the union, and Atlantaqua and Sa's daughter eloped. They had seven boys and seven girls. Sa remained angry and told his son-in-law, "You have taken away my daughter, though I treated you well. I have no children any more. From now on, you will offer yours to me every time I'll ask. I will choose them and they will obey me." Since then, by Atlantaqua's fault, death touches human populations all over the world. In this tale, death is Sa and life is Atlantaqua.

CONCLUSION

Anthropologists have obtained a great deal of information concerning the idea of death's origin from their studies. For primitive cultures everywhere, death has always been explained by means other than natural causes [43]. The various myths and legends focusing on the origin of death discussed in this paper demonstrate that death was not considered a necessity for the human species. Humans were believed to have been created initially without death. Death came into the world only because of mistakes made by messengers sent by God or by humans who refused to obey divine laws. Sometimes the origin of death was attributed to overpopulation, anger, jealousy, or selfishness of either humans or their gods. In the majority of African myths on the origin of death surveyed by Abrahamsson [44], a god or some other divine figure is typically the main character in the story and makes the final decision allowing death to enter the world. As Radin has indicated [45], nowhere can the idea be found among primitive cultures "that man himself is responsible for death as he is in the Old Testament."

There seems to be much similarity between the myths on the origin of death despite their origination from distant parts of the world. D'Alviella, as told by Abramsson [44], has rejected the idea of cultural connections between the various primitive groups espousing the tales, and attributes the similarities to the basic manner in which the human mind functions in all people.

Interestingly, under normal conditions, primitive peoples actually have more opportunities to observe people dying then does civilized man. For sophisticated, technologically complex societies, death usually occurs away from home under the sterile and sanitary conditions of the hospital and nursing home. It is rare for individuals, especially children [46], to experience first hand the death of a human. Nevertheless, primitive people were and still are incapable of drawing from their observations, and rely on legend and myth to fill the void which our own Baconian science and mechanism now fill. Myths discussing the origin of death often "assume a sacral character, and describe the original paradisiac state and its termination." [44] A myth has been defined as any part of the universe as seen from the point of view of primitive man [47]. Malinowski states that the myth is "a living reality, believed to have once happened, in primeval times, and continuing to influence the world and human destinies." [48] On the other hand, the myth may have simply lost its original sacred character and survives today as a narrative, its sole objective to entertain and amuse [44]. Landsberg has stressed that "consciousness of death goes hand in hand with human individualization, with the establishment of single individualities." [49] As long as the life of the clan in a primitive society was important, the most essential characteristic was the place primitive people held in it. Another necessary condition for the recognition of how death occurs was the emergence of logical reasoning [49]. Thus, from the many observations primitive people could make, in general, they failed to deduce that all humans eventually die from natural, rather than supernatural, causes. Learning of the inevitability of death is only the first stage of civilized humanity's discovery of death. The last stage of people's discovery of death may be the realization that death is total annihilation [50]. Legends and myths on the origin of death help maintain the structure of those prescientific societies using them. They account in a reasonable fashion for death continuing on the earth. Finally, they provide a basis from which the laws for the continuance of life and culture are to be dervied [44].

REFERENCES

1. W. R. Dawson, *The Beginnings, Egypt and Assyria*, Hoeber, New York, 1930.
2. M. Beckwith, *Hawaiian Mythology*, University of Hawaii Press, Honolulu, 1970.
3. J. P. Hallet and P. Pelle, *Pygmy Kitabu*, Random House, New York, 1971.
4. K. Langosh-Parker, *The Eualayi Tribe*, Archibald Constable and Company, London, 1905; also Australian Legendary Tales, Sydney, 1953.
5. B. Struck, *Das Chameleon und der Afrikanishen Mythologie*, Globus, 1953.
6. G. Lindblom, *The Akamba in British East Africa*, Archives d'Études Orientales, 1920.
7. H. Calloway, *The Religious System of the Amazalu*, Timbner and Co., London, 1870.
8. H. Stayt, *The Bevenda*, Oxford University Press, London, 1931.
9. R. Basset, *Contes populaires d'Afrique*, La Maisonneuve et Larosse, Paris, 1903.
10. E. Dayrell, *Folk Stories from Southern Nigeria*, Negro University Press, New York, 1969.
11. E. Perregaux, *Chez les Ashanti*, Neuchatel, 1906.
12. A. W. Cardinall, *Tales Told in Toyoland*, Oxford University Press, London, 1931.
13. W. Roth, An Inquiry into the Animism and Folklore of the Guiana Indians, *U.S. Bureau of Ethnology Annual Report, 30*, pp. 103-384, 1908-1909, 1915.

14. G. Brown, *Melanesians and Polynesians*, London, 1910.
15. A. Landes, *Contes et Légendes Annamites*, Excursions et Reconnaisances, No. 25, Cochinchine francaise, 1886.
16. C. Lunderman, cited by J. C. Frazer, in *Belief in Immortality and the Worship of the Dead*, 3 vols., 1913 (Reprint, 1968).
17. H. Nicod, *La vie mystérieuse de l'Afrique noire*, Libraria Payot, Lausanne, 1948.
18. P. Trilles, *L'âme du Pygmée d'Afrique, Les Editions Cerf, Paris, 1945.*
19. A. C. Hollis, *The Nandi*, Oxford, London, 1909.
20. W. B. H. Barrett, Notes on the Customs and Beliefs of the Wageriama, *Journal of the Royal Anthropological Institute, 12*, pp. 34-45, 1911.
21. T. Williams, *Fiji and the Fijans*, Second Edition, London, 1860.
22. A. W. Howitt, *The Native Tribes of South East Australia*, McMillan, London, 1904.
23. J. Frazer, *The Native Races of Africa and Madagascar*, Percy Lund Humphries and Co., Ltd., London, 1938.
24. J. Mooney, Myths of the Cherokee, *19th Annual Report of the Bureau of Ethnology, part 1*, p. 436, Washington, 1900.
25. M. Opler, Myths and Tales of the Lipian Apache Indians, *Memoirs of the American Folklore Society, 36*, pp. 1-293, 1940.
26. J. Teit, Folktales of Shalisman Tribes, *Memoirs of the American Folklore Society, 11*, pp. 1-134, 1917.
27. M. Opler, Myths and Tales of the Picarelli Apache Indians, *Memoirs of the American Folklore Society, 31*, pp. 1-45, 1928.
28. M. Beckwith, Mandan Hidasta Myths, *Memoirs of the American Folklore Society, 14*, pp. 1-80, 1920.
29. A. Marriot and C. K. Rachin, *American Indian Mythology*, New York, 1968.
30. V. Guerlach, Moeurs et Superstitions des Sauvage Bhamars, *Missions Catholiques, 19*, 1887.
31. R. H. Codrington, *The Melanasians, Studies in their Anthropology and Folklore*, HRAF Press, New Haven, 1957.
32. D. Harvey, The Mentra Traditions, *Journal of the Straight Branch of the Royal Asiatic Society, 10*, pp. 190-200, 1882.
33. N. W. Skeat and C. O. Blayden, *Pagan Races of the Malay Peninsula*, London, 1906.
34. C. P. Mountford, *The Tiwi, their Art, Myth, and Ceremony*, 1958.
35. E. Smith and A. Murray, *The Ila-Speaking Peoples of Northern Rhodesia*, 2 vols., McMillan, London, 1920.
36. L. Tauxier, *Les Gouins et les Towcouka*, Librarie Orientaliste, Paris, 1933.
37. J. Weeks, *Among Congo Cannibals*, London, 1913.
38. J. C. Scott and J. Hardiman, *Gazetteer of Upper Burma and the Shan States*, part 1, volume 1, p. 408 (s Rangoon), 1900.
39. C. Gouldberry and H. Sheane, *The Great Plateau of Northern Rhodesia*, London, 1911.
40. M. Beatti, *Tikaho Tales*, Wellington, New Zealand, 1939.
41. R. Decary, *Contes et Légendes du Sud Ouest de Madagascar*, Paris, 1964.

42. B. Hollas, *Penseés Africaines*, Textes Chosis, Paris, 1970.
43. L. Levy-Bruhl, *Primitive Mentality*, Allen and Unwin, London, 1923.
44. H. Abrahamsson, *The Origin of Death*, Studia Ethnographica Upsaliente, Vol. 3, 1951.
45. P. Radin, *The World of Primitive Man*, Schuman, New York, 1953.
46. M. H. Nagy, The Child's View of Death, in *The Meaning of Death*, H. Feifel (ed.), McGraw Hill Book Co., New York, pp. 79-98, 1965.
47. W. H. R. Rivers, The Sociological Significance of Myth, in *Studies on Mythology*, R. A. Georges (ed.), Dorsey Press, Homewood, Illinois, pp. 27-45, 1968.
48. B. Malinowski, *Magic or Science and Religion and Other Essays*, Free Press, Glencoe, Illinois, 1948.
49. P. L. Landsberg, *L'Expérience de la Mort*, Desdee de Browuer, Paris, 1933.
50. J. Choron, *Death and Western Thought*, McMillan Co., New York, 1963.

In our culture, we discuss natural deaths as resulting from illness or generally deteriorating health conditions, while other causes of death, such as suicides, accidents, or homicides, are, by implication, "unnatural deaths." Other societies make totally different kinds of distinction. For example, what we refer to as natural deaths may be viewed as deaths caused by either the sinful behavior of the dead person or by the acts of evil-wishers working through sorcerors or their own sorcery. Similarly, we describe physical death and social death, implying that social conditions may cause someone who still retains clinical life to be as though dead; other cultures also develop non-clinical definitions of death, but they differ considerably from ours. And even the more recent notion that some-one can die and be resuscitated is hardly limited to our culture; other societies are even more explicit than we are in recognizing this process.

Chapter 13 describes the definitions of death, as well as of aging, of the Kaliai, a tribal group of about 1000 persons living in New Guinea. At times the parallels to various cultures in North America seem considerable, while at other times the differences emerge most clearly. On balance, it is neither the similarities nor the differences that are important, but the ability to view constructions, or definitions, of aging and death within the broader cultural context that requires our attention.

CHAPTER
13

The Cultural Construction of Aging and Dying in a Melanesian Community

Dorothy Ayers Counts
and
David R. Counts

During the twentieth century, life expectancy has increased dramatically in the industrialized countries. Current figures show an average life expectancy of seventy-eight years for white American women [1, p. 74], seventy-six for Swedish women [2, pp. 49-50], and 77.5 for Canadian women born in 1976 [3, p. 124]. In the industrialized world, between 75 and 85 percent of us reach age sixty-five [2, p. 56] and in Canada this age group comprises 8.7 percent of the population [3, p. 134]. This situation is in contrast to the circumstances in tribal societies where only about 10 percent of the population live past the age of sixty and make up only about 3 percent of the population [2, pp. 55-56]. We in industrial societies are closing the gap between average life expectancy and the human life span (the age to which the average individual would live if there were no disease or accidents) of between eighty-five and ninety years [1, p. 3; 4, pp. 130-135], a potential that the human species reached approximately 100,000 years ago [5 (cited in 1), pp. 25-26 and 2, pp. 29-31]. We die of the degenerative diseases of old age rather than of infections, trauma, animal bites, childbirth, and childhood diseases. These and similar afflictions have been responsible for premature death for most of human history and are still the primary causes of death in most of the nonindustrial world. Most of us can expect to reach old age; most of them still cannot.

As a result of our increased life expectancy, we in the industrial societies increasingly associate death with the aging process. Death is perceived parimarily as the inevitable consequence of growing old, and the subject of aging is frequently treated with dread and avoidance [2, p. 56; 6, p. 1419]. In contrast, relatively few people in tribal societies die of the diseases characteristic of old age. As Simmons observed in 1945, in preindustrial societies death is more commonly associated with youth and vitality than with old age and decrepitude.

For these people ". . . life has been more often snuffed out suddenly than left to flicker and fade out by degrees." [7, p. 217] There is no necessary reason, therefore, for tribal people to connect death with old age or to assume its inevitability. It is entirely reasonable for them to search for an external cause to explain the deaths of their adult kin and neighbors.

Advances in medical technology are responsible for our increased life expectancy and, it is argued, for unique experiences of aging and dying as well. For example, Lofland argues that whereas death in modern society is often a prolonged affair, the dying period in premodern society is typically brief [8]. For people in this type of society, "we can quite legitimately deduce that . . . dying as well as living was mean, brutish and *short*." [8, p. 22] There are several reasons offered for this brevity. First, premodern societies commonly have a low level of medical technology. This delays diagnosis of terminal illness and prevents people from interfering with the dying process.

> The absence of medical gadgetry, the absence of a well-developed complex medical establishment, the absence of theories of living and dying that would promote attempts at "early diagnosis," the absence of bureaucratic control of large populations, all contributed to the likelihood that diseases or potentially fatal conditions could be "identified" rather late in the dying-to-death trajectory. . . . Most humans admitted to the dying category throughout human history and prehistory have probably been "sick unto death." [8, pp. 24-25]

In addition, premodern people are asserted to have a "simple definition of death," and when a person is diagnosed as dying the response is frequently for him to suicide or for his kin either to kill him or to respond to his condition with "fatalistic passivity." [8, p. 18] In contrast, modern society is characterized by:

1. a high level of medical technology;
2. early detection of disease or fatality-producing conditions;
3. a complex definition of death;
4. a high incidence of morality by chronic or degenerative disease;
5 a low incidence of fatality-producing injuries; and
6. customary curative and activist orientation toward the dying with a high value placed on the prolongation of life [8, p. 27].

Our experience with death in a village community in Papua, New Guinea suggests to us that Lofland's generalizations require modification. They are, we argue, based on overly simple assumptions about the ways in which people in nonindustrial societies diagnose illness, define death, and respond to the death of their members. We further argue that:

1. the diagnosis of illness and the criteria by which people are assigned to the category of the dying are cultural constructs that have more to do with ideology than with physiology or medical technology;

2. the contrast, that modern people have a complex definition of death while premodern definitions are simple, is a spurious one; and
3. the value that people place on the prolongation of life and their response to death has more to do with the perceived cause of death and the status of the dying person than with the society's level of medical technology.

Whether people respond to death as being "natural" may depend largely on the age status of the dying person. It appears to be common for people to accept as natural the death of some old people, but we must be very careful to distinguish between the categories of the aged. Amoss and Harrell observe:

> It is . . . nearly universally true that societies divide the category of aged into two classes. The first consists of people who are no longer fully productive economically (and who must consequently depend on others for at least a portion of their livelihood) but who are still physically and mentally able to attend to their essential daily needs. The second consists of the totally dependent. . . . There seems to be little cultural variation in the plight of the incompetent aged; they are everywhere regarded as a burden [9, pp. 3-4].

We will now turn to a brief discussion of the way in which the Lusi-Kaliai of West New Britain perceive the processes of aging and dying.

THE LUSI KALIAI

During the fifteen years between 1966 and 1981, we made four research trips to and spent about two and one-half years in northwest New Britain, Papua New Guinea. Most of our time was spent in the Kaliai village of Kandoka, one of five villages whose people speak the Lusi or Kaliai language. There are about 1,000 members of this linguistic group living along the northwest coast of the province of West New Britain. The people are horticulturalists who supplement their vegetable diet with sea food and with the flesh of birds and animals, especially wild pigs, hunted in the forest. They are ideally patrilineal, virilocal, and equalitarian, and they live in hamlets and villages of from about fifty to over three hundred people. Kandoka, with a population of 317 in 1980, is the largest village in Kaliai and the second largest one in the Kandrian-Gloucester area.

Death in Kaliai

The Lusi do not oppose life and death in the same way as do English speakers. They have no generic term for life, but oppose existence (-moro "to be") and the state of being called -mate, which may be translated as "to be dead," "to be unconscious," or "to be ruined." All living human beings are characterized by the presence of a spiritual component with two aspects: -tautau "spiritual essence" and -anunu "shadow." The Lusi do not have a simple definition of death. There are physical signs that signal when dying has occurred, but death is processual, it may begin long before the physical signs are manifest, and it is reversible. The process may begin with the social disaffiliation of the very old, a point we will return to shortly, or with the separation of an individual's spiritual component from his body. This separation of body and spirit usually occurs as the result of the actions of a sorcerer, or of a nonhuman spirit creature, and is manifest in any one of a number of physical illnesses. The Lusi are prepared to diagnose as potentially terminal any fever or internal pain or sickness that does not respond readily to treatment, either by traditional healers or personnel at the Kaliai medical clinic. We know of people whose dying took place over a period of up to three months; some of these recovered while others did not.

The death of a young person or an active elder is always considered to be premature death, to adopt the terminology of Fries and Crapo [1], and is always vigorously resisted. In all cases of which we are aware, the prematurely dying person himself made the decision that his illness was terminal. His subsequent activities—moving onto the beach under a tent or temporary shelter, sending for distant friends and kin to come and say farewell and settle accounts—and the response of his relatives made the dying person's condition a matter of public knowledge and community concern. Once the diagnosis of a terminal state has been made, relatives and friends vigorously seek to establish the identity of the causal agent and to effect a cure. They may travel for miles to engage the services of a healer or to negotiate with a sorcerer, and they may carry the dying person to medical help, to be given either by a healer or by a physician at the hospital in the town of Kimbe, 150 kilometers to the east.

In Kaliai the completion of the dying process usually begins with unconsciousness or "partial death" and moves on to "true" or "complete" death. This process is reversible. A dying person may return to life at any time, including after he is truly or completely dead. We know of a number of people of all ages who are considered to have died and returned to life, including two men for whom mourning ceremonies had already begun. Three of these persons, who are thought to have returned from death, reported being turned back from the world of the dead because it was not yet time for them to stay.

The dying process is well advanced if the person's breath smells of death (an odor that is also referred to as being salty or sweet), if he stares without blinking or shame into another person's face, if he is very restless, and if he loses bladder control. Death is complete when breathing stops, when heart beat ceases, and when the eyes or mouth open (the spiritual component leaves through the eyes or mouth, or occasionally, the anus). The corpse is usually uncovered for public viewing until it begins to bloat. Then it is wrapped in pandanas mats. Our consultants advised us that the dead body usually becomes tight and rigid within several hours, but sometimes this does not occur and occasionally people are buried whose limbs and body remain flexible. Adults are usually buried between twenty-four and thirty-six hours after death is complete.

The Lusi seem to think that death may be a natural occurrence—without human or spirit causal agents—for very young infants and for some very old adults. It is neither natural nor inevitable for people between these two age categories, and people assume that there is an agent (usually a sorcerer) involved in any serious, potentially fatal injury or disease, or death [10-12]. As one villager observed wistfully after he had named seven local sorcerers: "If we could only get rid of these men I think we'd have no more death."

Old Age in Kaliai

Lusi may respond quite differently to the death of an elderly person. There are two categories of old people in Kaliai, the elder and the decrepit (*taurai*). An individual enters the stage of elder when his parents have died or become dependent, and after the birth of his first grandchild. An elder, literally in Lusi a "big man" or "big woman," is at the peak of power and authority. Elders are responsible to and dependent on no one else and they have authority over and responsibility for the behavior of their dependents. Their ability to do strenuous and demanding physical labor begins to diminish, but this is compensated for by the help of others. Younger relatives are expected to do the heavier work involved in gardening and housebuilding. It is, indeed, a point of good manners and respect that no younger adult should sit by and permit an elder to carry a heavy burden or do truly strenuous work. The degree to which an elder is respected and obeyed depends both on his reputation for hard work, knowledge, and economic acumen acquired during early adult life and on his level of participation in community life. An elder is at the height of his powers, but not all elders are authoritative and well respected. People do not expect a man or woman who was foolish, lazy, stingy, or dishonest as a younger adult to become wise, active, generous, and honest as an elder.

There is ambiguity in the status of elder. The Kaliai share with other New Guinea people [13-16] the notion that the reproduction of human life and society is accomplished at the cost of the life of the older generation. The waxing strength and knowledge of young adults is literally at the expense of the waning capability and mental acuity of their parents. People specifically attribute the weakness of the very old to the fact that their vitality has been expended into their children. Embedded in the enjoyment of heightened authority, respect, and responsibility is the knowledge that prestige and faculties will soon decline and the fear that one's knowledge will be lost. Therefore, an elder is obliged to pass on knowledge, especially secret knowledge, to others so that it will not be lost with his death. He should also defer to the judgment of younger kin so that when the elder's strength and abilities are spent, others will be capable of taking responsibility. Our consultants observed that after a person becomes a grandparent, the risks of making enemies and becoming a sorcery victim that are the occupational hazards of community leadership become increasingly oppressive. It is then that a person begins to think with longing of a peaceful old age and begins withdrawing from competitive activities. So, it is

when a person is at the climax of his influence and authority that the process
of social disengagement is likely to begin.

When a person is classified as an elder, people begin to look for and to note the
physical changes of old age. These include dry, slack skin; white hair; loss of teeth;
failing eyesight; and mental decline including forgetfulness, inability to concentrate for long periods of time, and the condition called *vuovuo*. This term refers to
a state of mental incapacity, often combined with physical dependence, that is
characteristic of the very young and the very old. A person who is decrepit, inac-
tive, and dependent because of advanced age and who is *vuovuo* is said to be *taurai*.
The transition from the status of elder to that of *taurai* is not a function of chronological age, nor is it necessarily coincident with the death of a spouse or the failure
to maintain a domestic household. The *taurai* has ceased to act as a full social being.
Such aged people are excluded from active social responsibility. Decrepit old
people remain in the village, often cared for by children who provide them with
firewood, water, and food. Their deaths—like those of very young children—are
matters of concern and grief only to their close kin. The relatives of a *taurai* consider his death to be the inevitable and ultimate conclusion of the process of aging
and deterioration that is first noted when a person becomes an elder. In one sense,
the process of death—of social death through disaffiliation—has already begun for
the *taurai*. This process was given formal recognition by the children of a still-living
but aged leader who in 1981 began the cycle of mortuary ceremonies for their
father, ceremonies that usually honor an important person after his death. The old
man expressed ambivalence about his position. On the one hand he cooperated in
the mortuary ritual and danced with the masked ancestor figures who had come
to honor him. But he also bitterly protested his exclusion from the planning of his
grandson's initiation, and he continued to try to direct the proceedings even
though younger kin ignored his advice and gently led him away.

Death from old age is recognized, but is still relatively rare among the people
of Kaliai. When it does happen, the dying person's kin do not seek an external
cause or attempt to assign culpability for the death. Instead the family gathers
near to talk with the dying person and to hear his bones break one by one.
Finally the backbone breaks, the dying person crumples, and he is wrapped in
pandanas mats and soon buried.

AGING AND DEATH RECONSIDERED

We now return to and develop the points made briefly at the beginning of this
chapter.

Cultural Constructs

The criteria by which illness is diagnosed and people are assigned to the category
of the dying are cultural constructs that have more to do with ideology than with
physiology or medical technology. This is, or should be, a truism in anthropology;

certainly there are a number of classic anthropological studies that develop this point for people throughout the world, for example, in the Philippines [17], in Africa [18, 19], and in Papua New Guinea [20, 21]. As we have observed, the Lusi-Kaliai consider that a person has entered the dying category when he has an injury or illness that does not respond quickly to treatment. A dying person publicly acknowledges his condition by moving to a tent or temporary shelter outside his home. The time that a person spends in the dying state is not necessarily brief. He may remain in this condition, conscious and capable of interacting with those around him for days, weeks, or even months. He may even eventually recover. But while he is in this condition, he is involved in a process that, if not interrupted, will result in the permanent separation of his spiritual component, and his body will suffer true, complete death.

Definition of Death

The contrast between simple and complex definitions of death is a spurious one. Lofland argues that modern definitions of death are complex because modern technology has made "the complex issue of whether a brain is still functioning" rather than the "fairly simple issues of whether a body is breathing or a heart beating" to be the basis for the final diagnosis of death [8, p. 32]. The annals of the New York Academy of Science conference on brain death held in 1977 demonstrate clearly that in our society the definition of death is indeed a complex matter [22]. But it is complex because ultimately it is a matter of ideology and culture, not of technology. For instance, there is disagreement about whether the concept of brain death includes cognitive death [23]; concern is expressed about whether there is "a religious concept of brain death" [24]; various experts discuss death as being a matter of legal definition [25-27], a technical, moral, and ethical problem [28], and a matter of policy and concept [29]. One expert notes that there are historically four criteria for death: the irreversible loss of the soul, the irreversible loss of the flow of "vital" body fluids, the irreversible loss of bodily integration, and the irreversible loss of consciousness or capacity for special interaction [29, p. 308]. Furthermore, the observations that the final test of whether death has occurred is time [23, p. 4], and that the only certain signs of death are the appearance of rigor mortis [28, p. 422; 30, p. 281] and the beginning of bodily decomposition, are remarkably similar to the observations made by our Lusi consultants. There is no doubt that in modern society the definition of death is a complex issue—certainly a confusing and contentious one. This complexity is exacerbated by the ability of medical practitioners to transplant organs from mostly dead bodies into those that are (mostly) still living [31, p. 59; 32, p. 78; 33, pp. 396-397; 34, p. 33]. As Morison observes, the dying process does not proceed at a uniform rate throughout the body, and it is therefore critical that physicians be able to judge the time when somatic death has progressed sufficiently to be irreversible but still incomplete, allowing still-living organs to be taken for transplant [31, p. 59].

Lofland is correct that the medical technology of premodern societies is not yet sufficiently developed to make the confusion attending organ transplants a problem for their medical practitioners. Nevertheless, the definition of death for people in those societies is a complex cultural issue. In Melanesia, for example, the concept of *-mate*, usually translated as "dead" or "death," often includes the very sick and old as well as the deceased, and is a condition that may last for years. In some Melanesian societies the emphasis is placed on social disaffiliation rather than on death as such. The seriously ill, the aged, the insane, and the person we would identify as being dead share this condition: they are disaffiliated from the society of the living [35, p. 211; 36, pp. 33-34]. The Lusi notion that death involves the separation of body and spirit is widespread in Oceania [37-41] and, with one important difference, is similar to one of the criteria of death listed by Veatch, the irreversible loss of the soul. The difference is the notion of reversibility. Some Melanesians consider sleep, illness, and death to be transformations of each other, and death becomes a reversible process with boundaries that are contextually defined rather than an absolute and irreversible state [42, p. 124; 43, p. 133; 20, p. 137]. If death is defined as irreversible loss, then after-death or out-of-body experiences such as those reported by some Kaliai are by definition impossible. "Certainly if death is the irreversible loss of function, then individuals who are still alive are not, and never have been dead" [29, p. 309]. It seems, however, that this definition of death is not unanimously accepted among modern scientists and physicians, for there is debate over whether death is reversible [44-46].

Concept of Process

The response of people to the approaching death of a relative or friend has more to do with the perceived cause of death and the status of the dying person than with the society's level of medical technology. The Lusi, like North Americans, place a high value on the prolongation of active, meaningful life and desperately attempt to avert premature death. Lofland is correct in that pre-modern people may passively accept the deaths of some categories of people or even hurry them through the dying process by neglecting the dying elderly [47, p. 116] or the critically ill [40, pp. 229-230], or by the custom of premature burial [39, p. 171; 48, p. 131]. However, it does not appear that these practices are unique to premodern societies. It is argued, for example, that the segregation and isolation of the decrepit aged in institutions in North America is similar to customs of premodern people such as those noted above in that both types of practices result in a situation in which the infirm and impaired elderly are classified and treated as though they were already among the dead [49, pp. 128-129]. We also share with premodern people the idea that some categories of seriously ill persons should be classified with the dead. One theme that ran through the conference on brain death [22, pp. 50-52] was a concern with what we might call the Karen Ann Quinlan question, the question of at what point we should set aside our complex technology and permit the disaffiliated to become the truly dead.

In conclusion, we argue that anthropological data invite modification and reevaluation of some of the generalizations advanced in the literature on aging and death. We must attend more carefully to indigenous categories of old age and to native diagnostic categories, definitions of dying, and concepts of process if we are to formulate theories that have cross-cultural validity. The facile contrast of modern versus premodern society is too simple. If we are to learn anything about ourselves from the study of other people, we must focus on our similarities as well as our differences and not assume that a difference in form necessarily implies a difference in basic attitudes or that a simple technology implies a simple ideology.

ACKNOWLEDGMENTS

An abridged version of this chapter was delivered to the May 1982 meetings of the Canadian Ethnology Society, Vancouver, British Columbia. Research was supported by the Social Science and Humanities Research Council of Canada, The University of Waterloo, McMaster University, and the University of Victoria. Our research was also made possible by the people of West New Britain, especially of Kandoka village, to whom we owe our thanks.

REFERENCES

1. J. F. Fries and L. Crapo, *Vitality and Aging: Implications of the Rectangular Curve,* W. H. Freeman, San Francisco, CA, 1981.
2. K. M. Weiss, Evolutionary Perspectives on Human Aging, in *Other Ways of Growing Old,* P. Amoss and S. Harrell (eds.), Stanford University Press, Palo Alto, CA, pp. 25-58, 1981.
3. Statistics Canada, *Canadian Year Book 1980-81: A Review of Economic, Social and Political Developments in Canada,* Ministry of Supply and Services Canada, Hull, Quebec, 1981.
4. J. F. Fries, Aging, Natural Death and the Compression of Morbidity, *The New England Journal of Medicine, 303,* pp. 130-135, 1980.
5. R. G. Cutler, Evolution of Human Longevity and the Genetic Complexity Governing Aging Rate, *Proceedings of the National Academy of Science, 72,* pp. 4664-4668, 1975.
6. O. Pollock, Shadow of Death Over Aging, *Science, 207,* p. 1419, 1980.
7. L. W. Simmons, *The Role of the Aged in Primitive Society,* Yale University Press, New Haven, CT, 1945.
8. L. N. Lofland, *The Craft of Dying: The Modern Face of Death,* Sage Publications, Beverly Hills, CA, 1978.
9. P. T. Amoss and S. Harrell, *Other Ways of Growing Old: Anthropological Perspectives,* Stanford University Press, Palo Alto, CA, 1981.
10. D. R. Counts, The Good Death in Kaliai: Preparation for Death in Western New Britain, *Omega, 7:4,* pp. 367-372, 1976-77.

11. D. A. Counts, Fighting Back is Not the Way: Suicide and the Women of Kaliai, *American Ethnologist, 7,* pp. 332-351, 1980.

12. D. R. Counts and D. A. Counts, Aspects of Dying in Northwest New Britain, *Omega, 14:2,* 101-111, 1983-84.

13. A. Gell, *Metamorphosis of the Cassowaries: Umeda Society, Language, and Ritual,* Athlone, London, and Humanities Press, NJ, 1975.

14. J. C. Goodale, Gender, Sexuality and Marriage: A Kaulong Model of Nature and Culture, in *Nature, Culture and Gender,* C. MacCormick and M. Strathern (eds.), Cambridge University Press, Cambridge, MA, pp. 119-142, 1980.

15. ————, Siblings as Spouse: The Reproduction and Replacement of Kaulong Society, in *Siblingship in Oceania: Studies in the Meaning of Kin Relations,* M. Marshall (ed.), ASAO Monograph #8, University of Michigan Press, Ann Arbor, MI, pp. 275-306, 1981.

16. R. C. Kelly, Witchcraft and Sexual Relations: An Exploration in the Social and Semantic Implications of the Structure of Belief, in *Man and Woman in the New Guinea Highlands,* P. Brown and G. Buchbinder (eds.), AAA Special Publication No. 8, pp. 36-53, Washington, DC, 1976.

17. C. O. Frake, The Diagnosis of Disease Among the Subanun of Mindanao, *American Anthropologist, 63,* pp. 113-132, 1961.

18. E. E. Evans-Pritchard, *Witchcraft, Oracles and Magic Among the Azande,* Oxford University Press, England, 1937.

19. V. Turner, *Lunda Medicine and the Treatment of Disease,* Rhodes-Livingstone Institute Papers No. 15, 1963.

20. G. Lewis, *Knowledge of Illness in a Sepik Society: A Study of the Gnau, New Guinea,* Athlone Press, London, and Humanities Press, NJ, 1975.

21. S. Lindenbaum, *Kuru Sorcery: Disease and Danger in the New Guinea Highlands,* Mayfield, Palo Alto, CA, 1979.

22. J. Korein (ed.), Brain Death: Interrelated Medical and Social Issues, *Annals of the New York Academy of Sciences, 315,* 1978.

23. ————, Preface, *Annals of the New York Academy of Sciences, 315,* pp. 1-5, 1978.

24. S. Hauerwas, Religious Concepts of Brain Death and Associated Problems, *Annals of the New York Academy of Sciences, 315,* pp. 329-336, 1978.

25. H. R. Beresford, Cognitive Death: Differential Problems and Legal Overtones, *Annals of the New York Academy of Sciences, 315,* pp. 329-336, 1978.

26. A. M. Capron, Legal Definition of Death, *Annals of the New York Academy of Sciences, 315,* pp. 349-359, 1978.

27. B. Keene, The Natural Death Act: A Well-Baby Check-up on its First Birthday, *Annals of the New York Academy of Sciences, 315,* pp. 376-390, 1978.

28. F. J. Veith, Brain Death and Organ Transplant (and Discussion), *Annals of the New York Academy of Sciences, 315,* pp. 417-441, 1978.

29. R. M. Veatch, The Definition of Death: Ethical, Philosophical, and Policy Confusion, *Annals of the New York Academy of Sciences, 315,* pp. 307-321, 1978.

30. G. Pampiglione, J. Chalony, A. Harden, and J. O'Brien, Transitory Ischemia/Anoxia in Young Children and the Prediction of Quality of Survival, *Annals of the New York Academy of Sciences, 315,* pp. 281-292, 1978.

31. R. S. Morison, Death: Process or Event?, in *Ethical Issues in Death and Dying*, R. F. Weir (ed.), Columbia University Press, NY, 1977.
32. R. Roelofs, Some Preliminary Remarks on Brain Death, *Annals of the New York Academy of Sciences*, *315*, pp. 39-44, 1978.
33. M. D. Tendler, Cessation of Brain Function: Ethical Implications in Terminal Care and Organ Transplant, *Annals of the New York Academy of Sciences*, *315*, pp. 394-397, 1978.
34. J. Korein, The Problem of Brain Death: Development and History, *Annals of the New York Academy of Sciences*, *315*, pp. 19-38, 1978.
35. W. H. R. Rivers, The Primitive Conception of Death, in *W. H. R. Rivers*, R. Slobodin (ed.), Columbia University Press, NY, pp. 207-218, 1979.
36. M. Leenhardt, *Do Kamo: Person and Myth in the Melanesian World*, translated by B. M. Gulati, University of Chicago Press, Chicago, IL, 1979.
37. E. S. C. Handy, *Polynesian Religion*, B. P. Bishop Museum Bulletin 34, Honolulu, HI, 1934.
38. P. H. Buck, (Terangi Hiroa), *Mangaian Society*, B. P. Bishop Museum Bulletin 122, Honolulu, 1934.
39. J. Van Baal, *Dema: Description and Analysis of Marind-Anim Culture (South New Guinea)*, Martinus Nijhoff, The Hague, 1966.
40. K. Heider, *The Dugum Dani: A Papuan Culture in the Highlands of West New Guinea*, Viking Fund Publications in Anthroplogy No. 49, Wenner-Gren Foundation for Anthropological Research, NY, 1970.
41. P. S. Huber, Death and Society among the Anggor of New Guinea, in *Death and Dying: Views from Many Cultures*, R. Kalish (ed.), Baywood Publishing, Farmingdale, NY, pp. 14-24, 1979.
42. F. Barth, *Ritual and Knowledge among the Baktaman of New Guinea*, Yale University Press, New Haven, CT, 1975.
43. R. Wagner, *Habu: The Innovation of Meaning in Daribi Religion*, University of Chicago Press, Chicago, IL, 1972.
44. R. A. Moody, *Life After Life*, Bantam Books, NY, 1975.
45. K. Osis and E. Haraldsson, *At the Hour of Death*, Avon Books, NY, 1977.
46. E. Kübler-Ross, *Questions and Answers on Death and Dying*, MacMillan Publishing, New York and London, 1974.
47. P. Van Arsdale, The Elderly Asmat of New Guinea, in *Other Ways of Growing Old: Anthropological Perspectives*, P. Amoss and S. Harrell (eds.), Stanford University Press, Palo Alto, CA, pp. 111-124, 1981.
48. B. M. Du Toit, *Akuna: A New Guinea Community*, A. A. Balkema, Rotterdam, 1975.
49. W. H. Watson and R. J. Maxwell (eds.), *Human Aging and Dying: A Study in Sociocultural Gerontology*, St. Martin's Press, NY, 1977.
50. R. McCormick, To Save or Let Die: The Dilemma of Modern Medicine, in *Ethical Issues in Death and Dying*, R. F. Weif (ed.), Columbia University Press, NY, pp. 173-184, 1977.
51. P. Ramsey, On (Only) Caring for the Dying, in *Ethical Issues in Death and Dying*, R. F. Weir (ed.), Columbia University Press, NY, pp. 189-225, 1977.
52. G. P. Fletcher, Prolonging Life, in *Ethical Issues in Death and Dying*, R. F. Weir (ed.), Columbia University Press, NY, pp. 226-240, 1977.

The United States and Canada are both immense nations with well over 250 million people between them. These people differ in their responses to death based on age, ethnicity, gender, and many other factors. Equally important, there are, within the boundaries of these nations, small communities that manage to retain values held over the centuries. Sometimes these communities are confined to one geographical location, but often they consist of people who are spread out in many parts of North America and whose values are strongly influenced by their cultural antecedents as well as by the more general culture around them. Orthodox Jews are one such community; the Greek Orthodox is another; the Hispanics of Northern New Mexico form a third. Chapter 14 is a brief description of death and dying in still another such community. A suggestion: rather than judging whether these people have a "better" or "worse" response to death and dying, just consider how their responses are part of their general system of cultural values.

"He Died Too Quick!"
The Process of Dying in
A Hutterian Colony*

Peter H. Stephenson

The difficulties we have in coping with terminally ill patients are profound, and they stem from many conflicts, not the least of which is the basic conflict between the desire to alleviate pain and the knowledge that only death—the avowed enemy of every health-care professional—can ultimately release the terminal patient from pain. Thus we encounter the notion that persons in pain should ideally not suffer for long. The phrase "it was sad, but really a blessing in disguise" has so often been used that we can all recognize it along with its counterparts: "It was really a good thing, he suffered so," and "it was a mercy." The ideal death for us is as painless as possible, which also implies that dying should take place quickly. The ideal death also does not result from disease but is the product of so-called "natural causes," and occurs during sleep. We are presented with a portrait of isolated persons often gripped by profound fears, attended by others (strangers rather than family) who hope that death comes swiftly and painlessly, yet whose efforts often prolong life and with it, sometimes agony.

SOME BASIC HUTTERIAN VALUES AND
BEHAVIOR RELATED TO DYING

This portrait contrasts markedly with the process of dying among the Hutterian Brethren of the prairies. For the Hutterites the ideal death is a prolonged affair. During the period of dying a person is virtually never alone, for everyone is anxious to see "the fortunate" one. Hutterites do not distinguish between "natural causes" and disease categories because "all deaths are willed by God." Eaton reports that Hutterites show little fear of death and actually

*The fieldwork reported herein was conducted with the assistance of the Canada Council for the Arts and Humanities in 1976.

embrace it as their final reward for a life filled with tribulation and pain [1].
One Hutterite, in conversation with John Hostetler, summarized Hutterian
values as follows:

> We prefer slow deaths, not sudden deaths. We want to have plenty of
> time to consider eternity and to confess and make everything right. We
> don't like to see a grownup go suddenly [2, p. 248].

When severe illness strikes and a person becomes aware that he or she is dying,
word is sent to relatives and friends, who converge on the colony where the
person resides, often traveling from several hundred miles away. Small children
and adults are brought to see the dying person, who talks with them. Often the
subject matter of conversation is religious, and the "paradise of eternal life" is
stressed. Thus the visitors and the dying person mutually socialize each other into
an awareness of mortality and toward its graceful acceptance. Hutterites have
also preserved the bedside accounts of the deaths of some of their ancestors,
whose last words are often put to verse and sung [see 3, p. 44; 4].

The degree to which the dying person becomes the focus of activity is
stunning. The dying person may request favorite hymns to be sung, food to be
prepared, or a particular person's presence. Indeed, Hostetler reports an instance
in which a terminally ill person was sung to day and night by members of several
colonies in rotation until "the steadfast soul was ushered into the banquet of the
redeemed" [2, p. 172]. The dying Hutterite adult is also aware that those
visitors who now attend him or her will remain for the wake which follows.
Special funeral buns are being cooked and a coffin will be made later by a life-
long friend. Funerals are major social events, and, as every Hutterite knows,
courting takes place at them. Perhaps the dying Hutterite's children or grandchildren will meet their wives and husbands at the funeral.

The only exception to the ideal of a long death period (several weeks at least)
is the death of a child. Following the death of a seven year old girl by scalding, it
was said "She will sure be a beautiful angel," and a mature father noted, "when
these little ones die we know they are in heaven, but we never know what will
happen to them if they grow up. I sure wish I would have died when I was a
kid" [2, p. 249].

Hutterian values and behavior surrounding death appear to reverse our own.
Hutterites prize the deaths of children while we abhor them and they regard a
long death period as desirable while we regard it as unfortunate, particularly if
it is painful. Hutterites regard the ability to keep faith even in pain as the
hallmark of a true Christian martyr. One who has lived with much pain is regarded as special. I can recall commenting on the arthritis of one man's wife and
he replied, "Yes, but she'll sure walk fine in heaven!"

Some of the relative equanimity with which Hutterites greet death stems
from their practice of adult baptism, (*beigiessungstaufe*) which they term "a
dying of the old man and a putting on of the new." Hutterites baptize only

adults, who become accountable to God for their acts after they are reborn in baptism. After baptism one joins "the body of Christ" (*corpus christi*), participates fully in religious ritual (the Lord's supper) and is allowed to marry. Children's misdeeds are already forgiven through Christ's suffering, and so children automatically go to heaven. Adults, during their death-bed period, are essentially supposed to "relive" their lives, to forgive others and to be forgiven. Since the baptized adult has already died and been reborn in ritual once before, it is clearly implied that his or her final death is nothing more than a birth to eternal life. This is expressed in the funeral hymn itself. All assembled intone the lines:

> Each man and woman surely dies,
> For we know all flesh is hay.
> First this body must decay
> If it ever is to rise
> To the glory that awaits
> All the good at heaven's gates [5].

The dying person must slowly pass into eternity because he or she has a moral obligation to self and others to die socially before actually physically expiring. Old quarrels, grudges, mistakes, etc., must be acquitted, and in this respect a person's death corresponds to baptism. At that earlier ritual or rebirth the person died to the life of the child—a life of evil—and took up responsibility. At the deathbed the same time, writ large, must occur: a life must be shed.

PAUL'S DEATH: A CASE HISTORY

> Through Christ I live,
> Death is my goal.
> To him I give
> My joyful soul. (from a Hutterian Hymn)

During the autumn of 1975, Paul Stahl, a forty-eight-year-old Hutterite man whom I knew quite well, died from lymphosarcoma [see 6]. He was kept in the hospital in Calgary for nearly two weeks and finally taken by ambulance to his home colony, about forty-five miles outside the city. He arrived in the evening but died at approximately 4:00 a.m. The reaction of several of his kin, in particular one brother, was astonishingly atypical of Hutterians when confronted with death. This death was regarded as sudden despite the intervening period of two weeks after his initial collapse, partly because he was not at home during this period and partly because neither he nor his relatives were appraised of the mortal quality of his illness at the outset. The result was that all of the grief-work normally vitiated through the anticipatory procedures described earlier in this chapter could not be accomplished. Paul's brother John grieved in a manner inconsistent with the ideal. He showed anger, sullenness, and despair. Once he wept openly and uncontrollably, although briefly. Usually the public sobs of the bereaved are highly stylized, occur only at graveside, are given only by women (from oldest to youngest in sequence), and are meant to represent the grief of the living for their own sad plight.

Whatever had needed to be said between these brothers had been left unsaid. Over 500 people came to Paul's funeral.[1] The following are excerpts from my fieldnotes dated Sunday, October 26, 1976.

> There were over twenty-five people in the apartment, John sitting with one twin (grandchildren) on each knee. David (Stahl) brought me a beer and a girl brought juice for several of the men . . . quite abruptly a large contingent of visitors from Lethbridge left . . . all visitors . . . they shook hands with the Stahls, Dave and John, and left quickly and quietly. John's comments were, "He died too quick, too quick . . . he was so alive." "Well I've seen worse cases . . . men who went out in the morning to work and who never came back!" "But, he just died too quick!"

(later)

> We walked to my car . . . and shook hands . . . myself, John, and one of his younger sons. On the way, John pointed to the cemetery on top of the hill . . . silhouetted against the sky, in the snow, one could see a fresh grave dug in the frozen ground. He turned to me with a flushed face and said to me that "discrimination is a part of ignorance, maybe your work will help that. You wouldn't believe the questions people ask about us . . . do the Hutterites have cemeteries? They even say we feed them to the pigs!" To communicate his grief he would even let out such a horrible suggestion as that!

John was more depressed than other Hutterites following more "conventional" deaths. His grief was almost palpable and lasted for months. He was a sensitive man, so his grief reaction would perhaps have been more obvious than that of another even had his brother died more appropriately. However, his reaction was not the only one I witnessed. Several others from this family also showed clear signs of anxiety; not eating or sleeping well. The entire colony seemed somewhat confused, but kin were especially upset by this death. Paul was one of the most important men in the colony and would have been a likely candidate for an important administrative post in the new "daughter colony" which was being

---

[1] The name Paul and those of his brothers in the excerpts which follow are all fictitious.

constructed. Non-kin did not react as strongly to Paul's untimely death, and so a slight schism between the two kin groups in this colony became manifest. This division would not have been obvious had Paul been able to sustain a prolonged deathbed.

Generally Hutterite colonies divide in half when their populations double [see 7, pp. 118-161]. Ultimately, when this colony divided, Paul's kin-group moved away to the new colony. I think that the constituencies of the parties in this division were partly precipitated by Paul having died "too quick."[2] The choice of the word "quick" here is interesting, especially followed by "he was so alive." This conversation was in English, but "quick" in the sense of "alive" (*leben*) means much the same thing in both German and English. When Paul died he was still too much alive—he was still among the "quick" and not yet with "the dead." He did not have time to put his social *persona* to rest. As a result, more grief was shown than is normal in Hutterite life. Since close kin demonstrated this grief while non-kin did not, a gap was exposed between the kin groups in this colony which could not be closed, and which ideally should not have been there.

SOME RECOMMENDATIONS FOR TREATING HUTTERIANS WITH TERMINAL ILLNESSES

The recognition of cultural variation in the practice of medicine is widely espoused, yet specific recommendations are only rarely made. The following suggestions are meant to be broad enough to apply to Hutterian patients in general but specific enough to refer in application to discrete cases.

1. When Hutterian patients are diagnosed as terminally ill they should be returned to their home colonies as speedily as possible following some stabilization of their conditions.

2. When possible, visitation should be allowed or even extended. I have visited Hutterian patients hospitalized where "visitor's hours" were only for two hours during the evening and limited to three persons. Given their distance from home and the time necessary to travel to them, they received almost no visitors, and their isolation was almost total. For a Hutterite who has lived totally submerged in his or her *gemeinde*, an

---

[2] A number of other incidents involving the two groups also developed shortly after this including a *pshrien*, "evil-eye" suspicion which crossed kin lines. See [3, pp. 250-261] for a discussion of "evil-eye" beliefs among the Hutterites.

hour-long visit with several people is completely inadequate. The fear of isolation experienced by terminally ill patients in our society is quite profoundly compounded for Hutterites.

3. When children die in our society our emotional reactions are very strong, yet Hutterians regard the deaths of children as "a blessing." If this is recognized by health-care workers, the subdued responses to childhood deaths which the Hutterites sometimes demonstrate will not be misinterpreted as shock or lack of affect. This does not mean that all Hutterites gladly accept the deaths of their children. They are supposed to, but the conflict of the ideal value with emotional sense of loss sometimes leads to depression of a peculiar kind. The mother and father may be depressed because their feelings are not attuned to the values, and a sense of unworthiness may pervade them. This form of depression is termed "*Anfechtung*" (temptation by the devil) by the Brethren. In either case, simple lack of affect is not an appropriate reading of the behavior.

4. Should a psychiatrist have to deal with a Hutterite suffering from depression following what for ourselves would constitute an "appropriate death," he or she should treat the patient as any other patient whose loved one has died a sudden death where anticipating grief-work had not occurred. Assuming these cases to be "abnormal grief reactions" and pursuing a therapy where the relationship between the deceased and the patient is examined would be ill-advised—that relationship has already been hyper-cathected and at least initially should be avoided.

5. Outpatient care of Hutterians who can be put on maintenance schedules wherever possible is probably a wise policy. The use of "visiting nurse" procedures may assist health planners in this situation.

ACKNOWLEDGMENTS

The author thanks the council for their support and Skip Koolage and Margie Rodman for their comments on an earlier draft presented at the Canadian Ethnology Society meetings, February 1980, in Montreal. Most especially, this chapter is dedicated to Ira Goldhar (1947-1983).

REFERENCES

1. J. W. Eaton, The Art of Aging and Dying, *Gerontologist*, *4*, pp. 94-101, 1964.

2. J. A. Hostetler, *Hutterite Society*, Johns Hopkins University Press, Baltimore, Maryland, 1974.
3. W. R. Estep, *The Anabaptist Story*, Broodman Press, Nashville, 1963.
4. P. H. Stephenson, Like a Violet Unseen: The Apotheosis of Absence in Hutterite Life, *Canadian Review of Sociology and Anthropology*, *15*:4, pp. 433-442, 1978.
5. M. Holzach, The Christian Communists of Canada, *Geo*, *1*, pp. 126-154, 1979.
6. P. H. Stephenson, The View from Rattenburg-on-the-Inn and the Ethnography of Intuition, in *Proceedings of the Canadian Ethnology Society—1979*, Doyle G. Hatt and Marie-Françoise Guédon (eds.), National Museum of Canada, Ottawa, pp. 183-189, 1981.
7. _____, "A Dying of the Old Man and a Putting On of the New: The Cybernetics of Ritual Metanoia in the Life of the Hutterian Commune," Ph.D. dissertation, University of Toronto, Microfilm: National Library of Canada, Ottawa, 1978.
8. _____, Hutterite Belief in Evil-Eye: Beyond Paranoia and Towards a General Theory of Invidia, *Culture, Medicine and Psychiatry*, *3*, pp. 247-265, 1979.

Chapter 15 is unique in many ways in the literature on death-related issues. It not only describes the death system of Black residents of a small mountain community in the United States, but it describes changes in this system over the period of 100 years, with particular emphasis on the effects of urbanization, of in- and out-migration, and of technology. The historical perspective of the chapter seems of particular interest, especially since so many people tend to view concerns involving death as though these concerns had no history. This leads to the frequent belief that "things used to be wonderful but now they are awful." Thus, the dedication of physicians, the willingness of people to talk about death, the capacity to express emotions during grief, the desire to have elderly persons die at home, the introduction of death to young children, all these have been, at one time or another, described as "not as good as it used to be." Perhaps each of these trends is for the worse, perhaps not. But we often make such judgments without indicating when the particular historical trend began, without having good historical data, without having good contemporary data, without—in fact— knowing what we are talking about.

This chapter does suggest that the present difficulties of the community residents being described are greater than earlier difficulties in many ways. However, when we understand the historical context in which changes take place, we are likely to realize that the changes are not brought about by an evil plan by by social forces having end results often not foreseen at their initiation.

CHAPTER 15

The Impact of Urbanism
on Death and Dying
among Black People
in a Rural Community
in
Middle Tennessee

Arthur C. Hill

There is general agreement among social scientists that the impact of urbanism on the lives of rural people is often great. This discussion traces the changes brought about by urbanism in the observation of rituals associated with death and dying in an obscure mountain community located in middle Tennessee.

For many years this community was accessible only by train. Although located on the "main" line of a major railroad, few trains stopped there to discharge and receive passengers. At one time the community boasted a "sizeable" black population. Two of the community's largest employers, an iron foundry and two sawmills, moved away, and most of the black people followed the departed industries. Immigration, after the departure of the foundry and the demise of the sawmills, consisted only of displaced sharecroppers and bankrupt black farmers from the countryside.

During this time of cultural isolation, no significant changes could be noted in the celebration of rituals important to the lives of the people. Available data suggest that all important rituals, including those associated with death and dying, were community-wide affairs, and directly involved the total black population.

The present research is part of a study of the history of black people in three rural counties of middle Tennessee. The study was financed by a grant from the National Foundation for the Humanities. Among the techniques used in the study are taped and oral interviews, participant observation, questionnaires, and archival research.

The community under observation and study is one of five incorporated towns located in Franklin County, Tennessee. The county is a 500 square-mile stretch in Tennessee. One-fourth of the county is mountainous, covered by a thin layer of topsoil that nourishes red oak, scrub cedars, and a few hickory and black walnut trees. The soil is ideal for fruit growing and numerous peach and apple orchards have come to dominate the countryside. The principal crops are soy beans and crimson clover. Very little cotton is grown in the county today. There is also considerable strip mining and nearly all of the coal produced is purchased by the Tennessee Valley Authority to produce electricity at its steam generating plant at Stevenson, Alabama.

The first settlers in the county were "squatters" who came over the mountains from North Carolina. The first black brought to the county was a slave who was the property of a Lewis Finch. There are black people living in the county today whose surname is Finch, which strongly suggests that they are descendants of the first black to arrive there. Other blacks in the county also have surnames derived from former slave owners. The source of these conclusions is the United States Census for the years 1820, 1830, and 1840. The census data also suggest that a substantial amount of demographic stability has been experienced in the county through the years.

The community experienced only one sizeable influx of black people. The Davis, Hicks, and Green Lumber Company brought fifty black men, women, and children to the county during the last years of the nineteenth century. With this exception, the black population has survived by natural increase only. Prior to urbanization, family relationships were characterized by close cooperation and almost complete unaminity of purpose. Widespread sharing, borrowing, and lending of material goods was anticipated and expected.

The census of 1970 revealed a black population in Franklin county of 2104 with 316 blacks living in the community being studied [1]. Long-time residents recall times when the black population was significantly greater than it is today. Two informants said their grandparents had told them about the number of slaves in the county just before the Civil War. Their statements are verified in Table 1 [2, p. 19].

The population stability is further revealed by the census data for the decades of the 1950's and 1960's. In 1950, the black population of the county was 2167; in 1960, it was 2276; and in 1970, the number had dropped to 2104 [1].

Table 1. Franklin County Population in 1860

Number of Slaveholders	561
Number of Slaves	3,551
Total Free Black Population	48
Total White Population	10,249

GEOGRAPHIC CONSIDERATIONS

The studied community lies in the south central part of the county, and is surrounded on three sides by the Cumberland Mountains. It is on the main line of the Louisville and Nashville Railroad, less than an hour's drive southeast of Chattanooga, and not more than an hour and twenty minutes north of Nashville. While the town is not directly served by the interstate freeway system, the system is reached by a well-maintained hard surface road.

Franklin County contains 353,920 acres, 8,442 of which are owned by the federal government, 11,500 of which are built up or urban. The county has 1,583 farms, the average size of which is 120.9 acres. There are two black farmowners, neither of whom earns a living from the land [3]. A number of the black residents of the community are employed at the Arnold Air Research Center in Tullahoma, eighteen miles away. The University of the South is located seven miles away at Sewanee, on top of a mountain. There is also a community college less than twenty miles away in an adjacent county.

ECONOMIC ACTIVITY IN THE COMMUNITY

Around the turn of the century, lumbering in the Cumberland Mountains provided jobs for most of the black people who did not farm, work on the railroad, or work in the coal mines. In addition to these industries there was a "furnace" that turned out pots, pans, and other kitchen utensils made of cast iron. Black people were well represented in all of these industries, and unemployment was relatively rare. There were more than half a dozen grocery and dry goods stores, two drug stores, and a bank. There were a black boarding house, a black restaurant, an Elk's Lodge, and two black churches. It is said that most of the downtown area was at one time owned by a black family [4].

SPATIAL DISTRIBUTION

From the 1890's to the present the black population of the community has lived in two widely separated enclaves. One is known as the "Bottom" and the other is called "Newtown." Most of the residents of Newtown were employed at the Louisville and Nashville Railroad's roundhouse and "coal chute." All were classified as laborers or "helpers," although most could and did move the locomotives about the yard and performed other skilled jobs.

The Bottom received its name from the creek that skirts the edge of the community on its way to the Boiling Fork River. Most of the people who live in the Bottom were brought there by the Davis, Hicks, and Green Lumber Company in the late 1880's. With few exceptions, the houses were built by the lumber company and are typical company houses in size and design. Until quite recently the affluent blacks lived near the Bottom just beyond the reach of the creek's annual spring flood.

In addition to the predominantly black settlements of Newtown and the Bottom, a few black families lived in predominantly white areas near the abandoned black school and near the all-black cemetery that is adjacent to a swamp. Affluent blacks now live on the higher elevations, much nearer the affluent white settlement just off the highway that connects the community with the county seat. The shift in residential patterns has raised considerable rivalry between those who live there and those in the area near the Bottom who hope to move there some day [5].

For generations the black cemetery was allowed to become overgrown by weeds. Considerable difficulty was experienced by nearly everyone who sought to find a grave site. Conflict generally had to be resolved by consulting older citizens who had a knowledge of cemetery boundaries and of the location of burial plots. The cemetery has never been plotted, and no one knows exactly who is buried where.

LIFE AND DEATH IN THE COMMUNITY
IN THE LATE 1880'S AND EARLY 1900'S

The Boiling Fork Creek has long been closely associated with causes of death in the community. For most of the year it was a meandering brooklet. Heavy rains during the winter months made the stream a raging torrent. Its water spilled over the banks to inundate houses, and forced black people to flee to higher grounds. When the flooding was over, large pools of water were left to stagnate, and became breeding grounds for malaria-bearing mosquitoes. The dampness and mud contributed to development of pneumonia in the winter, and the stagnant water in the spring contributed to the causes of disease and death.

Nearly every household in the Bottom could expect to experience a death between November and May. If there was even a little flooding, the rains caused cellars, cisterns, and outdoor privies to fill; runoff from the outhouses contaminated the water supply. As a result, many of the young and the old could be expected to die [6]. Prescription medicines were not trusted, and the use of patent medicines and so-called "home" remedies may have on occasion contributed to some of the deaths. The Julius Rosenwald Fund's report on Health Education in Tennessee revealed in 1937 that blacks between the ages of five and fifteen died from pulmonary diseases ten times more than whites. Death rates did not equalize until age sixty-five [6].

In addition to the number of deaths caused by diseases of various kinds, farm, foundry, coal mine, railroad, and sawmill accidents took a heavy toll on black lives. Working for the railroad, men lost arms and legs in disproportionate numbers, mainly due to carelessness and the absence of safety regulations.

RITUALS FOR DEATH AND DYING
BEFORE THE 1900'S

A seriously ill person, regardless of the nature of the ailment, was a functioning member of the family and the community for as long as possible. Although confined to bed, an ill adult was kept informed of family and community affairs. Decisions were seldom made without the input of the ailing member, and all news except the most distressing was reported. If the ailing person was a member of the Elks Lodge, or a deacon, a steward, or a trustee in one of the churches, all proceedings were reported to him. The same rituals applied to females [7].

During illness, specially designed programs of prayer, song, and testimonials were carried on both at the churches and during home visits. In most cases, the church "brothers" came to the home of the ailing to sing and offer prayer. On alternate Sundays the ritual was performed by female church officers and members [7].

The children of the community played a role in this ritual. Promptly after Sunday school, children accompanied by their Sunday school teachers went to the homes of the ailing. They repeated their Sunday school verses, and sang songs they had memorized for the occasion.

The rituals were not performed for community citizens whose behavior was considered deviant, but the deviants were not ignored. Males were visited by the ministers, deacons, and trustees, and advised to repent through prayer. Females were visited by the female officers of the church and the minister. The rituals were modified and applied to those who repented.

In nearly all cases, responsibility for the welfare of the seriously ill and his or her family evoked patterns of behavior that were anticipated and expected. No one was excused from this responsibility unless he or she was ill. Women who worked as domestics, shared with the stricken, "delicacies" borrowed from their employers. Men who worked for the railroad "borrowed" fuel from their employer in the winter and "borrowed" ice in the summer to benefit the striken family. In addition to this "borrowing," chores, such as cutting wood, washing, and ironing were shared by the members of the community. The most important function, however, was not the sharing of resources, but the practice of "sitting up" with the ill.

"Sitting up" with the ill may be best understood if viewed in the light of present day visits to the hospital or nursing home by friends and relatives of the confined. In this community, however, "sitting up" carried with it sanctions of varying degrees of severity. Probably it was an outgrowth of practices that had originated in the slave system: the "master" assigned certain slaves the responsibility of "watching" over slaves who were ill during the night hours. Important to the "sitting up" practice was the severity of the illness and the perceived possibility of recovery. If it was anticipated that the illness was terminal, "sitting up" was intensified. This was done because it was felt that the family should not be alone when death came. This suggests, too, that there were a number of community residents on hand to offer solace to the family and to perform whatever duties the occasion called for [8].

Ministers sometimes criticized harshly those of their church who failed to respond adequately to the needs of the seriously ill. This criticism was sometimes carried out from the pulpit during the course of the somewhat lengthy sermons, at other times during the weekly prayer meetings. At all times however, the message was the same: ". . . it was the will of the almighty God that the strong and able see to the needs of the sick and shut in." [7]

In the 1890's the only doctor in the community was white, and the prevailing attitude of the community's black people toward him was quite ambivalent. While they relied heavily on him, few trusted him completely. The doctor's office was in the county seat and horse and buggy transportation probably lessened his availability. In any case, the interviews did reveal that he was called upon frequently.

As has been indicated, the time between the onset of illness and death generally involved a period of "sitting up" with the ill. This was more than a ritual. It was an institutionalized process involving the commitment of the black community as they mobilized to meet the needs of a family in crisis. Need assessment was based primarily on the age, sex, and function within the family of the ailing member. The men of the community were responsible for outdoor and strength-taxing chores. The women of the community took over the housekeeping and related responsibilities. Individuals with special skills were also important. Without being asked to do so, a woman with extraordinary skills in making soups and broths would appear at the sick person's home early each day with a container of her specialty. Should the disabled individual completely recover, generous praise was given for the therapeutic qualities of the soup or broth. This praise sometimes exceeded that which was accorded the doctor for his medical skills [9].

Most families carried "sick and accident" insurance and whole life insurance. The insurance agent functioned as an informal news source. Going from house to house as he did, collecting fifteen or twenty cents for each insured member of the household, he even knew the health status of the black people in the out-lying and more remote areas. In the event of the death of someone in the black community, the insurance agent was among the first to know.

DEATH AND PREPARATION FOR
THE FUNERAL RITES

The "sitting-up" practice previously discussed was a round-the-clock operation. It intensified as death approached, with more people involved for longer periods of time. The immediate family members expected to be grief stricken to the point of incapacitation. During the interval between death and burial there were so many people moving in and around the household that it was impossible for family members to sleep. The larger society defines this interaction process as a wake; for the people of this community it was known as sitting up with the dead.

It was the responsibility of the family to select the coffin, which involved a trip to the county seat by horse and buggy, and usually consumed at least four to five hours. During this trip a suitable wreath was purchased to be attached to the house near the front door. By the time the undertaker arrived several hours later the body was bathed and dressed and ready to be placed in the coffin. The undertaker brought along his cooling board, a length of plank on which the body was placed to cool. If the body was dressed and ready the board was not used. The date of the funeral was dependent upon the arrival of the family members who lived farthest away. Few people liked to postpone the funeral for more than two days after death. Some funerals, however, were postponed up to four days, by which time the body was noticeably smelly.

Depending upon the social status of the dead, the funeral could be quite elaborate. In the case of an influential black community members, for example, a railroad worker who was a homeowner with a bank account, a lodge member, and a deacon, the funeral ritual was emotional and exhaustive. In such an instance the best funeral preacher in the area was obtained. The local preachers deferred to the preacher of greatest reputation. In these events the regular pastor acted as a master of ceremonies. He read the order of the ritual, and acknowledged and read the telegrams from those who could not attend the funeral. High status funeral rites lasted from two to three hours at the grave site, and before interment a final ritual consisting of songs and prayers consumed an additional hour. The grave was dug by the men of the community. Few of the grave diggers attended the funeral rites at the church because they were dressed in work clothing and because most of them had indulged freely in alcoholic beverages. No one liked to appear in the vicinity of the church with the smell of alcohol on his breath. The pallbearers shared the grave-filling task with the grave diggers. The number and varieties of flowers depended on the season.

Lower status funeral rites were considerably shorter and not as well attended. Few whites attended, and most who came did so just to hear the singing. There were no pews set aside for them as there would be for the funeral of an influential member of the black community. Finally, the period of post-funeral mourning was brief. It was the dead of lower social status whom parents in the community alluded to when telling ghost stories to their children.

Death rites performed in the community were an institutionalized process that involved the total black population and a considerable number of whites. Undertakers by today's standards may not have been craftsmen but they were not considered parasites whose insatiable appetite for profit was unchallenged in the situation of grief.

TECHNOLOGICAL INNOVATIONS AND THEIR IMPACT ON DEATH AND DYING

By the mid 1920's most of the hardwood trees of the Cumberland Mountains had been cut down. The sawmills were running less than full time, and unemployment in the community was high and rapidly rising. Most of the hardwood finished at the sawmills went into the manufacture of spokes for automobile wheels, and it was widely rumored that the automobile would no longer be equipped with wood-spoked wheels. The rumor proved to be well founded, as auto makers cancelled their contracts with the lumber company. One night both sawmills mysteriously burned. Shortly afterwards the company passed out of existence [10].

The great migration from south to north that had begun during the first World War had not affected the community because there had been available jobs. With the sawmills gone, the pull of northern industry began to have an impact on the black people of the community. They went in ever increasing numbers to Chicago, Cleveland, Columbus, Dayton, and Detroit. This migration had a lasting impact on the lives of the migrants, and on those left behind. Those who moved were largely male, in their prime working years, and statistically they were the ones least likely to die. Those left behind were older and nearer to the end of their lives. To return home for the funeral of a loved one or relative was a desire and a duty, which was accomplished at whatever sacrifice or cost. The impact of outside exposure on the way funeral rites were celebrated was also important.

One of the most important technological innovations that came to the community during the decade of the 1920's was hard surfaced roads. With an improved network of roads, a few black people purchased automobiles. Equally important was the introduction of taxicab service. The taxicab made a variety of services available to community residents that had previously been denied them. These included visits to the black doctor and to the segregated hospital on top of the mountain.

It was during the 1920's also that the undertaker died. Almost immediately his struggling enterprise was taken over by an energetic and ambitious young black minister. It has been said that the financial backing of this minister was provided by a native of the county, himself a minister who had migrated to Nashville. The Nashville minister had not only achieved a reputation as an outstanding preacher, but had become the leading black funeral director in the city [11].

In the county, the young minister brought in a trained mortician, replaced the horsedrawn hearse with a motor driven vehicle, and added a funeral car to transport the deceased's family to and from the church and cemetery. A telephone was installed in his home and his wife assumed the role of receptionist. While no other black people in the community owned a telephone at the time, it was possible to make a phone call by going to the central office or to the home of a white and placing a call from there [11].

The funeral director/preacher blanketed the county with another innovation, known as the "Burial Association." This was a form of insurance that anyone could purchase by paying an initiation fee of $10 and monthy dues of $1. This new form of insurance guaranteed even the county's poorest a respectable burial. For twenty-five cents a week one could get a coffin, a shroud, and the use of the funeral car at the time of burial. The payment was painless enough and the policy could be paid up in ten years. The Burial Association was an instant success, as nearly everyone sought comfort in the knowledge that one had his or her funeral paid for and that one of life's major concerns had been put to rest [12]. Unfortunately for the subscribers, the Burial Association went bankrupt in less than five years [13].

Additional technological changes did not make their way into the county until the TVA brought inexpensive electric power. Economic changes, on the other hand, touched almost every black family in the county directly. Share-cropping dropped sharply as a way of life, due to consolidation of farm ownership as well as farm abandonment and bankruptcy by both black and white farmers. While sharecropping's death had been long overdue, it was the black sharecropper who suffered the most. Almost all black farmers and sharecroppers were forced to leave the land and to come to the stagnant communities where they literally had to beg or make application for admittance to the poor house [13].

THE IMPACT ON THE COMMUNITY OF ECONOMICAL AND TECHNOLOGICAL CHANGE

The community under study had to wait until the end of the second World War for dieselization of the railroad and the subsequent reduction of its economic base. As has been noted previously, the response of nearly all the young blacks to the closing of the lumber company was flight to the north. As soon as possible after arriving, growing numbers sent for their parents to join them "up north." While the economic and technological changes produced few manifest changes in the lives of black people, the latent functions realized in the celebration of funeral rituals produced far reaching changes.

One researcher has stated that "a black funeral in the South is like no other funeral in America." To justify this generalization the researcher added:

> . . . Usually held on a weekend—when mourners have a day off—it runs on interminably as friend after friend rises to 'testify' soulfully on behalf of the deceased. In some parts of the South, people who are not a part of the funeral procession will, nevertheless, respectfully pull over to the side of the road and park when meeting a hearse trailed by cars filled with mourners. Blacks and working-class southern whites also want to 'view' the dead, even accident victims, a challenge to the mortician's cosmetic ability. A particularly good job will bring forth quiet exclamations from passing mourners, such as, 'Oh don't he look natural!' [12]

Unquestionably, "viewing" the body was and still is widely practiced in the South. Testimonials, on the other hand, were never popular in the community, and were recalled only by the oldest citizens.

Economically, the community made sustained efforts to stave off the inevitable. The few influential whites managed to convince the less knowledgeable citizens to support a series of bond issues, the proceeds going to build a shirt manufacturing plant and a cement factory. The shirt factory proved to be a dismal failure; a failure that was doubly distasteful to black people. First, they saw their taxes increase to finance its construction, and second, only one black, a janitor, was given a job in the plant. The cement plant, on the other hand, proved to be the community's sole surviving industry [14].

Although the area was losing population, two black doctors came into it. One set up practice in the county and the other opened a hospital in an adjacent county not far away. No satisfactory explanation has been given to date for two highly competent doctors settling in what was shortly to become one of the nation's more impoverished areas. Black people rejoiced at the doctor's coming, although nearly all who died did so at home and not in the hospital. The arrival of the two doctors signalled the beginning of new procedures; among these were certification of births and deaths.

DEATH DURING THE AGE OF THE GREAT DEPRESSION

From 1930 to 1936 unemployment struck nearly every black household in the community. At one time less than a dozen black men held full time jobs [15]. The community residents recalled only one burial during the Depression. The burial was that of an elderly widower who had been a sharecropper. From the time of his wife's death many years before, he had lived alone on an abandoned farm that had been taken by the county for delinquent taxes. No one bothered to evict him, and he remained there in semi-isolation.

His death apparently was discovered too late for the community to mobilize a fund drive to bury him, and the alternative in this case was a "pauper's funeral." The old man had at one time been a deacon in the Baptist church and had lived a "good" life. His funeral was perhaps the last one held in the community where the mourners "testified" in his behalf. The "testimonials" may have been due to the absence of the regular minister; the lay preacher may have been called to preach the funeral, a task which may have been beyond his competence. Testimonials therefore filled in [15]. Respondents interviewed who remembered the funeral appeared to be more impressed by the appearance of the coffin in which the old man was buried than by the funeral rites. More than one said that the coffin was "the shiniest pine box" he or she had ever seen [15]. Some even held that a public solicitation should have been successful but available evidence does not support this supposition. The total population of the county in 1930 was 21,533, of which black people constituted 2,533. In 1955, about 1,110 families were on relief. While it is possible that black pride might have prevailed and the fund raising effort for the old man's burial may have succeeded, more realistic respondents quite frankly stated that it was time for the county to "do its duty." [16]

By 1936, the TVA program was under way and its dam building required the use of enormous quantities of cement. The cement manufacturing plant in the community began operating almost full time. The relief caseload fell to 485 families in the county [16]. Electricity was becoming available at prices the people could afford, and householders began to have their homes wired to accommodate electric refrigerators and radios. Rising expectations and black pride accounted for one of the most bizarre incidents in the community's history, centered on the death of a child and the subsequent funeral.

An unmarried mother of several children had allowed her son, about age nine, to roam about the community. Some believed the child to be retarded and therefore not responsible for his behavior. The child was a diabetic with an insatiable craving for sweets. He had been seen on numerous occasions eating from garbage cans at the rear of stores in the downtown section of the community.

The mother, unable to get a job in the community, had left the child in the care of his grandmother while she sought a job in the nearest city . The grandmother was a semi-invalid and was unable to keep up with the child. One day the child was found unconscious in an outbuilding behind one of the stores; despite the doctor's efforts the child died. A telegram was dispatched to the mother and she returned home on the first available train, bringing with her an expensive coffin and vault. The funeral rites for the child were reported to be the most elaborate the community had ever witnessed, complete with pall-bearers and a hastily organized children's choir. During the funeral ceremony the mother reportedly fainted several times.

The evening after the funeral, a special meeting was called by the officers of the church to which the mother belonged. The mother was in attendance and was called upon to explain her neglect. Citing her inability to find work in the community, she pleaded for sympathy and understanding. A vote was taken, and her membership in the church was withdrawn. As soon as possible afterwards the mother left the community and never came back. The sanctions imposed by the church through the action of its leaders are said to have been the most severe in the history of the community.

THE SECOND WORLD WAR AND AFTER

The World War II draft took from the area more than 150 men, and all but five saw service overseas [17]. Most were married and had families in their home towns, and they returned to their communities when the war ended. The impact of their exposure to other cultures was felt immediately in every aspect of social living, not excluding the rituals associated with death. For example, the black cemetery had been allowed to fall into neglect during the war. Referred to locally as the graveyard, the cemetery was a thicket of briars, sapling trees, and sunken graves covered by tangle-rooted sage grass. It was only with extreme difficulty that graves of loved ones could be found.

The veterans organized themselves, grubbed out the tree saplings, burned the sage grass, and filled the sunken graves. They also participated in church politics, attempting to overthrow the power structure of the churches. Through their efforts the Baptist minister was put on salary, tithing was made mandatory, accounting procedures were improved, and an annual financial statement was authorized and printed. Physically, both the Baptist and Methodist churches were rehabilitated and air-conditioners were installed.

While the funeral rituals were celebrated much as had been the practice through the years, some degree of professionalism could be observed. The use of commercial florists was increased; wearing of black arm bands, dark suits, and dresses, as well as the use of funeral wreaths, was discontinued.

The pomp, solemnity, and display remained much the same as before. Social status was still important, and as always, was directly related to funeral costs. Some rivalry crept into this, and although it has subsided, it is still present. The function of the funeral has not changed. The funeral rites are celebrated for sociability, religious fervor, and the reaffirmation of the social status of the deceased. Southern practices that were carried to the North by migrating black people and modified there have come back to the South and have blended with Southern traditions.

One researcher has concluded that "Southern blacks have fled to the North by the thousands, they are brought back in almost equal numbers when they die. Black youths headed North by train frequently find themselves waiting on the platform next to a newly arrived coffin." [12] In the community under study, this "one way trip" is taking place with ever increasing frequency today as the earlier migrants who have lived out their years up North are brought home to their final resting place.

Until quite recently the deceased were sent South by train with a family member or a close friend, as required by the railroad. At the destination the body was taken directly to the home of the closest relative. The funeral director was usually in charge, rather than people of the community. He busied himself doing small chores for the bereaved and often left a car and driver to be used for errands for the family. Sitting up with the dead was still practiced, and from the moment of arrival, friends and neighbors called to view the body. The same substantial quantity of food was brought in as had been in the past. In addition to the reduced roles of friends and neighbors in the funeral rites, the post World War II period was characterized by increased use of the automobile.

THE IMPACT OF THE AUTOMOBILE, THE AIRPLANE, THE TELEPHONE, AND THE FREEWAY

No effort has been made in this paper to rank the degree of impact on the celebration of funeral rites in the community related to the increased use of these innovations. Their impact has been far-reaching. The automobile came into widespread use during the 1950's. Before the decade passed nearly every family in the community either owned or had access to an automobile, and shortly thereafter more families had telephones installed.

The first noticeable effect of automobile ownership is related to the deceased who had migrated to the North and were shipped back home to be buried. Except for the accompanist on the train, family members of the deceased who lived in the North made the trip by automobile. In the days of segregation, black people could not use public accommodations in the South, and the automobile trip was made almost nonstop.

The day before departure a sufficient amount of food and water was prepared so that stops need only be made for gas. Having once arrived in the community, the car was made a part of the funeral procession. Immediately after the burial the nonstop trip back to the North was started. The previous practice of a prolonged stay and the train ride back was no longer prevalent. The flexibility of the automobile as a mode of transportation shortened the delay between death and burial, and at the same time, made it possible for more family members to attend distant funerals.

When the telephone came into widespread use it eliminated completely the need for the messenger who carried the bad news from house to house throughout the community. Telephone calls to distant relatives took the place of the telegram, and the time lag was substantially shortened. There was no need for black people to go to the central telephone office or to the home of a white to inform those at a distance of the bad news.

Since the second World War and, more importantly, since Medicare and Medicaid and the legal end of segregation, more and more black people who die in the community die either in a nursing home or in a hospital. The freeway has made it possible for black people to be more selective in their choice of hospitals. Nashville's black medical school is less than two hours away, and Chattanooga is forty minutes by ambulance. The hospital facilities in these two cities have the most modern equipment and the local facilities, by contrast, are quite primitive [18].

Nursing home facilities are in good supply and seem not to discriminate. The community does not have a black doctor, and the possibilty of a black doctor going there to practice is remote. The freeway has placed the community in easy commuting distance for those who choose to travel to Nashville or to Chattanooga for medical care, and while there is a black funeral director in the county, competitors from Chattanooga and Nashville aggressively seek business in the county.

This competition from city funeral directors has resulted in the local funeral director building a modern mortuary. The dead are no longer kept at home, and visitations are at the church or at the mortuary. Funeral programs are printed, and flowers are ordered from the florist.

Many additional changes have been effected by the widespread use of airline travel. Deaths that take place in the North frequently have a funeral ceremony in the city where death occurs. The body is then shipped South by air for burial. The members of the family accompany the dead on the same flight whenever possible. The local director meets the plane at the airport in Nashville and provides one or two cars to transport the members of the family from the city to the community. Deficiencies in family transportation are taken care of either by rentals or by friends from the local community. The practice of "sitting up" has almost disappeared. While there is much visiting with the bereaved family and huge quantities of food are still brought to the home for the family, instead of being home cooked it is more often from a nearby fast food outlet.

Last, there is less emotional display at the funeral, and the ritual is substantially shorter. The traditional black dresses and suits are no longer worn. The funeral director's crew digs the grave and graveside ceremonies are cut to a minimum. The local police provide an escort from the church to the burial place, and the family departs before the grave is covered and the funeral ritual is over. In most cases, those with planes to catch depart for Nashville in time to catch their flights back to the North on the same day of the funeral.

COST OF BURIAL IN THE COMMUNITY

Research is needed for an accurate analysis of burial cost in the community. It is believed that the cost of a burial is whatever the traffic will bear. The funeral director in the county has been, is, and will continue to be in direct competition with the city based organizations. The black population of the county is poor, and while economic well-being has not dominated entirely the decisions of those who must pay for burials, most tend to spend beyond their means. Like people in similar circumstances everywhere, there is no shopping around and no bargaining for lower prices. Many are influenced by the cost of the most recent burial and make their choices based on "how nice he or she was put away." Most of those who die today are covered by Social Security and have some kind of a burial policy as well. Social Security payments may be the minimum price on burial cost and the insurance policy may cover the upper limits; thus, an average funeral in the community now will cost about $1250 [19].

As had been noted, the far reaching impact on the community of urbanism is an ongoing process, and the migration out of the community by blacks has not been arrested. Future burials may be held in the large urban ghettos in the North with no more than a graveside ceremony in the community. Most assuredly, the trend seems to be in that direction.

REFERENCES

1. U.S. Bureau of the Census, *United States Census*, 1970.
2. W. M. Kollmorgen, *The German Swiss in Franklin County, Tennessee*, Washington, D.C., p. 19, 1937.
3. Interview with a black farm owner, December 1974.
4. Interview with a black farm owner, December 1974.
5. Interview with a black home owner, December 1974.
6. M. J. Brent and E. F. Greene, *Rural Negro Health: A Five Year Experiment in Health Education in Tennessee*, issued by the Julius Rosenwald Fund, Southern Office, Fisk University, Nashville, Tennessee, pp. 11-12, 1937.
7. Interview with the son of a retired minister, December, 1974.
8. Interview with the community's oldest citizen, Hattie Watkins, December 1974.
9. Interview with the community's folk historian, December 1974.
10. Interview with a former employee of the lumber company, March 1977.
11. Interview with a relative of the funeral director, March 1974.
12. J. Perry and E. Perry, *Face to Face: The Individual and Social Problems*, Educational Associates, Boston, Massachusetts, p. 518, 1976.
13. Interview with a former Burial Association member, March 1974.
14. Interview with the janitor, March 1974.
15. Interview with a railroad station porter who was one of the few fulltime jobholders in the community throughout the Depression, February 1973.
16. H. Ray, "An Economic, Educational, and Social Survey of Franklin County, Tennessee," unpublished master's thesis, University of Tennessee, Knoxville, Tennessee, p. 69, 1937.
17. Draft Board Records of Franklin, Lincoln, and Moore counties, Tennessee.
18. Interview with patient recently discharged from the local county hospital, December 1974.
19. Interview with an employee of the community's funeral director, April, 1976.

Among the many tens of thousands of persons in the United States and Canada who provide counseling and psychotherapy, only a very small number specialize in working with the dying and the grieving. Nonetheless, virtually every counselor and psychotherapist will find that death, dying, and grief are involved in his or her practice on innumerable occasions. For example, a family therapist learns that the tension between the husband and wife began at the time of a sudden infant death; a school counselor realizes that the student who has come for counseling has not dealt effectively with the death of his mother ten years earlier; a psychotherapist is told by her client that he has made three suicide attempts; a child is referred to the school psychologist when he begins to become troublesome in class, a situation that began just after the death of his father; a young businesswoman informs her therapist that her physician has just given her about one year before her cancer becomes incapacitating.

A couple of decades ago, death counselors didn't exist. Now a small number are in practice. Of greater importance, a couple of decades ago, there was little information available for counselors and psychotherapists who were concerned about issues related to death; now there is a great deal of information.

The question inevitably arises as to who is providing the death counseling: what are their credentials, what had they been doing prior to beginning this work, what kinds of education and training have they had. Answers are not easy, since the field is so new. However, it seems as though these individuals often have a background either in counseling or social services or in some form of health care. Most of them probably integrate the death counseling they do with their other work, for example, a hospital chaplain, a social worker in a senior center, a charge nurse at a hospice, a psychologist in private practice. Very few limit their professional roles to working only with the dying and bereaved. And since they enter this work from a variety of backgrounds, they also tend to have a variety of educational experiences. The only bond that they have is the wish to serve people who have major concerns involving death and loss. However, it can probably be assumed that they have all had either formal college courses or in-service or community-based training and educational programs focused on these issues. The matter of certification also comes up in regard to death counselors: the Forum for Death Education and Counseling, the only national organization of its kind, has been developing a program that will eventually provide a certificate for those death counselors who qualify. The extent to which this certificate, which has no legal power in the way a license does, will influence other relevant people in the community is still unknown.

PART 4
Counseling and Psychotherapy

Dying persons have always had access to the informal counseling services of the clergy, of close family members and friends, and of health professionals who were providing treatment. The more formal counseling programs that have developed recently offer something quite different. First, they offer as counselors people who have made themselves available for this specific task; second, for the most part these individuals have had some training in working with dying persons; third, the very fact that they are available for this task makes it easier to request their services; fourth, as time has gone on, the services they provide have tended to reach out to other members of the family, in addition to the dying person; fifth, there has been an increasing awareness that counseling dying persons requires more than a one-to-one talking relationship and may extend to advocacy with hospital authorities or staying with the dying person for an extended period without talking; and sixth, related to the previous statement, some counseling techniques and approaches have been developed that are specifically directed at dying persons.

Chapter 16 discusses the background of counseling with the dying, then looks at this relationship through various counseling models. It provides a useful overview of death counseling. What it doesn't do adequately, what in fact has not yet been done adequately by anyone, is to indicate the extent to which counseling dying persons "works," that is, the extent to which the person who is dying and others involved in that person's life are helped by the counseling. This will be very difficult to determine, in part because any kind of evaluation of helping programs is difficult and in part because many of the individuals who have been served are, obviously, unable to report how much help the counseling provided.

What can be begun, however, is to understand more about the counseling process and, through this understanding, to begin to offer relevant training and perhaps some supervision. At the present, we have some general ideas and a very few specific notions of counseling approaches that appear to work well with persons who are dying or grieving, but most of what we believe we know is really based primarily on the observations of the counselors themselves (hardly an objective group of people) and on our basic theories as to the nature of good counseling.

CHAPTER
16

Counseling Dying Clients

Daniel McKitrick

The use of counseling/psychotherapy with dying clients has only recently begun to gain in popularity. Kastenbaum and Aisenberg suggest several reasons why attention to death and the non-medical treatment of the dying has not paralleled the rapid growth of the mental health movement in the United States [1]. For instance, death has traditionally been the realm of other professionals such as funeral directors, physicians, and clergymen. Also, the spirit of the country has been centered around progress, optimism, and productivity, not "morbid" concern with death and the unproductive disvalued factions of the population, such as the ill and the aged. More specifically, LeShan and LeShan [2] suggest that two major reasons for clinicians' avoidance of the dying are:

1. the clinicians' own fear of death, and
2. the dying clients' inability to use counseling as a springboard to a long future of improved functioning.

Whatever the reasons for the delayed involvement of counselors and psychotherapists in working with the dying, the pubescent state of the literature reflects the delay. Very little was done before the mid-1950's, and much of the work has been done since the mid-1960's. Contributions to the literature almost exclusively have been accounts of approaches to counseling and discussions of issues on counseling dying clients. There has been almost no integration of different approaches, and even less empirical research.

The present chapter offers a critical review of methods of counseling dying clients. The main purposes of the chapter are to:

1. identify each method, pointing out possible strengths and weaknesses;
2. discuss some controversial issues in the literature as they relate to approaches;
3. integrate the approaches with each other by speculating as to which treatments might be suited best to which clients;
4. suggest directions for research on counseling dying clients.

Several possibilities exist for studying which counseling procedures might be suited best to which clients. An obvious method would begin with using traditional diagnostic terms or defense mechanisms to categorize clients. Precedence for such a scheme is suggested by research studying the dying person [3-6], which largely consists of classifying dying people into categories of psychiatric diagnosis and defense mechanisms. This scheme is further reinforced by the thesis developed by Meyer [7] that "dying and death play an important part in the development and course of the neuroses."

However, as is true for counselors in general, many counselors working with the dying vehemently oppose using diagnostic labels and defense mechanisms to categorize clients. Zinker [8], for instance, in reference to the literature on studying the dying, decries the "negative approach" to studying the dying in which the focus is "usually on psychological 'deteriorization,' 'regression,' unsatisfactory coping techniques, and psychopathology." Zinker argues for adopting a viewpoint which recognizes the possible positive aspects of dying, that considers the dying person's ability to grow and reach closure. Bard shares Zinker's bias against the negative focus of classifying dying clients with diagnostic labels and defense mechanisms [9]. He suggests that attention be given to the process by which the client tries to adapt to dying.

Similar to Bard's idea of focusing on the process of adaptation to dying is the notion of looking at the process of relating to dying. Kastenbaum and Aisenberg suggest that four of the most important ways one relates to one's dying and death are by *overcoming, participating, fearing*, and *sorrowing* [1]. Using these four ways of responding to one's dying, then, provides an alternative to using traditional diagnostic terms or defense mechanisms in order to determine which clients are best suited to which counseling approaches. These four ways of relating to one's dying and death will provide the framework within which the present chapter will review ways of counseling dying clients. No claim is made that a given client will assume only one way of relating to death. Rather, the assumption is made that at the point of entry into counseling, the client is apt to be reacting to dying in a manner characterized largely by overcoming, participating, fearing, or sorrowing.

Four limitations of the present review are that the only approaches to be considered are those:

1. used with adults,
2. used to counsel dying clients, not families or friends of dying clients,
3. originating from sources other than pastoral counseling, and
4. used for individual counseling.

OVERCOMING

Kastenbaum and Aisenberg focus on religion and one's striving for immortality as some primary ways of trying to overcome one's death [1]. However, they emphasize that "We have many individual and social strategies for getting past death. We bribe, trick, or bully him aside." Eissler [10] and Norton [11] with psychoanalytic approaches, Pattison [12] with a crisis procedure, and Schoenberg [13] with a treatment focusing on the client's feelings of loneliness and isolation offer counseling alternatives for clients who might be inclined toward overcoming their deaths. These alternatives involve the strategies of overcoming death by confronting it and/or avoiding it.

Psychoanalytic

Eissler's approach is among the earliest contributions to the literature on counseling the dying client. Working from Freudian theory, Eissler reasons that during the dying process a person's libido is drawn into the task of stopping the impending release of self destructive energies of the death instinct. This leaves no surplus of libidinal energy to maintain normal libidinal function. As a result, it is nearly impossible to produce enough libidinal energy on one's own to cope with dying.

The approach which Eissler derives from this theory differs, depending upon whether or not clients overtly acknowledge that they are dying. If clients do not acknowledge that they are dying, the counselor has two main functions. One function is to augment the clients' libidinal energy by providing external energy through appropriate displays of concern. Counselors should show their concern primarily through emoting sorrow and pity. This, says Eissler, will give the clients trust, courage, and consolation. However, counselors should avoid letting their emotions turn to grief and despair, as these emotions will burden the client. Concurrently with the first function, the counselor should show a strong conviction in the clients' immortality. It is a burden on the counselor to show these conflicting attitudes, but if it can be done, Eissler assures, it will not seem strange to clients and it will bolster their energies.

If clients do acknowledge that they are dying, Eissler, understandably, feels uncomfortable using the same tack. Instead, he suggests that counselors be flexible about their countertransference reactions to dying and let themselves identify to a degree with the client. Although the identification is partial, it must not be superficial. Indeed, it must be deep enough to make the client actually feel its existence, so that the client can make the counselor a companion on the "last leg of his sad journey."

Norton pursues Eissler's identification technique and further theorizes that the counselor is functioning to help the client defend against object loss [11]. Whereas the process of dying entails much object loss, the counselor can be one object that stays until the end. The counselor can establish a regressive relationship in which the client can rely on the counselor to always be available to provide succoring comfort to emotional and other needs.

The modes of counseling offered by Eissler and Norton, then, give clients two options for overcoming death. For clients who do not openly acknowledge that they are dying, Eissler offers the maintenance of the fantasy of being immortal, while at the same time giving the emotional support necessary to sustain the clients through the energy draining dying process. For clients who do acknowledge their dying, Eissler and Norton offer the counselor's companionship with which to forestall death's greedy consumption of all that is close and familiar to the clients.

A potential problem with Norton's approach is the immensity of counselor time and effort it would appear to entail. In fact, this is a problem with all the approaches to counseling dying clients, and perhaps is intrinsic to working with them. However, Norton's treatment seems to require an extraordinary amount of counselor time and energy, as it involves forming a regressive relationship in which the counselor is the succoring figure who must always be available to the client.

A limitation in both Norton's and Eissler's theories is that they conceptualize death and dying as bad, as things to be denied if possible. An issue in the literature on counseling dying clients involves the adoption of this view versus the view that death is a natural aspect of living and has positive as well as negative characteristics. As will be discussed later in the present review, many of the other methods of counseling the dying [12, 14, 15] put dying into a positive light, as being the end phase of life and growth.

Eissler himself seemed dissatisfied with the negative conceptualization of death and dying suggested in his theory. He proposed the future development of a philosophical view, "orthothanasia," in which death is not conceptualized as either good or bad, but simply as a reality which one can choose either to face or not to face. By facing this reality without illusions, Eissler theorized, one can enjoy enlarged inner freedom.

A strength of Eissler's and Norton's approaches is the flexibility with which they use countertransference. The role of countertransference in counseling the

the dying is another issue in the literature. The issue is whether to allow some countertransference or to avoid any involvement with countertransference. Several clinicians [9, 10, 11] advocate consciously accepted countertransference (especially countertransference of the counselor's own 1. death wishes and 2. fears of death). Counselors' defenses against death will tend to distance them enough from the client, and it is good to maintain some distance. Other clinicians speak of countertransference only to warn the counselor of its dangers [16, 17]. Through countertransference, for instance, the counselor might:

1. assume the client's tendency to deny the client is dying;
2. regress to feeling helpless like the client and try to compensate through magical solutions such as increasing or lengthening counseling sessions and giving pep talks;
3. become so fearful as to being avoiding the client.

Reactions such as these from the counselor are real dangers and should be guarded against. However, the flexible use of countertransference advocated by Eissler and Norton guards against possible pitfalls while also enabling counselors to use countertransference to their advantage.

Crisis

The overcoming response offered in Pattison's counseling theory begins as an outright counterattack against the overwhelming crush of the dying process. Pattison conceptualizes death as a crisis event characterized by being:

1. insoluble;
2. a new experience, so that in dealing with it one cannot fall back on previous experience;
3. a threat to life goals because of its abrupt onset;
4. a source of great anxiety;
5. an awakener of unresolved problems in the near and distant past.

In facing death, then, people are faced with a problem that they do not have the resources to deal with. They experience "bewilderment, confusion, indefinable anxiety, and unspecified fear," so that they are unable to break the problem into manageable parts. A counselor, however, can help the dying client to break the dying process into parts and begin to cope with the parts.

Pattison identifies the parts of the dying process as different fears, including the fears of the unknown, loneliness, loss of family and friends, loss of body, loss of self-control, loss of identity, and regression. With the concerned support and guidance of the counselor, clients can focus their energies on these various parts. Pattison lists client goals and specific counselor tasks relating to each part.

While this crisis approach begins as a kind of counterattack against dying, it ends as a means of joining with and accepting one's death. Through successfully coping with the part-aspects of dying, the client can retain dignity and self-respect and can have what Weisman and Hackett [18] call an "appropriate death." "The importance of an appropriate death," say Pattison, "is that dying is not an extraneous foreign process but rather it is a process integrated into the style, meaning and sequence of that which has gone before."

As mentioned previously, the positive light in which Pattison views death and dying, the opportunity to face and master the crisis of dying and the ultimate goal of an appropriate death, provides a contrast for the comparatively negative view of the psychoanalytic counseling approaches, where death is something to be forestalled or to be dismissed with fantasies of immortality, and the dying person is to be pitied and sorrowed after. Of course death has its negative aspects in Pattison's scheme too, as is evident in death being conceptualized as a crisis which must be overcome.

A potential problem with this treatment is the energy it might require from the dying client. One of the controversies in the literature on counseling the dying client is whether the client tends to be weakened versus energized during the dying process. Some clinicians [14, 19] suggest that the client tends to be energized. However, most clinicians say that the client is weakened either psychically [10] or both psychically and physically [15, 20]. To the extent that clients are weakened rather than energized they may have difficulty facing and overcoming all of the part-aspects of the dying process.

A strong point of the approach is that if clients indeed have the energy to confront and struggle with the dying process, their task is made more manageable when death is considered in terms of its parts rather than being considered in its overwhelming entirety. In addition, the counselor's task is made more manageable not only through the breaking down of the dying process, but also through Pattison's identification of goals for the client for each part, and his explication of specific ways in which the counselor can assist the client.

Loneliness and Isolation

Schoenberg identifies the primary need of dying clients to be that of reducing their loneliness and isolation which result from the tendency of the clients and important others to withdraw from each other in anticipation of the clients' deaths. This tendency to withdraw is a natural protection against the pain of guilt, anger, helplessness, and the like which relate to the dying process.

The most important goals of the counselor, then, are to help clients overcome their feelings of loneliness and isolation by:

1. being available to offer support and comfort, and
2. helping the clients to renew "emotional participation in life" and "to live deeply and meaningfully in spite of distressing circumstances."

Additionally, the counselor can help to resolve other emotional concomitants of the dying process. The clients with whom Schoenberg has worked usually have been referred to him because of their emotional reactions to their dying. The counselor can help the client express and resolve feelings such as fear, guilt, shame, dependency, anger, and depression by being understanding, tolerant, patient, and reassuring with the client.

A potential strength of the isolation approach is that it offers the client a means of overcoming death that is a compromise between the crisis treatment's head-on confrontation of death-related problems and the psychoanalytic method's avoidance of death-related problems. Like the crisis counseling, the loneliness and isolation approach directs the client to confront many difficult aspects of the dying process. For example, Schoenberg encourages the client to explore unrecognized or unexpressed feelings of fear, shame, guilt, anger, and the like. Also, the client may be urged to discuss fantasies related to dying in order to compare them with reality, which usually is less frightening.

The crisis approach continues its confrontation to the point of confronting the negative image of death, the alien intruder into the familiarity of life. Pattison encourages clients to incorporate dying into the positive, familiar life process. In contrast, Schoenberg retains a negative image of death, by making the major focus of his procedure the avoidance of the death-related problems of isolation and loneliness. Schoenberg's suggestion that counselors always be available and supportive in order to help clients with their loneliness and isolation is reminiscent of Norton's instruction in her psychoanalytic approach that the counselor form a regressive relationship with the client in order to help the client avoid object loss. Further evidence of Schoenberg's encouraging a regressive relationship is his suggestion that the counselor take advantage of the positive aspects of the transference relationship, especially the image of the counselor being "a magical, omnipotent figure." However, unlike Norton, Schoenberg discourages the counselor from allowing any countertransference to develop.

A potential problem with the loneliness and isolation approach is that both the client and the counselor might become confused with the mixture of avoidance and confrontation of death. The treatment is not as fully developed as most other methods of counseling dying clients, and one result is that Schoenberg offers no comprehensive theory (such as psychoanalytic theory or crisis theory) which might help one fill in the gaps that Schoenberg leaves in explaining his approach. Perhaps the most reasonable explanation of the gap concerning the confusing mixture of avoidance and confrontation of death is that the approach primarily offers a means to avoid the problem of dying, while simultaneously acknowledging that certain emotional reactions, such as anger, fear, and depression are not healthy to avoid, or simply cannot be avoided, and therefore have to be confronted.

PARTICIPATING

An alternative response to overcoming one's death is that of participating in one's death. Participating does not necessarily mean giving up. In fact most examples discussed by Kastenbaum and Aisenberg are of positive participation, such as in forming a "partnership" with death, where death is a familiar beneficent presence, or "treasuring" one's death because it is something very personal and all one's own. Still another example of participating in one's death is the tendency to comfort oneself with a strong self-interest. The dying person cuts down on the external expenditure of energy and redirects the energy inwardly. Counseling approaches which could fit well with this last example, of showing a strong self-interest, are a "patient-centered" method developed by Feigenberg [21] and a self-actualization treatment developed by Bowers, Jackson, Knight, and LeShan [14].

Patient-Centered

Feigenberg developed his approach for use with the terminally ill cancer patient. Feigenberg theorizes that the physiological deterioration involved in a fatal illness is accompanied by a growing need to protect and emphasize the dying client's individuality. In other words, the clients need to feel all right about themselves and about how they relate to the world. Often in the course of supporting and strengthening their individuality clients will identify specific needs to be met and past and present conflicts to resolve.

The key factors in Feigenberg's approach are that the counselor:

1. establish a strong therapeutic relationship characterized by trust, empathy, genuineness, and respect;
2. let the clients determine the pace and direction of counseling.

While the establishment of a relationship as described above is basic to most counseling theory, Feigenberg stresses that his approach is different from "classic" counseling/psychotherapy in several respects. One difference, of course, is the above second key factor in Feigenberg's treatment. The dying client, not the counselor, is usually the one who decides what problems will be discussed and when the discussion will occur, since during the dying process the client is typically faced with a series of unanticipated problems, such as new symptoms arising or relatives reacting strongly to the situation. Another difference, mentioned earlier in relation to Pattison's crisis approach, is that Feigenberg is of the opinion that the dying process drains the client of physiological and psychic strength, so that the dying client probably will not have the energy to devote to treatment that another client might.

Perhaps the most significant difference between this approach and classic counseling is in the aim of the treatment. The central aim of classic counseling, says Feigenberg, is the removal of the psychic symptoms and problems, through insight and subsequent working on the symptoms and problems. In contrast, a primary aim of the patient-centered treatment is directed toward meeting clients' needs to develop their individuality to the greatest possible extent. Another aim, aided to a large degree by the first aim, is to help the client relinquish emotional ties. A small amount of traditional insight-oriented symptom removal may be appropriate with a dying client in order to resolve important past and present conflicts, but proper timing and discrimination in the choice of conflicts to consider is important, says Feigenberg, in order to avoid becoming sidetracked from the more important aim of developing the client's individuality.

In the present chapter Feigenberg's approach is discussed under the "participating" reaction to death because the clients are encouraged to focus attention and energy inwardly in reacting to the dying process. However, an argument could be made for considering his treatment as a means of overcoming death. In a sense clients could be overcoming death simply by refusing to give death much attention. To the extent that clients are turning their attention inwardly, toward developing their individuality, in order to deny and avoid their deaths, the clients may be trying to overcome their deaths. Feigenberg's approach is readily amenable to such a client overcoming reaction, in that the counselor is directed to give clients freedom to direct the pace and content of counseling, and the counselor is advised to help the clients deny their deaths if the counselor's "psychological judgment" deems it appropriate. In fact, though, Feigenberg reports that only a small percentage of his clients try to deny that they are dying.

The patient-centered procedure takes an extreme stand on a controversial topic in the literature, the issue of how to include the families of the dying clients in the counseling process. Many counseling theories [15, 22] advocate using the families as valuable support resources for clients. For instance, an understanding family member who is kept updated by the counselor on the client's changing needs and problems can provide much needed comfort and support for the client. Feigenberg is willing to sacrifice the help the family can offer in the counseling process in order to meet another end. Feigenberg recommends severing contact between the counselor and families at the beginning of the counseling process. In fact he prefers using his only meeting with the families to explain to them his reasons for avoiding further contact. He feels that this break between the counselor and the families is necessary in order for the clients to feel able to speak openly. He theorizes that most of the pain in dying involves the necessity of breaking emotional ties with loved ones. The clients will feel most comfortable discussing with the counselor the problems relating to their families, Feigenberg reasons, if the clients know that the counselor has no contacts with the family.

The flexibility and open-endedness of Feigenberg's mode of counseling, where the counselor is largely non-directive and clients are expected to set the direction and pace of counseling, offers clients the opportunity to meet their specific needs in their own way. The price that the clients must pay for this opportunity is the energy they must direct inwardly toward developing their individuality. It may seem ironic that Feigenberg, who recognizes the energy drain which accompanies the dying process, has designed a treatment which requires so much effort on the clients' parts. One must keep in mind, however, that his approach is intended for terminally ill cancer patients who most likely have many of their needs met by hospital staff, and who therefore can afford to direct much of their remaining energy inwardly. Also, Feigenberg thinks that the more one develops individuality, the better able one is to meet external demands, such as found in the dying process. Therefore the energy a dying client directs inwardly toward developing individuality indirectly helps the client meet external demands.

Self-Actualization

Bowers, Jackson, Knight and LeShan [14] and, to a lesser extent, LeShan and LeShan [2], advocate helping dying clients use the dying process as a growth experience. The Bowers *et al.* theory will be emphasized in this chapter because it takes the more extreme stand of encouraging dying clients not only to grow, but also to utilize the dying process as a means to self-actualization.

As in the patient-centered treatment, the clients in the self-actualization treatment turn their focus inwardly to develop self-awareness and individuality. However, Bowers *et al.* go on from there to provide the clients with a framework within which to conceptualize death. This framework takes on an almost religious air of "a sustaining faith in the validity of life."

LeShan and LeShan theorize that fear of death is positively related to a person's sense of never having lived fully. Bowers *et al.* continue on to say that for dying clients "Help is really needed in terms of how to live, not how to die." Thus is the counselor's role described, as a teacher, guide, encourager who helps clients learn to live fully. The counselor urges clients to look for patterns and meaning in their lives. In doing this the counselor is helping the client experience "his own inner nature, his full realization of positive resources, his own potential as a person." As clients begin to understand themselves and where they fit in life, they are able to participate in the final phase of life, the dying process. They are better able to find meaning and order in the experience of dying. Their "will to live" is stimulated, so that they are better able to let their bodies react naturally to the dying process. The body has a natural healing process, says Bowers *et al.*, which is easily stymied by a person's struggling against the inevitable symptoms of death. Although the goal of counseling should not be to stave off death, clients' increased will to live and their ability to let their bodies react naturally to dying may in fact help to prolong life.

Whereas the psychoanalytic approaches to counseling the dying conceptualized dying in a negative light, the self-actualization approach takes the other extreme of conceptualizing dying in a positive light, possibly to the extreme of denying negative aspects of dying. Earlier in this chapter it was noted that Feigenberg's patient-centered treatment could be considered as helping clients to overcome, rather than participate with, death by helping clients deny and avoid facing death.

A word of caution seems called for at this point concerning the possibility of unintentionally using the self-actualization approach in a similar way, to help the dying clients deny their dying.

The self-actualization counseling mode probably could be adapted to clients' effort to overcome death even more readily than the patient-centered mode, because, while the counselor is non-directive in patient-centered counseling, the counselor in self-actualization counseling actively encourages the clients to focus on the positive aspects of the situation, to focus on living fully in the face of death. Moreover, the counselor is encouraged to become intensely involved in the clients' quests for self-actualization. Counseling, says Bowers *et al.*, should progress quickly and the counselor should promote an atmosphere of "real encounter."

Given these directives for the counselor and the almost religious zeal with which Bowers *et al.* discuss the dying clients' need for self-actualization, one could readily imagine the clients dying the the midst of their quests for self-actualization without ever having faced the fact that they are dying. This is reminiscent of an attitude intentionally taken by some medical personnel [22] in which they tacitly agree with the dying patients that they will not discuss their dying. Instead, both staff and patient fill their days with the busy hospital routine. Verwoerdt and Wilson claim this tacit agreement has two advantages for the patients:

1. it renders the dying to be less real;
2. it spares the patients having to "lose face" by having to show their "emotional pain."

However, Erickson and Hyerstay note that the unspoken agreement not to talk about death puts the dying person in a double bind not unsimilar to the bind which, theoretically, could be responsible for causing schizophrenic reactions in some people [23]. While this bind is not likely to cause schizophrenia in a dying client, it is likely to cause considerable emotional stress.

Despite the distinct possibility that the self-actualization approach could be used to help dying clients deny their deaths, it appears unlikely that Bowers *et al.* had that intention. An indication that Bowers *et al.* did not intend to encourage denial of death is their entreaty to the counselor to take advantage of the press created by the natural time limit of the clients' imminent deaths to speed along the counseling process. The use of a time limit to facilitate counseling is a familiar notion in the counseling literature. Empirical research suggests that time-limited counseling can be as effective as or more effective than much more time consuming time-unlimited counseling. While little is known as to why time-limited counseling is so effective, unconfirmed theory suggests that time limits stimulate client and counselor activity as well as client responsibility [24].

The relationship is unclear between Bowers' *et al.* suggestion to use natural time limits in order to push the client and their extreme stand that dying clients are energized rather than weakened during the dying process. Possibly Bower *et al.* feel that the clients are somehow energized by the dying process and are therefore liable to respond favorably to time pressures. The most likely explanation, based on time-limited counseling theory, is that Bowers *et al.* expect the client to become more energized, more active through the influence of the natural time limits of impending death.

FEARING

According to Kastenbaum and Aisenberg, "Fear is the psychological state that is most often mentioned when clinicians or researchers discuss responses or attitudes toward death." Kastenbaum and Aisenberg distinguish between three types of death-related fearing:

1. fearing the personal suffering and indignity of the dying process;
2. fearing punishment and rejection in the "afterlife";
3. fearing extinction.

This fearing may be expressed directly or it may be displayed in ways that are peculiar to the individual. For example, upon fearing one's death one may not express the fear, but instead may show exaggerated concern for one's family.

Fearing in one form or another is a pervasive reaction that is probably common to almost all dying people, whether their characteristic reaction to dying upon entering counseling is fearing, overcoming, participating, or sorrowing. Fortunately, fearing is a limited reaction, in that usually one can only remain intensely fearful for a short period. The initial response of fear is likely to be replaced soon by other responses. However, some people become more preoccupied with their fear than others, sometimes to the point of becoming immobilized. Two methods of counseling which seem to be used especially with clients who have intense or prolonged fearing reactions to dying are an approach using LSD along with counseling [25] and a treatment focusing on resolving client guilt conflicts through insight [26].

LSD

Fisher and his associates developed their counseling approach to use with terminally ill clients having one of two problems:

1. strong fear reactions to their impending deaths, making them management problems for medical staff;
2. severe pain, where medical and surgical treatment of pain is difficult.

The theory behind the approach is similar to that of the patient-centered and self-actualization approaches. Fisher reasons that dying is essentially an identity crisis and that it can be treated by helping the client form an appropriate identity. However, here the similarity to the patient-centered and self-actualization treatments ends. Where the patient-centered and self-actualization methods encourage clients to turn their energy inwardly and focus on themselves, Fisher encourages just the opposite, to focus attention outside of the self and to identify with something beyond the ego and the body.

Fisher states that many people identify with their bodies and their egos. For these people death means annihilation (or extinction, the fear of which Kastenbaum and Aisenberg identify as the "basic fear of death") and naturally is reacted to with emotions such as fear, panic, and anxiety. The counselor can help such a person cope with dying by helping the person to identify with something beyond the body and ego, to identify with the life process, an identification familiar in Zen Buddhism.

Fisher's approach may appear unconventional, especially considering the wide disrepute of the drug LSD. However, in its uniqueness lies its strengths. For example, an unusual yet positive aspect of Fisher's treatment is that it offers dying clients a Zen Buddhist alternative to the traditional Western view of life and death. Also, Fisher's is probably the only approach more extreme than that of Bowers *et al.* in viewing death as positive. Whereas Bowers *et al.* ideally enable the dying client to accept dying as a part of the life process, Fisher ideally enables the client to not only accept dying but also to actually welcome the new equilibrium and consciousness that death brings. Another unique aspect of Fisher's theory is that he cites a large number of empirical studies which indirectly support the use of LSD with people who are fearful and anxious about dying. Other theorists in the literature typically offer either case reports or no research evidence at all in support of their counseling approaches.

Two unconventionalities of Fisher's counseling method may especially grate against some clinicians. First, the approach is quite manipulative, in that the client is drugged and convinced to adopt a new life view during an intensive marathon session. Second, the method breaks some rules of thumb followed in most other approaches to counseling the dying. Most notably, the counselor in Fisher's treatment does not attempt to establish a strong relationship with the client. The development of a strong, trusting client/counselor relationship is generally considered crucial in counseling, both with dying clients and with other clients. Also, Fisher's approach is a one-shot treatment which breaks the rule of thumb that the counselor should see the client through the dying process, rather than ending counseling before the client has died. Fortunately, these two breaks from conventional treatment compliment one another. As long as the counselor is going to leave before the client dies, it is probably best that a strong client/counselor relationship is not formed.

Insight

Rosenthal's theory only indirectly deals with the client's fear of death. Rosenthal reasons that the primary problem for the dying client is fear of death.

Often clients will try to repress their fear, and in the process stir up many negative feelings, including anxiety and feelings of rejection and abandonment. For clients who have strong negative feelings toward themselves and their pasts, guilt is usually a problem.

According to Rosenthal, the dying clients' guilt is the counselor's primary concern. The counselor is apt to have difficulty helping with the other problem areas. For instance, some fear of death is realistic in dying clients. Also, the clients are often justified in feeling abandoned by friends, relatives, and medical staff who cannot help the clients and who feel awkward being with them. However, the counselor is well trained to help clients resolve guilt through insight counseling techniques similar to those used with neurotic clients.

Rosenthal's tack, then, is a familiar one, consisting of establishing a good rapport, trying to uncover and understand the client's past lifestyle, and trying to promote the client's insight through clarification and interpretation. To the extent that the counselor and client are successful at achieving insight and reducing guilt, they will reduce the client's fear of death, says Rosenthal. A major difference between this counseling technique and insight counseling with non-dying clients is, of course, that the goal is not to cure the dying client, but rather to provide relief and support.

This approach seems to be well adapted to treating guilt which might be precipitated by dying clients' fear of death. However, one must wonder what happens to the clients' other manifestations of fear. For clients who are not so much bothered by guilt, and even for those who are bothered by guilt, the dying process involves a multitude of mini-crises, as exemplified in Pattison's [2] breakdown of the fear of death into "part-aspects." A danger with an approach having such a narrowly defined primary goal as reducing fear through resolving guilt is that the counselor may miss (or avoid) dealing with many crises of the client who is going through the daily stresses of the dying process.

In fairness to Rosenthal, one must note that he does briefly describe some alternative treatment techniques for handling other problems of the dying client, such as getting the client involved in creative activities in order to alleviate the fear of death and to prevent the client from giving up and waiting for death.

SORROWING

In using the term "sorrowing" rather than "depression," Kastenbaum and Aisenberg try to avoid connotations of psychopathology and to emphasize that one should discriminate between "human sorrow at the thought of death" and "depressive reactions" described on the basis of traditional clinical symptomatology. Kastenbaum and Aisenberg emphasize that despite the greater attention given to fear of death in the psychological literature, sorrow in the face of death is an equally important and typical response. An example of the significance of sorrowing to the dying client is provided in a well designed study in which 102 dying hospital patients and a control group of non-dying patients were interviewed several times [27]. Results indicated that dying patients were both more anxious and more depressed than non-dying patients, however, depression was the more salient differential. Also, patients who knew they were soon to die did not necessarily feel anxiety, but they did feel sorrow.

Kastenbaum and Aisenberg conceptualize three types of death sorrow along the same lines as death fear. In other words, one might feel sorrow in regard to:

1. the dying process;
2. the afterlife;
3. extinction.

An approach which emphasizes the treatment of sorrow in one form or a another with dying clients is that developed by Goldstein and Malitz [28] which focuses on the client's "anticipatory grief." While Goldstein and Malitz do not go into much detail in explaining their approach, they do make specific recommendations for the counselor who becomes involved with dying clients. First, they suggest the counselor pick a task which will structure the contact with the client, perhaps a task such as improving client-physician relations. Second, the counselor should be aware that the chosen task is likely to have emotionally charged overt and covert meanings for clients, concerning their impending deaths. Finally, the counselor should not force talk about death, but instead should be sensitive to when clients feel the need to talk about dying.

Perhaps the major contribution of the Goldstein and Malitz approach is its taxonomy of the natural sorrowing/grief process experienced by the dying person. Goldstein and Malitz identify many losses experienced by dying persons which contribute to their grief. One is reminded of Pattison's breakdown of the fear of death into many part-aspects. In fact several things which Pattison relates to the fear of death Goldstein and Malitz also relate to sorrow over death. Where Pattison talks of the fear of loss of body, loss of self-control, regression, Goldstein and Malitz mention grief related to an increasing loss of bodily functioning and a loss of independent functioning; where Pattison discusses fear of the unknown, Goldstein and Malitz speak of sorrow related to loss of the future; where Pattison talks of fear of loneliness and fear of loss of family and friends, Goldstein and Malitz mention grief over knowledge of impending separation from loved ones and loss of human companionship because of a mutual withdrawal of dying persons and those around them. Such similarities as these support Kastenbaum's and Aisenberg's notion that the same contexts that induce fear of death (i.e., the dying process, the afterlife, and extinction) also induce sorrow over death.

While Goldstein's and Malitz's taxonomy of death-related grief is similar to Pattison's taxonomy of death-related fear, unfortunately they neither discuss their part-aspects in as much detail nor do they relate the taxonomy to a counseling approach nearly as well as does Pattison. Pattison not only describes in detail the part-aspects of the fear of death, but also he discusses goals of counseling that are related to each part-aspect, and he lists specific patterns of assistance which the counselor can employ. In contrast, Goldstein and Malitz only list the components of death-related sorrow, and roughly outline one pattern of assistance for counselors.

STAGE THEORY

Kubler-Ross's [15, 29] Stage approach, the final approach to counseling to be considered in the present paper, does not fit well within any of the four categories of major client reactions to dying, overcoming, participating, fearing, and sorrowing. Rather, the stages of dying proposed by Kubler-Ross appear to include all four categories of major client reactions to dying. Therefore, the stage approach offers an alternative to considering dying clients primarily in terms of a single major response to death.

From interviews and observations of approximately 400 terminally ill patients Kubler-Ross and her associates developed several guidelines for counseling, and concluded that clients go through a series of five distinct stages between the diagnosis of their fatal illnesses and their deaths. The shorter the length of time between diagnosis and death the more quickly a dying person tends to move through the stages. The first stage is denial, where the clients think some mistake has been made and cannot face the truth. Denial is usually dropped soon and replaced by the second stage of anger felt about the outrageous injustice of having to die. The anger is usually displaced onto others who are not dying. The clients no longer say "No, not me" as they did in the denial stage. Rather they ask "Why me?" In the third stage the clients bargain, often with God, to get an extension of life or to avoid pain, or to get some special consideration. The fourth stage is depression, where the clients no longer are bargaining by saying "Yes, it is me, but. . ." and instead are saying "Yes, me." The clients' sorrow is in reaction to the impending loss of everything and everyone they have known and loved. The fifth and last stage is one of acceptance in which the clients are not afraid and are ready to die.

The stages of dying proposed by Kubler-Ross hold an interesting relationship with Kastenbaum's and Aisenberg's four primary reactions to death. First, the reaction of overcoming can be related to Kubler-Ross's initial stages of denial and anger. The dying person in both these stages rebels by avoidance or emotional attack. Note that the behaviors of avoidance and attack are exactly the strategies proposed by the psychoanalytic and the crisis approaches, respectively, in the preceding section on "overcoming." Next, the fearing reaction to death is evident in Kubler-Ross's third stage, bargaining. Dying people are still trying to overcome their deaths in the bargaining stage but they have lost their initial rebellious air and are more in touch with the potentially painful, fearful aspects of dying. Finally, the last two Kubler-Ross stages, depression and acceptance, correspond to the remaining major reactions to death mentioned by Kastenbaum and Aisenberg, sorrowing and participating. In all, it appears that Kubler-Ross is suggesting that dying people have all four reactions to death at different points in the dying process.

In fact, while Kastenbaum and Aisenberg did not attempt systematically to relate to each other the four major eactions to death, they gave some indications that people may pass from one way of reacting to another. As discussed in the "Fearing" section of this paper, Kastenbaum and Aisenberg suggest that the usual fear reaction is typically not maintained long and is soon replaced by another response. They also suggest that while the participating response may occur at any point in the dying process, it is most likely to become evident and dominant as a person comes close to dying.

Since Kubler-Ross's theory spans all four major reactions to dying, it is not surprising to find that it includes many techniques and ideas mentioned by other counseling theories. However it is by no means a conglomeration of other approaches. Rather, Kubler-Ross has fashioned her own unique treatment, focusing on facilitating the dying clients' movement from stage to stage. She has conceptualized the dying process as a natural movement from the first through the fifth stage. A person is best off not getting stuck in an early stage. Adherence to Kubler-Ross's approach need not necessarily preclude using other approaches to counseling dying clients, in that aspects of other treatments may prove valuable for working with clients who become immobilized in one stage.

A serious drawback to the Kubler-Ross theory is the unresolved question of whether dying people really go through the stages she proposes. As previously mentioned, Kubler-Ross bases her theory on her experiences with hundreds of dying people. However, evidence reviewed by Schutz and Aderman indicates that researchers using more objective techniques than Kubler-Ross's interviews and observations found little evidence of stages [30]. The only consistent finding of researchers using behavior observations, tests and questionnaires, psychological autopsies (interdisciplinary conferences on the psycho-social context of individuals' deaths), and the like was that dying people are typically depressed shortly before death.

Recognize that objectivity does not necessarily imply accuracy. There are a number of problems with comparing Kubler-Ross's subjective results to these more objective findings. One, Kubler-Ross and her associates spent much more total time with individual clients than did other researchers. She presumably saw clients several days per week rather than once a week or considerably less often, as was the case for most of the more objective researchers. Two, partly as a result of the greater time spent with clients, Kubler-Ross and her associates may have been better able to determine the continuity of the dying process. The counseling/therapy nature of their interactions with clients also may have enabled Kubler-Ross and her associates to get a better feel for continuity than the researchers cited by Schutz and Aderman. These researchers tended to interact with clients only be means of their measurement techniques or other research-oriented interactions. Three, as a result of differences in time spent with clients and continuity observed, Kubler-Ross and her associates may have been more likely than other researchers to detect subtle complexities of the dying process.

Despite factors which may have enabled Kubler-Ross and her associates to see stages where other researchers did not, the fact remains that no objective evidence of stages is available, and if clients are to be treated as if there were stages it is important to verify the stages. Furthermore, it is important to verify that dying people move through the stages as theorized by Kubler-Ross rather than, for example, skipping stages or moving back and forth between stages. Unfortunately, researchers have yet to complete successfully many of the necessary basic steps for researching this topic, such as providing objective criteria for determining in which stage a given client is functioning.

THE OUTCOME CONTROVERSY

A controversy implicit in the literature of counseling dying clients is what goal, what outcome to aim for in counseling. For instance, should the counselor primarily be working toward providing the client with hope and support, as Eissler [10] and Norton [11] suggest, toward helping the client cope with fear and guilt, as in Rosenthal's [26] approach, or toward helping the client self-actualize, as Bowers et al. [14] advocate?

At first glance there appear to be as many goals as there are counseling approaches. However, upon further inspection the outcome controversy can be simplified and clarified by considering it in light of the controversy over how to conceptualize death. The treatments discussed in this chapter can be divided into those approaches which conceptualize death as negative and those approaches which conceptualize death as natural, as having negative and positive aspects. Correspondingly the goals of the approaches differ, depending on how death is conceptualized.

Conceptualized as totally negative, alien, and unknown, death is potentially the ultimate in terrifying experiences, for unlike most experiences in our lives death is certain to happen. Approaches which view death in this traditional Western image tend to work toward helping people deal with this terrifying experience by:

1. providing support and hope [10, 11]; or
2. coping with overwhelmingly unpleasant emotional reactions to death, including fear and guilt [26], loneliness and isolation [13], and sorrowing [28].

Many factors can support the traditional Western image of death in counseling. For instance, clients or counselors may have religious or ethnic beliefs that render them unwilling or unable to see death as anything but negative. Another variable is the time available for counseling. If death strikes suddenly or the dying process leaves the client with little energy to devote to counseling, there may be no opportunity to help the client see death as anything but negative. Yet, another example is age of the client. People dying at an early age, feeling robbed perhaps of years of life, may have a particularly hard time seeing anything positive about death.

As the death education movement grows, and more people of all ages explore their own deaths, the traditional Western negative image of death is being replaced by an image of death having both negative and positive aspects, an image of death as the natural end of life. Seen from this perspective death loses much of its alien, fearful quality and becomes a unique part of the familiar life process. Approaches which adopt this mixed image of death can be seen as working toward the general goal of integrating the dying process with the living process by:

1. helping clients gain control over the overwhelming crisis of death and face their last days of life with some dignity and composure [12];
2. allowing clients to turn their attention and energy inwardly in order to come to terms with themselves and how they relate to the world [21];
3. turning clients' attention outwardly through identifying with the process of life [25];
4. encouraging clients to use the energy available during the dying process to work on their self-actualization [14]; or
5. helping clients through the stages of natural reaction to dying to a final stage of acceptance of death [15, 29].

SUMMARY AND CONCLUSIONS

The literature on counseling dying clients is still at an early stage in which treatment approaches have been developed primarily on the basis of clinical experience, rather than empirical data. Moreover, the approaches have been devised and developed autonomously from each other and from much of the general literature on death and dying.

The need exists for an integration of the approaches with each other in terms of controversial treatment issues and relevant theory from the death and dying literature. This chapter offers an initial effort at meeting that need. Furthermore, this chapter attempts to go beyond simple integration. It attempts to analyze the approaches to dying clients in terms of which one to use with which client. The literature has tended to speak of the "dying client" in much the same way that the general counseling/psychotherapy literature until recently has tended to speak of the "clients," as if there were not a multitude of variables differentiating clients.

In this chapter clients were categorized according to the typical reactions to death noted by Kastenbaum and Aisenberg [1], overcoming, participating, fearing, and sorrowing. The fit between counseling approaches and death reaction categories was by no means perfect. Some approaches could have fit into more than one category. For instance, Pattison's [12] crisis treatment could have been considered in relation to the fearing or participating categories as well as the overcoming category. However, it was placed under overcoming because the emphasis of the approach is to face and overcome the several facets of the fear of death. Also, Bower's *et al.* [14] self-actualization theory and Feigenberg's [21] patient-centered theory could be considered as means to help clients overcome dying if counselors were to take the treatments to the extreme of encouraging clients to deny their deaths by focusing only on living and growth. Instead, Bower's *et al.* and Feigenberg's treatment were considered as ways of helping clients to participate with the dying process because the approaches do not appear to be used to encourage denial of death. The match between approaches and death reactions presented in this chapter, then, was not intended as the only possible match, but rather it was considered to be appropriate in terms of how approaches have been described in the literature.

Certainly it would be valuable to consider the match between treatments and client dimensions other than how clients relate to death and dying. In addition to the traditional "mental health" variables of nomenthology and symptomology, other pertinent variables include reasons for dying (disease, accident, old age), specific reasons clients give for wanting counseling (adjustment, support, insight), and the like.

Whatever client variable is chosen to consider in interaction with treatment, it is important that the client can be accurately identified in terms of that variable. In regard to the variable of client responses to dying, categorizing clients can be difficult. While fearing and sorrowing are familiar emotions which one could expect an experienced counselor to detect, the reactions of participating and overcoming might be relatively difficult to recognize.

Fortunately, Kastenbaum and Aisenberg [1] have presented several theoretical propostions concerning general criteria to consider in determining whether a person is apt to show a participating versus an overcoming response. According to Kastenbaum and Aisenberg, the following criteria indicate a person will seek a participating relationship versus an overcoming relationship with death:

1. the person conceptualizes death as an internal versus an external contingency;
2. the anticipated death is associated with honor, reunion, or fulfillment versus failure, defeat, or humiliation;
3. the person likes to be with other people and is sharing and cooperative versus having a strong need for achievement and independence;
4. the person has social channels for participating with death and no readily available supports to fight against death versus readily available supports to fight and no social channels for participating;

5. the person's culture or identity group stresses the value of achieving natural harmony with one's environment versus the value of struggling against the threatening forces of the environment.

Even with such criteria for categorizing clients in terms of Kastenbaum's and Aisenberg's hypothesized major reactions to death, more work is needed to determine such factors as how easily and accurately clients can be categorized, to what extent the categories exhaust major client reactions to death, and to what extent the reactions to death interact.

In addition to the need for working on matching clients with treatments, much more work is needed in other areas of the literature on counseling dying clients. Research is needed to investigate the efficacy of the different counseling approaches, as well as to study the many controversial issues, such as those mentioned in this chapter. These issues include whether the dying process can be broken down into several different stages, whether to openly discuss the client's death with the client, whether to avoid countertransference, whether the natural time limits of the dying process energize the client in counseling, whether to encourage the family to participate in counseling, whether the crisis of dying is comparable to other life crises, and what goal to aim for in counseling.

Some important variables to consider when doing research in this area can be grouped into five major categories:

1. client variables, such as age, previous adjustment, religious beliefs, reason for death, and financial, social, cultural, and psychological background;
2. helper variables such as profession, age, experience with death, and views about death;
3. situation variables such as clients' knowledge and acknowledgement that they are dying; duration of dying process, physical environment of dying process, and clients' support systems;
4. treatment variables such as counseling approach and medical treatments;
5. research assessment variables such as assessment techniques and research methodologies.

REFERENCES

1. R. Kastenbaum and R. Aisenberg, *The Psychology of Death*, Springer Publishing Co., New York, 1972.
2. L. LeShan and E. LeShan, Psychotherapy in the Patient with a Limited Life Span, *Psychiatry, 24,* p. 318, 1961.
3. R. D. Abrams and J. E. Finesinger, Guilt Reactions in Patients With Cancer, *Cancer,* 474 ff., 1953.
4. D. Cappon, The Dying, *Psychiatric Quarterly, XXXIII,* pp. 466-489, 1959.
5. L. LeShan and M. Gassman, Some Observations on Psychotherapy with Patients Suffering from Neoplastic Disease, *American Journal of Psychotherapy, XII,* pp. 723-734, 1958.

6. H. Shands, J. Finesinger, S. Cobb and R. Abrams, Psychological Mechanisms in Patients with Cancer, *Cancer, IV,* pp. 1159-1170, 1951

7. J. Meyer, *Death and Neurosis*, International Universities Press, New York, 1975.

8. J. Zinker, *Rosa lee: Motivation and the Crisis of Dying*, Lake Erie College Press, Painesville, Ohio, 1966.

9. M. Bard, Implication sof Analytic Psychotherapy with the Physically Ill, *American Journal of Psychotherapy, 13,* pp. 860-871, 1959.

10. K. Eissler, *The Psychiatrist and the Dying Patient*, International Universities Press, New York, 1955.

11. J. Norton, Treatment of a Dying Patient, *Psychoanalytic Study of the Child, 18,* pp. 541-560, 1963.

12. E. Pattison, The Experience of Dying, *American Journal of Psychotherapy, 21,* pp. 32-43, 1967.

13. B. Schoenberg, Management of the Dying Patient, B. Schoenberg, A. Carr, D. Peretz and A. Kutscher (eds.), *Loss and Grief: Psychological Management in Medical Practice*, Columbia University Press, New York, 1970.

14. M. Bowers, E. Jackson, J. Knight and L. LeShan, *Counseling the Dying*, Nelson, New York, 1964.

15. E. Kubler-Ross, Psychotherapy for the Dying Patient, *Current Psychiatric Therapies, 10,* pp. 110-117, 1970.

16. W. Cramond, Psychotherapy of the Dying Patient, *British Medical Journal, 3,* pp. 389-393, 1970.

17. R. Renneker, Countertransference Reaction to Cancer, *Psychosomatic Medicine, 19,* pp. 409-418, 1957.

18. A. Weisman and T. Hackett, Predilection to Death: Death and Dying as a Psychiatric Problem, *Psychosomatic Medicine, 23,* p. 232, 1961.

19. L. LeShan, Psychotherapy and the Dying Patient, L. Pearson (ed.), *Death and Dying*, The Press of Case Western Reserve University, Cleveland, 1969.

20. A. Weisman and R. Kastenbaum, *The* Psychological Autopsy: A Study of the Terminal Phase of Life, *Community Mental Health Journal Monograph No. 4,* Behavioral Publications, New York, 1968.

21. L. Feigenberg, Care and Understanding of the Dying; A Patient-Centered Approach, *Omega, 6,* pp. 81-94, 1975.

22. A. Verwoerdt and R. Wilson, Communication with Fatally Ill Patients, *American Journal of Nursing, 67,* pp. 2307-2309, 1967.

23. R. Erickson and B. Hyerstay, The Dying Patient and the Bouble-Bind Hypothesis, *Omega, 5,* pp. 287-298, 1974.

24. D. McKitrick, Initial Client Expectancies of Time-Limited and Time-Unlimited Psychotherapy in an Audiovisual Therapy Analogue, unpublished masters thesis, University of Maryland, 1975.

25. G. Fisher, Psychotherapy for the Dying: Principles and Illustrative Cases with Special Reference to the Use of LSD, *Omega, 1,* pp. 3-16, 1970.

26. H. Rosenthal, Psychotherapy for the Dying, *American Journal of Psychotherapy, 11,* pp. 626-633, 1957.

27. J. Hinton, The Physical and Mental Distress of the Dying, *Quarterly Journal of Medicine, 32,* pp. 1-21, 1973.

28. E. Goldstein and S. Malitz, Psychotherapy and Pharmacotherapy as Enablers in the Anticipatory Grief of a Dying Patient: A Case Study, B. Schoenberg, A. Carr, A. Kutscher, D. Peretz and I. Goldberg (eds.), *Anticipatory Grief*, Columbia University Press, New York, 1974.
29. E. Kubler-Ross, *On Death and Dying*, MacMillan, New York, 1969.
30. R. Schutz and D. Aderman, Clinical Research and the Stages of Dying, *Omega, 5*, pp. 137-143, 1974.

Although the basic principles of counseling and psychotherapy are the same, whether the counselee is facing imminent death or has no expectation of dying in the foreseeable future, the ways in which these principles are applied differ considerably. The previous chapter provided an overview of these principles. The present chapter discussed more applied issues, viewed through the eyes of the clinician rather than those of the more impersonal observer.

However, as you might assume, even the experts in these endeavors are not in full agreement. For example, some believe that the counselor/therapist should serve simultaneously as advocate for the dying person with others in his or her milieu, such as health caretakers; others assume that the role should be restricted to one of personal interaction with the dying client. Some emphasize the interpersonal relationship that develops between counselor and counselee; others give most attention to permitting the free expression of feelings; still others focus on dealing with practical problems and/or medical issues.

The authors of this chapter deserve special attention. Dr. Feigenberg, A Swedish physician, has developed a model for providing psychotherapy to seriously ill cancer patients that has gained international attention. Dr. Shneidman is best known for his extensive pioneering efforts in developing the first suicide prevention center in the world and for important writing and research on this issue. Both men are presently engaged in improving psychotherapeutic services for dying persons.

CHAPTER 17

Clinical Thanatology and Psychotherapy: Some Reflections on Caring for the Dying Person

Loma Feigenberg
and
Edwin S. Shneidman

We begin with a personal note: It struck us as an extraordinary coincidence that each of us, in our respective recent publications about our work with dying persons had, independently, written a section entitled "Is this psychotherapy?" [1, 2] The occasion of our working together for a month at the Radiumhemmet of the Karolinska Hospital provided an opportunity to discuss, in somewhat extensive fashion, this question which we both deem to be an interesting and thought-provoking one: Is what we clinical thanatologists do when we psychologically care for (or work with) a dying person properly to be called psychotherapy? Or, to put it another way: Is the close psychological relationship with a dying person one which merits special rules, understandings and concepts, to the extent that it ought even have labels of its own? That question is the issue for this exploratory joint chapter. We would like to share these thoughts with others, especially those who have had direct experience working with dying persons.

DYING AND VARIOUS VERBAL MODES OF INTERVENTION

On the face of it, commonsense tells us that doing intensive psychological work with a person who is dying *is* different from working with any other kind of person. We need to state at this point — not a digression — that by a "dying" person we mean an individual who believes, in whatever way, or knows that he or she is in an inexorable life-threatening situation and that the probabilities of surviving are extremely remote, and that there is not an "indefinite" or extended (macrotemporal) period of time in which to live. In "dying," the essential point is not the nature of the disease or injury, but the individual's emotional state of mind, the phenomenological sense that one is in an imminently life-threatening situation. Psychologically, this is what dying is.

We might, at this point, mention cancer as only one example of what we mean, simply because cancer is often identified (and confused) with dying. The facts are that approximately half the people who have cancer are cured or have remissions (and are not dying), but some are, in fact, deemed to be incurable (after all sorts of vigorous treatment regimens) and are then living "on borrowed time," knowing their days are limited, and they can be said to be "dying." Obviously, from whatever cause of disease, such individuals are in a special psychological state, marked by many problems and moods, but certainly by a discernable amount of realistic dysphoria, fear and concern.

There is a demonstrable and important difference that needs to be identified and attended to between working psychologically with a dying person and the ordinary use of psychotherapy — or, at the least, a broadening of the concept of psychotherapy itself.

In a recent book, *Illness as Metaphor* (1978), Susan Sontag [3] (who has had cancer) invoked the image of two worlds: the world of the well and the world of the ill:

> Illness is the night-side of life, a more onerous citizenship. Everybody who is born holds dual citizenship, in the kingdom of the well and in the kingdom of the sick. Although we prefer to use only the good passport, sooner or later each of us is obliged, at least for a spell, to identify ourselves as citizens of the other place.

We would quibble a bit with her way of putting it. We would like to add a "third world" to this scheme: the world of the dying. There is admittedly a keen difference between being well and ill (feeling bad and having pain), but there is an even greater difference — a vastly greater one — between being ill and dying. The psychological distance between knowing that one has an illness (and is expected or hopes to recover) and understanding that one has a mortal enemy is enormous. "Being ill" and "dying" are quite different.

Quite obviously, both psychotherapy (with an emotionally disturbed person who is not physically ill) and working with a dying person usually involve a verbal exchange between two persons in a face-to-face relationship. To the extent that this is so, our first task is then to explicate the various types of verbal exchanges.

In principle, it may be said that there are at least four different kinds of human (essentially verbal) communication. They can be described briefly as follows:

COMMUNICATION EXCHANGE

Ordinary Talk or Conversation

In this kind of exchange, which makes up most of human discourse, the focus is on the surface content (concrete events, specific details, abstract issues, questions and answers of content). The individuals are talking about what is actually being said: the obvious, stated meanings, and the ordinary interesting (or uninteresting) details of life. Further, the social role between the two participants is one of essential equality, sometimes tempered somewhat by considerations of age, status or prestige. But each of the two parties has the social right to ask the other the same kind of questions which he or she has been asked. Some examples of ordinary talk might be two friends conversing with one another about the events of the day, or two lovers whispering intimate thoughts to one another, or two businessmen closing a deal, or two neighbors simply chatting.

Hierarchical

In this kind of exchange the entire focus (like in a conversation) is on the manifest content—on what is being said—but the situation is marked by an explicit or tacit acknowledgment by the two parties that there is a significant difference of status between them; one of them is "superior" to the other. Questions asked or suggestions made or information transmitted or orders given by one would seem inappropriate if attempted by the other party. Examples would be the verbal exchange between a supervisor and subordinate, between an army officer and enlisted man, or between an oncologist and a patient in the doctor's office. The officer can order the enlisted man, but not vice versa; the doctor can examine the patient, but not vice versa. The doctor-patient relationship is an hierarchical one in that a doctor and a patient do not exchange roles.

Professional (e.g., Psychotherapy)

Here the focus is on feelings, emotional content and unconscious meanings, rather than primarily on what is apparently being said. The emphasis is on the latent (between-the-lines) significance more than on the manifest and obvious content; on unconscious meanings, including double-entendre, puns and slips of the tongue; on themes that run as common threads through the content rather than on the concrete details for their own sake. Perhaps the most distinguishing aspect of the professional exchange (as opposed to ordinary talk) is the occurrence of "transference" — wherein the patient projects onto the therapist certain deep expectations and feelings. These transference reactions often stem from the patient's childhood and reflect earlier patterns of reaction (of love, hate, dependency, suspicion, etc.) to whatever the therapist may or may not be doing. The therapist (like the doctor) is often invested by the patient with almost magical healing powers, which, in fact, can serve as a self-fulfilling prophecy and thus help the interaction become therapeutic for the patient. The roles of the two participants, unlike those in a conversation, are not co-equal. The situation is hierarchical but the focus is not on the manifest content.

Thanatological

A person who systematically attempts to help a dying individual achieve a psychologically comfortable death (or a more "appropriate" death or an "ego-syntonic" death) — given the dire, unnegotiable circumstances of the situation — is acting in a special role. (This is not to say that many others — doctors, nurses, relatives, dear friends, church members, neighbors — cannot also play extremely important roles.) If the distinction between a conversation and a professional exchange is crucial, certainly the distinction between working with dying persons as opposed to working with any other kind of individual is a vital one. Working with a dying person demands a different kind of involvement. Our position is that there may be as important a conceptual difference between ordinary psychotherapy and working with dying persons as there is between ordinary psychotherapy and ordinary talk. Below, we have attempted to limn out some of the important nuances of these differences.

CLINICAL THANATOLOGY

Here are some of the main elements which we believe distinguish thanatological work from other forms of human interaction, including ordinary psychotherapy.

The Unique Nature of the Existential Confrontation

An exchange between any two people is always, in a sense, an existential event. Consider the very nature of the existential situation with a dying person: it is between two human beings, one of whom (the patient) is currently struggling with dying and the other (the clinical thanatologist) who is not dying, but *both* are, without any question, going to share the common fate of dying someday—and both know *that*. The thanatological situation is certainly a unique one, where both individuals share a common vital problem. (This is not so in working with, say, a schizophrenic or suicidal or neurotic patient.) That fact, in itself, seems to set working with a dying person apart from usual psychotherapy. "Doctor, doctor, will I die? Yes my dear and so shall I." This is not suggested as necessarily something to say to a patient; it is simply a statement of the nature of life.

The Dimension of Time

In psychotherapy we usually assume that there is unlimited time. We attempt to "work through" problems with the implicit understanding that the patient will continue to live — it is hoped better adjusted. In the dying situation, an irrevocable series of changes, from what has been to what may be, takes place along the dimension we call time. When a person is dying, the passage of time creates anxiety. Moreover, time does not pass uniformly and the experiences of sudden accelerations or decelerations lead to further feelings of insecurity, threat and helplessness.

The perception of time alters and disintegrates in the process of dying. The habitual and conventional idea of time as a linear process is broken up by the patient into sections, a relevant measure being the intervals between meals, visits, or medications. The subjective experience of time is filled with special inner experiences and becomes increasingly disconnected with the chronological time of those around the dying person and thus loses much of its usual significance.

The Possibility of Intense Transference

We believe that it is therapeutic if the dying person develops rather strong feelings of essentially positive transference toward the clinician who is seen as being potentially helpful "in the business of dying." That helper then becomes an admittedly exaggerated "key figure" in the dying person's remaining days.

The nature and intensity of the dying person's positive transference is indeed another key feature which distinguishes thanatological work from ordinary psychotherapy. The clinical thanatologist helps the dying person through this most important "rite-de-passage." We therefore feel that it is permissible, in fact desirable, to create a situation of intense transference from the very beginning which might, in ordinary psychotherapy appear to be unseemly or contraindicated. There is something ineffibly special (and sometimes rather dramatic) in the transference that occurs with a dying person.

Negative transference — feelings of anger or dislike or jealousy — may arise, and perhaps the handling of it, because of the very situation that the patient is in, further distinguishes thanatological work from ordinary psychotherapy. Fear of negative transference is only one of the reasons why many physicians eschew working psychologically with dying persons.

Of course, where there is strong transference there is also countertransference; the thanatologist's genuine positive feelings of liking and concern for the welfare of the patient; and there is also an unavoidable psychological price: the vulnerability and grief over the eventual loss. One cannot ever invest without running the risk of loss. Dealing with dying persons is abrasive psychological work and the clinician is well-advised to have good support systems in his or her own life: loved persons, dear friends, congenial work and peer consultants.

The Goals are Limited

Because for the dying person time is limited, the goals for the thanatologist are more finite. The omnipresent goal is the psychological *comfort* of the person, with, as a general rule, as much alleviation of felt physical pain as possible. Full psychological insight is not the goal. There is no rule that states that an individual must die with any certain amount of self-knowledge. In this sense, every life is incomplete. The goal is to make a dire situation go as well as possible; to give psychological succor; to permit the tying-off of loose ends; to lend as much stability to the dying person as it is possible to give.

The thanatologist needs to be able to tolerate incompleteness and lack of closure. No one ever untangles all the varied skeins of another's intrapsychic life; to the last second there are psychical creations and recreations that require new resolutions. Total insight is an abstraction. There is no golden mental homeostasis.

The Importance of Empathy

Without empathy one cannot really understand another person. Empathy partly has to do with identification and should be present in all psychotherapy. In the doctor-patient relationship empathy is important and a desirable component.

Empathy is comprehending another person, feeling one's way into and sharing the other's reality ("If I were he . . . "). It involves identification and at the same time a maintained awareness of one's own feelings. Empathy is essentially a feeling of warmth and emotional involvement; it is beyond simple befriending; it is true caring. In the process of dying, pity may be abrasive, sympathy of little use, whereas empathy is a necessary condition for really helping the dying person. To the best of one's ability, through an open relationship, one should try to comprehend who the dying person is and what, in dialogues at every level, that person wishes to convey.

The Special Place of Flexibility

In the care of the dying person, flexibility is paramount; to use a fixed system would be to misconstrue the art. One is not trying to help the patient to function better "afterwards," but to make the limited life that is left bearable, meaningful and self-fulfilling as possible. This calls for maximal flexibility in relation to the psychological and biological manifestations of dying.

Psychotherapy is a discplined undertaking. You meet at a fixed place, at scheduled hours, the patient sits or lies in the same place, and one usually has a program in mind for months ahead. Systematic work is done, guided by the therapist. On the other hand, for those who work with dying persons, everchanging pictures pass before the mind's eye. These pictures are evocative, causing psychological events to occur in both minds, albeit in different respects. Some of these are, by their very nature, anxiety provoking, but also linking one person to the other, making a common bond. The clinician needs to be as flexible as his own personality and controlled countertransference will permit.

The Importance of Being Concerned With the Significant Others

Death is seldom a uni-person event. In the dying scene there are two classes of persons: the person who dies and those who continue to live and are left to mourn and grieve. The algebra of death's suffering is a complicated equation. But more important than this theoretical point is the demonstrated fact that widows and widowers, especially in the first year after the death of their spouse, suffer pain and are seriously ill more often (requiring hospitalization) and more of them die (from a wide variety of causes) than non-bereaved men and women of their same age and general status. Mourners are, to use a public health expression, a population "at risk." It follows from this that working with a dying person ought almost always to include someone's also working with the mourner-to-be, both before the death of the loved one and after, for perhaps a year or so, at decreasing intervals.

The Ambience of the Dying Scene

Typically, dying persons become sicker, bed-ridden, tired and weak, and begin to take on the signs of approaching death. Depending upon the circumstances, the clinical thanatologist will, during these weeks or days or hours, witness another human being's down-hill course toward death. During this onerous process, one would naturally follow the patient's own moods (and content) more and more, With each visit, the clinician will meet unexpected questions, fresh memories that the dying person has never talked about before, and also expressions of a variety of emotions — rebellion, aggression, grief, submission, fear, ennui, etc. The thanatologist will resonate to the patient's expressions. Depending on the circumstances and the "dying trajectory," the thanatologist will change the schedule and come more and more often, toward the end as frequently as more than once a day. The drama of the dying scene can be shared by talk or by sitting nearby without saying a word.

And so the question remains: Is clinical thanatology sufficiently different in the persons involved, in its requirements for empathy and flexibility, in its relationships to time, in its content and in its goals to warrant a special designation? We are inclined to believe that it is. We can see the prefiguring of a new and separate art, discipline, specialty, practice or emphasis. It does not matter what it is called (someone will coin a felicitious term), so long as it is practiced more often by people working with dying persons in health-care settings, whether in hospitals, hospices, or (more and more) in the person's own home.

REFERENCES

1. L. Feigenberg, *Terminalvård: En metod för psychologisk vård av döende cancer patienter,* Lund, Liber Läromedet, 1977 (to be published in English by Brunner/Mazel under the title of *Terminal Friendships: Psychiatric Care of the Dying* in 1979).
2. E. S. Shneidman, Some Aspects of Psychotherapy with Dying Persons, C. A. Garfield (ed.), *Psychosocial Aspects of Terminal Patient Care,* McGraw-Hill, New York, 1978.
3. S. Sontag, *Illness as a Metaphor,* N.Y. Forras, Straus and Giroux, 1978.

In his review of the field, McKitrick (Chapter 16) describes the use of psycho-analytic therapy, crisis intervention, LSD, and a variety of other psychothera-peutic approaches; in Chapter 14, Feigenberg and Shneidman discuss some of the more important issues involved with counseling the dying. Neither chapter, however, considers the possibility of using a behavior-modification model. The authors of Chapter 18 provide a basic background both to counseling the dying and behavior modification, then apply this model on a step-by-step basis to working with clients who are near death.

There are other possible models for working with the dying: a psychoanalytic model, a self-actualization model, a Gestalt model. Is one better than another? Does one work better than others for any given counselor? For any given counsellee? We haven't even begun to develop answers. At this point, we are still learning to apply our knowledge of counseling and therapy to circumstances in which death is imminent. In the final analysis, however, we will probably find that each dyad of therapist-dying person has its own optimum approach and that even that approach may require modification as death becomes increasingly close. There is unlikely to be any model that is more important than skill, wisdom, and sensitivity to individual differences on the part of the therapist.

CHAPTER 18

Clients Nearing Death: Behavioral Treatment Perspectives

George W. Rebok
and
William J. Hoyer

Psychological factors in relationship to death and dying usually receive attention only in sudden unexpected death or when the physical etiology is obscure. Kastenbaum and Costa pointed out that this state of affairs has contributed to the misconception that there are two "types" of death—the "purely physical" and the "purely psychological." [1] A more satisfactory viewpoint is that *all* deaths involve a complex interplay of cognitive, social and biological processes. Thus, while all life styles terminate with physical death (e.g., heart or brain death), when and how people die can be related to psychosocial as well as biomedical risk factors.

In the psychiatric literature, terms such as Holiday Syndrome and Anniversary Reaction have been used to describe the "death dips" prior to important dates in a person's life [2]. Kastenbaum and Costa cited a number of other related phenomena that invite a psychological explanation [1]. For example, the practice of "voodoo death" as well as the act of "healing rites" needs systematic documentation. In addition "will to die" and "will to live" phenomena have received much anecdotal and little empirical support in the clinical literature [3]. It has been demonstrated in several studies that the mortality rates of elderly are abnormally high in the months immediately following a move to a new location [4]. The individual's perception of his relocation as voluntary or involuntary makes an appreciable difference in mortality rate [5].

CONTROL AND PREDICTABILITY

The emerging conception of the death event is that the individual can to some extent exert control over length as well as quality of life. Seligman's work on learned helplessness as well as other research on the effects of unpredictable and uncontrollable events on behavior is relevant to the notion of environmental mastery [6]. Seligman and his associates have provided evidence to suggest that exposure to uncontrollable events leads to an expectation of "helplessness" in both humans and infrahumans [7–9]. The individual learns that environmental events are independent of his actions and, consequently, response initiation and performance effectiveness are decreased [10, 11]. Glass and Singer, who provided further evidence that experience with unavoidable events produces a deleterious effect on performance, also found that the mere belief in control even if not exerted minimizes the negative consequences of exposure to uncontrollable events [12].

Three outcomes of exposure to uncontrollability as it affects subsequent mastery of situations have been identified [6]: (1) learning that one's behavior and one's situation are noncontingent, independent events interferes with subsequent learning of mastery or self-efficacy; 2) the motivation to initiate attempts at environmental mastery is reduced; 3) there is likely to be heightened arousal and anxiety attributable to loss of situational control. The learned helplessness model has been offered as an analog for human depression and there is some evidence to support this interpretation. Miller and Seligman, for example, found that depressed compared to nondepressed people perceived environmental outcomes as independent of their behavior, and that depressives took longer in the laboratory to learn that they can exert control over environmental outcomes [9, 13]. In a study with institutionalized aged adults, Schulz found that individuals who had control and predictability over the frequency and duration of visits they received were rated significantly happier, healthier, and more active than individuals who were on an unpredictable visitation schedule [14].

THERAPEUTIC INTERVENTIONS WITH THE DYING

The research on the negative consequences of uncontrollable events has important implications for working with the dying. With regard to biomedical practice, protecting a dying individual from the knowledge of his physical condition or preventing his active participation in treatment and care decisions may promote feelings of helplessness and hopelessness and may even hasten death. Physicians, nurses, and other health-care professionals frequently see their responsibility as the application of the most advanced medical technology. One potentially hazardous side effect of a purely medical treatment emphasis is that it results in lessened responsibility, involvement and control on the part of the terminal patient [15]. Some recent interest has been shown in developing a "holistic health care" perspective which incorporates biological, psychological, and social components into a system where the individual patient is seen as the active health agent [16].

The ability of the individual to control the experience as well as the actual trajectory of self-health also has important ramifications for psychological therapeutic interventions with the terminally ill. Traditional psychoanalytic systems have de-emphasized the use of intervention with dying individuals. Freud suggested that the unconscious cannot recognize its own death and regards itself as immortal [17]. Becker argued that life is an unordered chaos without predictability or control and that psychological intervention, unless it is oriented totally toward allowing the client to lower psychological defenses, is inappropriate in death [18]. Probably the most popular current description of psychological factors in dying is Kubler-Ross's overworked stage theory [19]. Kubler-Ross has suggested that a dying individual passes through a well-demarcated series of five psychological stages—denial, anger, bargaining, depression, and acceptance—prior to physical death. Kubler-Ross has recommended that therapy with the dying is "not as much doing as being." Although her theory is useful for descriptive purposes, it is limited in that it ignores the dying individual's past history and current psychosocial context [20, 21].

A broad range of therapeutic interventions has been used with the terminally ill. An early approach was reported by LeShan in his psychotherapeutic work with terminal cancer patients [22—24]. More recently, LSD drug therapy has been used to relieve anxiety and heighten awareness of the living-dying experience [25—28]. Various nontraditional forms of psychotherapy are being used with terminal patients at St. Christopher's Hospice in London and at other hospices [29]. Death education courses, which are now being offered at universities, hospitals, and retirement communities also serve a therapeutic function for terminally ill individuals and others who are personally and/or professionally concerned with death and dying. Although a wide variety of psychological tehcniques are currently being used with terminally ill clients, to date there has been little or no systematic comparison of the relative effectiveness of various therapeutic interventions [15].

BEHAVIORAL THERAPY AND THE DYING

Our main purpose is to recommend one treatment technique that has received relatively little attention with the terminally ill. Known variously as behavior modification, behavioral analysis or management, or behavior therapy, this approach places emphasis on the individualization of behavior and its consequences and on functional relationships between behaviors and "here and now" environmental consequences. Behavior modification is not one type of therapy but a set of techniques that can be used in conjunction with any treatment procedure [30]. Successful applications to a wide assortment of target behaviors (e.g., exercise, walking, verbal behavior, study habits, social interaction, screaming, crying) have been demonstrated with elderly and younger adults [31–33].

There are very few behavior modification studies in the clinical literature on death and dying. Preston has discussed a behavioral approach that is designed to increase staff (student) awareness and understanding of self-statements about death [34]. Whitman and Lukes described some behavior modification case studies in which health care professionals have applied reinforcement principles in order to alter undesirable behaviors in terminal patients (e.g., temper tantrums, sloppiness of appearance, improper eating, physical inactivity) [35]. Relaxation and desensitization techniques have also been employed to change the behaviors of the terminally ill [36, 37]. Finnberg provided some concrete examples of how these procedures can be implemented by paraprofessional change agents [37]. For example, a nurse-therapist first teaches a patient deep muscle relaxation. Next, (s)he begins the therapy by exposing the patient to slides or photographs of individuals in mildly threatening situations (e.g., an adult being diagnosed for suspected cancer). These slides are then paired with pleasurable scenes in order to reduce the fear produced by the earlier slides.

Traditionally, most experimental approaches to studying and treating the terminally ill have encountered strong resistance [1, 38]. Perhaps one of the reasons that behavior modification has not been used widely in treating the dying is because it is seen largely as a heartless, mechanical approach to a deeply human problem. However, behaviorism and humanism need not necessarily be viewed as incompatible. Recently, Mahoney [39], Meichenbaum and others have argued persuasively for the attainment of humanistic goals via a behavioral self-management perspective [40].

From any therapeutic perspective, dying is not a pathological problem behavior to be remedied [22, 24, 41]. Rather, the treatment is viewed as part of an overall concept of helping that involves "real world" everyday thoughts, feelings, and actions. Of course, behavior modification is not the treatment of choice with all dying individuals, and in some terminal cases the best treatment may be no treatment. Indeed, it is questionable whether professional intervention during the final months or years is in the best interests of the patient. As the patient nears death, control should be increasingly in the hands of the patient. Bandura has indicated that the restoration of self-control is the aim of all therapy [42]. In the past five years there has been much concern for developing and refining the methodology of self-directed behavior analysis and change [30, 32, 40, 43-45]. Choice of treatment is the domain of the client, and when the individual wants to manage his or her own behavior (e.g., pain, fear, or depression), behavior approaches might be particularly helpful.

BEHAVIORAL SELF-MANAGEMENT

Described below is an adaptation of behavioral self-management procedures for use with terminally ill clients. These procedures have been applied successfully to a broad variety of problem behaviors such as overeating, social anxiety, nervous tics, depression, fear, and passivity. Self-control techniques are particularly useful for older adult clients who live in isolated environments and who cannot rely on external feedback for evaluation of their own behavior [46, 47]. The most important goal of this approach is to help individuals achieve more self-direction or more "will power" over their lives (or deaths). In contrast to many clinical behavioral techniques which require close supervision, self-control techniques do not depend on an extensive background knowledge of psychological procedures. In order to maximize the effectiveness of these techniques, a general rule to follow is to use many different self-management strategies in conjunction with other clinical techniques and allow sufficient time for change.

As viewed here, learning principles, especially operant techniques, underlie self-modification and are used to account for behavioral change. Over the past five years, there has been a trend toward the incorporation of both behavioral and cognitive components in self-change strategies. The studies on learned helplessness discussed earlier can be seen as support for a cognitive view of behavioral change phenomena. Recently, Abramson and Sackheim considered the paradox of uncontrollability versus self-blame in the understanding of depression [48]. They concluded that neither the learned helplessness model of depression nor Beck's cognitive model was sufficient to resolve the paradox [49]. Ledwidge reviewed the usefulness of the cognitive behavior modification approach to therapy and research, but he was not able to definitely resolve the question of its effectiveness [50]. He urged caution in uncritically accepting the claims of cognitive behavior modification studies until valid comparisons are made with traditional behavioral therapy approaches.

The first step in any behavioral self-change program is to select a goal. With a dying individual, the restructuring of the self-system or personality is probably an inappropriate target. In addition, it is undesirable to attempt to strengthen or weaken specific behavioral skills such as crying or complaining. Rather, the goal may be to strengthen a response class consisting of communication, awareness, and self-acceptance by removing debilitating fears of helplessness.

A second step is to state the goal in terms of specific behaviors that need to be changed to reach the goal or target behavior. One of the problems with treating a dying person's fear is that fears are not often expressed in behavioral terms. It is possible to list some specific fears associated with the dying process that may be amenable to systematic manipulation. For example, Pattison and Schulz have considered some of the following fear-associated behaviors that are present during the living-dying interval [15, 51]:

1. fear of loss of self-control, awareness, consciousness
2. fear of suffering and pain
3. fear of loss of physical functions
4. fear of loss of family and friends
5. fear of nonbeing
6. fear of punishment

These target behaviors should be stated in terms that are objective, concise, and complete. A critical step in specifying the problem is to stop speculating about the behaviors and to begin observing them [45]. There are several ways of observing and recording one's behavior. Logs, diaries, and tape recorders can be used in the initial data gathering to formulate hypotheses about the behavior [52]. More systematic observation may include making simple counts of the frequency or duration of a response by using a wrist counter or other record-keeping strategies. Rating scales are appropriate when the intensity of the behavioral event is a relevant variable. "Intensities" can be measured by assigning each event a number according to a predetermined schedule in which each number has a precise meaning [45]. Watson and Tharp suggested that rating scales are a particularly appropriate method for observing and recording emotions and feelings. For example, complete total death may be given an arbitrary rating of 100 and all other dying fears evaluated against that figure.

A final step is to develop a plan for change and then revise and readjust that plan in light of new behavioral observations. Such a plan requires a thorough knowledge of the antecedent and consequent events that mediate the behavior. If the dying client's goal is to reduce fear of loss of control, consider the following example of an antecedent-behavior-consequent (or ABC) analysis. Antecedent events related to a feeling of loss of control may include medical staff not informing the client of his condition or making him a part of the treatment process, or a patient being moved from a familiar home environment to an institutional environment in which interactions with family and friends are limited. In addition, family, friends, or medical personnel may convey a sense of helplessness and hopelessness to the patient through very subtle behavioral cues (e.g., lowered voice, little eye contact, long silences). In this case, the therapeutic intervention may take the form of exploring the feasibility of self-directed versus other-directed care and home versus institutional care, as well as identifying and controlling the verbal and nonverbal cues to the terminally ill client.

The rearrangement of existing consequences and the selection of new reinforcers are also part of the self-management approach. Reinforcers may be of the physical (e.g., a good meal, alcoholic beverage) or social (e.g., interactions with significant others) variety. The selection of reinforcers is done on an individualized basis and the objective is to temporally connect the occurrence of the reinforcer with the target behavior. A dying individual may contingently reward himself for thinking more positive thoughts (e.g., "I do not fear death," or "I am in control"). In instances where no physical or social reinforcers are available or suitable, as in severe depression, imagined (covert) reinforcers may be used but they are generally less powerful and more difficult to control than real reinforcers. Alternately, the Premack Principle (i.e., high probability events are reinforcers for low probability events) may be employed. Perhaps for a dying person "doing nothing" may be a highly probable and reinforcing event so that "doing nothing" can be made contingent on "doing something" like communicating with the nursing staff, writing a letter, or reading.

RECOMMENDATIONS AND CONCLUSIONS

In selecting behavioral goals and programming the reinforcer environment, several modifications of orthodox operant learning principles are recommended. First, a dying person may be unable or unwilling to articulate precise behavioral goals and client-centered counseling or psychotherapy may be relatively more useful, particularly in the initial phases of intervention (see Dimond, Havens and Jones', 1978 discussion of eclectic psychotherapy) [53]. In addition, too much attention to negative behaviors (i.e., fear, depression) may exacerbate those behaviors; monitoring of such behaviors should be done infrequently and considerable attention should be focused on imcompatible responses (relaxation, joy, curiosity) if possible. Although it is generally advised that reinforcers should not be overused and should be delivered intermittently, continuous reinforcement scheduling may be a more effective as well as humane procedure with a dying person. Finally, since family, friends, and staff are so often deeply needed by the dying patient, their involvement in treatment is very important.

We have described some theoretical issues and given some practical examples of self-directed behavior modification with terminally ill patients. The usefulness of this approach has not as yet been fully determined. One of the most frequent criticisms of all behavior therapies is that they are said to ignore the whole person. Although a dying person's behavior and feelings are often death-specific and conditions frequently are not ideal for total change or reorganization, the thoughts and awareness of the dying individual are very much alive. The self-management behavioral approach outlined in this article is relatively uncomplicated and can be used with dying persons by psychiatrists, psychologists, social workers, nurses, or counselors with sufficient background training in the therapeutic modification of behavior. It is strongly recommended that those individuals who plan to teach self-control techniques be sensitive to the ethical implications of behavioral treatment methods with this clinical population [1, 51, 54, 55].

REFERENCES

1. R. Kastenbaum and P. T. Costa, Psychological Perspectives on Death, M. R. Rosenzweig and L. W. Porter (eds.), *Annual Review of Psychology, 8*, pp. 225-249, 1977.
2. M. M. Baltes, On the Relationship between Significant Yearly Events and Time of Death: Random or Systematic Distribution?, *Omega, 8:*2, pp. 165-172, 1977.
3. E. M. Pattison, Psychosocial Predictors of Death Prognosis, *Omega, 5:*2, pp. 145-160, 1974.
4. K. F. Rowland, Environmental Events Predicting Death for the Elderly, *Psychological Bulletin, 84,* pp. 349-372, 1977.
5. I. Wittels and J. Botwinick, Survival in Relocation, *Journal of Gerontology, 29,* pp. 440-443, 1974.
6. M. E. P. Seligman, *Helplessness,* W. H. Freeman, San Francisco, 1975.
7. D. S. Hiroto and M. E. P. Seligman, Generality of Learned Helplessness in Man, *Journal of Personality and Social Psychology, 31,* pp. 311-327, 1975.
8. D. C. Klein and M. E. P. Seligman, Reversal of Performance Deficits and Perceptual Deficits in Learned Helplessness and Depression, *Journal of Abnormal Psychology, 85,* pp. 11-26, 1976.
9. W. R. Miller and M. E. P. Seligman, Depression and Learned Helplessness in Man, *Journal of Abnormal Psychology, 84,* pp. 228-238, 1975.
10. D. Douglas and H. Anisman, Helplessness or Expectation Incongruency: Effects of Aversive Stimulation on Subsequent Performance, *Journal of Experimental Psychology: Human Perception and Performance, 1,* pp. 411-417, 1975.
11. C. S. Dweck and N. D. Reppucci, Learned Helplessness and Reinforcement Responsibility in Children, *Journal of Personality and Social Psychology, 25,* pp. 109-116, 1973.
12. D. C. Glass and J. E. Singer, *Urban Stress: Experiments on Noise and Social Stressors,* Academic Press, New York, 1972.

13. W. R. Miller and M. E. P. Seligman, Depression and the Perception of Reinforcement, *Journal of Abnormal Psychology, 82,* pp. 62-73, 1973.

14. R. Schulz, Effects of Control and Predictability on the Physical and Psychological Well-Being of the Institutionalized Aged, *Journal of Personality and Social Psychology, 33,* pp. 563-573, 1976.

15. _____ , *The Psychology of Death, Dying, and Bereavement,* Addison-Wellesley Publishing Company, Reading, Mass., 1978.

16. E. Shanas and G. L. Maddox, Aging, Health, and the Organization of Health Resources, R. H. Binstock and E. Shanas (eds.), *Handbook of Aging and the Social Sciences,* Van Nostrand Reinhold, New York, 1976.

17. S. Freud, Thoughts for the Times on War and Death, *Collected Papers, Vol. 4,* Hogarth, London, 1915.

18. E. Becker, *The Denial of Death,* Free Press, New York, 1973.

19. E. Kubler-Ross, *On Death and Dying,* MacMillan, New York, 1969.

20. R. A. Kalish, Death and Dying in a Social Context, R. H. Binstock and E. Shanas (eds.), *Handbook of Aging and the Social Sciences,* Van Nostrand Reinhold Company, New York, 1976.

21. R. Kastenbaum, Is Death a Life Crisis? On the Confrontation with Death in Theory and Practice, N. Datan and L. H. Ginsberg (eds.), *Life-Span Developmental Psychology: Normative Life Crises,* Academic Press, New York, 1975.

22. L. LeShan, Mobilizing the Life Force, *Annals of the New York Academy of Science, 164,* pp, 846-861, 1969.

23. L. LeShan and M. Gassman, Some Observations on Psychotherapy with Patients Suffering from Neoplastic Disease, *American Journal of Psychotherapy, 12,* pp, 723-734, 1958.

24. L. LeShan and E. LeShan, Psychotherapy and the Patient with a Limited Life Span, *Psychiatry, 24,* pp. 318-323, 1961.

25. G. Fisher, Psychotherapy for the Dying: Principles and Illustrative Cases with Special Reference to the Use of LSD, *Omega 1,* pp. 3-15, 1970.

26. G. L. Klerman, Drugs and the Dying Patient, *Journal of Thanatology, 2,* pp. 574-587, 1972.

27. H. S. Olin, Failure and Fulfillment: Education in the Use of Psychoactive Drugs in the Dying Patient, *Journal of Thanatology, 2,* pp. 567-573, 1972.

28. D. V. Sheehan, A Review of the Use of LSD for the Patient Near Death, *Psychiatric Forum, 3,* pp. 21-23, 1972.

29. C. Saunders, *Annual Report,* St. Christopher's Hospice, London, 1976.

30. G. W. Rebok and W. J. Hoyer, The Functional Context of Elderly Behavior, *Gerontologist, 17,* pp. 27-34(b), 1977.

31. W. J. Hoyer, B. L. Mishara and R. G. Riedel, Problem Behaviors as Operants: Applications with Elderly Individuals, *Gerontologist, 15,* pp. 452-456, 1975.

32. G. W. Rebok and W. J. Hoyer, Technology of Applied Behavior Analysis: A Review and Critique, *JSAS Catalog of Selected Documents in Psychology, 7:33* (Ms. No. 1460) (a), 1977.

33. B. F. Skinner, Intellectual Self-Management in Old Age, paper presented at the Nova Behavioral Conference on Aging, Port St. Lucie, Florida, May 1978.

34. C. E. Preston, Behavior Modification: A Therapeutic Approach to Aging and Dying, *Postgraduate Medicine, 54,* pp. 64-68, 1973.
35. H. H. Whitman and S. J. Lukes, Behavior Modification for the Terminally Ill, *American Journal of Nursing, 75,* pp. 98-101, 1975.
36. J. Cautela, A Classical Conditioning Approach to the Development and Modification of Behavior in the Aged, *Gerontologist, 9,* pp. 109-113, 1969.
37. E. E. Finnberg, Behavior Modification Techniques—A New Tool for Nurses Who Care for the Terminally Ill, paper presented at the Foundation of Thanatology Conference, New York, November 1974.
38. D. Dempsey, *The Way We Die: An Investigation of Death and Dying in America Today,* McGraw-Hill Book Company, New York, 1975.
39. M. J. Mahoney, The Sensitive Scientist in Empirical Humanism, *American Psychologist, 30,* pp. 864-867, 1975.
40. D. Meichenbaum, *Cognitive-Behavior Modification,* Plenum Press, New York 1977.
41. G. Engel, Is Grief a Disease?, *Psychosomatic Medicine, 23,* pp. 18-22, 1961.
42. A. Bandura, Self-Efficacy: Toward a Unifying Theory of Behavioral Change. *Psychological Review, 84,* pp. 191-215, 1977.
43. M. Mahoney, *Cognition and Behavior Modification,* Ballinger Publishing Co., Cambridge, Mass, 1974.
44. D. Meichenbaum, Toward A Cognitive Theory of Self-Control, G. Schwartz and D. Shapiro (eds.), *Consciousness and Self-Regulation, Volume 1,* Plenum Press, New York, 1976.
45. D. L. Watson and A. G. Tharp, *Self-Directed Behavior: Self-Modification for Personal Adjustment,* Brooks/Cole Publishing Company, Monterey Calif., 1977.
46. F. H. Kanfer, Self-Regulation: Research, Issues, and Speculations, C. Neuringer and J. L. Michael (eds.), *Behavior Modification in Clinical Psychology,* Appleton-Century-Crofts, New York, 1970.
47. _____ , Self-Management Methods, F. H. Kanfer and A. P. Goldstein (eds.), *Helping People Change,* Pergamon Press, New York, 1975.
48. L. Y. Abramson and H. A. Sackeim, A Paradox in Depression: Uncontrollability and Self-Blame, *Psychological Bulletin, 84,* pp. 838-851, 1977.
49. A. T. Beck, *Depression: Clinical, Experimental, and Theoretical Aspects,* Harper & Row, New York, 1967.
50. B. Ledwidge, Cognitive Behavior Modification: A Step in the Wrong Direction?, *Psychological Bulletin, 85,* pp. 353-375, 1978.
51. E. M. Pattison, *The Experience of Dying,* Prentice-Hall, Inc. Englewood Cliffs, N.J., 1977.
52. M. J. Mahoney, Some Applied Issues in Self-Monitoring, J. D. Cone and R. P. Hawkins (eds.), *Behavioral Assessment: New Directions in Clinical Psychology,* Brunner/Mazel Publishers, New York, 1977.
53. R. E. Dimond, R. A. Havens and A. C. Jones, A Conceptual Framework for the Practice of Prescriptive Eclecticism in Psychotherapy, *American Psychologist, 33,* pp. 239-248, 1978.

54. D. Harshbarger, Death and Public Policy: A Research Inquiry, N. Datan and
    L. H. Ginsberg (eds.), *Life-Span Developmental Psychology: Normative Life
    Crises,* Academic Press, New York, 1975.
55. B. F. Skinner, The Ethics of Helping People, *The Humanist, 36,* pp. 7-11,
    1976.

ACKNOWLEDGEMENT

Thanks are extended to Christine Jones, California State University at Long
Beach, for her assistance in the initial preparation of this chapter.

Self-help organizations have become increasingly common throughout the United States and Canada. They provide practical help and advice, general information, and—probably most important of all—human relationships and support from people who have shared a particular trouble or stress. Alcoholics Anonymous, usually considered the first nationally-established self-help group, has an extensive network of chapters and is extremely well-known. Other groups, while not achieving the status of AA, have also had considerable impact on many individuals.

The Compassionate Friends, a self-help group, has over 360 chapters that provide information and support for parents who have suffered the loss of a child through death. In initiating a chapter in the St. Louis area, a group of bereaved parents approached the author of this chapter for help and advice. In earlier writing (Klass, D., and Shinners, B., 1982-83, Professional roles in a self-help group for the bereaved. Omega, 13, 361-365), Klass outlined his role as a professional invited by the same organization to participate actively in their group process. He quickly learned that the group functioned extremely well without his participation, and he shifted his position to that of a resource rather than that of an active participant. In this chapter, he describes a framework that he developed to understand the process that members of The Compassionate Friends seemed to go through.

CHAPTER 19

Bereaved Parents and the Compassionate Friends: Affiliation and Healing

Dennis Klass

We know very little about the nature and results of intervention in bereavement. Hospice, bereavement support groups, self-help groups, self conscious pastoral care, and "grief counseling" or "grief therapy," have become part of the mental health movement; yet we have limited understanding about how such interventions relate to the nature of grief and loss in general, or how they relate to particular classes of grief or loss. This article is an attempt to examine one form of intervention with one severe type of bereavement to uncover the nature of the process. The bereavement is the death of a child. The intervention is The Compassionate Friends (TCF), a parents' self-help organization. This chapter is an attempt to describe the TCF process and the movement of individuals through that process.

TCF is a self-help group. As such it should be understood as distinct from support groups, which have predetermined outcomes and a strong separation between helpers and helpees. It also should be understood as distinct from professional counseling or therapy, which has as its basis a specialized scientific knowledge about human functioning. We can take Lieberman and Borman's definition as the most adequate for the self-help group:

Their membership consists of those who share a common condition, situation, heritage, symptom, or experience. They are largely self-governing and self-regulating, emphasizing peer solidarity rather than heirarchical governance. As such, they prefer controls built upon consensus rather than coercion. They tend to disregard in their own organization the usual institutional distinctions between consumers, professionals, and Boards of Directors, combining and exchanging such functions among each other. They advocate self-reliance and require equally intense commitment and responsibility to other members, actual or potential. They often provide an identifiable code of precepts, beliefs, and practices that include rules for conducting group meetings, entrance requirements for new members and techniques for dealing with "backsliders." They minimize referrals to professionals or agencies since, in most cases, no appropriate help exists. Where it does, they tend to cooperate with professionals. They generally offer a face-to-face, or phone-to-phone fellowship network usually available and accessible without charge. Groups tend to be self-supporting, occur mostly outside the aegis of institutions or agencies, and thrive largely on donations from members and friends rather than government or foundation grants or fees from the public. [1, pp. 14-15]

There are some nationally organized self-help groups dealing with death and bereavement such as Make Today Count and THEOS. Other self-help groups such as Candlelighters have a bereavement aspect since a portion of their members have lost a child. There are also local groups with no national connection. In one sense, the planned funeral societies as well as the euthanasia society are self-help groups, but the common condition, heritage, situation, symptom, or experience that brings them together may be too broad to include those two groups for our purposes. It is not known at this time whether parental bereavement is such a special case as to make the dynamics of TCF significantly different from other groups of the bereaved. Thus at this time, it is not clear if the findings from this study are applicable to THEOS or MTC.

METHOD

Matching research method to the TCF process is difficult, for three reasons. First, a member's course through the group does not proceed in a straight line. Second, groups go through natural cycles, so long-term acquaintance with a particular group is necessary to understand the situation of particular members within the group and their own grief at a given time. Third, the TCF process is difficult to study because some methods may be disruptive to the process.

Our research method, participant observation, is appropriate to the process studies. By now participant observation should need no methodological introduction, but readers interested in the method will find Whyte [2] , Wax [3] , Glaser and Strauss [4] , Powermaker [5] , and Becker [6] of interest. My relationship to the group is as professional advisor—a position created by the members and one that I was invited to fill. When two couples wanted to start a local TCF chapter, they asked me to assist them. I agreed, and along with social work practicum students, attended most meetings for the first two years. As the group split first into two chapters and eventually into five chapters, I attended at least one monthly chapter meeting while the practicum students attended the others. I have also attended all steering committee business meetings. A previous article detailed the roles in the group we have attempted to play and the nature of the research relationship to the process. [7]

The research is thus from the inside, in the sense that we are well acquainted with the participants and have entered into their social experience in an extended and significant way. Yet at the same time the research is from the outside, for there is a gap between those who have experienced the death of a child and those who have not. A central tenet of the TCF process is that only those who have lost a child can truly understand. From an existential viewpoint, the claim seems to be true. Though I hear stories each meeting, I find that my students (most of whom have children) and I protect ourselves from full identification with the experience. I have tried to be helpful to the process in which TCF members are engaged, but I am not a member and must hope that I never become one.

We utilized the insider/outsider role in which we were cast to listen to the lived experience of the TCF members. But we could also step back from the experience in a way the members could do only late in their TCF careers. We asked several members for whom the TCF process had been useful to help us by reflecting on their experience of bereavement and their interactions with the group. We taped interviews with ten people, typed up the interviews from the tapes, and returned the typescript to the individual for corrections. We then retyped the corrected interview and gave the individual a copy. Our interviewees were often eloquent beyond our own expressive skills, so in this article we have often let their words carry the argument. As the ideas that form the framework of this chapter were emerging, we published a short article in the local TCF newsletter and asked for comments by members. That article was reprinted in some other TCF newsletters. We received helpful comments and reflections from local chapter members and from members in other cities.

We also asked why some people did not find the TCF process helpful. We went back through the attendance records and randomly selected twelve people who had been to one or two meetings and had not returned. We phoned them and asked about their grief. We were able to draw some understandings of the person and to allow the person to report anything about TCF they wished. The findings of this aspect of the research have been reported previously and are incorporated into this chapter [8] .

THE COMPASSIONATE FRIENDS PROCESS

We can understand TCF process in terms of three decisions people made in relationship to the group. First we find a decision to attend the group. Second we find the interactions that help people decide to affiliate. Two dimensions of interaction seem to be operative in the decision to affilitate: a) a cathectic dimension—that is an identification with others or a particular person in the group, and b) an experiential dimension—that is a specific solution to specific issues, which though practical on the surface, reach deep into the existential situation of the bereaved parent. Third, there is a decision to help others. The TCF process hinges on a discovery most people make: that helping others is a way of retaining a relationship with the dead child and a way of healing the self. At a later point some of those who make that decision take on organizational leadership. Others tend to attend less frequently, but among this latter group, we find the decision to sever the link to the group is an ambivalent one.

The Process I: Attending

Parents come to the group from a variety of referral sources, but all come with a timidity and more than a little ambivalance. From some, the decision to come was merely an acquiescence to an invitation or suggestion from someone else.

Irene:
> Well, I enjoyed the newsletters, but I really didn't want to come to the meetings. I didn't want new friends. I wanted my girls. I didn't feel I needed anyone. I had been independent all my life. But Cathy called and invited us for dinner and said "Tell S. to come over from work and bring his good clothes. We are going to a meeting." So, we went. Sometimes I need a little push.

Frank:
> First a fellow at work whose son had died told me about it. Then a relative who had a son killed had notified someone who sent us a newsletter. I talked it over with my wife and we went to the first meeting.
> Q: Did you go willingly or reluctantly?
> I would say reluctantly. My wife wanted to, but I didn't. There was a lot of emotionalism over my son's death between my wife and myself that was impossible for us to talk about. We were extremely polite and quiet with each other, but there was a lot of unspoken anger.

Sometimes the newly bereaved parents feel an inner sense of rightness about their going to their first meeting. Messages from the unconscious seem to play a part in bringing many TCF members for the first time.

Helen:
> I would say the crash came in June—maybe May—because May was when I saw the article on TCF and first attended in June.

Q: What took you there?

Mainly because by then I didn't like myself. I was screaming and hollering at the two kids and taking everything out on them....I didn't know why I was acting this way. I asked the doctor about support groups. He told me what he knew, which wasn't really a lot. He didn't know if it could be helpful. Things got progressively worse at home. That became the only thing I could think of doing (going to TCF). When I found the listing and realized where it was I said to myself, "That's right in my back yard, so God must be giving me a sign to go."

Grace:

We went fairly early. I think in December. One of reasons, which was probably a silly one, was that the meetings were at the same address as N. once worked. The association made me feel that maybe I was meant to go.

Donna:

I went for the first time the following February. I didn't know anything existed like that, but somebody had sent me a newsletter. I read it, but thought, "Oh, this stuff is not for me. There's no way I could handle this group." I left it lay there, but about an hour before the first meeting started, I suddenly decided I was going to the meeting.

Sometimes there seems to be a rather strong feeling of estrangement from the natural support system that moves people to find places where they will fit in.

Alice:

My friends didn't understand and I felt lonely. I felt I needed somebody or something but I didn't know what. I wanted to talk to someone who had gone through what I had gone through. I felt it would be best to get out and get involved in some activities since I had so much time on my hands. O.'s care had taken up a great deal of my day, so I suddenly didn't know what to do with myself. I had read about TCF in the *North County Journal*. My son took me to the first meeting and attended two or three meetings with me after that.

For some, attending the first meeting is part of an inner conflict about accepting that the child is really dead. One person was sent a notice of the TCF meeting with a sympathy card a few days after the child's death. She tore up the card. Then she received a newsletter that featured articles on getting through the holidays. She tore that up too because:

Cathy:

There were not going to be any holidays for me! Finally, though, out of sheer desperation I had to do something. I couldn't survive the way I was going. I had lost 15 to 20 pounds, and the doctor was angry that I wouldn't take any medication. I simply couldn't function when I attempted to take the tranquilizers, so I told him, "I've dealt with things my own way for too long to begin dealing with them your way. I'll survive." He said, "I don't think you will."

She went to her first TCF meeting two months after the child died, though she sat resentfully and quietly through the first meeting. She vowed not to return, but did and at her third meeting began to talk about her loss.

For a significant number of the TCF leaders, this is not the first experience of a self-help group. For one person, the recommendation to TCF came from another TCF member in Al Anon.

> Bob:
> I'm glad you mentioned Al Anon. Someone there who had lost a child told me about TCF. Al Anon provided tremendous support right after E.'s death. Thus going to TCF was a very easy step.

Another had been active in Parents Without Partners.

> Joan:
> In PWP people bare their souls and talk about everything that bothers them. Having been in PWP and having met people who had gone through and were getting out of crisis helped me in my decision to attend TCF.

The self-help groups in which the TCF members have been involved include the Cerebral Palsy Association, AA groups, the Cycstic Fibrosis group and in one case the deceased child had been in SOB (Sons of Bosses).

Several TCF members have been in professional counseling or therapy at some point in their lives, while others have not. Some try professional counseling as well as TCF after the death of the child. In some cases professional intervention seems to help and in others it does not.

> Bob:
> C.'s anger showed up in May. Six months after E. died, he began acting out his anger, which was taken out primarily on his brother. We agreed to go to a counselor, a psychotherapist. She insisted on working with us as a group. When it comes to children, I think you pretty much have to depend on professional help. Younger children would probably be unable to deal within the framework of TCF.
>
> Joan:
> The kids have been greatly touched by T.'s death, but I don't think at their young age they can ever know for sure how much so. I went with my youngest daughter to a counselor for some months.
> Q: Was the counselor helpful?
> No, not at all, not to me. He couldn't relate at all to what my problem was. He didn't know how to relate to a teenager either.

Other TCF members have sought counseling prior to the death, usually for marriage counseling.

Losing a child seems to be a rather random happening. It can come to rich, poor, citified and countrified families. It is difficult to know the percentage of people in the general population who have had experience with self-help groups or with counseling. Thus, at this point, it is difficult to know whether or not those who affiliate with TCF have had more self-help or counseling experience than the general population. Studies on a wider population might be helpful here, but as we have seen, the new members come ambivalantly, so clearly, neither counseling nor previous self-help experience make attendance a simple matter.

The Process II: Affiliation

We define affiliation simply as the person returning to the group four or more times within an eight-month period and saying that they find the processes within the group helpful in their grief. Yet obviously this simple definition points to some very complex matters in a person's life. At any given meeting, one third may be attending for the first time. Rarely is there a meeting when there is not at least one new attender. They come rather hesitantly, often accompanied by a very supportive friend.

Affiliation A: Cathectic Dimension—The newcomer asks, "Are these people like I want to be?" while those who have been there longer say, "I was like that, but I am different now." It is this sense of identification with fellow travelers on the road through the valley of the shadow of death that we have called the cathectic dimension. Most theories of grief, starting with Freud's [9], have some reference to the cathexis that must be changed in some way after the loss, though little attention has been given to tracing the path of the change in cathexis within the resolution to grief. In a study of professional therapies, the study of the cathectic dimension would largely center on the transference and countertransference, though current studies often disregard this aspect [10, 11]. Previously we have distinguished this cathectic dimension of self-help from the transference of professional intervention [7]. Transference is the emotional attachment to significant figures in the past projected onto the professional and therefore available for use in the therapeutic interactions. In TCF, that cathectic dimension remains in the present, for there is very little sense of continuity that the bereaved parents feel with the personal past as they try to come to terms with their loss. The time factor, which may be several decades in the cathexis of therapy, is in TCF a matter of months. The self that is brought to the TCF meeting is not the old familiar self for who social skills and social position are well established. It is a new self; one that is not pleasant to behold and whose future is frightening to project. That new self is isolated from the interaction patterns of the familiar self. But the discovery that the new self can be socially validated within a group of others sharing the same condition provides a beginning place to rebuild.

Bob:

> The one thing that is probably the most helpful is that when you are with other parents who have lost a child you have a common base. It has nothing to do with the reason the child died. It has nothing to do with your socio-economic status. And it has nothing to do with anything in life except that you are all level at one point. It is similar to Al Anon. You are all there for one reason, which is a very leveling thing. It affects you in different ways. You recover from it in different ways, but you all have a common base. I think that is what is TCF's single most important factor. We all have different levels of devastation because of our character and our relationship to the child. But that isn't nearly as critical as the fact that you are all leveled and all are rebuilding lives that are shattered—attempting to get them back to some normalcy.

Because everyone else there has lost a child, the child who is dead is the bond between the bereaved parents. Thus, the identification can have some of the emotional energy that was formerly invested in the child.

Helen:

> One thing that appealed to me is that I knew I could go there and not say anything if I didn't want to....The leaders had lost a baby son named V. so there was an immediate rapport. I thought, "Here's someone that understands!" It was a great feeling. I was very frightened of the introduction, but I thought, "Well, this is one place I get to introduce *him,* I don't even have to mention the other two. This is for V....
>
> It was like a magnet I was drawn to each month. It wasn't always something I wanted to do. I wasn't always up to it because I knew there would be new pain each time, but it was the one time of the month I could talk about my child.

Irene:

> I didn't think I would say anything, but it felt good to be able to talk about the girls. It was good to be able to say, "I'm their mother." You don't have anything else left, but you are still their mother.

One of the activities that bonds members of TCF to each other is sharing pictures of the dead children. Some chapters have an album in which many of the members put a photograph of the dead child. The album is available at each meeting. At the national conferences, there are boards on which parents can pin a picture of the child. That board becomes a gathering place for many parents. At a regular meeting about twice a year, our chapter has a picture sharing session. Photographs are brought and passed around while stories are told about the occasion of the picture—the summer camp, the family baptism gown, or even the body after the tubes had been removed. It is hard to know what to say when people share pictures of living children, but these pictures of dead children seem to evoke appropriate admiration in the TCF meeting. The emotional energy that is invested in the group is thus clearly a continuum with the energy that was invested in the child. Cathexis to parental figures is different than the cathexis to the children we bear. It is that difference that creates the special ambience of TCF.

As members mature in the group, as we will note in the section on helping others, some find that their primary remaining attachment with the group is the growth of the new self that comes from helping others. The emotional attachment to the child, which has become part of the cathexis with the other TCF members, becomes part of the reason to remain with TCF in the helper role.

> Eva:
> It's the one place I can talk about Y. freely. One mother couldn't understand how I could cry so openly in a group setting and she couldn't. What she didn't know was that I couldn't cry about Y. openly at home, so the group was a release for me. Also, by doing something to help other grieving parents, it gives Y.'s death a reason.
> Alice:
> You feel if you can do something for someone else, it helps put some meaning in the heartache you have gone through. If you go through all sorts of hell and don't learn anything.... I tell myself that O. would have been pleased that I do this. He was a very caring person. He would have felt that helping others in this way was a good thing to do.

The emotional energy of the cathectic dimension has elements in addition to the emotional energy that was formerly attached to the child, and not all the cathexis to the child is given to TCF. However, it is clear that at least some of the affiliation with the group is in the form of energy attached to the child. Such a transference of cathexis, therefore has a radically different temporal aspect than the transferences of cathexis that are the usual focus of therapeutic literature. As TCF members often remind each other, "When your parent dies, you lose your past; when your child dies, you lose the future." When TCF members affiliate with that energy, they are not drawn back to the past. Their affiliation with parents who share the same condition is a decision about the present and about the future, not about the past. In this way, the TCF process differs radically from the grief therapy of Worden [10] or Feigenberg's psychotherapy with the terminally ill [11], for the focus of both of these is on the past, or the closing off of the past. The focus of TCF is on dealing effectively in the present and in opening up the future.

The cathectic dimension also has the universal human element of community sharing in a time of crisis. Many bereaved parents report a sense of isolation from their usual intimate networks. For many, TCF fills that void.

> Donna:
> After the third time, I knew I wanted to stay. It was kind of like having a family. No matter where I'm at, it hits me that I'm different. I feel apart.

There was this horrible thing that happened to me that makes me different. With TCF though, we are just all alike. We are all a family. You can act so together, but if I break down with my friends, they don't understand and think I should be more together. If I break down at TCF, they don't think anything about it.

That new self that the bereaved parent brings to TCF feels strange, so the fear of insanity is present even when it is warded off with humor.

Helen:
The most helpful thing was finding out that there are all these other people dealing with the same things. I got a lot of hope by seeing people who had made it. They hadn't ended up on a funny farm.

For some members, the identification with the group is heightened by finding very close models for behavior in the group. Informal networks form continually in any TCF chapter as parents whose experiences are very similar seek each other out. The group attempts to foster that subgrouping by occasionally offering meetings aimed at one specific group, for example the parents of suicide deaths. On occasion the group facilitates such hookups by having a meeting in which a panel of parents representing different kinds of deaths presents short speeches, following which the group breaks into smaller groups with a panelist leading each. At the TCF national conventions, special sessions are held for parents of specific kinds of death. Often we find that a person in the group who has experienced a similar death but is a little further along in the process is the focus of a more specific identification for a newer member.

Eva:
It was during the second meeting I attended that Darla and I talked. It had been about a year since Darla lost her baby. We started calling each other and that helped a lot.
Cathy:
For the first three or four meetings I just stored their words of hope and advice for later because I wasn't ready to accept them at the time. Then I noticed that June, another mother whose child was killed a month before mine, was beginning to heal. I wanted desperately to be like her. I didn't know what to do to make it any better, but decided I was going to try.

The cathectic dimension is a special part of the TCF affiliation process, for the new self of bereaved parents is a special part of losing a child. The sense of unity with those whose lives have been shattered, the sense of hope at seeing that others have made it, the sense of finding an appropriate object on which to attach the energy formerly given to the child, the sense of family in a supportive community, and the special relationship with someone very much like the self but further along are all part of the cathectic dimension. That dimension allows for great intimacy through which the healing process can work.

It seems, however, that for some individuals, the intimacy of the TCF process does not open up the self in identification, but threatens the defenses by which the pain is kept at bay. When we called those who did not return after attending one or two TCF meetings, we found that some said they already had the intimate relationships that they saw in TCF. But a significant minority of those we called said that they found attending the meeting stressful in that they found no relief of the pain in the meeting, but that hearing of the experiences of others only made them feel worse. Characteristic of these people was that they did not communicate about the child's death even within the family. Several of these parents indicated that the conversation with us was stressful, one saying, "Why don't you call the Compassionate Friends. They like to talk about it there." [8] Thus, without the cathectic dimension, pain could not be shared and another's pain could not be an occasion for expressing one's own pain. Instead of reaching out, the parents attempt to hold the self from pain including cutting the self off from potential healing relationships.

Though it is family-like, the cathectic dimension seems contained in a way other intimate relationships are not. The social life of the group is severely limited. While some TCF chapters have socials, most do not. Our chapter tried to have a picnic as a year-end meeting, but despite all the plans, very few people wanted to go, so it was canceled. Perhaps the bonds of bereaved parents are so deep that like other holy things, they must have fences about them.

Cathy:
> The people in TCF mean a lot to me. Though we are a tight-knit group, we don't send Christmas cards and socialize much outside the group. But there is a strong bond. There is a level of understanding and caring there that you don't get elsewhere.

Affiliation B: Experiential Dimension—The temporal perspective of the cathectic dimension in TCF is oriented to the present and future. As in all the interactions in TCF, the basis for that temporal orientation is complex. We have already noted the tranference of the attachment from the child to the group. The sense of shattered self also contributes to the temporal perspective. In effect, life starts over for the bereaved parent. As one of the members said, "Your life has changed. It's like moving from one town to another. You can't go back. Even if you did go back, it's not going to be the same." How does one learn to live in this new town, in this new self? One must learn by experience, and from the experience of others, how to find one's way around. It is this learning that we have called the experiential dimension of affiliation with TCF.

The experiential dimension has as its heart what one scholar has called experiential knowledge, that is knowledge acquired by direct acquaintance with the affliction or condition [12]. It is based in immediate experience and in the multiple ways an individual must respond in order to transcend the condition. Such experiential knowledge is very different from the knowledge-base used in professional intervention because it is from the point of view of the afflicted individual rather than from an outside point of view, and therefore it is holistic knowledge.

To an observer with a psychotherapeutic background, many of the interactions in a TCF meeting or in the phone conversations would appear rather directive. A person newly bereaved may cry and tell the story of the death and the group listens with little interruption. But after the emotions are drained out, a rather direct question is likely to be asked by one of the newcomers. "Does anyone else have problems going into the child's room?" or "What have other people done with the child's things?" After the emotional catharsis of the earlier part of the sharing, these practical and rather objective questions seem, to the psychotherapeutically inclined listener, to be too simple, for it seems that valuable group time should be spent on issues more central to the core of the self. Yet, many TCF members see the practical advice they received as one of the most helpful parts of the process.

> Joan:
> I came into TCF with all these blank problems that had no solutions. Such things like do we hang the stockings? Do we have the Thanksgiving dinner? I was so relieved to hear people at the November meeting talking about the stockings and how they handled it. It was a big thing to me, yet you certainly don't go to a friend with this problem. They would think you were stupid, or nuts, or both....I remember reading in Ann Landers about someone, after the death of a child, asking how many children the parents should tell people they had. To me it seemed foolish. I could not even see how this posed a problem for them, yet that turned out to be the biggest problem I had. I was always so proud of my five kids and it absolutely broke my heart to ever speak the words, "Four kids."

The two issues that seem to recur most often in the group are what to say when asked "How many children do you have?" and how to celebrate the holidays. Often when the TCF members speak of there being no right way to grieve, they are not talking about emotional expression—rather they are talking about how to deal with the practical issues that the death of the child raises in this culture.

> Frank:
> I don't see where it would be possible to deal with it constantly in the same setting (therapy), but can see that you could go to TCF for years and continue to get something new out of it. It's also less pressure oriented. You are also taking a risk in going to a counselor in only hearing one viewpoint. With TCF, the actors keep changing so you hear a variety of viewpoints.
> Cathy:
> It is the only place you can go and talk about your grief and your child as openly as you want. No one is going to make any judgments on you about how you are handling the situation. They reassure you that there is no

right way or wrong way. Whatever helps you the most is the right way. You take all the information and sift through it for what you need. Also, where else can you go to discuss major issues such as when someone asks how many children you have, what do you say?

The holiday issue is probably clearer to the nonbereaved parent, for most people have faced Christmas with someone away from home, and it is generally recognized that significant occasions such as birthdays or holidays are reminders of one who has recently died. Each year TCF has a meeting just before Thanksgiving in which the topic is getting through the holidays. Parents tell what they have done in the past that was helpful and other parents try to make plans that will suit them. For example one parent did not know whether to hang up the stockings, so she went to her son's drawer and found nineteen socks. She put a present in each and sent them to the VA hospital. Another parent wanted to remember the child, but did not want to make the rest of the family more uncomfortable, so she attached a black bow among many colored bows to the wreath outside the door. Many parents find it helpful to put a Christmas tree on the grave.

Parents often measure themselves by how well they are able to deal with the holidays, and the experiential advice given at TCF is central to that measuring.

Alice:
> After a year I was beginning to be able to get on with my life; I was able to have the Christmas celebration back at my house.

Irene:
> I also learned how to cope at Christmas. A lot of people had different suggestions on what worked for them. Putting a tree on their graves was helpful to me. We put on all the girls' homemade ornaments, then I could go home and have Christmas with the rest of the family.

Another of the major experiential issues is the relationship between spouses in the marriage. TCF members have examined the issue and have developed a set of teachings for newcomers. The issue, however, is too complex for adequate treatment in this chapter, and will receive full treatment separately.

The curative qualities of experiential knowledge are linked to the existential stance the bereaved parent takes within their world. The question about what to say when asked how many children the member has can be an example. At first, it seems a rather practical question. But in fact the question reaches deep into the nature of the parental bond—what does it mean when people say they "have" a child? After all, only under specific conditions do children understand that they "have" parents. Yet even if we were to "work through" the nature of that bond in therapy, the parent is still left with the problem of what to say in the social situation in which the question is asked. It is a casual question to the one who asks, while to the bereaved parent it is an issue of the degree of intimacy there must be in a relationship before the loss is shared. The issue of the degree of intimacy is related to factors in the culture that bring on discomfort in people when they hear about the death of the child, that is, it raises the marginal social role of a bereaved parent in a death denying society.

In the group are others who have faced the question and found answers. Not all the answers are the same. Each answer positions the parent differently toward the underlying nature of "having" a child and toward the problematic social role of bereaved parent. When TCF members say they listen to the information or opinions of others and then decide what might work best for them, they are saying that they are finding ways to position the new self in the world. The parent with the problem can thus choose a position from among several available models in the group. At the point of choice, the underlying issues are understood clearly in a way that is both concrete to the social situation and congruent with other existential positions the person takes in life. It is interesting to watch the face of the individual asking the question at a meeting, for very often when the option they will choose is mentioned, there is a nod and a grin with a light in the eyes that shows an instant recognition of the issues involved and the solution that is now lined up. The problem is not that the parents needed to understand what it means to "have" a child. They understand that all too well. They also understand all too well the marginal nature of their social role. What the experiential dimension has given them are options for existential action. To change the metaphor a bit, objective knowledge can analyze bodily movement and the effects of air pressure differential on moving objects. But the batter in a baseball game must integrate both of these into one experience when watching a pitch. Like bereaved parents at a meeting, the ball players work on their "stance" during practice. During the game they do the best they can, knowing that they can go over the problems later at another practice session. If they go into a slump, they may want to try a different stance for a while.

The experiential dimension does not provide answers set in stone, for different answers may work at different times in grief. A newsletter on preparing for the holidays had the following report:

> What a torment! Funny how you worry what your friends will think. For days I worried and finally I hung three on the fireplace wall, and laid one gently on the mantle.
> But that was last year! This year I shall hang all four above the fireplace. For this year the confusion of the mind has found new answers—with conviction! For it does not really matter whether my oldest daughter lives in Tuscon, or my youngest son is dead—these are my children, our family— and as long as we hang the Christmas stockings, we shall hang them all... with love.

The experiential dimension of affiliation with TCF is thus not a decision to act in a particular way, but a decision that TCF members have gathered some experience about the problems of being a bereaved parent and a decision to use the experience of other TCF members as a starting point for learning to manage the new self in the world. It is also, as the affiliation develops, a decision to share experience from one's own life with those who follow by a few months.

Wambach used the idea of "social construct" in her study of a widow's self-help group [13]. The idea is more simple and didactic than what we have called experiential knowledge, for it was a teaching about the grief process, which was "simple, linear, and unidirectional." She found very negative consequences when the group mobilized social pressure on a member to conform to a theoretic ideal of grief. In our observations, we have not seen a dynamic such as Wambach describes. The principles for TCF published by the national organization are specific in discouraging such practices: "We understand that each parent must find his or her own way through grief," and "We never suggest that there is a correct way to grieve or that there is a preferred solution to the emotional and spiritual dilemmas raised by the death of our children." In TCF the experiential dimension is sharing discoveries, not promoting conformity to an ideology.

The Process III: Transitions and Graduations

It is at this time difficult to know exactly what the end of parental bereavement is in TCF. Does one get over being a bereaved parent? The answer seems to be no.

> Grace:
> It's not over after a year or two years. It's an ongoing thing. Your life has changed. It's like moving from one town to another—you can't go back. Even if you did go back, it's not going to be the same.

Peppers and Knapp attempted to resolve the medical model of grief with the long-term sense of a missing piece we find in bereaved parents by inventing the term "shadow grief." The term itself is not useful, for it does not reach deeply enough into the dynamics of parental grief, but it does point to that sense of permanence that goes with parental bereavement [14]. One bereaved father said, "It's like losing my right arm. I can't grow a new arm, but I'm learning to live as a one armed man." The analogy of amputation offers an interesting insight into the difference between parental grief and other forms of grief. Parkes compared the grief response of widows and amputees. He found that while widows showed more distress in the first year, the distress tended to diminish after a year. The equivalent distress reported by amputees remained unchanged in the follow-up year [15]. TCF members seem more like amputees than widows, yet most literature on the duration of grief is derived from studies with widows.

What, then, is the continuing relationship with TCF? While parents do not get over it, neither do they remain in the condition that brought them into the group. A newsletter article comparing parental bereavement to the grief of an amputee concluded with:

> For the amputee, the raw and bleeding stump heals and the physical pain does go away. But he lives with the pain in his heart knowing his limb will not grow back. He has to learn to live without it. He re-builds his life around his loss. We bereaved parents must do the same. In time, the pain in our hearts will gradually ease, and we can learn to live again without our beloved child. Our lives will never be whole, but they can become full once more.

The transition toward fullness, if not to wholeness is, in part, also a transition in the relationship of the member to the self-help group. The transition within the group is a turn of energy toward others. We find that after some resolutions to the grief have been reached, the TCF members find help in helping others. As we noted in the discussion of the cathectic dimension, the way many parents find growth and meaning in the child's death is in the change in the self from being one of the helped to being a helper of others. TCF members often link the helper's role with their continued relationship with the child. The experiential dimension is also a part of this transition to the helper role, for as members were given options for existential stances in relation to difficult problems, they now present the options to others. Sharing a solution can be as simple as a sentence in a meeting or over the phone or in a short newsletter article, so it is an easy step to take. By listening to others and offering the solution to the other's situation, the TCF member puts his or her own life experience in perspective, for the individual can see the self more clearly when it is reflected in the lives of others.

The newsletter article with some early formulations of the ideas in this chapter brought a response from a chapter newsletter from another state:

> I came to realize that I could accept the things that I could not change or I could become a bitter old man. I refused to become that and made a conscious decision to go on living, to survive. I read books, I cried, I talked with bereaved parents, I cried, I wrote letters to other parents who had lost children, I cried, and a day at a time, I began to heal. The day came when all the mirrors that surrounded me, that reflected all times and events back onto me and my tragedy, began to become windows and I could see again out of myself and into the lives of others; first into the lives of other bereaved parents, but then gradually into all those whose lives touched mine.
>
> I came to realize too that in trying to help others, I was helping myself, that a very important part of that healing was putting love back into my life.

Cathy:

> Between six months and a year, my motive for going to TCF changed from taking to giving back—not that I ever quit getting something from the

group....I find that giving to others in the group is a healing in itself. It helps to give some purpose to I.'s death. At one point I decided that he couldn't be completely happy in heaven while he knew I was so unhappy.

Writing for the newsletters and talking to newly bereaved parents on the phone are important ways that many people find to give back.

Irene:
Writing the letter that they printed in the newsletter was helpful to me. I really like writing, but it wasn't until I was in the hospital (for breast cancer) that I took the time to write that letter to the girls. It also helps me to know I have helped others. Some people have told me that just seeing that I have survived has helped them.

Donna:
My writings have really helped to get it out of my system, and the fact that TCF thought enough of what I wrote to publish it. People would let me know that I wrote just what they were feeling and it helped them to read it. That helped me a lot. With others it's different though. My kids don't read what I write. I think it's too painful for them. With my family (mother and sisters) there has been a lot of fussing about my writing. They ask, "What do you write that stuff for? It just keeps reminding you." I don't need to write to be reminded.

The transition from being helped to helping is a key one in the TCF process, for reaching out to others in sympathy seems to be a first step in reinvesting the self in other relationships. The matter of reinvestment is obviously complex. For some TCF members, it comes at the very time they are also cutting ties to a spouse and getting a divorce. It also needs to be understood in terms of the degree of self protection TCF members say they have developed in their relationship to others. Clearly, then, investment of the self after the death of a child is a complicated affair with many interesting dynamics.

A great deal of the activity within TCF is premised on the transition to helper. A newsletter is written and mailed by members. There is a list of phone numbers for newly bereaved and those having a bad day to call. Each of the chapters has a leader and some have co-leaders. Those who have been with the group for a while are likely to be asked to give presentations in the community or to appear in the media. The chapter has business meetings three or four times a year at which everyone is welcome. Generally any person who comes to one of those meetings will go home with an assigned task.

For those who become central members in the leadership, the structure of the organizational details seems to provide a good way for them to consolidate their gains. In some cases the rebuilding of the self after the death of a child is a radical change from the self they were before the death, and the leadership in TCF is a stepping stone to what Erikson calls the generative stage.

Helen:
> Either you feel like you've been helped and think, "I don't need that any more," or you feel like you've been helped and feel a need to give back. In my mind, TCF is a way to keep V. close to me and I like that feeling. If I wasn't involved in TCF, I think I would have a lot of sadder memories of V. But I realize that because of what has happened to me I can do this for him, with him. I can help other people. You see, I'm not typically a leader; I'm a follower.
>
> Q: I think you are a leader, but just didn't realize it.
>
> Perhaps, but typically in the past I would belong to an organization but not even think of being involved in the leadership. What I'm doing leading it is beyond me, but now I'm even becoming more comfortable speaking in groups. I guess the need to do this because it might help someone else has outweighed my self-consciousness and embarrassment of knowing I'll break out in a flush from the nervousness. I'm a totally different person than I was in my 20s and I know this experience has a lot to do with it. I have rejoined the Children's Challenge group and put down V.'s name and introduce him. Another mother then introduced her deceased daughter. I thought, "Well good, maybe I gave her the courage to do that."

On the other hand, for some people taking leadership is something they were used to doing before the death. Indeed, some of the TCF leaders previously led other self-help groups.

Other parents do not move into the formal organizational leadership of the chapter, though usually their attendance drops off after about a year if they do not assume formal leadership. But those people who have stopped attending regularly do not seem to feel as though they have stopped being members and most keep in regular contact with other members. The difficulty seems to be that while they are over the grieving in the medical model sense of that word, they are not "over" the loss. The loss of the child is not something to be gotten over any more than one could get over the amputation of an arm. So when parents leave the group, they do not leave as they were before the death. On special occasions, birthdays or holidays or when they see a child about the same age or hear of a similar accident, the grief returns and it seems as if it were "only yesterday."

Donna:
> It wasn't something I wanted to do. To this day I still miss the group. I had to go to work a year ago when my husband left me, and I have to work nights tending bar. At first I arranged to be off on the meeting nights, but as of this last summer, I wasn't able to work it out any more and had to stop. I miss it something terribly. I feel so left out.
>
> Q: Over the period of time you went, did TCF's role change for you?
>
> I still need the group and get a lot out of it. I still need to be able to talk about it and be able to say the things I still feel. But I also need to be able

to do something for someone else. Then I don't feel like I'm a total failure in life. If anything good came out of this whole thing, it's being able to help others. It bothers me very much not to be able to do that now. I still want to write, but haven't because I am exhausted from working, yet I still need to do that. It will be three years soon, but at the same time it was only yesterday.

Other people see TCF as a continuing source of strength in their lives, but do not move into formal leadership. A woman whose daughter was murdered was on a phone list, but had stopped attending. However, when the trial drew near she began attending again.

> Grace:
> Part of why we went to TCF was to get in shape for the trial. It was a year and a half before it went to trial and it was important to us to be there and be prepared to handle anything that came our way....
> Q: How long did you attend TCF and why did you quit going to the meeting?
> We went pretty regularly when it was close, but after it moved up north we didn't go. The last time or two was after the trial. It helped us keep our equilibrium during that time. I felt we had to be reasonably strong before the trial so we wouldn't fall apart. I'd still like to attend at times, but one of the results of all this is I'm very uncomfortable going out alone at nights and my husband doesn't want to attend any more.

It may be that one of the opportunities facing TCF is to find a way to maintain contact with those people who have been aided in the first year or so of their grief, but who do not find a part of the new self in the leadership cadre. At this time, the informal nature of the group and the pressure of the crisis felt by those who come newly shattered has not allowed for a long term program to develop. There is a special bond with other TCF members that can only be shared by those who have been through the fire and survived. But at this time the group has not found a way to nurture that bond and at the same time allow the bereaved parent to reinvest in relationships and organizations not connected with bereavement.

Some self-help groups such as AA assume that membership is life long because they believe that addiction to the drug is never over. Other self-help groups such as THEOS understand their role as aiding the transition through a life crisis. Clearly TCF is somewhere between those two, for parental bereavement is a permanent condition. The optimal solution would be for the culture to develop rituals by which the child could be remembered and mourned periodically throughout the parent's lifetime. That does not seem likely at this time, however, so perhaps some intermediate relationships between bereaved parents would serve.

CONCLUSION

Many bereaved parents seem to find self-help to be an effective intervention. We have attempted to understand the TCF process in terms of the decision to attend the group, the decision to affiliate, and the decision to transform one's self into a helper within the group. The decision to attend seems to be rooted in a variety of expectations, though an invitation by parents who are already members or the support of friends and family members is often involved, as often are messages from the unconscious. New members attend with a variety of experiences with professional interventions. A significant number have had positive experience with other self-help groups. Affiliation has, first, a cathectic dimension that entails a sense of unity with those whose lives have also been shattered, a sense of hope at seeing that others have made it, a sense of finding an appropriate object on which to attach the energy formerly given to the child, and a sense of family in a supportive community. Second, affiliation has an experiential dimension that is an attempt to develop an existential stance in a problematic world based on shared solutions to concrete problems. The decision to become a helper is the key to the TCF process, for it is the concept that helping others is the best way to help the self that allows the cathectic dimension to become complete in reinvestment, and allows the experiential dimension to change from using the experience of others to sharing one's own experience. As time progresses, some members move to formal organizational leadership while others tend to become less regular in attendance, though they do so with some ambivalence.

It would seem that analysis of other interventions using schemas similar to those used in this study could be done. Those schemas would include: reasons and background for seeking the intervention, the decision to stay with the intervention, including the cathectic aspects of the grief and the experiential problem solving the intervention provides, and a study of transformations within the intervention including the transition out of the intervention. If thanatology is to move beyond altruism, various interventions must be understood with far more precision than is now the case. We must understand what we do in a more exact way. The categories used in this study would seem usable in studies of other interventions.

REFERENCES

1. M. Lieberman and L. Borman, *Self-Help Groups for Coping with Crisis,* Jossey-Bass, San Francisco; 1979.
2. W. F. Whyte, *Street Corner Society: The Structure of an Italian Slum,* University of Chicago Press, Chicago; 1973.
3. R. Wax, *Doing Fieldwork, Warnings and Advice,* University of Chicago Press, Chicago; 1971.

4. B. L. Glaser and A. L. Strauss, *The Discovery of Grounded Theory: Strategies for Qualitave Research,* Aldine Publishing Co., Chicago; 1967.
5. H. Powdermaker, *Stranger and Friend: The Way of an Anthropologist,* W. W. Norton Co., New York, 1966.
6. H. S. Becker, *Sociological Work: Method and Substance,* Aldine Publishing Company, Chicago, 1970.
7. D. Klass and B. Shinners, " Professional Roles in a Self-Help Group for the Bereaved," *Omega 13*:4, pp. 361-375, 1983.
8. M. Hoeppner and D. Klass, "Factors in Affiliation with a Self-Help Group for Bereaved Parents," in Arlington, R. Pacholske and C. Corr (eds.), *Priorities in Death Education and Counseling,* Forum for Death Education and Counseling, pp. 131-137.
9. S. Freud, "Mourning and Meloncholia" (1917) Standard Edition, Vol. XIV, Hogarth Press, London, 1957.
10. .W. Worden, *Grief Counseling and Grief Therapy,* Springer, New York, 1982.
11. L. Fiegenberg, *Terminal Care: Friendship Contracts with Dying Cancer Patients,* trans. by P. Hort, Brunner Mazel, New York, 1980.
12. T. Borkman, "Experiential Knowledge: A New Concept for the Analysis of Self-Help Groups," *Social Service Review 50*:3, 1976.
13. J. A. Wambach, "The Grief Process as a Social Construct," *Omega,* in press.
14. L. Peppers and R. Knapp, *Motherhood and Mourning, Perinatal Death,* Praeger, New York, 1980.
15. C. M. Parkes, "Psycho-Social Transitions: Comparison Between Reactions to Loss of a Limb and Loss of a Spouse," *British Journal of Psychiatry, 127,* pp. 204-210, September 1975.

The previous chapter described the program of The Compassionate Friends, a self-help group that makes little or no use of professional services and staff. This chapter describes another way in which people receive services through non-professionals: volunteerism.

For many decades volunteers have made significant contributions to the health-care and social-service fields. During the past dozen or so years, they have also been involved in working with the dying and the bereaved. For example, hospice programs depend heavily on volunteer staff, and many hospitals have developed extensive volunteer services, some of which are offered to the dying. In addition, certain groups, such as Shanti (mentioned in the following chapter), have provided substantial programs of outreach services to the dying and the bereaved. Shanti is especially interesting, since it has shifted its mission to some extent over the past few years from ministering to a variety of individuals concerned with death and grief to focusing its efforts on victims of AIDS, a condition that, at least at this writing, has an extremely high death rate.

The present chapter discusses volunteering in general and offers a variety of suggestions about ways in which people can volunteer. For more information on volunteering with dying or grieving persons, you need to call a local hospice or hospital, or contact an appropriate person.

CHAPTER
20

Volunteers and the Care of the Terminal Patient

Chwee Lye Chng
and
Michael Kirby Ramsey

Dying can be a lonely and painful act. Sometimes, despite the devotion of
family members for the dying patient, or the medical care hospital staff
provides, the patient may still experience acute loss and isolation:

> When I die, my husband will lose his wife, his confidante, his lover;
> my children will lose their mother; my sisters will lose their sister; my
> friends their friend, but I will lose everybody [1, p. 15].

The dying patient, who has an inordinate need for companionship and
community support greater than ever before, ironically is more alienated than
at any other time. Unfortunately, in too many cases family members may
inadvertently "reject" the patient when confronted with the reality of death,
while the professional staff may distance itself to avoid becoming too
emotionally involved.

Into this dismal scene enters the volunteer who can provide valuable
companionship and needed care, sometimes by virtue of simply not being
a professional or relative. When terminal patients can no longer interact
with the community, volunteers bring the community to them. Conse-

quently, they do not feel so isolated from the mainstream of life. As a dying patient shares with deep conviction, "The volunteers are my friends." Unlike some members of the family, a well-trained volunteer can cope emotionally with the finality of death, free from feelings of guilt, depression and fear. The motivation may sometimes be the product of a previous personal experience with tragedy. Thus, when a dying patient asks, "What is it like?" these volunteers have some answers, because of their experiences and observations.

The purpose of the chapter is to explore the role of the volunteer in the care of the terminal patient and among other aspects, will discuss the role of the volunteer in a health care team, qualifications and selection of the volunteer, training programs, and special problems faced by the volunteer who works exclusively with the dying patient.

THE ROLE OF THE VOLUNTEER

Today there is an acute demand for health care services. The high cost of health care has greatly reduced the number of paid medical personnel, and with the impending budgetary cuts there is little room for optimism for the consumers of health care today. In a time when taxes are inadequate to carry the full load, and when philanthropic contributions are not readily forthcoming, President Reagan has asked Americans to renew their "spirit of volunteerism" to pick up the slack created by his budget cuts.

Volunteerism has a strong tradition in the United States and volunteers still represent a significant pool of human resources, particularly in the fields of health and welfare. Today more than one fourth of all Americans volunteer. Volunteering is no longer a casual activity for people with leisure time, but rather an acknowledgement that community health services are important because they strengthen and enrich community life. Today almost every occupational, ethnic, and socioeconomic sector has its quota of volunteers. Volunteerism offers the opportunity for people from all walks of life to do something meaningful for others. It also provides personal growth for the volunteer, and in many instances, enriches the person with valuable skills from other disciplines.

In the case of the terminal patient, the volunteer plays three roles: companion and friend, advocate, and educator. Although these different roles are interrelated, they will be treated individually in order to highlight their unique aspects.

Companion/Friend

When facing death the patient often wants to talk about hopes, fears, anger, disappointments, and hurts—in essence, to have someone with whom he or she can comfortably unburden feelings brought on by the impending death. The need is even more acute for a patient without any family, one who is completely alone.

Health professionals are by no means immune to the emotional upheavals that beset the dying patient and family. Doctors, nurses, social workers, and clergy respond regularly to the needs of the terminal patient. Although they are less intimately involved than family members or close friends, the emotional demands on the staff are nonetheless tremendous. This stress, coupled with ever increasing demands on their time, often prevents the professional staff from providing the time and attention the patient may desire. This is where the volunteer can be most useful, providing nonessential supportive services, such as reading to the patient, playing games, letter writing, or just listening to the patient. The cost of hiring such services would be prohibitive.

The volunteer, therefore, contributes what most professionals cannot: an indefinite amount of time with the patient and family, and identification with them, their feelings, and problems. He or she helps to enhance the quality of life when there is so little quantity left. Sometimes it is nothing more than just "being there," assuring the patient and family that they are not alone in this painful experience, that someone cares and is there just as a friend. Through the time, effort and warmth offered, the volunteer contributes a unique variety of "treatments" to terminal patients. A skilled volunteer can greatly enrich the last days of life for a dying patient without compromising the integrity of either the patient or family.

There are also the needs of the family members after the patient dies: the spouse, siblings, significant others. These persons too need to have someone with whom to unburden all the deep emotions precipitated by the death — feelings, which if ignored, will incapacitate and interfere with the grieving process thereafter. Technically, the professional staff has no jurisdiction when a patient leaves the hospital, but volunteers can be a bridge for the family to other sources of help. This supportive atmosphere may also contribute to the immediate coping and permanent adjustment made by the surviving family.

Advocate

Beside serving as friend and companion, the volunteer is in an advantageous position to act as advocate on behalf of the dying patient and family. Overwhelmed by grief and pain, and riddled with confusion, the patient and family may feel lost and helpless in the intimidating environment of the hospital. In the patient's final days as death approaches, the volunteer′ advocate can help articulate the unmet needs of the patient. There are times when patients, afraid of annoying the medical staff, would not request help or mention discomfort until it became critical. Because the volunteer is trusted, the patient may disclose this information to him or her. Often terminal patients would like to die at home but are afraid to request it. Here the volunteer can speak up for the dying patient.

Of course, the volunteer should operate within the framework of the hospital or terminal care facility. The role of advocate is obviously not an easy, nor generally accepted position, for the volunteer. To be truly effective, the suggestions of the volunteer have to stem from knowledge and understanding of the intricate patient-family-institutional configurations. Under the careful guidance of professionals, the volunteer can serve a significant role as ancilliary to professionals.

Educator

The responsibility of the volunteer extends beyond the mere provision of support and companionship to patients and families, important as this is. The volunteer also serves as educator, a role that involves assisting the patient and family to cope with dying and bereavement. The basic philosophy of the hospital, however, is quite antithetical to the needs of the dying patient. Often the declaration that a patient is terminal is immediately construed to be an admission of failure. Although the emotional care of terminal patients and their families constitutes a part of medical/nursing education, some health care personnel involved with patient care may still experience difficulty accepting this fact. They are, after all trained to keep the patient alive, and to deem all else as failure or defeat.

The experienced professional and the well-trained volunteer can change this thinking. Together they can provide compassionate care and support for the terminal patient and family, care that affirms their autonomy and dignity. This shared role of educator is especially important in our death-denying society where an entire generation of Americans has never met a dying person.

The inevitable product of the denial of death is an extremely expensive health care system that performs technological miracles to heal the sick, but often is insensitive to the unique needs of patients who cannot be cured. Hopefully, through the educational efforts of the volunteer and the professional, the terminal patient will once again be accepted as a person, and attempts will be made to alleviate the symptoms, even when nothing can be done for the disease.

WHO ARE THESE VOLUNTEERS?

Volunteers come for all age groups, socio-economic classes, and work backgrounds. Today's volunteers include the housewife, student, retired person, and professionals such as social workers, psychologists, teachers, gerontologists, members of the clergy and architects. Each volunteer brings with him or her skills and experience that can greatly enhance the life of the terminal patient [2, p. 364].

Many volunteers have lost loved ones. They have decided to help make the lives of other dying individuals and families more meaningful and enjoyable. As a result, it is not unusual to find a large number of widows and widowers volunteering in hospitals [1, p. 19].

Students also make up a large percent of the volunteer staff in health care facilities. The reasons for student participation include such factors as course credit at their academic institutions, development of skills that can be used in a career, experience in a work setting that will enhance future employment, humanitarian desires, and many other reasons. Many health care students studying medicine, dentistry, and pharmacology are encouraged to participate in volunteer work to experience early exposure to patient contact [3, 4].

Retired individuals can make an important contribution because many of them possess the qualities needed for this demanding task. They bring to the health facility many years of valuable experience [5, p. 184]. Conversely, in many cases volunteer work gives the retired person a new meaning in life.

Finally, it is not uncommon to find terminally ill patients themselves participating in volunteer work in terminal care facilities. These individuals often staff telephone "hotlines" to give comfort to other terminally ill patients and their families [6].

Although volunteerism is increasing in our society and all segments of our population are involved in volunteer programs, not every person is suited, psychologically or otherwise, for work with the dying patient. Work in terminal care facilities can be both physically and emotionally exhausting. To be an effective volunteer in such agencies, it often takes more than just a humanitarian desire to help the less fortunate. Many terminal care programs have special screening sessions to evaluate the prospective volunteer [2, p. 363]. According to Charles Garfield of the Shanti Project:

> All prospective volunteers send us a statement describing why they want to work with patients and families facing life-threatening illness. They are subsequently invited to an interview in which one or two experienced volunteers and the codirectors of the project meet with each prospective Shanti volunteer. In addition to an evident sense of compassion, we look for many qualities, among them a high tolerance for ambiguity; an ease in talking about dying (as evidenced by discussion that is personalized rather than predominantly philosophical); the ability for introspection as reflected in extensive self-knowledge; a healthy sense of self-confidence; a high tolerance for frustration; a degree of psychological mindedness; a sense of humility that allows one to view sharing in someone else's dying as a joint process with learning occurring on both sides; the ability to speak and understand various metaphors (religious, cultural, or symbolic); and revelant professional training in counseling, psychology, social welfare, nursing, or medicine [2, p. 364].

WHERE TO VOLUNTEER?

Organizations involved in caring for the terminally ill and needing volunteers include both private and public organizations. Prospective volunteers should contact area helping organizations such as churches, community health programs, support groups, hospices, and hospitals. Many of these organizations have placement departments that try to match the volunteer with the type of environment and work desired. Also, private homes often desire volunteers to care for terminal patients who are financially unable to seek help elsewhere, or where such facilities have long waiting lists [7].

Various organizations and support groups are either partially or totally dependent on volunteers in order to function. The National Retired Teachers Association and the American Association of Retired Persons have been involved in the recruitment of volunteers in meeting the needs of newly widowed persons. The program, *Widowed Persons Service,* is operating in over 100 locations in the country. The focus of the program is the personal relationship between the volunteer "veteran" widowed person and the newly widowed. People who are bereaved may find support in *The Compassionate Friends,* while those who are suffering from a terminal illness support each other in *Make Today Count.* Various YMCA programs across the nation sponsor student visitation and work programs for older people who suffer from extreme age or from terminal illness. The students often participate in singing, games, and individual conversations with elderly individuals [8].

Many colleges offer courses that require student participation in volunteer community programs. These courses not only provide needed volunteer help for tightly budgeted organizations, but also give the student practical, on-the-job training. Such a program is found in the health education department at North Texas State University at Denton, Texas. In the freshman level course, "Introduction to Community Health," the student is required to volunteer 30 hours of work at an area community health organization.

WHAT TO VOLUNTEER FOR?

Just what can a volunteer expect to do in facilities involved with caring for the terminally ill? It depends on the regulations of the organization itself and on the experience, training, and skills of the volunteer. Generally, there are six categories of jobs in which the volunteer may perform. These jobs include: fund raising; leadership and management; clerical and manual; teaching; professional skills, and all else. Many medical professionals including physicians and nurses, volunteer their services to programs serving the terminally ill. These individuals can perform any or all of the medical responsibilities their professional expertise qualifies them to perform. Some physicians may function as medical director of such organizations, while nurses perform counseling duties as well as traditional nursing responsibilities [9].

For the nonprofessional volunteer, any nonmedical duty that the management feels the individual is qualified to perform may be made available. These duties include diverse chores ranging from household services, transportation, babysitting, laundry, letter writing, and errands to, perhaps even more important, the provision of friendship and support to the dying person and members of the family. For the family who is unable to be with the patient at the time of death, the volunteer often fulfills this most important task. Each of these tasks can be performed by most volunteers with minimal training [2, p. 379].

Most terminal care facilities require a certain amount of orientation and training; this includes not only the nonprofessional volunteer but the professional as well. Such training sessions may vary in intensity and length but most training sessions last from eight hours to several days or even weeks. The training programs may include films and cassettes, panel presentations by the facilities staff, and readings. Additional training may include workshops, seminars and in-service programs. The educational aims of such training programs may include part or all of the following [10, pp. 177, 183]:

1. Orientation of the volunteer to the facility and the services it offers;
2. Exploration of the volunteer's feelings concerning death and dying, pain, loss, and the dying patient so that the volunteer can be helped to recognize and deal with these feelings before attempting to assist the dying patient and their family;
3. Development of an attitude of optimism so that such feelings can be conveyed to the patients and their family;
4. Reduction of patient discomfort and loneliness through various techniques;
5. Acquisition of teaching skills in order to train patients and their families in self-care techniques;
6. Establishment of realistic limitation for one's own role and performance, and the encouragement of periodic relaxation and refreshment;
7. Development of skills needed by the terminal care facility for assisting the patient and the patient's family;
8. Encouragement of the volunteer's committment to the program;
9. Establishment of ethical standards to regulate the volunteer's performance in the program and his/her dealings with all patient matters.

A problem faced by many terminal care facilities concerns burn-out in the volunteer. Although many training sessions deal with this subject, burn-out is still a big problem in such programs. Mansell Pattison, in his book *The Experience of Dying,* speaks of "death saturation":

Another aspect of self-helping is to recognize the phenomenon of death saturation. That is, we can only work with dying persons for so long, and with so much personal investment, and with so much intensity, before we have reached the limits of our personal tolerance. Helping the dying is a personally demanding task. We each have limits to our intimate exposure to dying. We must be able to identify our personal limits of saturation. Then we need to back off, to gain distance, relief, reconstitution of ourselves [11, p. 316].

Pattison stresses the need for a realistic plan to give sociopsychological support of the staff who care for the dying. Different organizations use different approaches and some use none at all. Possible methods to combat burn-out could include one or more of the following [11, p. 316]:

1. Debriefing sessions in which the volunteer and staff members meet with other personnel to talk over their feelings and frustrations.
2. Relaxation techniques such as biofeedback, transcendental meditation, progressive relaxation, and exercise activities.
3. Limitations in the amount of time allowed for the person to work.
4. Change in duties performed by the volunteer (i.e., one day the person may work with patients directly, while the next day he/she may perform household duties or run errands) [11, p. 324].

The methods chosen by the health care facility may vary but there should be some attempt on the part of the program management to address this very important problem.

CONCLUSION

Volunteers play a singularly vital role in the creation of a meaningful support system for dying patients and their families. Beside helping these individuals, the use of volunteers in the care of the terminal patient is also a significant way of introducing community wide changes. Through the involvement of large numbers of people from a wide cross section of society in an educational process, attitudes and practices in the important field of death and dying can be gradually changed.

REFERENCES

1. D. Garret, The Needs of the Seriously Ill and Their Families: The Haven Concept, *Aging,* Nov./Dec., p. 15, 1978.
2. C. Garfield, *Psychological Care of Dying Patients,* McGraw-Hill Book Co., New York, p. 364, 1978.
3. G. Oliver, Odyssey of a Volunteer and Activist, *The Humanist, 40*:3, p. 58, 1980.
4. New Turn in Student Activism. *U.S. News and World Report, 75*:10, p. 31, Sept. 3, 1973.

5. S. Stoddard, *The Hospice Movement,* Vintage Books, New York, p. 184, 1978.
6. S. Wilding, The Most Precious Gift, *Good Housekeeping,* pp. 80-86, Dec. 1979.
7. N. Legg, The Gift of Time, *Working Women, 3*:12, p. 38, Dec. 1978.
8. M. Morain, Adolescents as Volunteers, *The Humanist, 39*:3, p. 58, May/ June 1979.
9. Working for Free, *Human Behavior, 8*:1, p. 85, Jan. 1979.
10. P. Rossman, *Hospice,* Associated Press, New York, p. 177, 1977.
11. M. Pattison, *The Experience of Dying,* Prentice-Hall, New York, p. 316, 1977.

In the past 20 years, death education has changed from an expression bandied about by a handful of people to a recognized, albeit small, sub-specialty within education. The introductory comments made for Section IV (Counseling and Psychotherapy) to the effect that, although there are only a few death counselors, virtually all counselors and psychotherapists need to know about death, could be made in the present context as well. Although there are very few specialists in death education, virtually all teachers and educators must deal with death.

Teachers and educators encounter death in two ways: first, their students and their colleagues encounter death and grief at personal levels, and effective teachers must rise to the challenge of helping these individuals cope with the stress that enters their lives; and second, death is a constant topic in the classroom, particularly in such courses as literature, social studies, and the biological sciences. Whether it is Willy Loman in Death of a Salesman *or Macduff in* Macbeth, *the assassination of Julius Caesar or the significance of thousands of deaths in Viet-Nam, the effects of arteriosclerosis or the meaning of vast ecological changes, death and grief are a constant part of school curriculum at all levels of education.*

The term "death education" can be applied to a formal college course or the sermon of a parish priest or a health education lecture to sixth-graders or an educational television production. The form is not the determinant of whether it is education or not. Death education can occur in innumerable forms, as long as the content is related directly or indirectly to death, dying, or grief.

PART 5
Death Education

Death educators are, first and foremost, educators among whose special areas of concern and expert background, are the issues of death, dying, and grief. They may teach in universities or colleges, or they may develop programs and workshops in hospitals or hospices or community agencies. Their backgrounds may be in education or psychology or social work or the ministry or nursing or medicine or some other field. They may spend full time as death educators or, much more frequently, this is only one of several concerns with which they work. Their efforts may be directed toward university or college students, toward pupils in high schools or even elementary schools, toward the terminally ill themselves or toward the health professionals who care for them, toward the family members of the terminally ill, toward clergy and hospital chaplains, or occasionally toward future death educators.

Whatever their origins and whoever their students, death educators resemble other educators in many ways. But not in all ways. The fact that the content of their educational processes is death or dying or grieving sets them apart from other educators. Not surprisingly, they themselves often appear unaware of the uniqueness of their circumstances, and—since they usually believe in promoting their views among colleagues and others—they sometimes seem confused and even hurt when their words are ignored or their mission thwarted.

This chapter describes the role and status of the death educator as comparable to that of a deacon in the church. Other models of course could be applied, such as death educator as child or death educator as patient or death educator as middle management, but the role of deacon appears particularly apt.

CHAPTER 21

Death Educator as Deacon

Richard A. Kalish

THE RELIGIOUS METAPHOR:
PRIESTS AND DEACONS

Death education is slowly beginning to take form as a field, while death educators and counselors are themselves so much involved in the process that they often have difficulty stepping back to observe the significance. This presentation speculates about the meaning of death education today. It takes the form of viewing the death educator as deacon and the physician as priest, and explores the interactions between the two.

Religion has been defined as "man's ultimate concern." At one point in history—and for many persons, still—the ultimate concern was passing through the vale of tears that is earthly existence in order to abide with God and Jesus in the next life. When ascending to heaven was "man's ultimate concern," the priesthood was constituted of those individuals best able to provide access to this ultimate concern (i.e., clergy and theologians). These persons had extremely high status and were powerful community leaders.

More recently, at least among persons whose opinions reach the general public, the ultimate concern is no longer that of heavenly immortality, but of a long and healthy life on earth, perhaps even of earthly immortality. In that case, the priesthood must change. When the god is secular, the priesthood must also be secular, and the individuals who provide access to ultimate concern are those in the medical profession, especially physicians. Their status, influence, and fees have risen commensurately.

One cogent model is that of the physician as the priest recently come to power and the clergy as the priest recently losing power. This reflects Sam Keen's comment that ". . . disease has replaced sin as the condition from which we must be saved . . ." [1, p. 67]. An application of this model to the work of death education is that the death educator and the death counselor perform the role of deacon in relationship to both the contemporary priest-physician and the traditional priest-clergy.

A priest is authorized to perform the sacred rites of religion. Initially conceived as representing the people to God, in the 13th Century, the priest began to become the representative of God to the people [2]. During the Middle Ages, the priest was ordained with what amounted to supernatural powers and functions [2].

The old clergy priesthood and the newer medical priesthood have much in common. Both have established large temples for worship, temples where rituals are performed, where neophytes carry out the orders of their masters, where helpers (usually women) serve in supportive capacities. People who enter these temples speak in hushed tones, sometimes arrive as supplicants, and often go away carrying prescriptions that bear Latin terms. The priests solemnly offer advice as to how to attain one's ultimate goal, frequently with admonitions on how to conduct oneself better on a day-to-day basis. Certain foods are proscribed and others are prescribed.

Both priesthoods are required to undergo rigorous training and socialization into their guilds, and the guilds of both emphasize humility. Both find on emergence from their training that their guilds are political organizations as much as professional organizations. Both sets of priests study diligently and serve a demanding apprenticeship. Both are permitted, sometimes required, to don vestments that signify their status and that serve to differentiate them from others who work with them. Both have developed significant healing rituals, using the jargon of their guilds. Both are permitted to withhold certain kinds of information from legal and judicial bodies; both are given preferences in the military and, in some instances, in tax law. Both have been essentially male enclaves into which women are pressing in increasing numbers. The parallels could be continued indefinitely.

Both are expected to be warm and caring human beings, even though their technical knowledge does not depend on their humanity. Yet it is generally recognized, although sometimes ignored in practice, that the effectiveness of each priest's work is in part the result of technology and in part the result of warmth and caring.

The shifting power and status balance between the medical priesthood and the clerical priesthood appears to have stabilized, but very recently a new element entered the picture. It is as though the very success of the new priesthood only serve to accentuate its failure. As the quantity of life appeared to out-distance the quality of life, more and more people began to question sheer quantity as an adequate ultimate concern. The lengthened survival was seen as leading to the spectre of slow deterioration in nursing homes, of living out lives of loneliness, and of turning control of one's fate over to an impersonal technician standing behind an impersonal machine. The knowledge, machines, power, buildings, rituals, in effect, the magic of the new priesthood was clearly inadequate.

Although many individual priests recognized this, their political representatives either did not or preferred not to recognize the changes, and the political controls that they had established over life remained. The ultimate concern of many people was still that of long and healthy life, and the medical establishment was seen as their best opportunity for receiving it.

Nonetheless, the new gods, that of long earthly life, were weakened, and a newly-emphasized concern (not a new concern, but a newly-emphasized one) was recognized, that of an appropriate ending to life. While far from an ultimate concern, it did develop significance as a legitimate ancillary concern, and the priesthood was expected to respond to it. Too often, however, the magic of the physician was not applicable to this concern, and the physician retreated from even attempting to find new magic, preferring to insist that the gods he represented would continue to dominate.

As people's concerns shifted, as many perceived the rituals of the physician as leading to false as well as true gods, a new calling developed: the death educator. It lacked the power of both the other priesthoods, since it led neither to long life on earth nor continued life after death, but its adherents are at least permitted to enter the temples and perform their rituals. I would consider them deacons who will never be priests.

Historically the deacon served under the priest or other clergy, with specified tasks assigned. These tasks involved assisting the priest and might include delegated administrative duties. Early in the history of the Christian Church, the deacons overstepped their bounds, and their powers were severely curbed. Their functions are variously defined in the different denominations, but everywhere they are subservient to the priests [2].

The new deacons have been accepted by many of the old priesthood and some of the new, although acceptance by the latter appears contingent on the deacons making it clear that they do not wish either to criticize the new priesthood nor to take over more powerful roles than the one already delegated.

HEALERS AND PREACHERS

We can cut at another angle and come up with another division: healers and preachers. Physicians and death counselors are primarily healers; clergy and death educators are primarily preachers. These roles are not at all rigidly defined, but we still tend to find the counselor working under the auspices of the physician, usually in a highly subservient capacity as far as potential power is concerned, while the educator works in a more or less egalitarian relationship with the clergy.

The priests and deacons have a well-defined power relationship, although individual circumstances occasionally offer reversals. Healers and preachers, however, do not have a well-defined power relationship. Indeed, historically, and to some extent today, the person who ministered to the physical body and the person who ministered to the soul were one and the same: medicine man, shaman, prayer leader. (We find this still the case among the followers of Chirstian Science, and it is returning to some degree among advocates of the various wholistic health programs.) In western culture, however, these roles were divided centuries ago, with medicine emerging as a totally separate calling. Nonetheless, illness and accidents continue to be viewed in religious terms, as the penalty for original sin and subsequent sinning, as punishment for evil thoughts and actions. If the cause of illness and accidents is religious, then it is logical for the cure to be in keeping. Cutting a hole in the skull permitted the evil spirits to leave the head; sneezing required "God bless you" as the devils were expelled through the nostrils; prayer and penance were perceived as the price for good health; Jesus healed the sick.

For the most part, however, healing became the province of physicians. Although they did continue to preach to some extent, these tasks were largely delegated to social workers, health educators, and others.

The clergy, for their part, did not fully abandon healing. The more contemporary shifted to pastoral counseling and became knowledgeable in the tools and techniques of psychotherapy; the less contemporary (or so they initially appeared) held to faith-healing and other forms of healing. Thus the old priesthood again divided, with some retaining the role of healer of the body, while other forsake this role and compensated by focusing on the mind and emotions.

Both priests and deacons, both healers and preachers, are committed to maintaining life, except that each perceives this in different ways. The physician is committed to maintaining life on earth. Physicians are concerned with the quality of life, but their training and socialization have encouraged primary responsiveness to the quantity of life. The clergy is committed to providing access to life after life on earth. They are primarily concerned with the quality of this life, a task which may or may not be interpreted in flexible fashion, and the clergy's concern for the quantity of life is not likely to differ from that of other individuals. That is, their calling does not require a position on the quantity of life, but it often requires a position on the quality of life.

The division among deacons is somewhat different. Both healers and preachers are more likely to share the views of the clergy in these regards than they are to share the views of the physicians. They are most likely to see their skills and their proper role to be that of improving the quality of life, although they occasionally veer into the physician's territory. The nature of the life that the healing deacons are committed to maintain, however, differs from that to which physicians are committed. For the most part, the counselor appears about the time the contemporary priest disappears, and the deacon works to serve the very stage of life that the physician often feels is no longer worth his or her attention. The death counselor, unlike his priestly counterpart, rarely has the option of extending life or otherwise affecting its quantity, and therefore inevitably focuses attention on the quality.

What we end up with, then, is one group of priests and both groups of deacons sharing a primary concern with the quality of life, with the remaining—but still the most powerful—group of priests most intent on the quantity. Thus the philosophic division is reflected in both power and income.

A CLOSER LOOK AT THE DEACONS

The new deacons are definitely serving in ancillary capacities. Even the term *ancillary* is derived from the Latin *ancilla* meaning handmaiden. The traditional priests had nuns; the contemporary priests have nurses; it is not difficult for priests to accommodate themselves to either new forms of handmaidens or new forms of deacons, as long as the power relationships and roles remain clearly defined, and as long as the newcomers recognize that any intimacy must come on terms established by the priests.

We deacons must also acknowledge the power of the priestly guilds, especially of the new priesthood. Power begats power. Someone once compared the Catholic Church to a rock inside a large snowball rolling down the hill. The snowball would pick up more snow plus some twigs and pebbles, would bump into trees and stones and snow, twigs, and pebbles would fall off, but the rock surrounded by snow would continue rolling and would maintain its hard core. The new priesthood is not unlike the Church. For example, watch what happens to the hospice movement, a movement developed by a priest, but whose message has been carried on by deacons, over the next few years.

Deacons have begun their move for visibility and—even though many may recoil from the term—power. However, before they can become successful, they need to know who they are. I would like to offer my belief that "death" is a modifier of "counselor" and "educator," not the other way around. A death educator is an educator who specializes in topics related to death; a death counselor is a counselor who specializes in working with people experiencing stresses related to death. They are not "death—experts" who decide to express their knowledge by counseling or educating.

Deacons will be permitted to fulfill certain tasks, but only tasks for which they have background and training. A person who "studies death" is unlikely to be competent to take her or his studies anywhere, except perhaps into the far reaches of scholarship. There is no field of "death" and there is no field of "thanatology." There are social workers, teachers, psychologists, nurses, clergy, funeral directors, anthropologists, physicians, and innumerable others—including various volunteers—who have developed expert knowledge and understanding about death and dying.

We also need to keep in mind that death educators and death counselors are not interchangeable roles. Preachers may be able to heal, and healers may be able to preach, but they are not synonymous, whether we are considering priests or deacons. And the needs of each are going to compete with the needs of the other.

ON SUCCESS AND FAILURE

It initially appears that the new priesthood has all the advantages, while the traditional priesthood has all the problems. Not so. The old priesthood was seen as always succeeding. After the earthly death, which they did not pretend to be able to counter, they proclaimed the individual's soul to be in heaven (or elsewhere, as befit the occasion). There was no evidence that they had erred; such proclamation was consistent with prevailing beliefs. These priests felt, in spite of some individual doubts, that their mission had succeeded; their constituents agreed. By virtue of representing God to the individual, they were able to intervene for the individual with God and thereby accomplish what they claimed they would accomplish, that is, to improve not only the end of this life but the conditions of the next life.

The new priesthood inevitably fails in its mission. The mission of the physician is to maintain life and, along with it, maximum health, but each of us dies, no matter what the priest does. All priestly knowledge, technology, ritual, temples, warmth and caring, all are insufficient to avoid failure. They may have initial success, but they are doomed to eventual failure. Their implicit promises of earthly life eternal turn out to be worthless. At some level of personal consciousness, each member of this priesthood recognizes his or her failure, but copes with it differently. And their constituents, all of us, also recognize their failure. We become angry that they appear to promise so much and deliver only failure in the long run. We resent their grand apparel and expensive temples and jargon journals, and we express our resentment in a variety of direct and indirect ways. These new priests don't mean to promise too much, but they get carried away by their successes, by the adulation they receive, by the money and the power, and they develop a kind of psychological denial of their inability to offer immortality.

With the old priesthood, the closer a person came to death, the closer the priest was to achieving success, and it became very important to remain with the dying individual to assure that death came appropriately and without damaging the potential for attaining immortality through an after-life. With the new priesthood, the closer a person comes to death, the closer the priest is to achieving failure, and it becomes very important to move on to other not-yet-dying person whose immortality (or at least mortality) on earth can be assured by medical ministrations. After the death, the old priesthood could acclaim its success; after the death, the new priesthood must acknowledge its failure.

Further, the new priesthood must have strong feelings of impotence. Here he or she has been trained at immense expense, has been pressed through a rigorous apprenticeship, has been provided the most elaborate and expensive instruments and technologies. And people still die! It seems as though the people must be at fault. The old priesthood had worked death into their scheme. Indeed, without death, their scheme would not have worked, and their power would have waned. It is interesting to speculate as to how much the popularity of churches would drop if they ceased their preaching of an existence to follow this existence.

If Ernest Becker is correct, this feeling of impotence, of vulnerability, of inevitable decay, is the most powerful of all motivating forces, and it can be summed up as a fear of death and decay [3]. The physician then perceives this from two sources: the constant reminder, from having dying patients, that achievements are only temporary, and the same constant reminder of personal mortality. Why, then, are we always so surprised and often outraged when the physician retreats from the dying person? We seem to expect the superhuman, and perhaps what we resent is not that physicians lack superhuman abilities, but that they won't admit their humanness, their impotence.

The old priests had no such difficulties, no such sense of impotence. It was not their task to maintain life on earth, although they were expected to minister to the survivors. If they enabled the dying person and the survivors to feel better about the ending of the life, they had achieved part of their goal. The death counselors (and to a lesser extent, and less directly, the death educators) have similar goals. Their expectations, their training, their self-esteem, in no way depends on maintaining a lengthy life, but rather on bringing satisfaction, pain reduction, pleasure, into the life that remains and the lives that survive. No wonder they can feel good, feel cleansed, after a death. They did their job, as did the clergy. No wonder the physician has already moved on to arenas where success is more probable.

Herein lies the strength, the satisfactions, the opportunities, the smugness, and the seeds of destruction of the deacons, especially the healing deacons. As handmaidens to the new priests, the deacons take over tasks that the priests prefer not to perform, and for this the latter are grateful. But deacons are expected to be loyal to their priests, and those in the death awareness movement are not especially loyal to physicians. In essence, they have attempted to persuade, even manipulate, physicians who were recruited, selected, educated, and socialized as healers of the body—hopefully, but not necessarily, caring and warm—to become healers of the spirit.

They ignore the existing process of creating a physician and attempt to install the process they prefer. And they forget. They forget that most patients, as long as they see the physician as having the ability to intervene between them and their god (that is, continued mortality) will select the priest over the deacon. Only after it becomes obvious that the priest cannot provide the communicant with his ultimate concern does the latter turn to the deacon for solace. They also forget that most of the dying want and need both priests and deacons.

HEALING DEACONS AND DEATH

Deacons have been given permission to enter the temple because they can successfully handle a task that the priest has neither the time nor inclination nor skill to handle. As long as they render unto Caesar the territory that Caesar perceives as his, their future will be assured, at least on earth; when they aggress against Caesar's territory, there will be holy warfare, and the priests control the arsenals.

The old priests, having lost much power, are often insecure and uncertain; they frequently welcome the deacons as allies and join the death awareness movement, which was once their movement, to regain a part of the vanished prestige and sense of competence. But not only has a significant proportion of our population lost its faith in the old priesthood, it is losing its faith in the new priesthood.

Some individuals may develop faith in their healing deacons, and this faith may affect their physical as well as psychological and spiritual health. Recent newspaper articles have even outlined a physiological explanation for the placebo effect for pain reduction, so the wholistic concept emerges again. As Jean Quint Benoliel once stated, "The experience of being cared for may affect the patient more than the direct effect of the care." [4]

But there are dangers in being deacons. They may become too subservient to the priests and never challenge or question their ways or assert themselves in their presence. Or, conversely, they may begin to feel that their magic is the true magic. Their love and support, their touching, their visualization techniques, their bedside vigil will suffice for life eternal. They may put themselves between the patient and his or her death, and become the priestly healer. The role of the healer, especially a healer with a divine mission, is very powerful and seductive, and deacons are not immune.

It is easy to develop the same kind of divine delusions that the priests have developed over the centuries. Any of us may begin to attribute our successes

to powers within us, rather than powers within the communicants that we may—
may—have helped become active. We begin to think that our laying on of
hands has power rather than remaining aware that it is the communicant's faith,
not our hands, that has the power.

We even become grandiose. We heed the voices in the land that claim that no
one dies who does not want to die, that there are not sick bodies but only sick
minds and spirits, that there is no such thing as disease but only dis-ease. In
trying to promote appropriate deaths, it is important to avoid trying to appropriate their deaths. Humility is required to enhance the effects of humanity.

And both the old and new priesthoods do understand something that others
have forgotten: that life exists until death occurs. If the priests are too capable
of ignoring death, some of the deacons are too capable of ignoring life. They
need to be careful that focusing on death and dying does not turn the remainder
of life into a game to develop a beautiful death. They also need to be careful
not to become the agent of a self-fulfilling prophecy, that by turning the attention
of the dying person to his or her own death, they not remove the fight to live
that some of these individuals might prefer. If deacons spend too much time
and effort facilitating acceptance of death, they may rob people of their remaining zest for life. Deacons are not there as ushers, to help them through the door;
they are there as waiters, to show them the variety on the bill of fare, than
making certain that their dishes are prepared skillfully and served expeditiously,
but the dishes must be the ones they select, not ones selected for them.

In other words, let's not be unduly hasty in dismissing the tendency of the
physician to support the denial of death in a quest for life, nor the tendency
of the clergy to support the denial of death in the quest for immortality.
Deacons are not the only ones with truth. One person's denial is another
person's immortality.

THE PREACHING DEACONS AND DEATH

Death educators remain one step further removed from the fray. They have
not impinged in any major fashion on the new and powerful priesthood, except
occasionally to irritate. "I don't want anybody like *that* to get between me and
my patient." "You stick to your writing; I'll take care of the sick." "The next
person who tells me that I shouldn't let a patient regress from Stage Three to
Stage Two will get punched out." Often the individual physicians approve of
the preaching, even when the medical profession is the devil, since they may
not perceive themselves as such individuals. Indeed, the death educator is telling
the physician that the task of caring for the ill is significant, all the way to the
end of life. The new priest will agree, even though deacons may wonder whether
the behavior observed supports the beliefs that are explicated.

But let's look more closely at the old priesthood. The preaching deacon does
impinge on these persons, since the role of telling people how to die, the art of
dying, is a sacred role, often maintained by the clergy. Now here is an entire

new wave of people coming along and saying, "Look, you didn't do your job very well, and we need to do it for you." How did the old priesthood respond? By agreeing. "Yes, you're right. We didn't do very well, and we are going to change." Seminarians and nursing students were probably the first two student groups to have heard of Elisabeth Ross, and it was seminarians who pressed Ross into her initial investigations.

Of course, not all of the old priesthood is aligning itself with the death educators and counselors. Among the conservative religionists, the clergy still have power, and they retain control of the passage into death. They are unlikely to ask for the support of death counselors and they are unlikely to attend to death educators, although they may be sensitive to the messages of writers like Edgar Jackson and Richard Dumont, as well as those of Moody and the recent Elisabeth Ross. Preaching about dying is a significant part of their work, and they don't need to call for either help or affirmation, although they are pleased when support is provided. They were never sidetracked by social issues in the first place. Indeed, some, perhaps many, of them feel that prayer and faith are more important than care and touch. Their own faith in themselves and the faith of their followers in them seem to remain high, which, if the wholistic model works, means that they will have a high success rate, not only in the spiritual realm but in the temporal as well. And this does follow, since it is from clergy that the faith-healers initially came, before the recent wholistic health movement catapulted a new group of faith-healers into the picture.

A FEW FINAL COMMENTS

There is no doubt in my mind that the concerns that surround death and dying, among them death education and death counseling, are among the most powerful concerns that exist in affecting human behavior. What can compare with feelings concerning death, dying, finitude, immortality? Sex? Power? Achievement? Love? Religion and God? And in comparing death to sex, power, achievement, love, and religion, it seems evident to me that death, as the negation of all else, becomes the most significant, the most powerful.

Using the religious metaphor strikes me as most appropriate, because it is the metaphor of life and death, of meaning and meaninglessness, of alpha and omega. The deacons have each made their own decision to enter the doors of the novitiate, but they are very much novices, and have a great deal to learn from both the successes and the failures of the other priesthoods. Indeed, deacons will probably never rise to the level of priest, which is likely to be fortunate rather than unfortunate. The priesthood has inequality with their constituents virtually built into its structure; they represent us to God and God to us. Deacons are equals who have special concerns or special skills. In this way, they have an advantage over the priests, since communicants will speak with deacons in ways and about things that they cannot communicate to priests.

However, death educators and counselors are treading sacred ground, and must expect to be attacked for their errors, their vanities, any signs of greed or lust or need for power. Just as they attack the old and new priesthoods. These attacks have begun. The media, which only recently carried nothing but laudatory articles on the death awareness movement, is now publishing subtle and not-so-subtle digs at the movement.

Those in the death awareness movement have selected a deeply-sensitive area in which to work, and they will find their motives impugned—not only as macabre, morbid, and sick, which are accusations they are accustomed to and which they share with funeral directors, proctologists, and garbage collectors— but as self-aggrandizing, greedy, manipulative, and riding the wave of popularity, perhaps even voyeuristic and sensation-seeking.

Those who enter the orders take on special responsibilities, and death educators have done that. It doesn't matter whether they have meant to or not, whether they believe they should be required to or not: they have done it. Like physicians, they will find any attempts to make substantial money criticized as greed; like clergy, they will find any attempts to be falsely self-effacing criticized as sanctimonious.

Death educators are no longer seen as cute toddlers or adorable pre-schoolers. They are now in their dirty, sweaty, over-active latency period. They are coming of age.

REFERENCES

1. L. Dangott and R. A. Kalish, *A Time To Enjoy: The Pleasures of Aging,* Spectrum Books, Englewood Cliffs, New Jersey, 1979.
2. F. L. Cross (ed.), *The Oxford Dictionary of the Christian Church,* Oxford University Press, London, 1958.
3. E. Becker, *The Denial of Death,* Free Press, New York, 1973.
4. J. C. Quint, *The Nurse and the Dying Patient,* Macmillan, New York, 1967.

ACKNOWLEDGEMENT

With thanks to Charles Garfield, Suzanne Stillinger, and Claude Welch for their comments on this chapter.

In Chapter 22, three physicians outline the processes and dynamics of a hospital-based course on death and dying. The chapter describes some of the tensions that existed among persons from the various disciplines, for example, between humanistically-oriented nurses and chaplains and less humanistically-oriented physicians, or between chaplains and those who viewed the chaplain's role as unnecessary.

What is described here represents the reality of teaching about death, whether in a medical setting or elsewhere. Not everyone involved in the process views the caring roles and responsibilities in the same fashion. The caretaker who is especially sensitive to budgetary issues may seem to have different priorities than the caretaker whose sole mission is to improve spiritual well-being. In fact, they both seek to improve the lives of dying persons, differing in how to achieve the goal rather than in the nature of the goal. These differences are challenging to the death educator who is responsible for teaching relevant persons, regardless of their orientation.

CHAPTER 22

Teaching about Dying and Death in a Multidisciplinary Student Group

David Barton
Miles K. Crowder
and
John M. Flexner

In the face of rapid technical advances in medical care, increasing numbers of persons dying in institutional settings, and increasing interest in the psychosocial, ethical and humanistic aspects of medical practice, there is a growing need to include instruction on the topics of dying, death and bereavement in the medical curriculum [1]. Actual descriptions of medical school courses remain relatively limited in number [2-4]. This in-depth course has been expanded to include medical students, student nurses, theology students and social work students. Because the care of the dying person and his family is most often provided by a number of disciplines and is heavily dependent on effective interaction among these caregivers, the multidisciplinary composition of the classes has significantly broadened the scope of the course. The purpose of this communication is to describe the important interactional dimensions and group process which became highly significant issues in teaching the multidisciplinary group.

For each of the sixteen one-and-one-half-hour weekly meetings, patient interviews, selections from medical and fictional literature, structured group experiences such as role playing [5] and interdisciplinary presentations were used to provide focus and direction for the extensive group discussions and interpersonal transactions in the class. Enrollment in the course was limited to a workable size of fifteen to twenty students.

The group process which occurred in the course represented the most important dimension involved in teaching a multidisciplinary class. The work of the group in the classroom was in effect a microcosm of the relationships among caregivers from various disciplines in working with dying patients and their families in clinical settings. The intensity of the subject brought these transactions into bold relief and made them more available for use in the teaching and learning process.

In the course, three stages in the evolution of the students' transactions were apparent. Initially, there was a stage in which members of the group related to one another in terms of preconceived stereotypes. This was followed by a stage of conflict in which widely divergent views and intense feelings were expressed. After considerable group interaction, a stage of rapport developed. This stage was characterized by collaborative and cooperative effort, and the group members began to commit themselves to a deeper exploration of their observed transactions and the primary task of learning how to provide better care for the dying person and his family.

PRECONCEIVED STEREOTYPES

Interaction in the early phases of the course involved not only attention to the material utilized as focal presentations. In addition, there was obviously a considerable amount of interchange aimed at testing preconceived stereotypes held by the participants, determining the orientation of the individual's discipline and eliciting responses in the transactions which would either validate or invalidate the perceived role or purpose of the group member in caring for the dying patient. Clearly, the medical student was viewed as an expert on the physical dimension, the nurse as the compassionate physical comforter, and the chaplain as the theological expert. The group learned later, however, that although the questions and comments of the participants appeared to reflect the language and position of their discipline, there was a striking underlying commonality.

Students, however, entered the class with preconceived stereotypes. The medical student and physicians in general were stereotyped by the group as being aloof and emotionally unavailable. They were viewed as unfeeling, technically oriented and always "too busy" to become involved in issues related to psychosocial care. Appearing self-sufficient, they were viewed as needing little emotional support and were felt to be insulated and unaffected by dying and death and the matters surrounding it. To the rest of the group, their technical knowledge represented a readily available defensive position in which they might hide from their deeper feelings.

The nursing student and nurses in general were viewed by others in the group as the physicians' assistants and the patients' comforters. They were seen as being dependent on the physician, always available, compassionate, passive and often required to serve the needs of the patient at the expense of their own needs. They were viewed as lacking direct responsibility for the patient's care and as persons who took vital signs, administered medications and provided physical comfort for the patient. Their role as an information-giver, a middle person between the physician and the patient and his family was often not acknowledged, but always expected. They were also expected to possess extensive information about patients' conditions and to be endowed with an ability to perceive the gravity of a situation without having communicated directly with the physician.

The chaplains were viewed as the spiritual comforters. Their role in the hospital setting was poorly defined and understood. They were viewed as frequently tampering with areas outside their realm, intrusive, evangelistic and often in the way. Their form of caring for the dying patient and his family was sometimes viewed as contrived. They were seen as "God's Representative" and as such, evoked strongly ambivalent feelings in other members of the group. At times these evoked feelings approached the level of fear. Their role in caring for the dying while extensive, and often necessary and effective, was little understood.

The social work students were viewed as persons representing extensions of society's social organization. They were stereotyped as individuals who might guide a family through a myriad of social agencies or assist the person and his family with such matters as insurance and financial distress.

CONFLICT AND THE WORKING-THROUGH PROCESS

The position of an individual in a discipline was not only defined and perceived in terms of the individual himself but also was considered in terms of the social structure of the medical institution. Issues related to institutional hierachy and the traditional lines of authority and responsibility quickly emerged. As they were discussed, many of these issues appeared related to institutional routine rather than patient need.

Institutional tradition has established what may be viewed as essentially legitimate role expectations. Patients' needs, on the other hand, at times establish a differing set of legitimate expectations. Typically, this might be illustrated in a situation where the nurse is questioned about the condition of the patient by the family. Due to poor communication between physicians and nurses, the nurse may or may not have the information. If the nurse has the information, she may well be expected to refer the question to the physician on the basis of tradition and hierarchy. On the other hand, the expectation that a nurse should be knowledgeable about a patient's condition is a legitimate one. Such situations, numerous in the context of dying and death, give rise to considerable role conflict and were the focus of considerable discussion in the group.

As the conflicts emerged, subtle and blatant evidence of hostility and divisiveness appeared. Resentment of the traditional hierarchy was expressed by nursing, social work and theology students. Resentment toward a theological approach or a less technical, more humanistic approach was expressed by many of the medical students. For example, at one point in the discussion, in a sweeping act of control, one medical student launched on a long discourse on the pharmacological properties of one of the minor tranquilizers while the nursing students and theology students wished to discuss more humanistic issues involving how the patient was dealing with his family about his dying.

The effects of varying levels and different sets of knowledge and language differences were apparent. Frequently these differences were utilized by members of the group to retreat to a defensive and sometimes inpenetrable position. In this position, the expression of their feelings diminshed; they avoided struggling with difficult issues and interacting with other caregivers. Role conflict and the resultant anxiety and hostility, knowledge and language differences often created a sense of separateness and interfered significantly with the communication process in the group.

Through the process of group interaction, stereotypes and role expectations were more clearly defined, scrutinized and reevaluated. The discussion and working-through process allowed the group to begin to overcome their conflict and move in the direction of more cooperative and collaborative efforts.

The most striking and difficult issue involved in teaching in the multidisciplinary group entailed working-through divisive transactions and communication difficulties related to stereotyped role perception and role conflict. Role playing exercises designed to highlight and work-through these areas were particularly useful in dealing with these problems. In these vignettes, clinical situations were devised in which someone played the patient and other participants in the course exchanged roles [5]. For example, a student chaplain would act as a physician, a nurse as a student chaplain and a medical student as a nurse. These exercises underlined the positive and negative aspects of roles, the varying levels of knowledge, communication difficulties, and the need for a collaborative approach.

Gradually, the group reached a stage of rapport. In this phase, the work of the group, the determination of common purpose and the development of a concept of solidarity of purpose were achieved. In essence, this phase represented the individuals' acceptance of their roles, but involved the ability to relate to one another within the role and outside of the stereotype.

RAPPORT AND COLLABORATIVE EFFORT

Recognizing that conflict among caregivers often compromises the ability to discern and meet the needs of the patient, the group began to move toward the determination of common goals. This phase included the individuals' acceptance of their roles but involved the ability to relate to one another within the role and outside of the stereotype. Rather than focusing on the conflict, the discussion shifted toward evaluating the varying and unique individual needs of the dying patient and his family. Important questions began to be raised: What tasks in caring for the dying should be shared by caregivers? Who is to communicate certain types of information to the patient and his family? How are caregivers to obtain reliable information? Should a chaplain see every dying patient? Who is to deal with the family and their questions? How might communication among caregivers be facilitated? How is emotional support for caregivers to be achieved? How might traditional lines of hierarchy and delegation of responsibilities be dealt with or altered in order to provide better care?

The group came to see the importance of roles; it was seen that roles, while in some ways restrictive, often provided a social structure which allows the individual an established identity and a secure base from which to explore his feelings and utilize his skills. At times, the manner in which the patient perceives the role of the caregiver allows access and approximation in a way in which specialized types of interventions may be employed.

COMMENT

The divisiveness so apparent in these student groups was seen as growing out of stereotypical views of one another, role conflict, problems related to traditional hierarchy and delegation of responsibility, differences in language and levels of knowledge, individual differences in attitudes, poor communication, and focusing on the conflict rather than the care process. These difficulties are reinforced by the numerous uncertainties and intense feelings surrounding the death situation.

Through the process of the group, the students came to recognize that there are shared affective responses evoked in the context of dying and death inherent in being human and present no matter what the discipline or role. The recognition of shared feelings and the development of solidarity of purpose in the course led to the emergence of a mutually helpful support system for the caregivers involved. Mutual support and collaboration is particularly important in caring for the dying person, for the wide range of uncomfortable feelings experienced by individuals working in this area can lead to avoidance of the patient and emotional unrest in the caregiver. In an area where the coordination of a wide variety of knowledge, attitudes and skills is necessary, divisiveness and isolation, if not overcome, can seriously compromise care.

REFERENCES

1. D. Barton, The Need for Including Instruction on Death and Dying in the Medical Curriculum, *Journal of Medical Education, 47,* pp. 169-175, 1972.
2. D. Barton, J. M. Flexner, J. van Eys, et al., Death and Dying: A Course for Medical Students, *Journal of Medical Education, 47,* pp. 945-951, 1972.
3. E. H. Liston, Psychiatric Aspects of Life Threatening Illness: A Course for Medical Students, *International Journal of Psychiatry in Medicine, 5,* pp. 51-56, 1974.
4. S. Bloch, A Clinical Course on Death and Dying for Medical Students, *Journal of Medical Education, 50,* pp. 630-632, 1975.
5. D. Barton and M. K. Crowder, The Use of Role Playing Techniques as an Instructional Aid in Teaching About Dying, Death and Bereavement, *Omega, 6:*4, pp. 243-250, 1975.

Chapters 21 and 22 describe specific death education programs, both directed at healthy adults and both in a medical setting. Chapter 23 shifts gears abruptly. Rather than describe a particular program, the author discusses the implication of the arts—drawing, fiction, poetry, film—for children who are learning to cope with death and grief. Bertman does not go through the steps for using the arts, nor does she discuss the meaning of death for children at any length. Rather, she offers an extensive discussion of the meaning of the artistic process and of artistic products, both those that the children create themselves and those created by others, for the children. Her comments shed light on how we may use the arts to understand what children are experiencing and to help them through some of their most stressful times.

It would be a serious mistake to assume that use of the arts for learning about death should be restricted to children. People of all ages can benefit from involvement with the various arts to learn about death. And, as with children, this involvement can be that of the creator or the observer or both. Some of the world's masterpieces have depicted death in pictures or in words. Just consider the vast number of great paintings, icons, and statues of Christ on the Cross, or the power of fiction like Moby Dick, Hamlet and Macbeth, A Death in the Family, or the outstanding film, All That Jazz. The anticipation of distant death, the encounter with immediate and personal death, and the experience of grief have all led to great works of art and literature by those who are competent to create these, and to personal expressions through form and word by those whose skills are not notable but who benefit by the opportunity for expression.

CHAPTER
23

The Arts:
A Source of Comfort
and Insight for Children
Who Are Learning
about Death*

Sandra L. Bertman

Death education is in many ways a misnomer. There is little we teachers can tell children or adults about death. There is, of course, information to share and research to be considered. But this knowledge serves primarily as a foundation or framework; death education really means permission to share attitudes, fears and concerns. The classroom provides a condusive yet structured setting in which to become aware of varied views of life and death, different styles of coping with loss, and the grieving process.

The expressive arts convey a rich variety of human experience. Who of us has not wondered what it feels like to be dead nor pondered the significance of being? Who of us has never felt afraid, alone, uncomfortable, or at a loss for words? The realities of coping with loss perceived by the artist can elucidate

* This article is expanded from a presentation to educators and clinicians at a conference, *Children and Death,* March 17-19, 1978, University of Chicago, Chicago, Illinois.

those of the students. Fictional images can serve to reduce the individual's sense of isolation and open the mind to previously unconsidered ideas and behaviors. This aesthetic language or language of the human spirit is not the exclusive province of the professional artist. It exists within us all. Expressions in the form of dialogue and drawing, for example, give focus and vision to deeply felt feelings and concerns present in the student of any age.

Working with the visual and literary modalities (story, song, painting, film), this chapter.

1. identifies sources of concern and consolation;
2. presents materials and techniques for eliciting and expressing emotion; and
3. underscores the "mutuality" — the universality and yet individuality — of each subjective experience.

THE LIFE CYCLE:
A NON THREATENING "GRABBER"

The *Life Cycle*, an abstract animated film, is an involving, non-threatening instrument that can help students focus on perceptions of life and death [1]. The animation, restricted to blobs which move to a musical soundtrack, presents a framework; a structure devoid of verbal exchanges or much in the way of human characterizations. However, emotional connotations and intent are quickly ascribed to the pulsating blobs by the viewers. Details of individuality such as age, sex and values are debated. The responses range from being moved by the blobs ("they seem so real") to being unaffected ("they seem so generalized, non personal"). One of the blobs dies — "at home," "with husband," and "is the grandmother," or "in a hospital," "alone," and "is the grandfather." The students' experiences of/and fantasies about death emerge in giving the animation personal definition.

THE LIVED VS. THE UNLIVED LIFE

Students are concerned with whether the blob which dies had a "full" life; a life marked by warm relationships, a loving marriage, children and grandchildren. But not all students evaluate the blobs' lives with such tenderness. The blob which dies is ascribed an "empty" life — one of form: born, schooled, married, grandparented, and died. This unlived life assessment is reminiscent of the Solomon Grundy of the nursery rhyme ("born on Monday . . . married on Wednesday . . . died on Saturday") [2].

Some people conclude (and console themselves) that the blob which dies had a "good" life. But what constitutes the good life? Surely the long life is not necessarily the good life. If death occurred any other place along the life cycle, far earlier or far later, could it appropriately be called "a good life?" Is it merely a matter of number of years, or is it, rather, what one does with those years? When faced with the diagnosis of acute leukemia, Ted Rosenthal concludes in the biographical film, *How Could I Not Be Among You?*, that it is not death people fear, it is the "incompleteness" of their lives [3]. Completeness to Rosenthal, has nothing to do with living out one's four score and ten; it has to do with not having lived fully "in the moment," with not having lived those years well whatever their number. In *The Magic Moth*, a children's story, the mother recounts how special and happy her daughter's short life was for the family [4]. When questioned by her son about his sister's death, she answers that some people do not seem to be meant to live very long:

> "Then why was Maryanne born?"
> Mother smiled, "Maryanne was like the plants in our garden," she said. "They only last a short while, but they make us happy while they are here." [4, p. 56]

In *Annie and the Old One*, another story for children, an Indian grandmother feels her time has come and prepares the family for her death: "When the new rug is taken from the loom," she says, "I will go to Mother Earth." [5] Annie tries to hold back time by undoing the weaving each evening, her grandmother completed during the day. But Annie eventually comes to understand — and accept — the appropriateness of a timely death:

> The cactus did not bloom forever. Petals dried and fell to earth.
> She knew that she was a part of the earth and the things on it. She would always be a part of the earth, just as her grandmother had always been, just as her grandmother would always be, always and forever. And Annie was breathless with the wonder of it [5, p. 41].

No matter what their individual ideas of afterlife or death, most readers come to appreciate Annie's feeling that all living things are intimately connected with each other.

It is not always easy to die in one's time. Others may not understand, especially people who work in highly structured institutional environments. *In Dying In Academe*, an intern is no more able than Annie to accept an old person's readiness to give up life [6]. The patient, Mr. Kahn, explains metaphorically to the young physician, "you see . . . the engine is broken down; it is time for the engineer to abandon it." His more direct statement of intention to die leads to the following discussion:

> " . . . it's not allowed. You are in a hospital, a university hospital, equipped with all the latest technology. Here you must get well."
> "My time has come."
> "Time is measured differently here." [6, p. 56]

Violating the old man's wishes, by recusitating him as she'd promised not to do, is simply a sophisticated way of unraveling the weaving, of undoing the careful arduous work of dying. Unfortunately, for the young physician, the consequences are more far reaching than the awareness that death is no enemy. The intern is left with a sense of tension between certain taught professional roles and the inherent human value of honoring another's autonomy.

WHAT DOES IT FEEL LIKE WHEN YOU DIE?

The last vignette of *Life Cycle* slowly freezes and the animated blob becomes quite literally, in-animate. This is the first time the pulsating blob is seen not moving. What is death? In fact, "your heart stops beating." BUT DOES THE DEAD PERSON STILL FEEL? This question often becomes an obsessive one for younger students.

Children's drawings and accompanying explanations reveal a continued concern for the comfort and safety of the body. One six year old explains why, in the picture he constructed, the men are carrying the dead body to the cemetery high over their heads: "she shouldn't be dragged; that would be bad." [7] A bit later, examining why a river of tears is coming from one figure whose mother had died, he says, "That was his mother and she's watching them. She feels sorry." He quickly corrects himself, "I mean, *he* (the grieving son) feels sorry."

Children's literature deliberately addresses this concern. In *The Magic Moth*, after burying William, the guinea pig, Mark-O is thinking about how uncomfortable his pet must be under the wet, heavy dirt. A conversation with his mother reveals this worry and his continuing doubt in spite of her reassurances:

> "Momma, do you think William is cold out there?"
> "No, I don't," she answered.
> "Why?"
> "Well, because after guinea pigs die, they don't feel anything anymore."
> "Are you sure?"
> "I am very sure." [4, p. 24]

In another novel, *Growing Time,* a mother comforts her son, Jamie, with the consolation that their pet dog is no longer feeling the aches and pains he suffered in his aged life: "his teeth don't hurt him and his legs don't hurt him anymore." [8] Unfortunately, she prefaces these words with "He is happy now," a statement which causes confusion in the classroom. Students, even the youngest ones, pick up the contradiction. If he is not able to *feel hurt,* how can be *feel happy?*

It is not only children who wonder whether the dead body might feel pain or discomfort. A recently bereaved nursing student confessed an affinity to Mark-O when she told the class of her overwhelming urge to run out during a rainstorm in order to cover her dead sister's mound. Rationally, she "knew" her sister was immune to cold. Nonetheless, she was haunted by the thought that her sister was cold and getting wet. In *Gifts,* the speaker exhibits concern when the funeral people come to collect her mother's body [9]. Reminiscent of the six year old who insisted a body not be "dragged," she and her father actually rearrange heavy furniture so the corpse can be removed without being twisted or discomforted in any way:

> ... Daddy was horrified, and he said, we'll have to move the bookcase, but it's heavy, because he was worried about how they'd get her out on that cot, if they had to fold it to get it in [9, p. 68].

WHERE DO YOU GO WHEN YOU'RE DEAD

Not only might the dead one still feel, but where is he now? What happens after death is a major question. In the children's book, *The Tenth Good Thing About Barney,* one youngster envisions his cat in the ground helping flowers grow and he consoles himself with the thought, "you know . . . that's a pretty nice job for a cat." [10] His sister pictures Barney "in heaven with lots of cats and angels, drinking cream and eating cans of tuna."

The Confusion with place, with literalness, is voiced by Mark-O (*Magic Moth*) who is trying to make sense of his sister's death. In this story, an adolescent brother tries to respond to Mark-O's insistence that Maryanne will come back:

> "Well, no, she won't. But where she is going it will be nice."
> "Is she going to China?"
> "Creepers! Don't you know anything? Of course she's not going to China. When people die they go to heaven."
> "Is heaven under the ground?"
> "Of course not. Quit asking questions." [4, p. 17]

Using this conversation as a focus for role play in the classroom, a ten year old girl responded to Mark-O's next question, "Do you think she's in heaven?"

> Well, I really don't think so. I think that she goes in the ground and goes to little pieces of the soil but the heart goes to the family and makes them think about the good times with the person who dies and finally they feel better and go out and just have a good time. And the person who dies stays in the other people so they don't forget her and always think of the good times [7].

In another classroom setting, a fifteen year old adolescent picked up on the conversation by composing a dialogue:

"No, not exactly. Maryanne is not alive anymore. She's not with us here on earth. There is only one part of Maryanne that is alive, and that is her mind."

"You mean her brain."

"More than her brain, but her other thoughts and what she believed about the people and things on earth. Her ideas are alive."

"Yes, but where did she *go?* I saw her go into the ground."

"Her body went into the ground, but where do you think her mind went?"

"I bet it went to that place Dad used to take us to on the cape. You know, the place with the flowers!"

"That's probably what Maryanne's mind is thinking now. Wouldn't that be nice for her to think about forever?"

"Yes, cause that was her favorite place! I'm glad she's happy now. When I die, will Dad let me have a new bike?"

I laughed and said, "Why don't you ask Dad for the bike now?" [7]

The concern with where the being is, where that self, that spirit of a person or animal has gone, is not so easily dismissed. The issue frequently arises both in the literature and in the classroom. If king's old worn out body buried beneath the apple trees is "nothing to him anymore," (*Growing Time*), then what is something to him? What and where is the "him" that once was? In much the same way as the nine year old and fifteen year old explained to Mark-O that Maryanne still existed in memory and essence, Jamie's grandmother (*Growing Time*) helps him understand how King's spirit did not get buried with his body underground but remains alive and at home with them:

Well, look here child, I can't see a thing, without my glasses. I can't see the stove over there, but I know where it is, all right. I can't even see my own shoes right now, but I know my feet are in them, don't I? Well, I know what's in my heart, too. And I know King still has a home to come to [8, p. 23].

Not having had the benefit of exposure to the nine year old and fifteen year old students, or to Jamie's grandmother, Mark-O (*Magic Moth*) again raises the question when the minister consoles his family with a prayer voicing the concept that life never ends, it just changes:

"Is that really true?"

"That is what I believe," replied the minister. "I believe that when people die they step through the door into another place that we can't see with our eyes."

"Could they go through a window, too?" Asked Mark-O, remembering the moth.

"Yes. Windows let in light, and I believe there is light where people go. But not the kind of light you see with your eyes. It is more like the kind you feel inside when you love someone, like Maryanne." [4, pp. 45-46]

Just such warmth, love, and presence is felt by the speaker in *Gifts* when she is uncomfortably cold and puts on one of her dead mother's sweaters and thinks "its like having her arms around me." [9, p. 69]

COPING: STAYING IN TOUCH

Responding to the assignment "describe in picture or words someone dead," one third grader wrote the following letter to his (dead) grandmother:

Dear Grandmother

Where did you go. Will you come back, Please come back. I will give you a cake a car as much gold as you want and a lot of house and everything you want. Are you in havin or in your grave or are you a ghost.

If you are in havin I will send you a letter to havin. If you are in you grave I will put the letter on your grave and if you are a ghost I will be scerad [7].

The letter reveals how badly the boy misses his grandmother and how much he wants her back. It does not deny the fact of death; rather, it tries to make sense of where the grandmother is now in actuality or in essence. The letter is a way of feeling the strength of being in touch with the lost person, just as is wearing a piece of clothing and gaining the comfort of "having her arms around me." [9]

This youngster's letter is in spirit much like Maxine Kumin's poem in which she tells her dead friend how it is without her:

Shall I say how it is in your clothes?
A month after your death I wear your blue jacket.
The dog at the center of my life recognizes you've come to visit, he's ecstatic . . . .
I think of the last day of your life,
Old friend, how I would rewind it . . . . [11]

In the story, *Dusty Was My Friend,* the main character resolves his sorrow and emptiness after his friend's accidental death, by the same vehicle: a written communication directly to (dead) Dusty, despite parental challenge:

"You can't do that."
"Yes I can."
"But Dusty is dead. He couldn't read it," Mom said.
"I know that." Of course I knew that. Sometimes mothers act dumb [12].

and symbolically, delivering it

> . . . I wanted to put it on Dusty's grave . . . But he is buried where the accident happened, far away. Maybe someday I'll go there. I'd like to. I have the letter in my secret treasure drawer in case I ever do. Otherwise, I'll just keep it.

This is an explicit illustration of the healthy working out of one's grief, no matter what the age.

COPING: PARTICIPATING IN THE LAST RITES

In a book for the very young, *The Dead Bird,* a group of children experience sadness when they happen upon a newly dead bird. The thought of performing a ritual makes them feel better [13] :

> The children were very sorry the bird was dead and could never fly again. But they were glad they had found it, because now they could dig a grave in the woods and bury it. They could have a funeral and sing to it the way grown-up people did when someone died [13].

In the classroom, it becomes apparent that quite a large percentage of students have never attended a funeral. Nervous laughter punctuates the discussion as students of all age identify with Mark-O (*Magic Moth*) whose stomach hurts when he thinks about his sister's funeral ("He had never been to a funeral and he *knew* he would not like it." [4, p. 48] In this novel, the mother does not heed Grollman's advice of allowing the young child to attend the burial "if he chooses." [14] Explaining the details of what to expect from the event and well aware of the value of family participation, she insists five year old Mark-O attend:

> "Do I have to go?" he asked Mother.
> "Yes, you do," she replied firmly. "Anyway, it will not last very long. You will feel better if you go. Remember how you always bury Guinea Pigs when they die? You read poems when you put them in the ground, and you say a prayer. They you feel better. This will be like that." [4, p. 49]

In *Gifts,* the relevant rite which arouses anxiety for the author precedes the funeral. The father does not insist on participation:

> . . . Daddy had taken me out on the porch and said: there's a tradition of our people. We wash our own dead. It's a last act of loving kindness. I plan to do that for your mother. Would you like to help me? I was stunned into silence. Then, I said hesitantly, I want to do it, but I don't know if I'm able. He was silent. Finally I said: yes. You don't have to if you don't want to, he said. I can do it alone [9, p. 69].

Seeing her mother dead initially overwhelms this young adult:

> I was stunned and terrified that I would scream or cry; fail him, and
> her. I stood there, clutching the prayer book and praying for strength not
> to fail them . . . . [9, p. 71]

The participation in washing her mother's body transformed a "distasteful
chore" into a "last act of loving kindness." Even more, the act of participation
is perceived as a reciprocal gift showering the giver with unexpected feelings of
contentment and mastery:

> . . . I feel a certain strength in myself that I never thought I'd be capable
> of, just because I helped . . . . [9, p. 71]

REMEMBERING AND ALLOWING ONESELF TO FORGET

> . . . and if thou wilt, remember [15].

Remembrance and the solace and contentment it brings is a concern of many
students. This issue, is addressed in part, in *Where is Dead,* a film exploring the
ramifications of an accidental death of an older sibling [16]. The younger sister
Sara tests her mother's explanation of what memory is with both her
grandfather and Anne her best friend. Anne's mother had warned Anne not to
remind Sara of David (the dead brother). In the classroom, we freeze the film in
these two instances (after the friend's revelation of her mother's admonition and
before the grandfather's healthy answer about the value of memory) and students
role play their responses. The ensuing conversation, graphically exposes the
discomfort of the consoler, the horrors of not mentioning painful memories, and
ultimately the benefits of sharing. It becomes apparent that the burden of small
talk widens the gulf between bereaved and friend, and even may evoke anger.

Role playing the grandfather's explanation of memory to Sara, an eleven year
old said:

> Your brain keeps on thinking of him even though he's not a physical
> being. In the mind there has been a place set aside for him and you
> usually don't think of it until he dies (then it stands out) [7].

To Sara's (role played) response, "I don't want to remember David because it
makes me sad," the same youngster explained:

> Well the more you don't think of him the sadder you'll get. Because in
> this place in the mind (it's like water leaking out of a dam — if you don't
> stop it will leak out more and more until it will all come out and it will
> explore the dam). Well, that's sort of like a person. If you don't think of
> him you'll get sadder and sadder and finally it has to all come out. Some
> way or other [7].

In strikingly similar imagery, Shakespeare acknowledges the value of sharing grief and the danger of repressing painful memories:

> Give sorrow tongue
> The grief that does not speak
> Whispers the o'erfraught heart
> And bid it break [17].

The film *Where Is Dead* opens at the playground with David's encouraging Sara to attempt the slide. Positioning himself at the foot of the slide, he reassures his sister, "Don't worry, I'll catch you." In the final scene, once again at the playground, the film demonstrates the positive incorporation of memory. Sara pauses, briefly, at the top of the slide and relives the time David was there to assist her. The memory is not so painful that she is unable to complete the slide. To the contrary, recalling how her brother made it safe for her to come down, Sara slides and then positions herself at the foot of the slide exactly as David had done. She reassures another child with his words, "Don't worry. I'll catch you."

"And if thou wilt, forget" is the concluding line of Rosetti's couplet [18].

After the ritual burial of a dead bird in Margaret Wise Brown's book *The Dead Bird,* we find the following description of the children's behavior:

> And every day, until they forgot, they went and sang to their little dead bird and put fresh flowers on his grave [13].

The illustration on the following page focuses not on the grave in the woods (though it is visible in the distance), but on the children happily involved in a ball game. Both the parenthetical phrase, "until they forgot," and this pictured scene declare, unjudgementally, it is O.K. to forget. Forgetting is in the natural order of things. And one does not have to feel guilty for enjoying ongoing life.

In the film *The Day Grampa Died,* the rabbi consoles young David with the idea that "Grampa doesn't die as long as we remember him." [15] The discomfort in the classroom exposes an unintended implication of the rabbi's words. Students infer from this that the grandson now has the responsibility of remembering. As long as he does so, grandfather is "alive" somewhere — in limbo or a waiting place of some sort. The minute David forgets him, his grandfather will *really* be dead. And David, then, would be saddled with the guilt of having caused the death.

As in the final scene of *Where is Dead,* the filmmaker demonstrates that one needn't be preoccupied with the sadness of loss and that memories aren't always painful. The suggestion of time lapse is indicated by the details of season change — foliage, birds, and lighter weight clothing. David is playing with a friend. Seeing a man that resembles his grandfather, David pauses from his play. But he is only slightly distracted. He smiles to himself at the reminiscence, and continues playing.

Figure 1.

COPING: ALLOWING ONESELF TO CRY

The idea that giving way to tears is a sign of weakness, especially for males, is directly voiced in Hamlet when Claudius rebukes a grieving son for "obsequious sorrow." "Tis unmanly grief." [19]

To the student, letting go means quite literally, "crying our eyes out." The fear of giving way to tears seems to be connected to losing control and the possibility of *never* being able to stop. In this six year old's picture (see Figure 1), grief is overwhelming. Notice the number of tears flowing from the mourners and the percentage of space they occupy in the drawing. Lest the viewer miss the

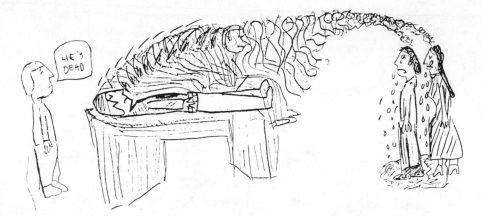

Figure 2.

Figure 3.

young artist's intention, the word "CRY" is incorporated into the composition.

Being overwhelmed by grief is depicted somewhat differently in this eleven year old's set of drawings. The first picture (Figure 2), quite Duchamp-like in technique, focuses on the process of the boy becoming memory to his parents. While this is happening the parents are crying profusely. The extent of their sorrow is indicated by the number and detail of tears flowing from the parents eyes accumulating in a puddle at their feet.

In the second drawing (Figure 3), no tears are visible. But circles under their eyes, the occupation ("making sad balloons"), and the protruding stomachs signify great desolation. The youngster explains that the parents have big stomachs because they are still "eating to feel better" and are consumed with their sadness "a long time later."

This youngster's final drawing did not indicate that all those tears had succeeded in washing the sadness out of the grieving parents. Grief is so overwhelming in its early stages, so all encompassing, that it is hard to believe the pain will be mitigated with time and that life will again hold meaning. Quite incredulously, George Herbert writes "Who would have thought my shrivel'd heart could have recover'd greeness?" Giving way to tears and to whatever other discomfort one is feeling, is the strange mystery of the healing process.

Some people don't cry. A person might wonder, as she looks around and realizes that no one else has dry cheeks, "Am I some kind of monster?" Being *under*-whelmed by grief is also cause for anxiety. Students fear being exposed as less than human, as callous and unfeeling, if expected behaviors (such as crying after a death or at a funeral) are not displayed. As Mark Twain, tongue in cheek, guides us:

> Where a blood relation sobs, an intimate friend should choke up, a distant acquaintance should sigh, a stranger should merely fumble sympathetically with his handerchief [21].

Twain's satire brings a smile to one's face, for we all recognize the pressure of the expected response. Peter Ivanovich felt it (and behaved accordingly) when he visited Ivan Ilych's widow in Tolstoy's novel, *The Death of Ivan Ilych:*

> And (he) knew that, just as it had been the right thing to cross himself in that room, so what he had to do here was to press her hand, sigh, and say, "Believe me . . . . " [22]

Priority has little to do with sincerity, and students sometimes feel that the *shoulds* should be eliminated: grief work is not etiquette. Yet, it also should be remembered that expected, recognized forms of behavior are very comforting in times of unusual stress. Although manners are sometimes used hypocritically, they remain the currency of concern, and they are an indispensible mode of expression for many.

The intense mood swings and inconsistency of feelings that accompany loss are acknowledged with a tinge of guilt by the mother in the short story, *The Bad Baby* [23]:

> You know, she says, her face suddenly troubled, there are days when I think it would be a relief to rend our clothes and walk around with ashes on our heads — when I want no part of my sanity, when I don't want to function at all. And there are other times, like today, when I want to skate and make lunch and laugh, even though . . . .

Helga Sandberg comments on her own behavior at the news of her father's death, "When they told me to come, I could not weep." Again, after the wake, she mentions leaving the funeral parlor "unweeping." [24] Similarly, in a children's novel, *The Taste of Blackberries* [25], Chuck notes that he was unable to cry at his friend's funeral. Feeling guilty, he tries to make the tears come by pressing his face into his father's coat buttons.

The classroom responses to Chuck's dry eyes range from logical explanation "What good is crying? It's not going to bring his friend back."), to empathetic statements ("I couldn't cry either. I'd be too shocked."), to intimations of what does, indeed, happen ("It's O.K. not to cry now. At one point he'll cry. If It's not now, later. Maybe tonight."). If a class member does judge or berate Chuck for not caring (e.g., license to forget, not crying, or not displaying the expected behavior), tolerance for a multiplicity of responses and styles warrants special consideration.

Tears are not the only way for pain to be relieved. Sadness and tenseness may be handled by surprising and unusual responses. Young Mark-O's behaviors after Maryanne's funeral (*Magic Moth*) were frenetic physical activity and displaced anger:

> When he got out on the playground at recess, he ran faster, yelled louder, and played harder than he had ever done before. When he went home he was happy until he got to his porch. There were more people in the house! How he hated all these people! It was his house. Why wouldn't they leave him alone? He could hear them laughing, too . . . . He went in and stomped loudly up the stairs. When Mother called him down to lunch, he did not answer [4, p. 46].

Concern may even be expressed by bizarre outbursts, such as a sacrilige or a piece of macabre, "sick" humor. The anxiety at the time of President Kennedy's death was addressed in the high school classroom by such Mad Comic jokes as "What did Caroline Get for her birthday? A jack-in-the-box." To an assignment to describe death, a thirteen year old boy responded with this drawing (Figure 4). This adolescent's grandfather had recently undergone open heart surgery.

Crying is sometimes for oneself. In her poem *Death*, one sixth grade girl reveals a tolerance for the range of responses exhibited by her family when faced with the illness and death of her grandfather. With remarkable clarity and not a tinge of guilt, she attributes her own tears, not to sadness at her grandfather's death, but to the awareness of her own vulnerability:

> My grandfather's gone
>   Never to return.
> He was in the hospital
>   Getting better.
> He died though I
>   Knew he would.
> My mom hated it.
>   He was her dad.
>
> She kept saying
>   "I wish I could cry."
> She never cried.
> I didn't either except
>   When I thought
> THIS will happen to
>   Me Too [7, G].

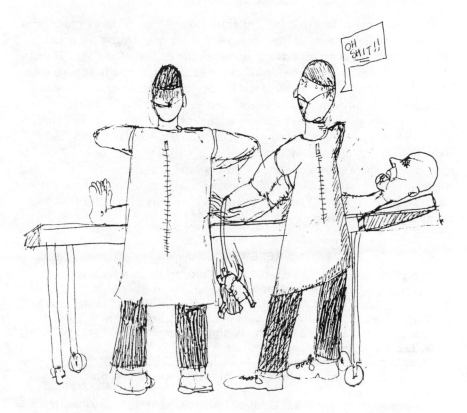

Figure 4

In *A Taste of Blackberries,* Chuck, who had not cried at his friend's funeral was surprised to find his "tear faucets" turned on by the sight of his mother tucking him in that evening. "The strange thing is I wasn't crying for Jamie," he confesses. "I was crying for me." [25, p. 47] Gerard Manly Hopkins points out in his poem *Spring and Fall: To A Young Child,* that when meditating on any loss, one is intimately confronting one's own mortality [26]. Hopkins affirms the experiences of the sixth grade poet and of Chuck when he, gently but directly, concludes to Margaret, weeping over the passing seasons ("Goldengrove unleaving"):

> It is the blight man was born for,
> It is Margaret you mourn for.

CONCLUSIONS

The classroom can be a repository of death experiences, anxieties and feelings. Art expressions in the form of film, dialogue and drawing can give focus and voice to deeply felt concerns that are present in the student of any age. The use of one art form quickly leads to identification of similar themes in another form. Through the stimulation of pictorial and literary media, students find they can articulate sentiments that may have been previously unshareable. Death education is not group psychotherapy; nonetheless, open expression in a once taboo area can ease feelings of fear and loneliness. Sometimes students find a community of mutual ideas with one another as well as with the artist. Provoked by an artistic image or by a classmate, "the ease and discharge of the fullness and swellings of the heart," can occur in the classroom. Francis Bacon phrased it in his essay *Of Friendship:* "Friendship words two contrary effects, for it redoubleth joys and cutteth griefs in halves." [26]

REFERENCES

1. *Life Cycle,* film animation created by E. Zinn, production pending, Equinox Institute, 159 Ward Street, Newton, Massachusetts.
2. Solomon Grundy, *The Real Mother Goose,* Rand McNally, Chicago, 1916.
3. T. Rosenthal, *How Could I Not Be Among You?,* Braziller, New York, *45,* film distributed by Benchmark Productions, Scarsdale, New York, 1973.
4. V. Lee, *The Magic Moth,* Seabury, New York, 1972.
5. M. Miles, *Annie and the Old One,* Little Brown, Boston, *41,* 1971.
6. N. Caroline, Dying in Academe, *New Physician,* Amer. Med. Student Assoc., Virginia, pp. 654-657.
7. Collection of Student Work, Equinox Institute, Newton, Massachusetts, cf. S. L. Bertman, *Death Education: A Primer For All Ages,* unpublished manuscript.
8. S. S. Warburg, *Growing Time,* Houghton Mifflin, Boston, 1969.
9. D. Linett, Gifts, *MS. Magazine,* pp. 67-71, March 1978.
10. J. Viorst, *The Tenth Good Thing About Barney,* Atheneum, New York, 1972.
11. M. Kumin, How It Is, *New Yorker Magazine,* New York, p. 58, March 3, 1975.
12. A. Clardy, *Dusty Was My Friend,* unpublished manuscript.
13. M. W. Brown, *The Dead Bird,* Young Scott, New York, 1958.
14. E. Grollman, *Talking About Death,* Beacon, Boston, p. 32, 1970.
15. *The Day Grampa Died,* Bailey Film Assoc., California.
16. *Where is Dead,* Encyclopedia Britanica Educational Films, Chicago, Illinois.
17. W. Shakespeare, Macbeth, In: G. Harrison (ed.), *Shakespeare The Complete Works,* Harcourt, Brace, New York, p. 1212, 1948.
18. C. Rossetti, Song, In: M. Van Doren (ed.), *An Anthology of World Poetry,* Reynal & Hitchcock, New York, p. 1245, 1928.
19. W. Shakespeare, Hamlet, In: G. Harrison (ed.), *Shakespeare The Complete Works,* Harcourt, Brace, New York, p. 889, 1948.

20. *Anthology of World Poetry,* Reynal & Hitchcock, New York, pp. 1086-1088, 1928.
21. M. Twain, At the Funeral, *Letters from the Earth,* Fawcett, New York, p. 152, 1932.
22. L. Tolstoy, *The Death of Ivan Ilych,* New American Library, New York, p. 99, 1960.
23. R. Stilman, The Bad Baby, *New Yorker Magazine,* New York.
24. H. Sandberg, Father, Once You Said That in the Grace of God, *McCalls Magazine,* New York, p. 96, October 1968.
25. D. Smith, *A Taste of Blackberries,* Crowell, New York, 1973.
26. F. Bacon, Of Friendship, *Oxford Anthology of Prose,* Oxford University Press, New York, p. 66, 1935.

Many death educators operate on the implicit assumption that having high death anxiety is distressing and that successful efforts to reduce high death anxiety provide benefits to program participants. Chapter 24 describes such a process, based on the tenets of behavior modification (which was discussed in another context in Chapter 18). The major significance of the chapter is the research findings in which it is shown that death anxiety can, in fact, be reduced. The research reported in Chapter 24 is not only interesting in its own right, but also suggests numerous other research possibilities that might add important knowledge to our understanding of the meaning of death anxiety and the potential for death-anxiety-reduction programs.

A Group Desensitization
Procedure for the Reduction
of Death Anxiety

Ronald L. Peal
Paul J. Handal
and
Frank H. Gilner

Apparently, death anxiety is not a problem faced only by the dying since one consistent finding among researchers in the area of death anxiety is that many non-dying individuals in western society are sorely lacking in resources for dealing with fears about death [1]. In addition, death anxiety appears to be quite prevalent among all segments of the population [2-5].

The current rise in the number of college courses dealing with death and dying [6] may also be a response to the underlying need for ways of dealing more directly with individual's concerns about death. Yet, by itself, death education has not been shown to be very effective in reducing death anxiety levels of college students or of children [7]. In fact, investigations focused on the alleviation of death anxiety in non-terminal populations are rare.

Behavior therapists have suggested a useful adjunct to recent educational and clinical trends toward more open and less regressive approaches in dealing with death anxiety. Specifically, Cautela proposed the general use of desensitization and thought stopping in aiding the elderly in dealing with death anxiety [8]. Templer, Ruff, and Franks also indicated that behavioral techniques such as desensitization may provide ways of directly reducing death anxiety [9]. In addition to these suggestions, a successful desensitization of a death phobia in a non-dying person has been reported by Wolpe [10].

Although desensitization may be an appropriate technique to reduce death anxiety, our review of the literature has revealed no published experimental studies dealing with the use of desensitization to reduce death anxiety in any population. In response to this apparent need, the present investigation was designed to examine the efficacy of group systematic desensitization in reducing death anxiety levels of highly death anxious individuals.

The design entailed pre- and post-intervention assessment of death anxiety on each of three death anxiety measures [11-13]. Treatment interventions consisted of systematic desensitization, relaxation, and test-retest groups. Specifically, it was hypothesized that following intervention only the desensitization group would evidence a significant reduction from their pre- to post-intervention death anxiety scores; and that the desensitization group would obtain significantly lower death anxiety scores at post-intervention assessment than both the relaxation and the test-retest groups.

METHOD

Participants

Participants were selected from a pool of 247 undergraduate students on the basis of their scores on two different measures of death anxiety [11, 12]. All potential participants who scored in the high death anxious range were approached to participate in the remainder of this investigation and approximately 74 per cent of those approached volunteered to participate. This resulted in a total of twenty-four female and fifteen male participants who were placed into one of three groups; desensitization (8 females, 5 males, mean age 19.45); relaxation (8 females, 5 males, mean age 20.62); test-retest group (8 females, 5 males, mean age 19.09). There were no significant age differences among the three groups.

Scales

The Death Anxiety Scale is a modified version of the Livingston and Zimet Death Anxiety Scale [14]. This scale was revised because several items proved unsuitable for administration to a general population since the test was originally designed for administration to medical school students and, therefore, contained very specific references to medical terminology [12].

The revised form consists of twenty items in the form of statements to which there are six possible responses range from "strongly disagree" to "strongly agree." Some examples of the questions are:

1. When I see a funeral procession, I never particularly wonder who the dead person is;
2. Death hardly concerns me; and
3. Dying people don't make me uneasy.

Responses are scored on a six-point scale yielding a minimum score of 20 and a maximum score of 120.

The test-retest reliability coefficient for the revised death anxiety scale has been reported to be .85 [12]. Validity data for the scale has been provided by Handal [15], Handal and Rychlak [16], and Handal [17]. Tentative norms were developed by Handal such that participants scoring 74 above are defined as highly death anxious, those scoring 64-69 are defined as moderately death anxious, and those scoring 61 and below are defined as low death anxious [16].

The second measure of death anxiety employed was Templer's Death Anxiety Scale [11]. This scale was designed to be appropriate for a number of different populations and consists of fifteen true/false type questions. Scores range from 0 to 15, with 0 indicating no death anxiety and 15 indicating high death anxiety. Average scores generally range from 4.5 to 7.0 with a standard deviation slightly more than 3.0. The test-retest reliability coefficient was found to be .83 and a considerable amount of validity data has been provided by Templer [5, 9, 11].

The third measure used to assess death anxiety was Feifel and Branscomb's color-word interference test (CWIT) [13]. The CWIT is purported to be a preconscious measure of death anxiety. The CWIT requires the subject to respond to the color a word is printed in, and to disregard its content. In the original CWIT, ten death words and ten neutral words equated for color representation, frequency of usage, and syllable content are used. Five lines of ten death words are alternated with five lines of ten neutral words. The cumulative time differential in verbalizing the color of the two sets of words is used for scoring purposes and a constant of 50 is added to avoid negative scores. The computational formula is the total time of non-death word color naming minus the total time of death word color naming, plus the constant of 50. Thus, lower scores indicate greater disruption caused by the content of a word being related to death. Reliability coefficients of .79 and .83 are reported by Feifel and Branscomb [13] and validity data for the measure have also been provided [18].

Another measure, the Death Hierarchy Scene Question was devised specifically for this study. The questionnaire consists of fixty-four death related scenes (e.g., "You're lying in bed and notice that your heart is skipping beats"). Participants were asked to rate each scene on a four-point scale as to how much anxiety they would feel if they were actually experiencing what is described. Items from the questionnaire were used to form a common hierarchy of death scenes for all desensitization groups in this study. The bottom portion of the hierarchy was formed by taking the five scenes that most participants agreed caused them "some anxiety" while the middle portion of the hierarchy is composed of seven scenes that most participants agreed caused them "moderate anxiety" and finally, the upper portion of the hierarchy consists of the nine scenes that most participants agreed caused them "great anxiety."

Procedure

Potential participants in undergraduate psychology classes were administered both the revised Livingston and Zimet DAS and the Templer DAS. They were also asked to indicate if they were colorblind. Participant's scores on each DAS were converted to z-scores, then the two z-scores for each individual were averaged. Only participants who had a combined z-score $> .50$ standard deviation above the mean of the entire pool of respondents were considered "high death anxious." These potential participants were then randomly contacted and asked if they would participate in the investigation and a total of thirty-nine participants agreed. These participants were individually administered Feifel's CWIT then given the Death Hierarchy Scene Questionnaire. Three subjects were then randomly selected and assigned, respectively, to a desensitization group, a relaxation group, and a test-retest group. Each threesome was yoked to the participant in the test-retest group to control for differences in treatment exposure due to working through the hierarchy at different rates. Participants were divided into smaller groups based on their available meeting times. Participants in the test-retest group were told that they had been placed in a group to see if anxieties about death would change with the passage of time and would be retested in about ten weeks.

At the first meeting of the relaxation group, the relaxation procedure and rationale were briefly explained and participants began learning the deep muscle relaxation technique described by Goldfried and Davison [19]. Likewise, the desensitization groups were told the rationale and the procedure to be used, then taught the same relaxation technique. The rationale given was that the investigation was looking at procedures that might decrease anxieties about death. All groups spent the second session learning to deepen their relaxation. The relaxation groups spent the first half of the third session deepening their relaxation, while the second half and subsequent sessions were spent "maintaining" and "enjoying" the relaxation.

The desensitization groups also spent the first half of the third session learning to deepen their relaxation, but the second half of the session involved beginning to work through the death anxiety hierarchy in the prescribed method of desensitization [19]. The desensitization groups continued to work through the hierarchy in the subsequent sessions. Working through the hierarchy was geared to the slowest person in each of the groups. When a desensitization group finished the hierarchy, each individual was retested immediately along with the individuals they had been yoked with in the other groups (relaxation and test-retest). The average number of sessions to complete the hierarchy was eight with a range of six to ten sessions. Sessions for the groups were approximately thirty-five minutes long.

RESULTS

Table 1 presents pre- and post-treatment means and standard deviations for each of the three participant groups on each of the death anxiety measures. As can be seen from the table the z-score transformation and averaging on the revised Livingston and Zimet DAS and the Templer DAS resulted in pre-treatment scores on these measures for all groups that fell within the high death anxiety range according to the norms for each measure.

In order to determine the existence of significant differences on death anxiety scales among treated groups at pre- and post-treatment assessment, and to determine the existence of significant differences from pre- to post-treatment assessment for any one of the three treatment groups, a 3 $\times$ 2 (treatment groups $\times$ time, pre/post) analysis of variance was computed for each of the three death anxiety measures. Results, using the Templer DAS as the dependent variable, revealed significant main effects for treatment groups (F = 3.54, df 2,36, p $<$.05), time (F = 15.08, df 1,36, p $<$.001), and a significant treatment by time interaction (F = 3.54, df 2,36, p $<$.05). Further analysis to determine the nature of significant differences, using the Newman Keul's Test, revealed no significant pre-treatment differences among treatment groups, but yielded significant post-treatment group differences. Post-treatment, both the desensitization group and the relaxation group, were significantly less death anxious than the test-retest group (p $<$.01 and p $<$.05, respectively). The desensitization and relaxation groups did not differ significantly from one another at post-treatment; however, pre-treatment to post-treatment significant differences existed within both the desensitization and relaxation groups (p $<$ .01 and p $<$ .05, respectively,) but not within the test-retest group.

Results of the ANOVA with the Revised Livingston and Zimet DAS revealed no significant main effects for treatment groups (F = 1.15, df 2,36), but a significant main effect for time (F = 30.98, df 1,36, p $<$.001) and a significant treatment by time interaction (F = 5.21, df 2,36, p $<$.02). Results using the Newman Keul's procedure revealed that although there were no significant pre-treatment differences among groups, there were significant post-treatment differences. Post-treatment, the desensitization group was significantly less death anxious than both the relaxation group (p $<$.01) and the test-retest group (p $<$.01). The latter two groups did not differ significantly at post-treatment assessment and only the desensitization groups revealed a significant pre-to post-treatment decrease in their death anxiety scores (p $<$.01).

Results of the ANOVA using the CWIT as the dependent variable revealed no significant main effects for treatment (F = .73, df 2,36), or time (F = 3.73, df 1,36), and no significant interaction for treatment by time (F = 1.88, df 2,36). Since the main effect for time approached significance (p $<$.10) and because a priori hypotheses were made regarding the CWIT pre- and post-

Table 1. Means and Standard Deviations on the Templer DAS, the Revised Livingston and Zimet DAS, and the Feifel CWIT Measure of Death Anxiety for the Three Experimental Groups Pre- and Post-Treatment

| | | Treatment | | |
| | | Pre- | Post- | |
Measures		Pre-	Post-	Sig. Level
Templer DAS				
Desensitization group	$\overline{X}$	9.00	6.23	.01[a]
	SD	1.08	2.74	
Relaxation group	$\overline{X}$	9.31	7.46	.05[a]
	SD	1.75	2.50	
Test-retest group	$\overline{X}$	9.54	9.39	ns[a]
	SD	1.20	3.07	
Revised Livingston and Zimet DAS				
Desensitization group	$\overline{X}$	78.46	66.54	.01[a]
	SD	5.64	10.73	
Relaxation group	$\overline{X}$	77.85	75.00	ns[a]
	SD	7.77	8.45	
Test-retest group	$\overline{X}$	78.00	72.92	ns[a]
	SD	5.21	7.60	
Feifel CWIT				
Desensitization group	$\overline{X}$	46.98	49.62	.01[b]
	SD	3.50	2.58	
Relaxation group	$\overline{X}$	47.49	47.26	ns[b]
	SD	3.97	3.23	
Test-retest group	$\overline{X}$	46.40	47.48	ns[a]
	SD	4.03	3.08	

[a] Newman Keul's test of significance.
[b] Planned comparison t ratio test of significance.

treatment means for the desensitization group, pairwise t comparisons were computed to test the hypotheses. Results of these analyses revealed that the three groups did not differ significantly on pre-treatment assessment; that, on post-treatment assessment, the desensitization group was significantly less death anxious than both the relaxation group ($p < .02$) and the test-retest group ($p < .025$); and, that only the desensitization group evidenced a significant decrease in death anxiety from pre- to post-treatment assessment ($p < .01$).

DISCUSSION

Results from the present investigation reveal that systematic desensitization is clearly an effective intervention for the short-term reduction of death anxiety when the revised Livingston and Zimet DAS is the criterion measure. Since there were no significant decreases in death anxiety scores from pre- to post-treatment assessment for either the relaxation or test-retest groups it does not appear that the decrease in death anxiety by participants in the desensitization group can be attributed to the passage of time, the non-specific effects associated with learning the relaxation technique, being in a research project, and/or meeting with the therapist.

Although the pre- to post-intervention death anxiety scores on the Templer DAS showed a significant decrease for the desensitization group, there was also a significant decrease of death anxiety from pre- to post-intervention on this measure for the relaxation group. This finding may be the result of the psychometric nature/properties of the instrument, rather than reflecting that relaxation alone is an effective treatment for death anxiety. The Templer DAS has high face validity and its content is primarily limited to conscious anxiety related to self dying and/or death of self [2] and previous research has demonstrated [20] significant changes in desensitization study control groups on face valid measures similar to the Templer DAS.

The results for the relaxation group on the Templer DAS may also be attributable, at least partially, to the tendency for post-intervention assessments to regress to the mean [21]. This regression is most clearly evident in Table 1 for the relaxation and test-retest groups on the revised Livingston and Zimet DAS. It is possible that the psychometric properties of the Templer combined with the tendency for post-assessments to regress to the mean and yielded the significant results for the relaxation group on the Templer. However, it is clear that relaxation alone had no effect on the death anxiety scores, as measured by the revised Livingston and Zimet DAS, of the relaxation group in this investigation. These findings reflect the need for additional investigation of the Templer's psychometric properties and the need to replicate these results.

The fact that no significant main effects or interaction effects were found using the CWIT as the dependent variable is intriguing, particularly since later pair-wise comparisons revealed significant differences in the expected direction for all three groups. It may be that the increased variance, which occurred on all three death anxiety measures at post-treatment assessment, masked the effects of desensitization on the CWIT. This would account for the failure to obtain significant F values using the ANOVA while still obtaining the predicted significant pair-wise comparisons.

It may also be that the post-intervention assessment, taken immediately following the completion of the Group Death Hierarchy, did not allow enough time for incubation effects to occur, particularly since the CWIT is purported to be a measure of pre-conscious death anxiety. Future research, designed to allow for incubation, may prove fruitful regarding this interpretation and may shed some much needed light on the relationship among these three measures of death anxiety. By using only high death anxious participants, the present study was not designed to obtain intercorrelations among the three death anxiety measures. However, the mixed results regarding the effectiveness of systematic desensitization on each of the three measures of death anxiety indicates the need for additional data concerning the relationships (correlations) among these three measures.

The question may be raised as to whether the changes in the desensitization groups' death anxiety level actually represent a reduction of death anxiety rather than general anxiety. Prior research on the Templer DAS [11] and the revised Livingston and Zimet DAS [15] indicates that the two measures have relatively little common variance (13% and 9%, respectively) with measures of general anxiety. Thus, any change on either of these death anxiety measures is unlikely to reflect a reduction in general anxiety.

Overall, the present study has shown that group desensitization is an effective procedure for the short-term reduction of death anxiety as measured by the revised Livingston and Zimet DAS. This procedure, as part of death education classes (which have failed to demonstrate significant death anxiety reduction), may be effective in reducing death anxiety levels. Moreover, this study has provided initial data regarding the development and successful use of a *group* death desensitization hierarchy which may be applied to various populations. However, whether the effects of group desensitization are lasting remains to be determined by future investigations.

REFERENCES

1. H. Feifel, Attitudes Toward Death: A Psychological Perspective, *Journal of Consulting and Clinical Psychology, 33*, pp. 292-295, 1969.
2. J. Durlak, Relationship between Various Measures of Death Concern and Fear of Death, *Journal of Consulting and Clinical Psychology, 41*, p. 162, 1973.
3. H. Feifel and L. Hermann, Fear of Death in the Mentally Ill, *Psychological Reports, 33*, p. 931-938, 1973.
4. D. Lester, Studies in Death Attitudes: Part Two, *Psychological Reports, 30*, p. 440, 1972.
5. D. Templer, Death Anxiety in Religiously Very Involved Persons, *Psychological Reports, 31*, pp. 361-362, 1972.
6. R. Craddick, Symbolism of Death Archetypal and Personal Symbols, *International Journal of Symbology, 3*, pp. 35-44, 1972.
7. M. Mueller, Death Education and Death Fear Reduction, *Education, 97*, pp. 145-148, 1976.
8. J. Cautela, A Classical Conditioning Approach to the Development and Modification of Behavior in the Aged, *Gerontologist, 9*, pp. 109-113, 1969.

9. D. Templer, C. Ruff, and C. Franks, Death Anxiety: Age, Sex and Parental Resemblance in Diverse Populations, *Developmental Psychology, 4*, p. 108, 1971.

10. J. Wolpe, *The Practice of Behavior Therapy*, Pergamon Press, New York, 1969.

11. D. Templer, The Construction and Validation of a Death Anxiety Scale, *The Journal of General Psychology, 82*, pp. 167-172, 1970.

12. A. Tolor and M. Reznikoff, Relation between Insight, Repression-Sensitization, Internal-External Control and Death Anxiety, *Journal of Abnormal Psychology, 72*, pp. 246-430, 1967.

13. H. Feifel and A. Branscomb, Who's Afraid of Death, *Journal of Abnormal Psychology, 81*, pp. 282-288, 1973.

14. P. Livingston and C. Zimet, Death Anxiety Authoritarianism and Choice of Specialty in Medical Students, *Journal of Nervous and Mental Disease, 140*, pp. 222-230, 1965.

15. P. Handal, The Relationship between Subjective Life Expectancy, Death Anxiety and General Anxiety, *Journal of Clinical Psychology, 22*, pp. 39-42, 1969.

16. P. Handal and J. Rychlak, Curvilinearity between Dream Content and Death Anxiety and the Relationship of Death Anxiety to Repression-Sensitization, *Journal of Abnormal Psychology, 71*, pp. 11-16, 1971.

17. P. Handal, Individual and Group Prolem Solving and Type of Orientation as a Function of High, Moderate, and Low Death Anxiety, *Omega: Journal of Death and Dying, 10*, pp. 365-377, 1979–80.

18. H. Feifel, J. Freilich, and L. Hermann, Death Fear in Dying Heart and Cancer Patients, *Journal of Psychosomatic Medicine, 17*, pp. 161-166, 1973.

19. M. Goldfried and G. Davison, *Clinical Behavior Therapy*, Holt, Rinehart, and Wilson, New York, 1976.

20. A. Kazdin and L. Wilcoxin, Systematic Desensitization and Nonspecific Treatment Effects: A Methodological Evaluation, *Psychological Bulletin, 83*, pp. 729-758, 1976.

21. J. M. Oliver and B. Burkham, Depression in University Students as Measures by Random Samples: Duration, Relation to Calendar Time, Prevalence, and Demographic Correlates, *Journal of Abnormal Psychology* (in press).

ACKNOWLEDGEMENT

The authors are grateful to John G. Napoli for his helpful comments and to Herman Feifel for his assistance concerning the Color Word Interference Test of Death Anxiety.

Do you want to teach a workshop or course on death? The author of Chapter 25 offers some very specific suggestions, although you may need to modify them to fit your own preferences and the nature of your audience. Not only are the suggested exercises practical in getting points across, but author Koenig uses a very light touch in his writing. Moreover, he isn't even above catching you, the reader, or your eventual students in traps of your own making. That is, he sets up one kind of task and, when you have finished, you realize that his purpose was quite different from what you had assumed. So read ahead. You're on your own.

However, as you read this chapter, ask yourself some questions. For example, how long do you believe the changes found by the authors lasted? For weeks? Months? Years? A lifetime? And do you assume that the measures of death anxiety were valid? Also, do you believe that a follow-up desensitization program, perhaps six months later, would have led to greater reduction in anxiety or for reduction for a longer period of time? Would this approach work for corporate executives? For women lawyers? For construction workers? For persons who had attempted suicide? And finally, if you were developing a comparable program, what changes would be made in the process? You don't need to be a researcher in order to begin to evaluate the adequacy of any given research study. And you can, on the one hand, be critical of the research that has been reported while, on the other hand, recognizing the value of the information that it offers.

CHAPTER
25

Counseling in Catastrophic Illness: A Self-Instructional Unit*

Ronald Koenig

Those who have already acquired some clinical and teaching experience "the hard way" are in a position to help students who stand on the verge of their first relationships with people suffering from catastrophic illness. One possible technique could be the self-instructional unit. Here, then, is such a unit that the author has devised, applied, and found useful. Perhaps it will have some interest for others as well.

TO THE INSTRUCTOR

While this procedure is termed a "self instructional learning unit," it is important that the instructor assume considerable active responsibility to prepare the student for initial interviewing assignments. It can be used without much preparation, but is most useful and effective if students have first

* Supported in part by Clinical Cancer Training Grant T 12CA08096, National Cancer Institute, U.S. Department of H.E.W., at Darling Memorial Cancer Center, Grace General Hospital, Detroit, Mich.

participated in discussions dealing with life-inventory interviewing concepts, or provided with guidelines for review of important psychosocial areas of life. In clincial situations, this unit is particularly useful for students who are learning to apply the problem-oriented record system.

In classroom situations some preliminary operations are necessary. After discussion of the eroding effects of illness on the lives of patients, students are asked to imagine they have recently been told that they themselves have a potentially fatal disease such as leukemia. The symptoms and normal course of the disease are discussed. Next, they are directed to write a brief (300-500 word) anonymous, *now*-oriented, cross sectional autobiography. The students should be encouraged to describe all important areas of their lives, including problems that concern them, and relating these to the disease and its implications. It is helpful to make specific suggestions to add details about family relationships, work, finances, religion, recreation, future plans, attitudes about dependency, etc. Occasionally a student may find it too threatenting to consider the issue of his or her own fatal illness. In such a case it may be desirable to offer the student the option of developing an imaginary case description if they are in considerable discomfort about the autobiographical approach.

The anonymous cross-sectional autobiographies are then redistributed to the class. Each student receives an autobiography from an unidentified fellow student of the same sex. This information is used to play the role of patient. Half of the class is assigned to be the "counselor," and half "patient." It is important to emphasize the need to "get into" the role of counselor, establish rapport, and develop the relationship toward the goal of understanding the "patient" and his social and emotional troubles.

Students who are playing the role of patient should be encouraged to improvise when there is not enough detail in the autobiography distributed to them. In the next class session, students change partners and reverse roles. Careful matching of "patient" to interviewer will avoid problems that could arise if students receive their own or their interviewer's autobiography. It is generally better if students are asked to find a private place, outside of the classroom, to conduct the interviews.

Finally, the "patient" is asked to write a frank evaluation of the strongest and weakest points of the interviewer. This provides feedback to the student interviewer, and useful group discussion about the interview experience tends to follow. Additionally, of course, each student is asked to complete the tasks spelled out in the self-instructional unit. This can be done in less than one hour. The interviews themselves usually require an hour or a little longer. The instructor may want to request that interviewers prepare a "case report."

Note that the pre-test section of the self-instructional unit is intended to orient the student to troubles associated with illness; it is not intended as a research tool.

THE SELF-INSTRUCTION UNIT

Introduction

The following unit is designed to help you "get over the hump" as you begin to help patients deal with the personal troubles that come along with their illness. It is intended to help you to look at yourself and your ideas about sickness. It is mainly intended to help you get started to identify the problems which your patient may have in getting along with his illness. From time to time you will be asked to complete brief exercises and do some thinking for yourself. Please complete each exercise before going on to the next section. Do the Pre-Test now.

Pre-Test

The following is a list of problems which have been known to trouble patients who have a catastrophic illness. (One which could cause them to die.)

You may regard some to be serious problems and others not to be serious at all. If you think a problem is not serious or that an issue does not really come up, mark it at zero per cent (0%). For example:

a. Are patients troubled because they don't know how to order breakfast?

0% |—|—|—|—|—|—|—|—|—|————— 100%

If you think a problem is serious but comes up only in 10 per cent of patients or less, put a mark in the first segment of the line. If you think a problem comes up with ten to twenty per cent of patients, put a check in the second segment (10% to 20%)—and so forth.

1. Are the patients troubled and upset about undergoing tests, procedures and therapies?

0% |—|—|—|—|—|—|—|—|—|————— 100%

2. Are patients concerned about losing their active role in life, like their ability to work, travel, take care of children or other responsibilities?

0% |—|—|—|—|—|—|—|—|—|————— 100%

3. Are patients upset about being a burden on family, friends or others?

0% |—|—|—|—|—|—|—|—|—|————— 100%

4. Are patients concerned about money issues, such as paying for medical care, insurances, medicine, or providing enough income to take care of family and other responsibilities?

0% ├─────┼─────┼─────┼─────┼─────┼─────┼─────┼─────┼─────┼───── 100%

5. Are patients concerned that important relationships with others will be jeopardized by changes related to their illness (for example: changes in sexual performance, ability to join in shared activities) or concerned that already unstable and poor relationships will get worse?

0% ├─────┼─────┼─────┼─────┼─────┼─────┼─────┼─────┼─────┼───── 100%

6. Are patients concerned that others are patronizing toward them, that others are too cautious or protective toward them, or in other ways make them feel "different"?

0% ├─────┼─────┼─────┼─────┼─────┼─────┼─────┼─────┼─────┼───── 100%

7. Are patients troubled about causing sadness, worry or guilt in family members or those who they are emotionally close to?

0% ├─────┼─────┼─────┼─────┼─────┼─────┼─────┼─────┼─────┼───── 100%

8. Are patients concerned that they may not be adequately cared for when they are sick, or that their basic needs (foods, medicine, nursing care, shelter, etc.) will go unmet?

0% ├─────┼─────┼─────┼─────┼─────┼─────┼─────┼─────┼─────┼───── 100%

9. Are patients concerned that they will be lied to or that they will not be told all of the important facts about their situation?

0% ├─────┼─────┼─────┼─────┼─────┼─────┼─────┼─────┼─────┼───── 100%

10. Are patients troubled by the feeling that there may be no good times ahead for them?

0% ├─────┼─────┼─────┼─────┼─────┼─────┼─────┼─────┼─────┼───── 100%

11. Are patients concerned that their doctors may not be competent, that they may make a mistake or fail to understand what is wrong with them?

0% ├─────┼─────┼─────┼─────┼─────┼─────┼─────┼─────┼─────┼───── 100%

12. Are patients troubled that, as they look over their life, they feel it has been a failure, worthless or without meaning?

0% |—|—|—|—|—|—|—|—|—|——— 100%

13. Does the idea of being in the hospital and away from their familiar surroundings trouble patients?

0% |—|—|—|—|—|—|—|—|—|——— 100%

14. Are patients concerned that their illness causes them to be isolated and cut off from others emotionally or physically?

0% |—|—|—|—|—|—|—|—|—|——— 100%

15. Are patients concerned that they *will* get well again and have to go back to the way things were before they were seriously ill?

0% |—|—|—|—|—|—|—|—|—|——— 100%

16. Are patients troubled because they feel responsible or to blame for their illness?

0% |—|—|—|—|—|—|—|—|—|——— 100%

17. Are patients concerned about being unable to provide for their family if they do not survive?

0% |—|—|—|—|—|—|—|—|—|——— 100%

18. Are patients concerned about the loss of independence and that they have to rely on others?

0% |—|—|—|—|—|—|—|—|—|——— 100%

19. Are patients concerned that they will not be treated as an individual; that their personal feelings will not be taken into account, or concerned that they are regarded as a guinea pig?

0% |—|—|—|—|—|—|—|—|—|——— 100%

20. Are patients concerned that they may soon die, either because of worry about the experience of dying itself, or worry about non-existence or punishment in the here-after?

0% |——+——+——+——+——+——+——+——+——+——— 100%

21. Are patients concerned about the changes in the appearance of their body, because of surgery, major loss or gain of weight, or other changes in the way they look to themselves or others?

0% |——+——+——+——+——+——+——+——+——+——— 100%

22. Are patients concerned that their situation may be much worse than they realize, and fear bad news?

0% |——+——+——+——+——+——+——+——+——+——— 100%

23. Are patients troubled because they can no longer be in full control of their life because their illness demands that they go through hospitalizations, treatment regimens, tests and other activities that interrupt their plans and routines?

0% |——+——+——+——+——+——+——+——+——+——— 100%

24. Are patients concerned that their emotional reaction may be inappropriate. That they may be wrong to be so sad and tearful, nervous, demanding, angry, fearful and so forth?

0% |——+——+——+——+——+——+——+——+——+——— 100%

25. Are patients troubled by the loss of confidence in their body, or by a point of view that their body is in a revolt against them?

0% |——+——+——+——+——+——+——+——+——+——— 100%

26. Are patients concerned that their doctor or others may give up on them, consider them hopeless or in some way cause them to feel abandonment?

0% |——+——+——+——+——+——+——+——+——+——— 100%

27. Are patients troubled about getting nursing care for themselves when they are out of the hospital, either at home or in a nursing home?

0% |——+——+——+——+——+——+——+——+——+——— 100%

It may be mildly frustrating to learn that there is currently no way to determine whether you did well on the foregoing test. While some of the problems you checked cause serious troubles for sick and dying patients, we can only guess how often this may happen. What is more frustrating—so far as predicting problems is concerned— is that one patient who has a problem may regard it as serious while another who has the same problem may regard it as trivial.

Going through the experience of dying is likely to cause people quite a lot of trouble, inconvenience, and worry. Patients, like the rest of us folks, are about as likely to be concerned about one important thing as they are another. In order to understand which difficulties are troubling any particular patient you have to be with them, talking, listening, observing. It is easy to assume that because a patient knows that he has an incurable disease that he is mainly worried about dying. It is natural for you to assume that the patient who has a fatal illness is worried about the same thing that would trouble you if you were dying with the disease. That is probably not the case. If the patient's problems with his disease were the same kinds of problems that you would have, then it would not be so very important to talk to him about his difficulties in order to understand him. If you want to communicate with a patient, you have to understand *his* point of view about his situation.

EXERCISE

List six problems which you think would be most likely to trouble you if everything in your life was as it is now except that yesterday you were told you have Stage III Hodgkin's Disease.

1. _____
2. _____
3. _____
4. _____
5. _____
6. _____

Now in the space below rate your six problems from one to six with one being the most important to *you* and six the least important.

Do your rating this way: If, for example, the first problem you listed is one of of the least important to you, then you would write something like; 1. = 6. If it was the most important you would write; 1. = 1.

Do your rating on this sheet because next I want you to ask a fellow student or someone else around here to rate the importance to *them* of the problems you have listed, so keep your ratings to yourself for the time being.

1. = _____
2. = _____

3. = _____
4. = _____
5. = _____
6. = _____

Ahah, did you rate them? Now, ask someone else to rate the importance of your list of problems to *them*. At first you should not let them know the way you rated the list of problems. After they do so compare your ratings together. Discuss your reasons for agreeing or disagreeing with each other.

(Note: If there is no one around here you feel you want to rate your problems then I suggest you ask your mother. Mothers are usually very nice for that sort of thing.)

As you were making the list of problems you thought would most trouble you, did you notice that it was not so much fun to think about your Hodgkin's Disease? Lots of patients feel the same way, so if you only ask them to talk about their *troubles* they don't always like to do it. It is usually much easier to talk about work, family, fun, hobbies. Talking about these kinds of things is a lot better way to get acquainted with someone than talking to them only about their miseries. You need to develop a trusting relationship with a patient before he can tell you how he really feels. If you were going to talk to someone about the problems of your Hodgkin's Disease and how you feel about it you would probably like them to get to know you some first.

Look at your list of problems. Why did you pick these instead of some of the other problems you can think of? The uncomplicated answer to that question is: These problems have special importance to you because you are the special person you are. They feel right for you. When you get to know the way your patient's life has been going you can begin to see *why* their disease causes their special troubles. Other peoples' problems are exactly appropriate for them. Imagine whether your worries about your Hodgkin's Disease would be different if:

1. You were twenty years older or younger.
2. You got a divorce last month.
3. Your brother also died of Hodgkin's Disease last year.
4. You were poor.
5. You were a millionaire sweepstake winner.
6. If your Blue Cross had been cancelled.
7. If you also had just learned that your two-year old son was severely mentally retarded.
8. If you were whatever sex you are not.

I hate to leave such an interesting topic, but let's stop talking about you for a minute and talk about me. What are the main points I have been making? (Before you turn to "The Convenient List of Main Points I Have Been Making" which follows, try to write two or three you think I have been making!)

A CONVENIENT LIST OF THE MAIN POINTS
I HAVE BEEN MAKING

1. There is considerable likelihood that the patient who is dying with a chronic fatal disease does not look at this situation in the same way you would.
2. If you want to understand his point of view about his illness, you have to talk with him. You have to develop a relationship. (These usually occur together.)
3. Talking with a patient about his life in general rather than just his problems is a good way to form a relationship that will help you understand each other when you get around to talking about the trouble of his disease.
4. The troubles that dying patients run into are not just related to their disease. Their troubles are related to all the important issues in their life.

It would be interesting to me to know whether the main points *you* thought I was making are the same as the main points *I* thought I was making. I don't want to grade you yet, but leave your main points on the work sheet so we can both see how we are doing.

Getting Started

If you have not talked to a lot of people who have a serious illness, there are a few ideas that can make the experience easier for both of you. For example, pick a time when your patient is not having severe pain, nausea, etc. You will like each other better if you are both comfortable. Explain exactly why you are there.

Can you answer the following questions?

1. How do I start?
2. What do I say?
3. Why should this patient talk about himself to me?
4. What if he cries or gets upset or angry?
5. Will I make him feel worse?
6. Will he make me feel worse?
7. What am I doing here!?

If you cannot answer these questions, do not pass go, do not collect two-hundred dollars. Read the next section.

When your new patient seems not too talkative, a question such as, "What do you understand to be the matter with you that causes you to be in the hospital?," can be a good one for openers. You are not so interested in the specific answer as you are in the topic. Probably the only person more interested in that topic than you is the patient, so it is often a good way to get the ball rolling. Patients usually have a lot to say about their experiences with their disease. Talk about when it started, how they noticed it, what the doctor told them, what treatments they had, what they expect from it, what they call their disease (cancer? a tumor?), and so forth. If you have to do a medical history, this information will be useful anyway. If you stick with it a while patients get the idea that their illness is important to you. They usually like that, and already you have a basic issue on which you agree. Feel free to be sympathetic and understanding. Throw in at *appropriate* moments comments such as "That must have been tough" or, "That would have made me mad, too." Patients often appreciate it and it makes them feel closer to you. The alternative—not to be sympathetic—does not seem worth considering.

It also makes sick people feel more relaxed and comforted if you touch them. Handholding is pretty asexual when one is sick. It is also appropriate to touch children and old people, but if you do it much to other nonsick people who you don't know too well they tend to act odd about it. Handholding works best when patients are talking about things that make them feel like crying or when they seem to need affection.

You may have some concern about boldly intruding on people's private lives by asking them a lot of questions about personal matters, things like, "How do you get along with your wife?" or, "Have your bills been getting behind since you have been sick?" It would be out of place if you were asking because of personal curiosity, but you should ask these kinds of questions because you need to know how their life is going in order to form strategies to help them. I would like to give now the rule of thumb that, "The better you understand the patient's situation from *his* point of view the better will be the rapport in your relationship."

(Rules of thumb are likely to be true in more than 6 per cent of cases and therefore, make excellent digital computers.)

Talking to patients about the relevant personal circumstances of their lives usually causes them to feel that you are really interested in them. They like that. It also can offset the impersonal nature of most hospital experience. Nobody likes to be a case number.

When patients start to talk about emotionally loaded things, things that are sad, frightening, or make them feel guilty, or angry, you may notice a temptation to change the subject. If you feel the inclination to pull back, if you are tempted to avoid emotionally loaded issues, the chances are you feel either:

1. that they cannot deal with talking about emotionally upsetting issues, or
2. that *you* cannot deal with talking about emotionally upsetting issues, or
3. both of the above.

Patients are usually a lot tougher than we think they are. Their problems and hardships are their own. They are familiar with them and they can tell you what things are troubling them without falling into the depths of depression and despair. Often talking about things that worry them can make troubles seem less frightening and hopeless. Words have a way with people.

If you feel that some issues are too difficult or too delicate to discuss, then the patient will soon feel the same way, too. If you feel that you will mishandle the situation, that you will damage the patient and your relationship together by saying the wrong thing, you are probably wrong. After all you are in this business because you are interested in helping people. Remember? That's how you got into this mess. This like any other relationship you have been in. If you fail to find just the right thing to say, you get a chance to fix that up the next time you see your patient. You have the big advantage that the patient already knows that you are in the business of helping him. By the "Rule of Placebo Benefit" almost anything you do will prove to be helpful at least 33 per cent of the time because the patient expects that it will be helpful.

There is no rush, take it easy. Your patient has probably had his problems for a long time before you arrived. The most common mistake you are likely to make is to give in to the temptation to leap in and solve a problem for a patient too soon, before you agree about what the problem is and which would be the right solution. Don't plug in your solutions until you see how the rest of his life fits together. Premature efforts to solve problems are usually calculated primarily to make yourself feel better. A more effective approach to dealing with your bad feelings is to:

1. (Very discreetly) sob into your hanky when no one is looking.
2. Go find an attractive member of the opposite sex and invite them to have coffee.
3. Talk to someone around here who has been through the experience.

Feeling bad some of the time about other people's troubles is one of the occupational hazards of this business. It is allright if the patient notices you feel bad about him, so long as he doesn't have to help you deal with it. Patients can get into very serious trouble with the American Psychological Association for practicing psychotherapy without a license. So long as you keep in mind that, for this moment, your patient comes first, things will probably be allright. The preceding section includes at least thirteen humanistic, homeopathic hints to help you get a handle on talking to patients. They are listed in abbreviated form on the next page. Before turning to the next page:

1. List five hints which make sense to you. Read the section again if you had to peek.
2. Think of, and write below, one or two mistakes that you might make yourself if you are not careful.
3. You already knew a great deal about establishing relationships. See if you can come up with two original hints of your own which you think might be helpful to fellow students as they talk to their patients.

HUMANISTIC HOMEOPATHIC HELPFUL HINTS

1. Catch the patient when he is comfortable.
2. Tell him why you are there (honestly).

3. Discuss what the patient already knows about his disease.
4. Be reassuring and supportive about the troubles he talks about.
5. Touch patients.
6. Be interested in their life, not just their disease or problems.
7. Don't worry too much about asking personal questions—it's expected.
8. Don't be afraid to talk about feelings of sadness, anger, anxiety, or guilt.
9. Patients are not too fragile to talk about what troubles them.
10. Stop worrying about being stupid or insensitive, your're O.K.!
11. Being a designated helper helps the patient to trust you.
12. Don't leap in prematurely to solve problems.
13. If the patient makes you feel bad notice it, deal with it yourself in the way that suits you—after you leave him.

Pretty soon you will be asked to formulate a list of problems that are presented by the patient who you are assigned to help. The problems you are prospecting for are likely to be medical, emotional, or financial. They may involve home nursing care, control of disease related symptoms, tension in family relationships, or the way the patient feels about himself. Problems which will concern you may have existed before the onset of the patient's disease or they may come up primarily because the patient has become ill. There is a whole symphony of problems which may exist. Fortunately most patients experience only a few serious troubles, but since the possibilities are astronomical your search of their life must be systematic. Here is where your wise professional demeanor, your evident warm regard for the patient, and your winsome smile come in.

If the patient has decided that you are an ally, that you share common goals, and a common enemy (the disease) you're on. If the patient is uncertain of your motives or doubts your benevolence you have to clean that up before you can go on and get into his life. The relationship is your tool and you have to keep it clean or it won't work. Of course, some patients will take a lot longer to check you out than others. Not every patient will choose to be frank and open with you. Your charm, your wit, your warmth, and your wisdom have been evident to all of us since the day you got here. Patients, however, are not always so perceptive. You can't win them all.

The chances are that, (and this may hurt) the patient who refuses to relate to you doesn't give a damn about you one way or the other. It's not that he decided to reject you, but he never considered relating to you in the first place. He does not *really* regard you as incompetent, so your secret is still safe. If you had read the patient's chart carefully, including the nurses' notes, and if you had talked to some folks who know the patient, you would likely have discovered that others had also enjoyed the humbling benefits of this patient's indifference, resentment, and disdain.

If you are the first to encounter these problems, then it makes very good sense to ask the patient what's going on. Since you will probably assume if you are not getting along, there is something wrong with you personally, it may be hard to convince yourself and the patient that you really want to know what is wrong in the relationship between you. If you do want to know and you can convince the patient that you really do, the chances are he will tell you what's wrong. Patients are usually very honest that way. In general it is better to accept criticism and go on trying to do better than to try to explain it away or justify your actions to the patient. Remember, you are both more interest in *his* problems than *yours*. Anyway, don't worry too much now about your rapport with your patient. The chances are you will get along fine from the start.

Look at your life for a minute, think about the good things that you draw pleasure from. Think about it. The goodies come from;

1. Your relationship with others,
2. your professional performance,
3. your body,
4. your view of yourself,
5. your interests and recreation,
6. your material resources and financial security,
7. your hopes and dreams for the future, and
8. your happy remembrances.

It's enough to make you grin if you think about all those rich, honey-gold, happy resources. A serious, prolonged illness can erode these sources of comfort and pleasure. What emerges instead are the problems you are trying to identify. For the most part patients will tell you what their troubles are in each of these areas if you ask them.

If you think you only half understand what your patient means or why a particular issue is so important to him, he will usually help you if you ask him to break it down. Some ideas are too big to get in your mind all at one time. For example, your patient volunteers, "I am afraid to die." That is too large a problem to manage all in one chunk. You can break it into more manageable pieces by saying something like, "Most everyone would feel that dying is a scarey idea. When you think about dying what part is most worrysome? What ideas are going thorugh your mind when you are thinking about dying?"

They may then talk about being afraid of pain, about leaving their family, about not being able to look forward to enjoying the future or their uncertainties about the hereafter. Some issues like pain, finances or plans to see that their children are cared for, can become part of your problem list to be solved. Others can only become part of your understanding of your patient.

If this approach seems too direct for your style, then you can probably help the patient to narrow and specify the issues by encouraging him to elaborate in more subtle ways. Perhaps an approach you have used in the past when trying to persuade a teacher to describe what he meant by the questions on his final exam will be more appropriate to your style.

PROBLEM LIST AND TREATMENT PLAN

At the end of this section you will be asked to prepare a problem list and an initial plan of treatment for a patient who you are working with. The following kind of note, while characteristically found under the heading "Social History" in many medical records, will not be sufficient: "Patient smokes one pack of cigarettes a day for the past twenty years, had gonorrhea in 1936, admits to being a 'heavy drinker'."

The kind of problem list which you develop should be a product of your detailed understanding of the patient's life history, the problems that existed at the time of onset of his illness and those life troubles that seem to be a consequence of his illness. Often the troubles that occur in a patient's relationship with his family, his financial trouble, or emotional stresses may be more important to him (and to you) than his disease and its symptoms. This should become a part of your general medical assessment. Your strategies for helping the patient ought to be based upon an understanding of the full spectrum of important issues that affect him. Medical problems and other troubles merge in the patient's life and one of your jobs is to figure out how they fit together.

For example: Mrs. G., a fifty-one year old, divorced ex-nurse with breast cancer, came to the out-patient clinic when her left breast had all but eroded away. She admitted it had been difficult to take care of the lesion and tolerate the smell of the necrotic tissue. Her reply to the question, "Why did you wait so long?" was, "I wanted to die and when I didn't, I had to come here." She felt that her fatal disease was of low priority of importance in relation to other problems in her life. Painful feelings of guilt, loneliness and sadness over her divorce were issues which most troubled her.

I would like to provide a check list of points which would guide you as you talk with your patient about the important issues in his life. I would like to do that just to make things easy for you, but, unfortunately, we are all helpless victims held captive by the bell curve. In most respects, the patient who you are about to talk with will not be an average patient. You will have to sort out what it is that makes him different than other patients. That kind of sorting cannot be done in the abstract so, it's time to go see your patient.

If you would like to think a bit more about how to plan strategies for helping patients who are dying and you don't think you are ready to see your patient yet get a copy of the journal article [1, 2] : if you read it, it will shorten the ride home on the bus.

When you finish your interview, make a list of problems which you and/or the patient have identified. (It's all right to make some notes as you talk to the patient if you want to.) You may want to talk to members of the patient's family, his primary physician, nurse on the ward, etc.

You may want to talk to the patient again. As you go along, note each problem as you become aware of it. When you feel you have a complete picture, review your problem list and number them in order of their importance to the patient. You may have a different opinion than the patient about what importance to place on certain issues. As soon as you can, discuss the problems you have identified with the patient's doctor. When the patient seems to place different importance on one of his problems than you would, discuss those issues in depth and attempt to develop a theory to account for the difference in opinion between you and the patient.

When you feel you have a fairly complete problem list and after you have numbered the problems in order of their priority go back to the pre-test and check in the margin each problem which you think applies to your patient.

REFERENCES

1. Ronald Koenig, "Dying vs. Well Being" Omega, 4:181-194, No. 3, 1973.
2. ──────────── , Nursing Digest 2:49-54, May 1974, No. 5.

Seldom is a single study definitive. In fact, it usually requires a number of studies to even approximate a good answer to a research question. Also, since there is probably no research investigation in the behavioral and social sciences that is not flawed in some fashion, a follow-up is almost always necessary to fill in some of the blanks. At times we expect too much from individual research projects; at other times, we accept the results of research without being adequately critical. Research can advance our knowledge a step at a time, and it is important to evaluate each study on its merits and to gain whatever information the study provides, avoiding the common tendencies to reject or accept the results without careful critical thought.

The introduction to an earlier chapter emphasized the importance of good research and evaluation in death education and outlined some significant researchable questions. Durlak has conducted this study in an attempt to gain some answers. However, we need to offer some initial attention to various kinds of research methodologies. For example, we can obtain tentative answers to some questions right after the program is over, perhaps by asking the participants about the educational experience or by developing a questionnaire to determine what they learned. A more complete evaluation can be provided only some years after the program has ended, by which time many of the participants will have had death-related experiences; a competent research investigator could develop a research design that would determine whether the death-related behavior was influenced by the earlier death education. The latter kind of research, while very important, is also extremely difficult and expensive to conduct. However, studies like the one reported in Chapter 26 provide a start.

Comparison between Experiential
and Didactic Methods
of Death Education*

Joseph A. Durlak

Although 20,000 death education and training programs have been offered in the United States, there are few systematic investigations of the effectiveness of these various programs [1]. For example, Murray found a reduction in death anxiety for nurses involved in a death education course [2], but there was no control group against which to compare and measure the significance of obtained findings. Subsequent to an academic course on death and dying, Bell reported that college students changed significantly more than controls in frequency of thinking about death and interest in death-related discussions, but there were no significant intergroup differences or within group changes in students' feelings and attitudes toward death [3]. Aside from using college students, which limits the generality of findings, Bell offered no evidence in support of the reliability and validity of his specially-constructed death questionnaire measures [3]. This report improves upon the shortcomings of previous studies in an attempt to examine the impact of a death and dying workshop on individual attitudes toward life and death. Pre and Post questionnaire data were obtained from workshop participants and a

*This study was conducted while the author was assigned to the Psychology Service of the Eisenhower Army Medical Center, Fort Gordon, Georgia.

nonparticipant control group. Two widely-used death scales [4, 5] were used in conjunction with Crumbaugh and Maholick's Purpose in Life Test as outcome measures [6]. Due to changes in workshop format on two occasions, it was also possible to examine the differential effects of an educational approach emphasizing didactic versus experiential components. This latter aspect of the experimental design was considered important from a research standpoint. Although several authors have implied that an emotional, personal approach to death is more effective than didactic presentations in death education and training programs, there is no empirical data supporting these claims [7-11].

METHOD

Instruments

Test packets were prepared containing an information facesheet, a series of questions assessing concern and contact with death, and four psychometric scales appearing in randomized order. The data relevant to the death concern and contact measures are not reported here. The information facesheet sought the respondent's age, sex, marital status, occupation, religious affiliation, and a self-rating of religiousity along a 4-point scale (1 = nonreligious; 2 = somewhat nonreligious; 3 = somewhat religious; and 4 = religious; cf Feifel / Branscomb) [12].

The four psychometric scales consisted of Templar's Death Anxiety Scale [5], Lester's Fear of Death Scale [4], Crumbaugh and Maholick's Purpose in Life Test [6], and the Marlowe-Crowne Social Desirability Scale [13]. The Lester and Templar scales are two widely-used research instruments that have been developed with considerations of reliablity and validity in mind. The Purpose in Life Test is an attitude scale that measures the degree to which a person experiences a sense of meaning and purpose in life. Crumbaugh and Maholick [12] have presented evidence that the instrument is a reliable and valid operational measure of the existiential concepts of meaning and purpose in life as proposed by Frankl [14, 15]. Frankl theorizes that true meaning and purpose in life is associated with an individual accepting and finding meaning in suffering and, ultimately, death. Death actually becomes a factor in life's meaningfulness. Previous research has supported Frankl's theory in this regard [16-18]. The Marlowe-Crowne Scale was included within the test packets to measure the possible influence of social desirability response parameters on questionnaire scores.

Respondents

A total of fifty-one individuals who participated in five successive workshops completed the test packets from one to three days before and from one to three days after attending the workshop. A nineteen member nonparticipant control group completed pre-post testing during a comparable time period. The workshop group was divided into two experimental groups consisting of nineteen participants from two didactically-oriented workshops (didactic group) and thirty-two participants from three experientially-oriented programs (experiential group). The total sample averaged thirty-two years of age; 67 per cent were female; 43 per cent were married; mean religious self-rating was 2.58 (midway between "somewhat nonreligious" and somewhat religious"); 38 per cent were nurses, 14 per cent physicians, 24 per cent paramedical staff; 9 per cent administrative and secretarial employees, and the remainder consisted of other hospital personnel. Experimental and control groups did not differ on the above characteristics.

All respondents completed the materials voluntarily and anonymously after being told that individual attitudes toward death and dying were being studied.

Death And Dying Workshop

The death and dying workshop under study is part of a continuing education training program at a large southeastern medical center. The workshop is held monthly from September to June, publicized throughout the hospital, and open to every hospital employee. It is an eight-hour small group experience conducted for four hours on each of two, successive, weekday mornings and is attended by eight to sixteen participants selected from a waiting list to represent a cross section of hospital personnel (physicians, nurses, ward medics, laboratory technicians, etc.). A psychiatric nurse, psychologist, general physician, and two chaplains lead the workshop and assume personal responsibility for separate presentations during the two day program.

The psychologist and one chaplain simultaneously decided to change the nature of their presentations in two of the five workshops from an experiential to a didactic focus. This change made it possible to compare the differential effects of workshop programs that emphasized didactic versus experiential components. In didactic presentations, the chaplain spoke about helping patients to deal emotionally with impending death, and the psychologist talked first about personal feelings regarding death and then about emotional reactions involved in mourning and bereavement, including anticipatory grief. The didactic presentations also included a discussion of social factors influencing the treatment of dying and grieving persons, psychological styles of adaptation to death, and the frequent denial of the reality of death.

During the other three workshops the chaplain and the psychologist used an experiential rather than a didactic focus with the groups. The chaplain led the group in two hours of role playing similar to that described by Barton and Crowder [7]. Roles involving care-givers and dying and grieving persons were described on separate index cards and volunteers were solicited. Participants frequently exchanged roles as both actors and observers shared their feelings in each situation.

In his experiential presentation, the psychologist began with a 15-minute discussion of emotional aspects of grief and bereavement. He than asked group members to perform Berman's death awareness exercises [19], in which each individual is asked to imagine he has only 24 hours to live and then is asked to share first with one other group member and then with the entire group how he would spend his last day. As noted by Berman this exercise produces strong affective reactions among participants and leads to intense personal discussions concerning anxieties, insecurities and fears about death and dying [19].

After reactions to this exercise were shared and processed, the group was asked to participate in a grief-related exercise. Participants were divided into small (two to four person) groups and asked: (a) to relate their past, personal experiences in which someone close to them had died; and, (b) to imagine how they would feel and react if the person closest to them was going to die soon. One of the five workshop leaders monitored each small group discussion in this exercise, which, similar to the death awareness exercise, aroused strong emotional reactions among group members. Experiences and feelings discussed in each of the small group discussions were shared with the total group.

The presentations of the other workshop leaders did not change during the five monthly workshops. The nurse began the workshop with videotaped interviews of dying patients and their spouses followed by a group discussion, and a didactic presentation of Kübler-Ross's work [20]. After a short break, the physician spoke about the need for honest and direct communication with dying patients and problems encountered by medical staff in this regard. He also indicated the general lack of training for medical personnel in the psychosocial aspects of dealing with terminal illness. The first part of the psychologist's presentations ended the first half of the workshop.

On the second day, the psychologist completed his presentation, and the two chaplains presented their material. The second chaplain concluded the workshop by discussing theological and philosphical concerns of dying patients and their families.

In summary, the primary difference between the didactic and experiential workshops lay in the methodology rather than the content of instruction. Each program dealt broadly with such topics as emotional reactions to grief and death, and communication with the terminally ill. However, during a critical three and one-half hour time period in which the psychologist and one chaplain led the workshop, the didactic group learned about grief and death through lecture and small group discussion—a method of instruction that continued the didactic emphasis of other workshop experiences. This same time frame was spent differently in the three experiential workshops. Here, participants were assisted to confront, examine, and share their own feelings and reactions to grief and death. Role playing, and personalized death awareness and grief exercises were used for this purpose. The experiential workshop thus sought to provide participants with both a cognitive *and* emotional encounter with death while the didactic program emphasized only the former component.

RESULTS

Table 1 presents the pre- and post-test scale correlations for the total sample. Correlational data indicated that social desirability response parameters were a relatively unimportant influence on questionnaire scores. Only the post-test relationship between the Death Anxiety and Marlowe-Crowne scales reached significance and this correlation was small in magnitude ($r = -.30, p < .05$). The Purpose in Life Test was significantly and negatively correlated with both death scales (r's $\geqslant -.36$). These data replicate previous findings regarding the relationship between "purpose in life" and death-related concerns and feelings [16-18]. The significant pre- and post-test correlations between the two death scales (r's = .24 and .33 respectively) indicated some, but not a major degree, of measurement overlap between these two instruments. The significance of this finding is discussed later.

One-way analyses of variance were performed on pretest questionnaire scores to assess initial comparability of groups. No significance between group differences was found. To study the effects of the workshop experience, scores on each life and death questionnaire were subjected to a 2 X 3 analysis of variance with groups (experiential, didactic, and control) as a Between-Subjects main effect and time of evaluation (pre- and post-) as a repeated measures, Within-Subjects main effect. Duncan multiple range tests with significance set at the .05 level were applied to inspect mean differences following significant F ratios.

All F tests were nonsignificant for scores on the Purpose in Life Test. A significant main effect for time ($F = 14.06, df, 1/67, p < .001$) and a significant group by time interaction ($F = 12.15, df, 2/67, p < .001$) appeared in the analysis of scores on the Templar scale. Post hoc mean comparisons indicated the didactic group differed significantly from the experiential but not the control group. The latter two groups did not significantly differ from one another.

Analysis of scores on the Lester scale also yielded a significant main effect for time and a significant group by time interaction (F's = 24.76, df, 1/67, $p < .001$, and 113.27, df 2/67, $p. < .001$, respectively). Duncan tests indicated that the experiential group differed significantly from the other two groups who did not differ from one another.

Table 1. Pre- and Posttest Scale Correlations for the Total Sample

	SDS	DAS	FOD	PIL
SDS		−.14	−.06	.01
DAS	−.30[a]		.24[a]	−.59[b]
FOD	−.11	.33[b]		−.49[b]
PIL	.00	−.54[b]	−.36[b]	

Note. The upper half of the matrix contains pretest and the lower half posttest correlations. SDS = Social Desirability Scale, DAS = Death Anxiety Scale, FOD = Fear of Death Scale, and PIL = Purpose in Life Test.
[a] .05
[b] .01

Table 2. Pre and Post Means and Standard Deviations for Experiential, Didactic, and Control Groups on the Life and Death Questionnaires

	Measures					
	FOD	DAS	PIL	FOD	DAS	PIL
Groups		Pre			Post	
Experiential						
M	5.56	6.40	106.03	4.92	6.78	107.78
SD	1.01	2.28	14.71	0.72	2.89	15.24
Didactic						
M	5.38	6.57	106.42	5.73	7.68	106.42
SD	0.87	2.34	15.52	1.13	2.05	17.69
Control						
M	5.39	6.63	104.31	5.56	7.26	103.95
SD	0.92	3.56	19.38	0.89	3.23	13.89

Note. FOD = Fear of Death Scale; DAS = Death Anxiety Scale; PIL = Purpose in Life Test.

Table 2 presents the pre and post group means on the life and death questionnaires. Inspection of group means indicated that the pattern of results differed on the two death scales. On the Templar scale, scores increased over time for all groups, but the experiential group demonstrated the smallest and the didactic group the greatest amount of change. On the Lester scale, however, whereas scores rose for the didactic and control groups from pre- to post-testing, scores declined over the same time period for the experiential group.

In summary, results indicated that the experiential workshop decreased participants' fears and concerns about death while only slightly heightening their anxieties about death. In contrast, the didactic workshop had negative effects since participants reported greater fears and anxieties about death at the end of the workshop than when they began it. Controls showed slight negative changes on these death measures over time. No changes appeared in purpose in life scale scores for any of the groups.

DISCUSSION

Results suggest that a death education program with experiential exercises to assist individuals in confronting and sharing their personal feelings about death and dying was significantly more effective in changing attitudes toward death than an educational workshop not containing such components. These data lend empirical support to the view that an emotional, personal approach to death is an important element in an effective death education program [7-11]. Current findings therefore encourage further investigations on the value of experiential exercises within the context of other death-related, educational and training paradigms.

Although this research is a step forward in the systematic evaluation of death education programs, there are several experimental limitations. The death and dying workshop studied here was conducted in a hospital setting by a multidisciplinary teaching staff for an eight-hour period with small groups of voluntary, heterogenous participants. Current findings may not replicate if any of these factors, such as group composition and workshop length, differ in other settings.

In addition, program evaluation was confined to immediate, self-report measures of death attitudes and feelings. The durability of obtained changes and their relation to subsequent behavior was not assessed. Although several thanatologists believe that positive modifications in care-givers' death-related feelings and attitudes does improve the care given to dying and grieving persons, the direct connection between attitudes or feelings and behavior has not been demonstrated empirically.

Current outcome data illustrate the difficulties involved in attempting to assess attitudes and feelings toward such broad concepts as life and death. For example, in retrospect, it was perhaps naive to assume that significant changes on the Purpose in Life Test would occur as a result of the death workshop. According to Frankl, acceptance of death is but one aspect in the development of personal meaning and purpose in life [14, 15]. Modification of death attitudes may not necessarily affect the larger construct of purpose in life, although the reverse may be true. However, the significant negative correlations that were obtained in the present study between the Purpose in Life Test and Lester's Fear of Death Scale replicate previous findings and suggest the utility of the former measure in future death research [16-18].

Problems of interpretation also arise with findings on the two death scales. Although the present study found a significant but low correlation between the Lester and Templar death scales, other studies have reported nonsignificant correlations between these scales, indicating these two instruments are not measuring the same dimensions [21, 22]. Krieger, Epting and Leitner developed a threat index for use in death research and reported significant positive correlations among their threat index, Lester's death scale, and a direct, specific, self-report of fear of death, but Templar's scale was significantly associated only with the latter measure [22]. The authors interpreted these findings to mean that Lester's scale is more a measure of the conceptual meaning death holds for individuals, including the elements of fear and threat, than it is a measure of death anxiety per se.

There is both theoretical and empirical support for the view that individual reactions to death are multi-dimensional. For example, Ray and Najman report data to indicate that anxiety about death and acceptance of death may coexist within individuals [23]. Therefore, current data for the experiential group that reflect a reduction in test scores on the Lester scale concomitant with a rise in scores on the Templar scale over time, are plausible. Nevertheless, much further work is needed to determine the exact components of death-related concerns that are being assessed by different measuring instruments.

It is unclear exactly how workshop experiences exerted changes in reactions to death, but some speculations can be offered. Personal consideration of dying appears unsettling, and the context in which individuals approach death affects personal reactions to the topic. Controls who merely completed pre- and post- questionnaires displayed negative changes on scales measuring death anxiety and death fear, but didactic group members who were involved in a more intense, personal exposure to death-related topics demonstrated even greater negative changes. In contrast, experiential workshop experiences seemed to minimize anxious reactions to death and to positively affect concerns and fears about death.

It is believed that positive changes occurred in the experiential group because participants benefited from a nonthreatening atmosphere in which they could "work-through" their death-related feelings. Workshop leaders observed that although the experiential exercises produced a significant ventilation of personal fears, anxieties, and insecurities about death and dying, the sharing of these reactions was beneficial to individuals in recognizing and resolving these feelings. Individuals were relieved that others shared similar feelings about death and they felt supported in coming to terms with the personal meaning death had for them. Future research attempting to evaluate the above (and other) speculations regarding factors responsible for changes in death-related feelings and attitudes would be useful.

In summary, current findings and implications must be offered tentatively due to limitations in the experimental design and the lack of strong, pervasive program effects. Nevertheless, even on an exploratory basis, this research represents a more objective assessment of effects then is currently available in most other death programs. We hope this report will encourage further systematic investigations of other death-related educational programs.

ACKNOWLEDGEMENTS

The author wishes to thank Majors Joyce Burchard and John Danner, successive workshop coordinators while this study was undertaken, for their cooperation and assistance in the data collection.

REFERENCES

1. R. S. Somerville, Book Review, *J. of Marriage and the Family, 37,* pp. 1042-1044, 1975.
2. P. Murray, Death Education and Its Effect on the Death Anxiety Level of Nurses, *Psychological Reports, 35,* p. 1250, 1974.
3. B. D. Bell, The Experimental Manipulation of Death Attitudes: A Preliminary Investigation, *Omega, 6,* pp. 199-205, 1975.
4. D. Lester, Fear of Death of Suicidal Persons, *Psychological Reports, 20,* pp.1077-1078, 1967.

5. D. I. Templar, The Construction and Validation of a Death Anxiety Scale, *J. of General Psychology, 82,* pp. 165-177, 1970.

6. J. C. Crumbaugh and L. T. Maholick, An Experimental Study in Existentialism: The Psychometric Approach to Frankl's Concept of Noogenic Neurosis, *J. of Clinical Psychology, 20,* pp. 200-207, 1964.

7. D. Barton and M. K. Crowder, The Use of Role Playing Techniques as an Instructional Aid in Teaching About Dying, Death and Bereavement, *Omega, 6,* pp. 243-250, 1975.

8. S. Bloom, On Teaching an Undergraduate Course on Death and Dying, *Omega, 6,* pp. 223-226, 1975.

9. K. Kopel, W. O'Connell, J. Paris and P. Girardin, A Human Relations Laboratory Approach to Death and Dying, *Omega, 6,* pp. 219-221, 1975.

10. M. A. Simpson, The Do-It-Yourself Death Certificate in Evoking and Estimating Student Attitudes Toward Death, *J. of Med. Education, 50,* pp. 475-478, 1975.

11. H. B. Weiner, Living Experiences With Death—A Journeyman's View Through Psychodrama, *Omega, 6,* pp. 251-274, 1975.

12. H. Feifel and A. B. Branscomb, Who's Afraid of Death?, *J. of Abnormal Psychology, 81,* pp. 282-288, 1973.

13. D. P. Crowne and D. Marlowe, A New Scale of Social Desirability Independent of Psychopathology, *J. of Consulting Psychology, 24,* pp. 349-354, 1960.

14. V. E. Frankl, *Man's Search for Meaning,* Knopf, New York, 1965.

15. V. E. Frankl, *The Doctor and the Soul,* Washington Square Press, New York, 1963.

16. J. A. Blazer, The Relationship Between Meaning in Life and Fear of Death, *Psychology, 10,* pp. 72-73, 1973.

17. J. A. Durlak, Relationship Between Individual Attitudes Toward Life and Death, *J. of Consulting and Clinical Psychology, 38,* p. 463, 1972.

18. J. A. Durlak, Relationship Between Attitudes Toward Life and Death Among Elderly Women, *Developmental Psychology, 8,* p.146, 1973.

19. A. L. Berman, Crisis Interventionists and Death Awareness: An Exercise for Training in Suicide Prevention, *Crisis Intervention, 4,* pp. 47-52, 1972.

20. E. Kübler-Ross, *On Death and Dying,* The MacMillan Company, New York, 1969.

21. A. L. Berman and J. E. Hays, Relation Between Death Anxiety, Belief in After-Life, and Locus of Control, *J. of Consulting and Clinical Psychology, 41,* p. 318, 1973.

22. S. R. Krieger, F. R. Epting and L. M. Leitner, Personal Constructs, Threat and Attitudes Toward Death, *Omega, 5,* pp. 299-310, 1974.

23. J. J. Ray and J. Najman, Death Anxiety and Death Acceptance: A Preliminary Approach, *Omega, 5,* pp. 311-315, 1974.

Chapter 27 describes the effectiveness of another death education program. Like the program presented in Chapter 26, this one had some positive effects, at least as of the end of the course. Evaluations of death education programs have numerous limitations: For example, participants may learn the "proper" response to an attitude item and will give that response, even though it does not reflect their actual attitude or feeling, or any given study will evaluate only one or a very few programs, so that the results are strongly influenced by that one program or by that particular set of instructors. Nonetheless, as studies accumulate over a period of time, each based on a different program and using different instructors and applying different instruments to measure change, we will eventually acquire enough sets of findings to draw some useful generalizations.

CHAPTER
27

Coping: Effects of Death Education

Larry A. Bugen

INTRODUCTION

Questions regarding the effects of death education have remained either unasked or unanswered. Death educators have been content to liken themselves to early explorers and thereby merely describe the new terrain. Descriptions of courses abound. Recent elaborations by Leviton [1]; Leonard [2]; Barton [3]; Jeffrey [4]; Bloom [5]; Leviton [6]; and Somerville [7] have profiled the rich array of methods, targets and materials characterizing the field. Diversity rather than sameness in approach certainly seems to be the rule. But what of the outcome of such diversity?

What can the typical student enrolled in a death education seminar expect to gain from the experiences? Death educators must examine what is happening to their students, in what situations and for how long. Results to these needed inquiries have been inconclusive for at least three reasons. First, a variety of unreliable and invalid instruments have been used to assess death education effects [8-10]. Secondly, certain expected outcomes are simply unattainable. Leviton has pointed out as an example that "some of the most significant outcomes—how the former students actually feel and behave when death comes forcefully into their lives—have yet to be reached in most instances."[1]

A third problem appears to lie in the preoccupation with apparent trait rather than state measures of personality. Bugen [11] for instance, has found that Dickstein's [12] measures of Death Concern possesses a high test-retest reliability and appears to be measuring a rather stable characteristic. Its use as a sensitive outcome criterion would consequently be ill-advised.

In light of the above inconclusiveness, a more systematic approach to assessing death education effects was deemed necessary. The purpose of the present study was to:

1. construct a scale expressing the valid death education gains of a student population;
2. monitor the effectiveness of a death education seminar in creating changes in participants; and
3. emphasize "coping" as a desirable outcome to a death education experience.

It was hypothesized that an experiential/didactic seminar on death and dying would enhance student coping capacity on each of thirty items measuring coping skills. It was further hypothesized that a matched control group not experiencing the complete seminar would demonstrate non-significant changes in coping capacity.

METHOD

The participants for the experimental group consisted of twenty-four graduate and undergraduate students enrolled in a death and dying seminar. The fifteen female and nine male participants represented a variety of academic disciplines. Included were Nursing, Health Education, Psychology, Sociology, Anthropology and Religion. Exposure to terminality among participants ranged from none to a great deal (e.g., a minister with a service history in Vietnam).

The control group (N = 30) consisted of twenty-two females and eight males enrolled in a Fall 1977 seminar on death and dying. The control group was similar to the experimental group in that:

1. all students self-selected into the experience,
2. a wide range of academic backgrounds were represented, and
3. exposure to terminality was widely varied.

All participants were informed of the research questions and were assured that all data would be confidential and anonymous. Participants granted written permission prior to the completion of questionnaires and prior to exposure to course content.

Procedure

Both the experimental and control groups were similar in that participants completed the "Coping with Death Scale" (see instrumentation) during the first class session. Completion of the questionnaire takes approximately five minutes. Three weeks subsequent to the pretest, both groups were again administered the posttest of the "Coping with Death Scale." The two groups differed greatly, however, in their exposure to the course content.

The experimental group experienced the entire fifteen unit death and dying seminar during their three-week interval while the control group was exposed to only two course units. This methodology was possible since classes were permitted to meet for three hours every day during summer academic sessions. This procedure allowed the experimental group to cover all course content in a very intense manner during a three-week interval. The control group, by comparison, met for three hours, once a week, during the Fall semester. Only the "Epidemiology of death and its statistical presence" could be covered during the first two class sessions. By utilizing only enrolled students in both experimental and control groups, it was believed that motivation was held constant as a contributing variable. Exposure to course content would appear to be the only experimental manipulation as a result.

The death and dying seminar at the University of Texas at Austin consists of both didactic and experiential components. Students are exposed to presented material in the first half class-session and meet in small groups the second half. Didactic material covers such topics as:

1. the epidemiology of death;
2. fundamentals of human grief;
3. crisis intervention;
4. process of dying;
5. community resources for prevention and coping;
6. children and death;
7. religious and parapsychological views of death and
8. organizational and societal constraints.

Experiential components consist of structured exercises designed to encourage exploration of attitudes and feelings related to living and dying. Students are administered death concern scales, visit cemeteries and funeral homes, listen to terminally ill and bereaved guests, and participate in life-planning workshops. Participants create and maintain the same small group throughout the course of the entire semester. These "support groups" are vital due to the very personalized sharing expected of the members. No formal assessment is used in the course and limits are placed on enrollment each semester. Personalized logs and group projects provide a basis for grades.

Instrument

The "Coping with Death Scale" is a thirty-item measure with responses arranged along 7-point Likert Scales. The diverse items appear to fall into two categories: 1. coping with self and 2. coping with others. Coping with self includes items relating to increased understanding, knowledge and expressivity of emotions. Examples include "I understand my death-related fears, "I am familiar with funeral prearrangement should I prefer to use it," and "I can express my fears about dying."

Coping with others includes items related to increased abilities to communicate with and/or help the bereaved and terminally ill. Example items included: "I can communicate with the dying," "I can help someone with their thoughts and feelings about death and dying," and "I know how to speak to children about death."

Each item on the "Coping with Death Scale" represents a personal gain reported by students who completed a death and dying seminar. The author had asked students as part of a final exam to indicate what "they had gotten from the course which would justify continued instruction in this area." Responses were tabulated and composed as a scale. Content validity appears to be guaranteed as a result of this procedure.

RESULTS

Pretest vs. posttest scores were analyzed for both experimental and control groups using the Statistical Package for the Social Sciences. T-tests were applied to the mean differences for each group. Table 1 present pretest and posttest Means, Standard Deviations and T-values for both the experimental and control groups.

Statistically significant differences were found for twenty-three of the thirty items for the experimental group. As Table 1 reveals, the majority of these differences are significant at the $p < .001$ level. When the thirteen most significant differences are dichotomized, it appears that participant's report enhanced capacities to cope with *both* a) self and b) others. Items 2, 4, 5, 10, 11, 12 and 13 reflect the former; while items 21, 23, 26, 27, 28, and 29 reflect the latter.

The control group, in comparison, reported only one significant difference out of the possible thirty items. As Table 1 reveals, item 1 for the control group is significant at $p < .02$ level. Two class sessions appear to be sufficient to strengthen already firm convictions ($m = 2.33 \rightarrow m = 1.50$) that "thinking about death is not a waste of time."

DISCUSSION

Results strongly suggest that individuals enrolled in a death education seminar can acquire and/or enhance a variety of coping capacities in regard to self and others. Exposure to a full array of experiential and didactic components appears to be a necessary means to this end. A control group experiencing only the first fourteen per cent of the seminar were not able to manifest these significant gains.

Table 1. "Coping with Death" Means, Standard Deviations,
and T-Values for Experimental and Control Groups

Item	Pre-Score		Post-Score		T. Value
	Mean	S.D.	Mean	S.D.	
1. Thinking about death is a waste of time	2.33 (2.33)	1.58 (1.67)	1.67 (1.50)	1.05 (1.01)	-1.72^a $(-2.34)^{b,c}$
2. I have a good perspective on death and dying	4.25 (3.73)	1.73 (1.91)	6.00 (3.97)	.83 (1.96)	4.47^e (.47)
3. Death is an area which can be dealt with safely	4.38 (4.37)	1.81 (2.14)	5.71 (4.33)	1.49 (2.94)	2.78^d (−.06)
4. I am aware of the full array of services from funeral homes	2.54 (2.40)	1.77 (1.97)	5.88 (2.67)	1.57 (2.09)	6.91^e (.51)
5. I am aware of the variety of options for disposing of bodies	3.88 (3.77)	1.80 (1.98)	5.88 (3.20)	1.96 (1.99)	3.68^e (−1.11)
6. I am aware of the fully array of emotions which characterize human grief	5.00 (3.93)	1.75 (2.07)	6.08 (3.80)	1.56 (2.09)	2.27^c (−.25)
7. Knowing that I will surely die does not in any way effect the conduct of my life	2.63 (3.30)	2.10 (1.99)	3.13 (2.47)	2.40 (1.74)	.77 (−1.73)
8. I feel prepared to face my death	3.50 (2.87)	2.23 (1.98)	5.13 (3.13)	1.68 (1.83)	2.86^d (.54)
9. I feel prepared to face my dying process	3.38 (2.63)	2.24 (1.92)	4.83 (3.07)	1.47 (1.74)	2.67^d (.92)
10. I understand my death-related fears	3.79 (3.50)	1.72 (1.87)	5.63 (4.10)	1.01 (1.85)	4.50^e (1.25)
11. I am familiar with funeral pre-arrangement	3.13 (3.03)	1.92 (2.31)	6.17 (2.80)	1.09 (2.07)	6.75^e (−.41)
12. Lately I find it O.K. to think about death	5.25 (4.13)	1.70 (2.16)	6.54 (4.87)	.51 (1.79)	3.57^e (1.43)
13. My attitude about living has recently changed	4.00 (4.20)	2.27 (2.19)	4.50 (3.97)	1.79 (2.21)	.85 (−.41)
14. I can express my fears about dying	4.79 (3.97)	1.91 (2.16)	5.58 (4.83)	1.64 (1.93)	1.54 (1.64)
15. I can put words to my gut level feelings about death and dying	4.13 (3.87)	1.80 (2.26)	5.75 (4.00)	1.30 (2.00)	3.59^e (.24)
16. I am making the best of my present life	4.75 (4.93)	2.09 (1.87)	5.71 (4.23)	1.52 (2.05)	1.82 (−1.38)
17. The quality of my life matters more than the length of it	5.87 (5.60)	1.75 (1.87)	6.54 (5.53)	.83 (2.24)	1.68 (−.12)

[a] A negative value reflects increase in disagreement with the statement; a postiive value, an increase in agreement.

[b] A value in (parentheses) reflects the control group; a value without parentheses reflects the experimental group.

[c] $p < .05$ [d] $p < .01$ [e] $p < .001$

Table 1. Cont'd.

Item	Pre-Score		Post-Score		
	Mean	S.D.	Mean	S.D.	T. Value
18. I can talk about my death with family and friends	4.63 (4.27)	2.14 (1.93)	5.83 (3.83)	1.47 (1.91)	2.28[c] (-.87)
19. I know who to contact when death occurs	4.42 (3.97)	1.99 (2.34)	6.00 (3.73)	1.35 (3.08)	3.22[d] (-.41)
20. I will be able to cope with future losses	4.45 (4.40)	1.72 (2.03)	5.75 (4.23)	.74 (2.03)	3.38[d] (-.32)
21. I feel able to handle the death of others close to me	3.96 (3.57)	1.68 (1.92)	5.67 (3.43)	.87 (1.81)	4.42[e] (-.28)
22. I know how to listen to others including the terminally ill	4.79 (3.67)	1.93 (1.92)	5.96 (4.13)	.99 (2.05)	2.63[d] (.91)
23. I know how to speak to children about death	3.25 (2.93)	1.89 (1.96)	5.38 (3.20)	1.41 (1.63)	4.41[e] (.57)
24. I may say the wrong thing when I am with someone mourning	3.21 (4.20)	1.79 (1.83)	3.33 (4.00)	1.74 (2.05)	.25 (-.40)
25. I am able to spend time with the dying if I need to	4.83 (4.30)	2.01 (2.25)	6.13 (4.53)	1.19 (1.91)	2.70[d] (.43)
26. I can help someone with their thoughts and feelings about death and dying	4.42 (3.80)	1.72 (1.73)	6.17 (4.10)	.87 (1.83)	4.46[e] (.65)
27. I would be able to talk to a friend or family member about their death	4.42 (3.96)	1.93 (2.01)	6.08 (4.33)	.88 (1.77)	3.85[e] (.75)
28. I can lessen the anxiety of those around me when the topic is death and dying	4.16 (3.67)	1.52 (1.65)	5.75 (3.90)	.94 (1.87)	4.33[e] (.51)
29. I can communicate with the dying	4.21 (3.56)	1.69 (1.85)	5.92 (3.67)	.88 (1.75)	4.38[e] (.22)
30. I can tell someone how, before I or they die, how much I love them	5.08 (5.23)	2.21 (2.40)	6.63 (5.36)	.65 (2.04)	3.29[e] .23

[a] A negative value reflects increase in disagreement with the statement; a positive value, an increase in agreement.

[b] A value in (parentheses) reflects the control group; a value without parentheses reflects the experimental group.

[c] $p < .05$; [d] $p < .01$; [e] $p < .001$

This study's focus on coping capacity represents a new and crucial dimension in the assessment of death education effects. The dearth of evidence validating positive benefits from death education may in part be due to an excessive focus on attitudes toward bioethical issues and trait measures of death concern. These curriculum goals may not be as sensitive to change as is coping.

Bugen [13] has underscored the importance for death educators to design their courses, select target populations, and develop methods of instruction *after* goals for the course have been established [13, 14]. One of the goals underlying the present study was to enhance the ability of students to cope with their own death and/or the death of others. Methods of instruction were chosen accordingly. It was hoped that ability to cope would also generalize to other life crises as well.

A crisis such as death represents a threat, a challenge, and a call to new action. Individuals must explore their previous methods of solving problems in order to cope with a given dilemma. If previous means of coping prove inadequate, new coping capacities must be acquired. Students enrolled in death education seminars learn to appreciate the inevitability of death for themselves and others. By exploring their present feelings and reactions to death-related issues, students gain valuable information about themselves and others. They begin to anticipate and practice new response patterns. These patterns may include "expressing fears about dying" or "speaking to children about death." The benefits of such rehearsals prior to a death crisis may actually lessen the intensity of the crisis itself and the resulting grief process. These psychological benefits resulting from preparation for coping have been well documented in the literature since Janis' pioneering study with surgery patients [15]. The present study is further evidence that exposure to pre-crisis dynamics can enhance coping capacities with self.

The ability to cope with others was an additional goal in the present study/seminar. Morlea has described four approaches which might be taken during crises by helping persons and agencies [16]:

1. *environmental manipulation* requires someone who knows the resources of a community;
2. *general support* requires working in a limited way with the person in crisis. The primary behavior of the helper is interested listening without deep probing or confrontation;
3. a *generic approach* requires the helper to have a knowledge of crisis in general and specific crises in particular; and
4. the *individually tailored* approach requires a knowledge of personality theory and abnormal psychology.

Death education effects demonstrated in the present study, reveal that students can learn to function at the first two levels described by Morley. In the area of environmental manipulation, students learn to "be aware of the full array of services from funeral homes," "be aware of the variety of options for disposing of bodies," and "know who to contact when death occurs." By having this information, students represent important resources for others who may need assistance in making decisions at the time of a crisis.

In the area of general support, students report a variety of skills which can be helpful to others in crisis. These include such capacities as "knowing how to speak to children about death," "helping someone with their thoughts and feelings about death and dying," "being able to talk to a friend or family member about their death," or "being able to lessen the anxiety of those around me." Table 1 reports numerous other gains reported by participants in the present study. Though many of the items in the "Coping with Death Scale" are presented as behavioral objectives or outcomes, the reader must be cautioned that the results of the present study were obtained through self-report and not behavioral analysis.

Death educators must set appropriate goals for their instructional efforts. We must then carefully evaluate our outcomes. These outcomes will hopefully blend the problems of living with the problems of dying. Knott urges us to be accountable and believes that "thanatologists of all persuasions need to put more into the evaluation of educating others for living by education them about and for dying." [10] The present study reflects that this goal can be humanistically attained!

REFERENCES

1. D. Leviton, Death Education, H. Feigel (ed.), *New Meanings of Death*, McGraw Hill, New York, pp. 253-272, 1977.
2. V. R. Leonard, Death Education in the Helping Professions, *Australian Journal of Social Issues, 11:*2, pp. 108-120, 1976.
3. D. Barton, Death and Dying: A Course for Medical Students, *Journal of Medical Education, 47*, pp. 945-951, 1972.
4. D. Jeffrey, Death Education: Teaching a Course on Death and Dying, paper delivered at the 85th Annual Meeting of the American Psychological Association, 1977.
5. S. Bloom, On Teaching an Undergraduate Course on Death and Dying, *Omega, 6:3*, pp. 223-226, 1975.
6. D. Leviton, Education for Death, or Death Becomes Less a Stranger, *Omega, 6:3*, pp. 183-191, 1975.
7. R. Somerville, Audio Visual Materials on Aging, Death, Sex Roles, *The Family Coordinator*, pp. 86-88, January 1977.
8. B. D. Bell, The Experimental Manipulation of Death Attitudes: A Preliminary Investigation, *Omega, 6*, pp. 199-206, 1975.
9. N. Silberman, Effects of Thanatology Instruction on Attitudes and Fears About Death and Dying, unpublished manuscript, University of Wisconsin, Oshkosh, 1977.
10. J. E. Knott, Death Education: Accountable to Whom? For What?, *Omega, 7:2*, pp. 177-181, 1976.
11. L. A. Bugen, Death Education Effects Upon Death Concern Stability, *Psychological Reports, 43*, p. 1086, 1978.
12. L. S. Dickstein, Death Concern: Measurement and Correlates, *Psychological Reports, 30*, pp. 563-571, 1972.
13. L. A. Bugen, Innovative Trends in Death Education, paper presented at the 85th Annual Meeting of the American Psychological Association, San Francisco, 1977.

14. L. A. Bugen, *Death and Dying: Theory, Research and Practice*, Wm. C. Brown, Dubuque, 1979.
15. I. Janis, *Psychological Stress*, Wiley and Sons, New York, 1958.
16. W. E. Morley, Theories of Crisis Intervention, *Pastoral Psychology, 21*, pp. 14-20, 1970.

Epilogue

This book has been about death, the process of dying, and grief: the basic issues they create, the influences of culture, how we can intervene to improve the quality of life through institutions and through counseling, and how education can add to the effectiveness of the ways people cope with these circumstances.

But, since no book can hope to cover all of such a wide territory as death and grief, some issues have not been addressed. For example, although the twentieth century is certainly an era of specialization, there is danger in over-specialization. The boundaries of personal and vocational interests need to be broad enough to encompass related sources of information and understanding. Thus, those individuals who wish to become death educators need to know about educational processes; those individuals who wish to become death counselors need to know about counseling and psychotherapy. Being sensitive, knowing about death and dying and grief, and having good intentions are all important ingredients and may enable the individual to be an extremely important friend, but they are not sufficient by themselves to enable an individual to be a death counselor or death educator. Relevant professional training and experience are also needed.

Another issue is the tendency to move from one untested truism to a slightly, although perhaps only temporarily, better untested truism. Therefore, before Elisabeth Kübler-Ross proposed her five stages for an optimum dying process, many people viewed the process as murky and unstructured; after the stages were described and recognized, *they* became truth. No longer seen as useful guidelines or testable hypotheses (and, of course, the consensus of research and expert opinion is that the stages are not observed with sufficient frequency to be accepted as a basic structure for the dying process), these stages are sometimes seen as "right and necessary" processes for dying people who are, as a result, evaluated in terms of what stage they are in and whether that is where they "should" be. Other truisms obscuring important individual differences are that dying people want to be touched, that grief should be expressed overtly immediately after the death, that dying at home is better than dying in institutions, and that death education enables people to confront their own death more effectively. On the whole, I personally believe that—for the most part—each of these statements is true, but I also believe that such generalities require verification for each individual when we are concerned about individuals.

Nor have we dealt at all adequately in this book with what I refer to as individual theology, the belief system that an individual develops concerning those issues the causes of which he or she cannot adequately understand to make sense of the issues. The meaning of death is very much such an issue, and we develop a variety of explanations so that death makes sense: it's God's will, it's required to avoid over-population, it's an absurd act in an absurd universe. Many of us move from explanation to explanation or combine two or more explanations or have only hazy explanations. Death educators and counselors need to understand the alternative types of explanation in order to understand what their clients/ students are afraid of . . . or not afraid of. How do people organize the universe of death in their heads so as to comprehend its meaning and how does this organization affect their feelings and behavior?

And finally, at least for the moment, I don't think this volume has said enough about how much we use different words to mean the same thing when, in fact, they mean different things. Death and dying, grief and mourning, fear and anxiety. Meanings overlap and it is inevitable that words sometimes are used without precise meaning. But if we are educators or counselors, it is important that we have in our own minds a clear knowledge of what a word means and that we use it, with permissible slippage, correctly. So we should be the last ones to refer to "fear of death" when what we really mean is anxiety concerning the dying process. And, to close with another deep concern of my own, we should be careful to avoid attributing fear of death to someone when all that we have observed is that the person does not want to die.

The topic is endless, but this book must eventually end. Here.

Appendix

Education in general, and death education in particular, can be most effective when it combines the intellectual base for ideas, as learned through theory, description, speculation, and research, and the experiential understanding for practice, as learned through actual experience away from the reading chair or outside the classroom or through experiential exercises within the classroom.

With a few exceptions, the previous materials have provided an intellectual base. This appendix will offer some suggestions of ways to learn about death, dying, and grief in more experiential ways.

You may be reading this book to inform yourself of some issues that involve your work: you may be using the book in a classroom setting; or you may wish to expand your knowledge of some of these concerns for personal reasons. Regardless of how much each of these circumstances is influencing you, you can find ways to make use of these exercises.

Volunteer Opportunities

1. There are likely to be groups or organizations in your community that offer counsel for the dying and/or bereaved. Check to see if they provide an opportunity for you to volunteer your time and energy.
2. Look into possibilities of volunteering to cover the telephone for your local Suicide Prevention Center.
3. See if the local hospice can use your volunteer services.
4. If you find that there is a significant gap in the services provided in your community, consider the possibility of planning and developing those services yourself.

Visits

1. Visit three or four nearby cemeteries. Consider ways in which they are similar and ways in which they differ. Notice the arrangements of the tombstones, the messages on the tombstones, how well maintained the facility is, what you learn about local history, and so forth.
2. Find out which of the local mortuaries encourages visitors and, with a group of interested persons, plan a visit. Many funeral directors are eager hosts and excellent instructors. You can learn about the technology of the funerary process, the financing and related issues, and its psychology and sociology.

3. When you make arrangements to visit the funeral home, make additional arrangements to meet with one of the staff to arrange your own funeral. This is "for real," not just a game . . . unless, of course, you are the one person in the world who is absolutely certain of not dying tomorrow.

4. Visit the offices of the local coroner. Find out what these people do and how they serve the community. Check out the accuracy of the well-known television show, *Quincy*.

Find Out About . . .

1. The living will. What is its status in your state.

2. Academic and professional journals that carry reports of studies on death, dying, and grief. Read some research articles from *Omega, Death Studies* and other appropriate journals. Use the *Psychological Abstracts* or the *Sociological Abstracts* to help you find these articles.

3. Death-related training programs held at nearby facilities. It is very possible that death education programs are being provided at local colleges and universities, hospitals, professional meetings, social agencies, churches, and elsewhere. It's not unusual for a well-known person in the field to be talking to the local hospital staff or at a local church. Although the public is not always invited to these programs, a telephone call can usually lead to a personal invitation.

4. Organ donations. How does this work? What possible problems can arise? Do you wish to make personal arrangements? How can this be done?

5. How one dying person really feels. There is often someone in the community who has been diagnosed as terminally ill and who is capable and willing to discuss his/her experiences and feelings with people like yourself. Check into this and set up a small gathering of concerned persons.

6. The hospice nearest to you. What are its policies? How is it funded? What services does it offer?

Develop a Discussion Group To Talk About . . .

1. The right to "death with dignity." What does this mean? How can it be accomplished? Try to avoid diatribes and "horrible" experiences and develop reasonable plans.

2. The right to die sooner. Is suicide ever justified? Is a physician or a family member ever justified in speeding up the timing of a death? How should such decisions be made? By whom? Under what circumstances? How useful is the living will?

3. The opportunity to live longer. Can you extend your life by an effort of will? By improving your lifestyle?

4. What you want to be remembered for after your death.

5. To whom would you donate a kidney. From whom would you request a kidney? Discuss some of the issues in being an organ donor or recipient.

6. The depiction of death and dying on television, in adult literature, in children's literature, in the newspapers, in magazines. Don't be satisfied with general impressions, but develop a systematic way to look into this matter.

7. The evidence for life after death. What is the nature of life after death? How do you know? What would you want life after death to be? Why?

8. The possible hazards of death education programs. How can they be avoided?

9. Unexplainable experience with death or dying. Have you ever had a death-related dream or premonition that seemed to come true? Have you ever had a vision or feeling that someone was going to die? Have you ever seen or heard or "sensed" the presence of someone who had died? What does all this mean? How can it best be explained?

10. How best to cope with your own death when it is imminent. In any group of five or six adults, at least one will have had the experience of believing that she/he was going to die shortly. Find out how the experience affected that person and consider how it might affect you.

11. A slow death trajectory versus a rapid death trajectory. What are the pros and cons of each? On the person who has died? On the survivors?

12. Funeral and burial customs and rituals in various subcultures in the United States and in other nations.

13. What there is about death itself, as opposed to the process of dying, that frightens, angers, upsets, or intrigues you.

14. The definitions and meanings of death, dead, dying, grief, bereavement, mourning.

Exercises

1. How are you going to die? Write an account describing your death.

2. Develop your own research study. Get help from an appropriate person. Carry your study out and write it up.

3. Write the description of the death of a person you knew personally. What specific things did you do when you heard about the death? How did you feel? (Don't set this up to make yourself look good—be honest.)

4. Make out a living will for yourself, after finding out what you need to in order to do so intelligently and within the laws of your state. (However, be careful to avoid doing anything with this living will until you are certain you want to.)

5. You died yesterday. Write your obituary for the local newspaper. You may wish to read some obituaries first.

6. You died at the age of 80. Write your obituary.

7. Divide the group/class/gathering into triads and designate each person A, B, or C. Begin by having Person A tell Person B about a loss, any loss, e.g., a parent or spouse through death, a job through cutbacks, a car that was stolen, a pet that was hit by a car, or even the loss of a hope or dream.

   Person B helps Person A understand the loss and ways of coping with the loss, or ways that the loss might have been handled. Person C listens without comment until Persons A and B have finished. Then Person C offers feedback to the others as to what seemed to be happening. After Person C has finished, the roles are shifted so that each person can perform each of the three roles. Anticipate spending at least an hour for this exercise.

8. Find out about guided fantasies. If you know someone who is skilled with guided fantasies, have that person develop one for dying. Make certain that it is a positive fantasy, not a threatening or frightening one.

9. Create a make-believe friend who is approximately your age, of your religious and ethnic background, earns about the same amount of money as you, and so forth. Call this person, for now, Jane Friend or John Friend. Now create another person, also very much like you and Mr./Ms. Friend. This person has an elderly parent who is dying, so we will, for now, refer to him/her as Mr./Ms. Child. Bill/Barbara Child visits John/Jane Friend and asks about seeing someone to help him/her deal with the coming death and the dying process more effectively. Friend tells Child to see you, and Child asks why.

   Now write Friend's description of you. Be honest in both positive and negative comments. After all, Friend wants Child to know what kind of person you are. Pair off with two other persons, and read your descriptions to each other. Then discuss what they imply.

10. You are a consultant to a long-term care facility. One of your clients tells you that whenever a resident of his home dies, all he can think about is filling the bed. "It takes 75% occupancy to break even, and we are hovering around 80%; how can I make a profit when residents keep dying. I like these people, and I don't want them to die, but when they do I think in terms of money, not of human lives. And that makes me feel guilty." What kind of advice, counsel, help, etcetera would you offer this person? How would you go about it?

11. You are a high school principal. One of your most popular students committed suicide Saturday evening, and it was carried in the Sunday newspaper. It is now Monday morning, before school begins. What do you do?

12. You are the director of a nursing home, and one of your patients is the father of a physician. The old man has a serious heart condition and could die at any time; he is confused and incontinent. His physician-son tells you that if the father has a heart attack or seems to be dying, he

would prefer that you not call in heroic methods to save him. What do you say to the son? What do you do if the circumstances occur?

13. A close friend of yours is part of a very warm and devoted extended family. When his grandfather dies at the age of 91, a very large and expensive funeral is planned, even though no one in the family is wealthy and many of them are near poverty. Your friend is upset about the cost and also about the pomp of the ceremony and asks you for your thoughts. How do you respond? What do you think to yourself?

14. You are a hospital chaplain of whatever denomination you prefer, and you notice that a middle-aged woman is sobbing as she walks down the corridor. You introduce yourself and ask her if you can be of service to her. She notices your chaplain insignia, and she shrieks at you, "I hate God!! He let my son die!! I prayed and prayed and prayed and begged Him to save my son, and He didn't!! He could have and He didn't!! and I hate Him!! Get the hell out of my way!!" How do you respond? What do you think to yourself?

15. Go to an art museum or look through art books and notice all the ways in which death, dying, and grief are depicted. Consider the implications.

16. Investigate the other arts: poetry, drama, dance, music, opera, fiction. Consider the implications of the ways in which death, dying, and grief are depicted.